Globalizing Resistance

WGG

The **World Forum of Alternatives** (WFA) is an international network of research centres that support the emerging process of the international convergence of social movements. It provides opportunities for reflection and coordination and puts information and analytical tools on the dynamics of these convergences at the disposal of the movements and citizens in general. Along with the *Globalizing Resistance: The State of Struggle*, the WFA has developed, together with other networks, the **Directory of Social Movements**, which brings together and organizes information on the movements and struggles at the world level. The aim of the directory is to promote the communication, mutual understanding and the building of bridges between the social movements of different countries or continents working on similar issues, as well as different ones. This collective and interactive project hopes thereby to contribute to creating dynamic international networks and coalitions that are effective in promoting rights and justice against neoliberal globalization. It can be consulted on www.social-movements.org

The **Tricontinental Centre** (CETRI) of Louvain-la-Neuve is a centre for research, publication and documentation on North/South relationships. It has a twofold aim to disseminate viewpoints from the South on the crucial issues of our times, and to participate in the analysis of social movements and their alternative proposals. It belongs to the movement of critical opinion and action vis-à-vis the current globalization of the neoliberal development model. CETRI runs a documentation centre of over 500 reviews from the South and publishes the quarterly *Alternatives Sud*, as well as other works linked to specific research projects. It also participates in numerous conferences and seminars with social actors. It functions as the secretariat of the World Forum of Alternatives and can be consulted on www.cetri.be

Globalizing Resistance

The State of Struggle

Edited by François Polet
with translations by Victoria Bawtree

Pluto Press
LONDON • ANN ARBOR, MI
in association with
THE TRICONTINENTAL CENTRE (CETRI)
LOUVAIN-LA-NEUVE, BELGIUM

First published 2004 by Pluto Press
345 Archway Road, London N6 5AA

www.plutobooks.com

Translator's note: Chapters 4, 7, 11, 12, 14, 17, 18, 22 and 23 have been translated from French; Chapters 10 and 19 from Spanish; and Chapter 16 from Italian.

British Library Cataloguing in Publication Data
A catalogue record for this book is available from the British Library

ISBN   0 7453 2356 1 hardback
ISBN   0 7453 2355 3 paperback

Library of Congress Cataloging in Publication Data applied for

10   9   8   7   6   5   4   3   2   1

Designed and produced for Pluto Press by
Chase Publishing Services, Fortescue, Sidmouth, EX10 9QG, England
Typeset from disk by Stanford DTP Services, Northampton, England
Printed and bound in the European Union by
Antony Rowe Ltd, Chippenham and Eastbourne, England

Contents

Introduction   vii

Part One: The State of Struggle Around the World

1 Political Diversity, Common Purpose: Social Movements
   in India, by *Vinod Raina*   3
2 Resistance to Globalization in Rural China, by *Lau Kin Chi*   15
3 NGOs and Social Movements in Southeast Asia,
   by *Francis Loh*   27
4 Central Asia and the Southern Caucasus: US rearguard
   Bases? by *Bernard Dreano*   42
5 Resistance to Neoliberalism in Australia and Oceania,
   by *Verity Burgmann and Andrew Ure*   52
6 Social Movements in the Arab World, by *Azza Abd
   el-Mohsen Khalil*   68
7 Struggling and Surviving in the Democratic Republic of
   the Congo, by *François L'Écuyer*   85
8 Social Movements: Experiences from East Africa,
   by *Opiyo Makoude*   91
9 South Africa's New Social Movements, by *David Coetzee*   103
10 Neoliberalism and Social Conflict: The Popular
   Movements in Latin America, by *Clara Algranati,
   José Seoane and Emilio Taddei*   112
11 Proletarian Resistance and Capitalist restructuring in
   the United States, by *Pierre Beaudet*   136
12 Europe: The Challenge for Social Movements,
   by *Bernard Dreano*   145

Part Two: The Dynamic of Convergence for Another World

13 The World Social Forum: Towards a Counter-Hegemonic
   Globalization, by *Boaventura de Sousa Santos*   165
14 The World Social Forum: A Democratic Alternative,
   by *Francine Mestrum*   188
15 The African Social Forum: Between Radicals and
   Reformers, by *Mondli Hlatshwayo*   206

16 Convergences and the Anti-war Movement: Experiences
    and Lessons, by *Paola Manduca*   212
17 The Trade Union Movement and the Social Movement:
    Towards a New Dialogue? by *Pierre Beaudet*   222
18 The New Agrarian Issue: Three Billion Peasants Under
    Threat, by *Samir Amin*   226

Part Three: The Strategic Challenge

19 The Alternative Movement and its Media Strategies,
    by *Victor Sampedro*   243
20 The European Union and the 'Internal Threat' of the
    Alternative World Movement, by *Ben Hayes*
    and Tony Bunyan   258
21 Police Measures Against the New Global Protest,
    by *Donatella della Porta and Herbert Reiter*   272
22 New Powers, New Counter-powers, by *Raoul-Marc Jennar*   289
23 International Law, a Decisive Issue for the Alternative
    World Movement, by *Monique Chemillier-Gendreau*   294

Contributors   303
Index   305

Introduction

Gone are the days of the hegemony of *la pensée unique* (or the one-and-only-way of thinking) and the euphoria created by the globalization of markets. Rising unemployment and insecurity, the insidious dismantling of public services, repeated financial crises, ecological imbalances and US unilateralism: all these have helped to undermine the neoliberal discourse. People have lost their confidence in the capacity – or will – of those who govern to guarantee priority for collective security, even rights, over the interests of powerful private groups. This is responsible for the emergence of a 'world citizens' movement' that seeks new forms of collective and democratic regulation. It has taken only a few years for the 'alternative world galaxy' to force its way, often in a spectacular fashion, on to the international scene and attract responses from broad sectors of the population.

The alternative world 'events' that have had the greatest impact – counter-summits, demonstrations and social forums – show the range and diversity of the various forms of resistance to liberal policies. However, we perceive the characteristics and potential of the struggles against globalization only partially and are often conditioned by national viewpoints and the generalizations of the media. Mobilizations against neoliberal hegemony have their own peculiarities, in range, social composition and political culture, according to the different regions. To understand the dynamic of social conflicts, certain aspects of the various national societies have to be seen in perspective, such as the evolution of the social and economic structures resulting from the type of modernization adopted by the elites, the way in which liberal policies have been put into practice – rapidly and radically in certain cases, more hesitantly and partially in others – and the various impacts that these policies have had on different social groups.

The kind of political power and the type of relationships that have been historically established between the power structures – parties and State – and popular organizations affect the margin of manoeuvre and the mode of expression of these organizations. In many countries, particularly in Africa and the Arab world, they are far from having acquired the right to express their views and make their claims. The holding of elections, more or less regularly, as well as concessions made to external fundraising bodies, have in no way hindered numerous regimes from controlling and blocking the political and social life of their countries through a subtle combination of clientelistic practices, co-optation and intimidation. In such authoritarian and paternalistic environments, participation in political activities outside the control of political power is an everyday challenge. The presence of 'apolitical' NGOs that loudly proclaim their role as actors in civil society contributes to the marginalization, even asphyxiation of popular initiatives contesting structural adjustment.

In countries where there is more massive contestation of neoliberal policies, it is often led by trade unions or popular movements – movements of peasants, women, students and indigenous people – that have been organized over a long period of time. These struggles against neoliberalism are thus part of a broader project for political and cultural emancipation, in the same way that they are the prolongation of historical struggles against the unequal social structures that liberalization and privatization are reproducing and accentuating. It is through a long process of confrontation of ideas and experiences that these actors have identified the new dynamics of the global powers, made the linkages with their local situation and incorporated these new realities into their agendas.

In the North as in the South, the question of how to translate these struggles into political action lies at the heart of many of the discussions. The militant organizations are sometimes linked to political parties, to which some identify as being in the same broad political movement. These alliances are important, as they give greater publicity to the demands being made by the movements. However, they do imply allegiances that can be very ambiguous, for example when competition between parties leads to a fragmentation of social forces (as in the *piqueteros* of Argentina or the mass movements of India). Also, sharing power with 'allied' parties leads to the institutionalization of movements and trade unions, who are invited to give their opinions, but also to soft-pedal some demands so as not to weaken their political partner (as in the Cosatu trade union confederation in South Africa or the CUT in Brazil).

At the same time, new forms of organization – more autonomous and less formal – are emerging, from day to day, in the field, to oppose privatization policies and the pillage of natural resources. Whether they are the unemployed, the precarious, the urban poor or rural communities threatened by the construction of dams and the destruction of their natural environment, they often take direct action such as occupying the land or official buildings, barricading roads, sit-ins, diverting water or electricity supplies. It is also necessary to stress the tendency for flexible and decentralized coordination between organizations that normally work on different issues but decide to join forces to make progress on cross-cutting issues. These new groupings, like the Coordination for Water and Life in Bolivia (Coordinadora por el Agua y la Vida de Bolivia), Jobs with Justice in the USA and the Assembly of the Poor in Thailand, go beyond specific interests, rise above particular struggles and promote new forms of solidarity.

Moreover, campaigns against regional integration projects that are dominated by liberal principles – like the Free Trade Area of the Americas, the proposed European constitution and the NEPAD for Africa as well as the campaigns against the WTO and Third World debt – greatly contribute towards creating political ties between the movements that are emerging and operating in very different national contexts. In this respect, the development of the international movement against the war in Iraq – which culminated in the demonstrations of February and March 2003 – provides valuable lessons. The extent and synchronization of these demonstrations were the result of a long process of networking by organizations and movements at the world level. Reaching beyond national contexts and specific *problematiques*, this method of horizontal coordination makes it possible to form and reinforce flexible and effective international coalitions and even to mobilize millions of people on the same issue at the same moment.

The convergence of these different movements in the same demonstrations and in the same public places is indisputably an important development, linked to increasing awareness of the global and interdependent nature of problems – socio-economic, cultural and ecological – which used to be considered separately. Clearly, it is also linked to the disappearance of a doctrinaire and exclusive concept of militancy. This convergence does not come about automatically, however. Simply bringing people together under the same banner condemning neoliberalism and affirming that 'another world is possible' is not enough to produce political proposals or development strategies that are unanimously accepted.

The discussions now taking place in world, regional and national social forums are certainly the best way of tackling the divergences between organizations that are pursuing the same general objectives while expressing their own ideas on citizen action and its relationship to politics. Such debates should contribute to the political maturity of these convergences. Not, however, as an artificial alignment of everyone on one position or another: there must be an effort to distinguish what separates and what unites them so that the struggles for another world are articulated more effectively.

In treating these different aspects lucidly but from a committed standpoint, *Globalizing Resistance* sees itself as a crossroads between the militant and the academic. The authors include key actors in various mobilizations who have undertaken to step back for a moment from their daily activities in order to understand them better, as well as researchers who have been close to the movements and contribute original analyses of how they are developing. They hail from all five continents and show their involvement and understanding of the struggles for another world, so they are particularly well qualified to present their findings to a wider public.

The first part of the book invites readers to take a trip round the world to sample the resistance to the neoliberal model of globalization. This unusual circuit consists of a series of 'incursions' into the dynamics of resistance that are at work in the different regions of the world. Concise and representative presentations give an idea of the vigour and diversity of these struggles, which are not given much publicity or not well understood, whether it is the 'gas war' in Bolivia or the claims of the Maori in New Zealand, the coalitions against privatizations in South Africa or the *dalit* movement in India, not forgetting the new forms of opposition to unbridled capitalism in China. These accounts go beyond the purely anecdotal in order to give readers an overall and consistent framework of interpretation, to help them grasp the sense and range of these struggles.

In the second part we focus on key discussions that bring together networks, movements and unions in the social forums, as well as in the anti-war movement. What kind of relationships should there be with the State or with international institutions? How to articulate local or national struggles with global campaigns? Which is better, direct action or action through the institutions? What positions should be adopted on such issues as global governance, international trade and the solidarity economy?

In the third and last part of the book the emphasis is on several of the crucial challenges faced by the social movements, of which media strategies are one of the first. How to make use of the mass media at the same time as developing their own information channels? The climate created by the 'war on terror' is another such challenge.

This has now become generalized, giving numerous governments the opportunity of setting up new mechanisms for control and surveillance and to adopt measures to criminalize the actions of those who oppose the state. At the same time international institutions have been trying for years to co-opt part of what they call 'civil society' in order to domesticate NGOs and marginalize those who 'refuse to dialogue'. And finally powerful private actors impose the rights of business over the rights of peoples. Another challenge faced by social movements is to recover the principle of the common good and to develop its applications in texts that are universally relevant.

Contestation of neoliberal globalization is no passing phenomenon. It is highly contemporary, as it is gradually integrating the 'global' dimensions of today's problems, in both analysis and practice. And it is a long-term proposition, to bring social forces gradually together, across frontiers and above political sensitivities. This collective work stems from the conviction that the different viewpoints involved need to be put into perspective and disseminated, and the belief that this is an indispensable stage in the long process of exchanges underpinning the political, cultural and thematic convergences that are taking shape today.

François Polet

Part One

The State of Struggle
Around the World

I

Political Diversity, Common Purpose: Social Movements in India

Vinod Raina

The methodological problem of identifying and defining a social movement is always difficult, and it becomes particularly complex in Asia. Given its multi-ethnic, multi-lingual and multi-political reality and the bewildering multiplicity and diversity of social movements in the region, this is hardly surprising. After all, social movements must necessarily be firmly embedded in the social, cultural and political realities of a nation. Whereas a mere description of the movements is a matter of collecting information and presenting it systematically, an analysis of the 'embeddedness' and linkages of the movements with wider socio-political processes is a tougher, long-term proposition, especially when dealing with Asia. The region is so vast that to capture its variety in one single overview is quite impossible. Accordingly, this chapter will try to convey an idea of such complexities by focusing on social movements in India, on the assumption that much of the analysis can also be extended to other areas of Asia.

Nevertheless, it seems necessary to have some kind of a guideline, if not an exact definition, of a social movement in order to explore its complexities. We shall therefore use the following: *A social movement is any explicit or implicit persuasion by non-institutionalized groups seeking public gain by attempting to change some part of 'the system'*. Hence:

- social movements are an attempt to bring about institutional change, mainly from *outside* the social structure;
- change may be limited to reform. It may alter some practices or policies of an institution, but leave the institution itself intact;
- change advocated may also be radical or revolutionary, demanding fundamental change in the existing social/ institutional structures and relationships.

Obviously, a large number of social movements in Asia would come into at least one of the above categories; and many may overlap all three of them.

In general it could be said that the scope and concerns of the social movements in the Asian region are not very different from those of other continents. The more historical movements, involving industrial workers, peasants and *adivasis* (indigenous people), since independence from colonial rule in many countries in the region, have been supplemented by the women's, environmental, human rights and peace movements. A particular characteristic of South Asia is the *dalit*, the religious reform and religious fundamentalist movements.

Religious fundamentalist movements pose a particular problem in any attempt to list the movements in the region: should they be included, or not? In terms of the numbers of people involved, they are large movements; but, as far as their objectives go, they show up the inadequacy of the guideline or definition of a social movement as presented above. Many of them are quite radical, as they even demand a structural change in the system itself – from a secular state to one based on a particular religion. But, in the process, they have also to be seen as movements that promote enmity and violence among people of different religions, so the legitimacy of including them in any list could be questioned. If *'public gain'* is to be interpreted as the *'common good for the majority of the oppressed and of those facing injustice'* in the above definition, it would be difficult to include religious fundamentalist movements as they seem to be promoting the *'public gain'* of only one particular identity; that is, if their work can be characterized as promoting *'public gain'* at all. But their reality, extent of penetration within the society and linkages with state politics cannot simply be dismissed, particularly in present-day India.

THE NATIONAL MOVEMENT FOR INDEPENDENCE

One aspect of Asia that must always be kept in mind while discussing its social movements is the various national liberation movements that combated colonial occupation in many countries of the region. Contemporary social movements cannot really be understood without identifying the elements of continuity and change in such liberation movements. And nowhere is this as important as in India.

The Indian national independence movement, as is well known, was greatly influenced by the leadership of Mahatma Gandhi. A staggering number of people participated in this movement, particularly from about 1910 until independence in 1947. Apart from gaining the country's political independence, the movement influenced a nation of 300 million people in 1947 and still influences its population of over a billion today in nearly all aspects of politics and life. Apart from its main characteristics of non-violence and struggle based on truth – *satyagraha* – Gandhian thought penetrated areas such as governance, decentralization, ethics and morality of politics, education, rural and national development, self-reliance, volunteerism, caste and untouchability and much more.

After gaining independence, and even after Gandhi's assassination by a Hindu religious fanatic in 1948, his thought inspired a wide variety of Gandhian movements and civil society formations that continue today. The persistence and resilience of his thought can also now be seen in movements even if they are not direct descendants of Gandhian movements, as in the environmental, *adivasi* and local governance movements. The more direct Gandhian movements include the *sarvodaya* movement that concentrated on the redistribution of land in the 1950s and 1960s but is somewhat dormant now, the movement for *Panchayati Raj* (local governance), and a plethora of Gandhian institutions all over the country, among which the Gandhi Peace Foundation in Delhi, Sewagram Ashram in Wardha, Gandhigram in Tamil Nadu, Gandhi University and Sabarmati Ashram in Gujarat are prominent. His notion of self-reliance, symbolized by the hand-spun local cloth, *khadi*, and other locally produced products, is promoted by the State through a huge organization called the Khadi and Village Industries Commission, with an extensive network of popular retail outlets.

Gandhian thought is appreciated among groups and movements that want to establish a more ethical, moral and harmonious relationship between human activities and nature, and who are seeking 'another world' that avoids the centralization of political power and economic production. It therefore seems to confront and resist both forms of capital, private and state-owned, putting much greater emphasis on community ownership.

DOMINANT POLITICAL TRENDS

A brief outline of the trends dominating the Indian polity can help towards a deeper understanding of the continued impact of the independence movement, and make it easier to situate other contemporary movements in the country. The main organization that canalized the masses of people towards India's independence was the Congress Party: through it, Gandhi was able to reach out and consolidate the movement for independence. But when the country was close to its goal, it became clear that the Congress Party had little faith in Gandhian beliefs concerning power, governance and development.

The modernist Jawaharlal Nehru, although with undiminished respect for his mentor, Gandhi, strongly differed with him on his ideology. The preference of the 'progressive' elements like him within the Congress Party was for a Soviet-style industrial modernization process, combined with a secular, socialist approach. Gandhi's vision was thus seen as utopian, even by those in his own organization. And, despite Gandhi's efforts to reconcile Hindu nationalists and Muslim elements demanding a separate nation, the country was finally divided along religious lines. Thus, instead of one country, there were two, India and the mainly Muslim Pakistan that emerged in 1947, foreshadowing a politics that would be based on religious fundamentalism and intolerance.

But Gandhi and his thought faced, and continues to face, strong criticism and opposition from another sector of society, namely the *dalits*, who see B.R. Ambedkar as their true leader. They believe that Gandhi's concern for the untouchables (*harijans* or 'the people of God', as he called them) was based on upper-caste compassion, rather than a recognition of their social, political and economic rights as equal citizens of India. The left was mostly critical of Gandhi as he did not explicitly talk of class and, worse, his preferred form of resistance, *satyagraha*, was different from the concept of class struggle. Gandhian thought thus differs from both that of the *dalits* and the left.

The left has been, and continues to be, a persuasive political force within the country, without perhaps ever being dominant. Quite clearly, the national independence movement was dominated by the Congress Party. After independence, as has often happened with other multi-party democracies, the single Communist Party of India split, and now has three main strands: the CPI, the CPI (Marxist) and the CPI (Marxist-Leninist), the last being recognized as the Maoist party in other countries and which itself has many factions. Formed in 1967 and coinciding with the campus revolts of the late 1960s, with an explicit justification for the the use of violence for capturing State power, at that time the CPI (ML) caught the imagination of many academics, intellectuals and students, who enrolled in it to work alongside peasants in remote areas of the country. The CPI and CPI (M), on the other hand, have participated in the electoral process, with the CPI (M) having had greater success in the states and the centre. It has continued to rule the state of West Bengal for the last twenty-five years and alternates with the Congress party in governing Kerala. Apart from the three left-wing parties, there are also many left and left-oriented non-party groups and organizations all over India, active on a wide variety of issues.

State power, however, continued to remain largely with the Congress Party, who paid the usual lip service to Gandhi, but moved the country in directions far away from his ideals. The biggest exception occurred in 1994, when Rajiv Gandhi was Prime Minister and the country's constitution was amended to pave the way for local governments, the *Panchayati Raj*, that had been favoured by Mahatma Gandhi. The Congress Party leadership remained mostly and firmly upper caste, with a centrist approach that sometimes leans mildly to the left, as in the case of the nationalization of banks. However, it was the Congress Party that ushered in the era of neoliberal globalization in India at the beginning of the 1990s. There have been two departures from this trend of Congress domination in recent years: the emergence of the lower castes and the rise of Hindu nationalist forces in electoral politics. These developments have completely changed Indian politics.

The Hindu nationalists have not been very prominent in state politics, but they were strongly represented in society, mainly through their 'social movement', the RSS. However, in recent years, after a series of acts heightened communal tensions, such as the demolition of the Babri Masjid (a historic mosque) by Hindu fanatics, and with the rise of Islamic fundamentalism, together with continued hostility towards Muslim Pakistan, the way was opened for their political party, the Bharatiya Janata Party (BJP) to take power at the centre, and in a number of states. At the same time, the lower castes and the *dalits* gradually distanced themselves from the 'benevolence' of the Congress Party by organizing their own parties, including the Bahujan Samaj Party, the Samajvadi Party and elements of Janta Dal. They tasted electoral success in states including Bihar, Uttar Pradesh and Haryana, and began influencing national politics.

Gradually, therefore, political polarization, instead of being based on class, poverty and development, has moved increasingly towards issues based on identities: of religion, caste and ethnicity. And it is in the context of this extremely complex system of politics, religion, caste, poverty and cultural diversity that the social movements operate – attempting social transformation!

THE MOVEMENTS

The most easily identifiable movements in India are those connected with the political parties. Thus the three Communist Parties each have an allied trade union, a student/youth union and a women's movement. But this trend is common for other parties too, including those whose presence may be more dominant in state rather than central politics. Thus both Congress and the right-wing BJP have their trade unions, student unions and women's movements. These are further reinforced by unions of professional workers affiliated to political parties, like those of school, college and university teachers, etc. Having deep loyalties to their parties, with a high degree of control, these movements tend to reflect the traditional tensions and competition existing between their parent parties. Though the student, labour, women's and other issues expressed by each one of them could be the same or similar, there is a tendency to compete with each other. This is not to say there are no common agendas or collaboration from time to time. But the need for unity is a common refrain, particularly from those who are concerned about fragmentation and subsequent loss of political strength.

The contradictions, however, appear when the parent party is in power. The allied movements, vociferous when their parent parties are in opposition, have to muzzle their views to support their party when in power, negating the definition given at the beginning of this chapter that a social movement is one that is 'outside the system'. Party-allied movements are therefore not seen as independent.

Apart from such 'traditional' movements there are the 'new' and 'independent' movements that tend to distance themselves from the traditional party linkages in order to innovate, in terms of organizational structures, leadership roles and proximity with the most oppressed in remote areas. The environment movement comes quickly to mind as one such example.

REVISITING CHIPKO ANDOLAN

Andolan is the common term for a movement in India. The well-known Chipko Andolan literally means 'Hug the Trees Movement', which originated from an incident in 1972 in Reni, a remote village high up in the Himalayas. To recapitulate the story briefly, there was a dispute between the local villagers and a logging contractor who had been allowed to fell trees in a forest close to the village. One day, most of the menfolk had gone to a meeting with government officials at some distance from their village. In their absence, the contractor's workers appeared in the forest to cut the trees. Without hesitating, the women of the village rushed to the forest and clasped the tree trunks, thus preventing the workers from cutting them down. Thwarted, the workers had to withdraw.

News of the incident spread like wildfire through the communities and media, forcing the government, which owned the forest, to negotiate with the community, most of them women. The latter began setting up committees in the region that were soon tackling larger issues, such as eco-friendly development, as a partnership between the community and the government. In spite of the usual ups and downs, the movement has become a major environmental movement, inspiring people elsewhere in the country and the world over.

What underpinned this movement is not always understood, particularly by the elites in India and in the Western world. There is a tendency to cite it in the same breath as, say, the Sierra Club, as a shining example of environmental conservation. But in fact conservation is just one of the underlying elements in the women's action. What they were expressing above all was their 'right to use'. So the issue may be seen as a competition for the right to use, in this case betweeen the State-approved contractors and the local community. It was not as if the women were fighting so that the trees remained untouched. In fact, they themselves needed these trees, as a source of firewood for their hearths and the leaves for fodder. The contractor, on the other hand, was going to clear-fell the trees for timber to be used for manufacturing sports goods. The women were posing the question: 'whose use comes first? Ours, for cooking food, or that of a distant sports goods factory?' In this competition to control a natural resource the conservation of a replenishable resource is inherent, but it is also a question of the kind of use, rather than its non-use. The contractor would have clear-felled the trees, destroying them for ever. The communities traditionally lop the branches and pluck the leaves, allowing the resource to replenish over time.

Chipko therefore provided a blueprint for future movements, both in expressing the tensions between State and communities over the right to natural resources, as well as embodying newer forms of mass action and organizational forms, in which the gender aspect is the most remarkable.

In a different context, the anti-dam movements in India and other Asian countries articulate similar concerns regarding the contending rights of community and State in decisions affecting common property resources that provide subsistence to local populations. Starting with the Narmada Bachao Andolan (NBA, the Save the Narmada Movement), Indian anti-dam movements have propelled the environmental movements to centre stage, through their radical redefinition of development itself. The success of the NBA in forcing the World Bank to withdraw its financial support for the dams on the Narmada river has reverberated throughout the world, and largely contributed to the setting up of the World Commission on Dams, which produced a convincing report in 2000. Largely through the efforts of the NBA, hundreds of resisting movements in the field of natural resources and the environment are today allied under the banner of the National Alliance of People's Movements (NAPM).

THE *DALIT* AGENDA

The caste system is an ancient legacy closely bound up with Hinduism, and still dominant in Indian and other South Asian societies, as well as in Japan (the *burako*). This is a system of four *varnas* (groups): namely, the *brahmin* (the elite, learned and landed), the *kshatriya* (the warriors), the *vaishya* (the traders) and the *shudra* (the menials and the lowest), in that order of hierarchy. At the very bottom are the *dalits*, the untouchables. One of the problems of the left in India has been its inability to combine caste with class in an inclusive political agenda. In other political formations there has been, at best, compassion and sympathy, including – as mentioned earlier – from Gandhi, but they were not for political empowerment that could lead to political rights. The two most influential thinkers and leaders in this respect have come from within the *dalits*, namely Jyotirao Phule and B.R. Ambedkar.

The influence of the older *dalit* political party, the Republican Party, has dwindled over the years and has been supplanted by the more successful Bahujan Samaj Party (BSP). The RP was mostly active in the state of Maharashtra, whereas the BSP has extended itself over large parts of north India and has actually been in power in the country's most populous state, Uttar Pradesh. The backward castes, as they are designated officially by the government, have also changed the political scene in Bihar, another populous state of India, where their party, the Rashtriya Janata Dal, has ruled for many years now. Similarly, it is another party that espouses the cause of the backward castes, the Samajvadi Party, that is in power in Uttar Pradesh today.

The *dalit* social and cultural movements have remained robust and active within civil society, drawing their strength from Phule and Ambedkar. But, as with the left movements, different currents have developed, often in disagreement with one another. They attracted international attention for their fierce protests at the International Conference on Racism in Durban some years back when the Indian Government refused to have the issue of *dalits* included in the conference agenda. They formed an important part of the World Social Forum in Mumbai in January 2004.

RESISTING GLOBALIZATION

With almost all Indian political parties implementing policies of privatization, liberalization and promoting foreign direct investment and markets since 1990, the conflict between the marginalized and impoverished on the one hand and the government on the other has visibly increased. With the closure of thousands of older industries, an increase in agricultural inputs and a decrease in the purchase price of domestic agricultural produce, workers and peasants are bearing the brunt of neoliberal policies. With the urban middle class reaping whatever few benefits the neoliberal world can offer, the rural–urban divide is further deepening.

India has a labour force of some 340 million people, of which only about 30 million are organized. This leaves over 300 million in the unorganized sector, most of whom are agricultural workers. The trade union movement is therefore unable to reach out to most Indian labourers, many of whom are *dalits*, women and *adivasis*. They thus express themselves through their allied social movements, which may be concerned with the environment, *adivasis*, peasants or *dalits*. Increasingly in the last fifteen years, these movements have had to deal with issues related to globalization. However, with the national media firmly under the control of neoliberal interests, their voices have been stifled and they have become more invisible, as they are of no interest any more, meriting barely any mention in the frenzied news industry.

The Gandhian legacy of volunteerism spawned many development voluntary agencies, particularly after the heyday of the Maoist uprisings in the early 1970s. Many city professionals migrated to rural areas and worked directly with the local people through these voluntary agencies. In the beginning these agencies had meagre funds available, and they worked in the spirit of volunteerism, close to the communities. But in the early 1980s, the central government recognized their importance as delivery agencies for rural development and began to set aside funds for them. With funding available from agencies abroad, the voluntary sector quickly mushroomed into the more familiar NGO sector, particularly in numbers. It is estimated that there are as many as 200,000 NGOs in India.

The funded, professionally staffed NGO contrasts greatly with the large social and mass movements that are cash-starved but much more broadly based. Very often the two collaborate on issues in their geographical areas, but there is mutual tension, sometimes bordering on mistrust. The movements generally find the NGOs less radical and prone to taking decisions determined by their funding needs. The advent of globalization seems to have heightened such tensions, as the NGO sector is heavily favoured even by institutions like the World Bank.

The situation has become further complicated by the advent of the local government institutions, the Panchayats, since the 1994 constitutional amendments that facilitated their emergence. As they are elected bodies with five-year cycles, movements and NGOs are confronted by these democratic institutions in precisely the fields in which they themselves work. Governments, often irritated by the presence of NGOs and movements, have been quick to raise the legitimacy of civil society organizations in the midst of such democratically elected bodies. Many NGOs have either ignored the Panchayat institutions or come into conflict with them. But some have recognized their political importance, however inefficient they may be, and tried in various ways to collaborate with them.

One such movement is the People's Science Movement, which appears to be unique in the world: certainly it is difficult to find a similar movement outside India. It consists of a large number of science professionals – engineers, doctors, scientists and many teachers, who have worked with the local people and communities – and in many instances the Panchayats. As many as 300,000 such professionals have been engaged in such work almost over the whole country. The movement, combining reconstruction and struggle, is involved in education, literacy, water, health, rural production, energy and local governance systems, and it uses various forms of struggle to resist the neoliberal onslaught. Whenever feasible, the movement collaborates with the government, but also confronts it when in disagreement. With a definite left leaning, the movement has tried to be inclusive in bringing together people of all political opinion from centre to left, and its intellectual efforts have tried to synthesize Marxist and Gandhian thought. In particular, it has experimented actively in local people's planning methods, in collaboration with the Panchayats, as a means of resisting the centralizing tendencies of the neoliberal paradigm.

A major upheaval occurred among the social movements in India, confronted as they were by the challenge of the World Social Forum in Mumbai in January 2004. With the international community favouring India as the venue for the fourth forum, after the first three in Porto Alegre, Brazil, there were many who doubted whether the process could remain inclusive in the highly diverse and somewhat divisive world of Indian social movements and NGOs. This is hardly surprising, given that there are divisions even among the movements sharing the same ideology, and the historical differences between the left, the Gandhians, the *dalits*, the Socialists, the environmentalists, as well as the new and the traditional among the women, worker and peasant movements. In the end, nearly 200 mass movements, social organizations and NGOs from diverse ideologies combined to form an Indian working committee to collaborate to make WSF 2004 happen. This is quite unprecedented and it is interesting to note that the Brazilian counterpart organization has only eight member organizations.

But WSF is obviously not everyone's favourite space. As it excludes groups who believe in violence as a means of action, and given the deep mistrust of Indian movements towards foreign funding agencies in general, some groups and movements came together, with other countries like the Philippines, to organize a parallel event to the WSF 2004, which they called the Mumbai Resistance 2004. Their claim was that their agenda against imperialist globalization was more radical than that of WSF.

However, as long as movements against neoliberalism are prepared to mobilize more and more people for the purpose, the WSF does not claim or want to be the only platform or space from which to operate. This has clearly been the attitude of the movements that have come together for the first time in such large numbers for the

WSF in India, and it indicates how the movements are beginning to see the value of keeping the main objective in view rather than quibbling over who is in control. If such an attitude continues after the WSF, one could say that it has had a positive impact on the Indian movements. One can only hope so.

2

Resistance to Globalization in Rural China

Lau Kin Chi

The term globalization has entered everyday vocabulary in China in the last decade. After the Reform was launched under Deng Xiaoping's helmsmanship in 1978, although reservations have been voiced about negative impacts on China's development, the overall view in the official media and from the metropolitan centres was to welcome this development as restoring China's 'global citizenship', attaining probable world power status, and possibly liberalizing society. Favourable reports have cited China's 9 per cent annual economic growth rate, and the emergence of a substantial middle class whose values and lifestyles are influenced by perceptions of Western modes of modern life, apparently representing a promising future for the country's ascent to modernity.

At the same time, the media cannot avoid being deeply troubled by the increasing polarization of Chinese society, acknowledging the irreducible existence of *san-nong*, 'the three rural dimensions', that is, problems relating to rural population (peasants), rural production (agriculture), and the rural world (countryside). Dr Wen Tiejun, among the first scholars to draw national attention to these three dimensions, explained the need to highlight the predicament of large sections of the rural population and the deterioration of conditions in the countryside. Public concern is not, in fact, only about the economy.[1]

This chapter attempts to focus on the rural dimension by exploring resistance to globalization spearheaded by the powers from above and from outside. It is by scrutinizing the rural dimension that one can see the processes in which large sections of the population are being relegated to irrelevance in social development, and natural, human and capital resources are being increasingly drained away from the countryside. Alternatives need to be explored to counter the logic of this situation.

Many discourses on resistance to globalization tend to identify the source of the problems as being, for example, the policies of powerful G7 states or the influential World Trade Organization, the World Bank, International Monetary Fund and multinational corporations. Resistance is seen as being organized against these institutions, hence the protests at Seattle and Genoa, or advocating changes in IMF policies or the restructuring of United Nations institutions. While institutional or legislative changes at these high levels are desirable and do have positive impacts of scale, ordinary people are likely to be remote from such interventions, or find them irrelevant – even working against them, for they are rarely, if ever, confronted directly by these powerful institutions and high-level politics. Instead, they have to combat the consequences and effects of globalization processes that are mediated through local networks of power relations and institutions. Their everyday negotiations inevitably seem fragmented or incoherent but they may contain elements that are enabling, as well as being confined by the context in which they are embedded.

It is the purpose of this chapter to try and make sense of this innovative resistance from the people as they confront the mediating effects of globalization. It is true that alternative ways of thinking and action cannot be divorced from the local situation, which is embedded in a complex web of polemical or contesting power relations. However, such innovative responses and initiatives point to the possibilities of different forms of agency in the pursuit of self-organization as a group or community, outside the confines of the mentalities and practices of globalization.

The overall State policy defining economic and social development strategies in China since 1978 has been the Reform. The key turning point was the introduction of the household responsibility system for agriculture by dissolution of the People's Communes and redistribution of land and other resources, initially on a per capita basis, and subsequently allowing concentration in the hands of a so-called 'competent' minority in order to enhance productivity. It should, however, be stressed that this system did not become State policy through initiatives from the centre. Many reviews cite, for example, Xiaogang Village in Anhui Province as one of the first experiments in introducing the household responsibility system in December 1978. A document with the fingerprints and seals of twenty people from this village is now to be found in the Chinese Revolution Museum, bearing witness to the secret oath taken by the twenty families to practise this system, with mutual support, at risk of imprisonment for contravening the mainstream practice of People's Communes at that time.[2] As is often the case, local practices resist obsolete central policies before they are subsequently acknowledged by the authorities, or even adopted as State policy. But in the process of institutionalization, certain essential elements are lost, such as the co-operative spirit and appropriate division of labour among the families. The baby (communal co-operation and mutual trust) is thrown away with the bath water (State-imposed extraction of rural resources in the name of collectivism and through the People's Communes).

It should also be stressed that the pressure of globalization, though much more visible in the last two decades, had already had an impact on China before the Reform. The first three decades of China's practice of 'socialism in one country', presented as embarking on a road of self-reliance, were more the result of necessity than of choice, because of US isolation and the hostility of the USSR. The exclusion, apparently ending in failure in 1978, was itself a response to the challenge of globalization but it was not necessarily a resistance – or even an effective one – against the essence of globalization, which is modernization. The dream of modernizing China, confronted by imperialist domination and occupation, has been based for over a century on China emulating its rivals: hence the slogan of the 1910s of acquiring Science and Democracy, and the slogan of the 1950s of Catching Up with Britain and the USA.

Industrialization, urbanization and militarization follow the logic of modernization and globalization. The advocacy of self-interest and greed and the reduction of human relationships to monetary ones, which have been legitimized and promoted in the last two decades since the Reform, are but the more flagrant emulation of the values and cultures of modernization. In this bold march towards it, what is forgotten are the values of traditional cultures that hold communities together: giving, reciprocity, tolerance, mutual aid, collectivity and sustainability.

Resistance to globalization can be seen in places where the logic of modernization is frustrated or countered. Overall State policies and strategies are mainly responsible for the overwhelming tide of the globalization of the modern, from images of modern life together with the desires and fantasies it embraces, to the use of science and technology for the building of military might. But the colonization of social processes by globalization has various impacts in the different areas of China and evokes various reactions. The tensions and disputes reflect the constraints as well as the possibilities for resistance.

The first two developments examined here have been carried out on a fairly large scale. The Two-Land-Use Scheme is concerned with land use, and the Rural Cooperative Fund has to do with rural finance. Neither originated as a State policy, but developed as an initiative at the local level in an attempt to meet local needs. In both cases, promotion of the schemes, which had varying effects elsewhere, later provoked the intervention of the central government, and both were banned in the 1990s. However, they do represent an alternative vision of the possibilities for the collective use of resources and people's voluntary participation in social life. They resulted from people's efforts to find solutions to problems created by the imposition of directives and organization from above, according to the ideas serving the objectives of modernization in competition with the West.

These local initiatives always contain elements from the traditions of rural communities. It is these elements, once rooted in people's knowledge and practice, which can constitute the resistance to becoming completely engulfed by globalization. They can lead to openings for alternatives by engaging with everyday life, reviving such elements in a different context. This makes the innovative moves of the people neither traditional nor modern, but contemporary – that is to say, in order to grasp innovative resistance from the people, as pointed out by Frantz Fanon, we must be able to recognize the contemporaneity of the people.[3]

Pingdu County in Shandong Province, northeast China, is a good illustration of these two developments. With a population of one million, Pingdu deferred implementing the Reform decree of contracting land to individual households because its existing collective economies had been quite developed before the Reform. In 1984, when implementation of the household responsibility system became compulsory, as an indication of allegiance to the Reform, it was launched over the whole county, but some collectively owned processing factories, orchards and farms remained collective.

From 1986 onwards, the township governments in Pingdu launched an experimental policy. Instead of a more or less equal distribution of arable land, a per capita 0.8 acre of 'subsistence land' was allocated to the villagers. This should normally produce 350 kg of grain for each person and enough for the rearing of two pigs and ten chickens for each household. The remaining two-thirds of the land was graded according to fertility and plans formulated for a different use. These activities were conducted by all the villagers collectively. Some land was designated for growing vegetables, some for orchards. The land was then put to open bidding as 'contract land', with the rent assessed at 35 to 40 per cent of the net profit expected, to be paid in advance to a collective development fund. The average scale was 2 to 2.5 acres for each working hand, for a contract term of five years. Conditions were attached: for example, for every 0.8 acre of land contracted, two pigs, one cow or fifty chickens had to be raised.

This combination of farming and livestock rearing helped to defend them against the negative effects of market fluctuations. (Indeed, since 1989, there have been substantial fluctuations in market prices for chilli, ginger, cabbage, chicken, pork, beef and other agricultural products.) At the same time, organic manure was produced so that the peasants did not hand back impoverished land to the collective. This two-land-use scheme of subsistence land and contract land, while assuring individual subsistence, collective income and fairness of income distribution, also subjected land use to collective planning, individual implementation and greater efficiency.[4]

When this result was promoted as a success, in many other places where Pingdu's traditions or conditions for a collective economy and participation did not exist, the scheme was often used as a pretext by local authorities to give minimum subsistence land to peasants and the rest of the land to a small minority. In 1997, to halt this, the central government banned the scheme and Pingdu was also obliged to give it up.

In the case of Pingdu, there was a different practice of collectivism than the reductive, levelling-of-differences collectivism imposed by the Communist regime. Collectivism based on the levelling of differences was prescribed as a cure against the injustice of capitalist individualism. But, inevitably, there are differences because of the heterogeneity of the members of a collective. By reducing consensual relations of equality (which can only come about through negotiations between the people themselves) to relations of numerical equality between individuals, the back door is opened for the worst kind of individualism to creep in. It led to a grudging spirit, which was against other people getting a greater share than oneself. Such calculating control stifles the spirit of giving and generosity cultivated in communal traditions of reciprocity and mutual aid, based on the acknowledgement of difference.

The Pingdu case was an experiment in the art of making a collective that upheld the principle of equality for all members while acknowledging the differences created by the heterogeneity of the collective. It was a question of finding a formula of the minimum numerical equality guaranteeing the material existence of each member of the collective and serving as the basis on which differences are allowed to work to the benefit of all. Playing on differences is very much a pedagogical process and it is well understood by the villagers: mapping the difference of resources from land to people, acknowledging the differences and abilities of other members of a community, and taking risks. It is also a pedagogical process because it cultivates the open mind that comes from giving and a generous spirit.

As for rural finance, agricultural banks had withdrawn from the agricultural sector and there was little government investment. Hence alternative ways had to be sought for local finance and accumulation. Rural Cooperative Funds (RCFs) were developed in the early 1980s because of this need for rural credit. With the approval of the central government, collective assets from the People's Communes were audited as credits in these fund organizations, which also took contributions from collectives and individual households. As co-operative funds, they were initially promoted at the grassroots levels in provinces specializing in agricultural production. In Pingdu, RCFs began to be set up in 1988 and by 1992, when they were formally established, the total membership contributions amounted to 263 million yuan (US$1 = 8.3 yuan), of which 12 million yuan came from village collectives and 66 million yuan from peasant households. Of these funds, 83 per cent were invested in agricultural production, infrastructure and machinery, as well as in the generation of electricity. This enabled the irrigated area in Pingdu to cover 64 per cent of the total cultivated area.

This community-based RCF is a good example of the self-management of collective assets. It was reported that by 1992, 17,400 townships and 112,500 villages in China had co-operative funds as their main financial institutions, representing 36.7 per cent and 15.4 per cent respectively of Chinese townships and villages, with a total capital of 16.5 billion yuan.[5]

After 1992, however, while RCFs at the village level were mostly subject to collective monitoring by villagers, those set up at township levels were in the main controlled by township authorities and used to fund rural enterprises or pay off local government debts. The whole country gave way to a fever of speculative economic growth resulting in chaos and bad debt in the financial sector. According to research, in 1997 the average debt in seven provinces was 2 million yuan for the township governments and 0.2 million yuan for the village governments. Their total debts were to exceed 30 billion yuan in 1999. The central government finally intervened at the end of 1996 to close down 21,000 RCFs at the township level and 24,000 RCFs at the village level, their total capital amounting to 150 billion yuan. Formal dissolution was announced in January 1999.

These two examples provide a glimpse into the complexity of what happens on the ground. The Reform is politically compulsory, but local situations vary, determined by a complex interplay of diverse actors and forces. Different authorities intervene in various ways, producing different results. Banning the two-land-use scheme may be strangling a good practice in Pingdu, but it protects the land rights of peasants against the expropriation of their land elsewhere. It is important to recognize the constraints while identifying all the possibilities for alternative practices to evolve locally. It is also necessary to consider the cultural factor in deciding whether practices are accommodating globalization or resisting it.

Take, for example, a very well known case that has been publicized as alternative practice. Nanjie Village in Henan Province has a population of 3,000 and has been in the spotlight of both the domestic and international media.[6] Called a 'mini communist community', it is apparently a pocket of communal ownership and distribution that has persisted, despite the general flood of privatization and atomization. It is reported that each year the village receives 300,000 visitors interested in its experience.

As in other similar cases, the Nanjie example is inextricably linked to a charismatic leader. Wang Hongbin, the village party secretary, carried out the State policy of distributing land to households and contracting enterprises to individuals in 1981. Within a few years, he was receiving complaints about social polarization and inequities. In 1984, after consultation with the villagers, the local party leadership contracted village enterprises and started to recover land for collective planning. Its motto was 'square internal discipline and round external relations'. Internally, it is one big collective, with everyone being employed as wage-earners, and agricultural labourers replacing small peasants. Starting from a brick and a flour factory, there are now 26 enterprises based on food processing and related services. The value of their output has almost doubled each year, from 0.7 million yuan in 1984 to 1.42 billion in 1999 – increasing 2,000 times in 15 years.

While the workforce numbers 12,000, almost 90 of them are migrant workers from outside, who do not share in the benefits enjoyed by the Nanjie villagers. The latter enjoy a life of 'communist' egalitarian sharing: from cradle to grave, everything is taken care of by the collective, including education, housing, health and job security. The incomes and benefits of the leaders are the same as those of an ordinary villager. Private life is closely monitored, marriage and family planning must be approved by the leadership, and deviant behaviour is criticized at mass assemblies. Dissident villagers have the 'right' to leave the collective, but lose all welfare benefits.

As for 'roundness' in external relations, Nanjie presents itself as a successful corporation, playing according to the rules of the domestic and global market, modern management and capital accumulation, with decision-making vested in a body that combines party authority, village administration and entrepreneurship. For example, cadres take turns to play mahjong to entertain Japanese investors in a special guest-house, although all forms of gambling are banned in the village. Thus, the imposition of ideological control and work discipline is instrumental in capital accumulation, although Nanjie's business 'success' goes back a long way.

Since the 1950s, the village had developed a sound economic base through mobilizing collective input – hence the strong reaction of most villagers against the inequalities of the 1981–84 period. However, the fact is that the general feeling in favour of justice and equality has turned into unquestioning submissiveness to authority, which betrays the egalitarian collective spirit of the village. For the collective, shaped by decades of practice in rejecting an outright return to individualism, is based on a secret individualism characterized by a grudging spirit against difference, against having less than others. It is the irony of such collectives, formed by the aggregates of identical numbers, that their world can only be maintained by submitting themselves to the iron hand of an absolute authority.

Heilongtan (Dark Dragon Pond) in Yulin County, Shaanxi Province gives an idea of the way communities can organize themselves in providing public services. A local folk legend has it that a Dark Dragon inhabits a natural spring and gives its blessing to this area, where annual rainfall is a mere 300 mm. Nine villages in the vicinity of the Dark Dragon Pond took part in renovating the temple in 1981, organizing the rituals, and attracting 200,000 visitors every year to the Dark Dragon Festival. After 1995 voluntary contributions to the temple by villagers and visitors amounted to one million yuan a year. This wealth has been used by the communities for social investments such as installing TV transmission stations, setting up scholarships for clever or poor students, building a secondary school and renovating several primary schools, sponsoring adult education, opera performances, sports activities and old people's clubs, and working on infrastructure for agriculture such as irrigation, roads and electricity. All this was done by villagers headed by the architect of the temple, Wang Kehua, acting outside the government administration. There has been no lack of problems, such as the temple being compelled to define its religion. In the end, Taoism, one of the five officially endorsed religions in China, was self-designated.

This example is significant, not only in the way folk culture plays a role in the organization of life in the community. It is also well known for its environmental concerns. In this arid area there is a great need for trees. Using contributions to the temple and volunteer labour, trees have been planted and now cover 300 acres.[7]

The Dark Dragon as the guardian of the community stands for the well-being of each and every member of the community. But it does not represent them in the same way that the Party claims to represent the people. It is not an agent, like the Party, which can do things in the name of the people. The public authority it has over the people is more like an empty space that can receive the aspirations, visions and discourses addressed to it for the safekeeping of the community as well as the well-being of individuals, which is understood as being rooted in the community and given meaning by the folk beliefs in the Dark Dragon. This makes the authority of the Dark Dragon dialogic and collectively grounded. It also means that people are linked to the Dark Dragon, not simply as visitors coming as individuals for their own interests, but that they are also connected to the habitat of the Dragon and the community that claims to be its protégé. Thus it is more likely that the actions of the authority of the Dark Dragon can mobilize forces for conservation rather than the relentless modernization that is destroying traditions and communities through the processes of globalization.

What the Dark Dragon guards, against blind allegiance to globalization, is the language, knowledge and experience of sustainable livelihoods that are organically linked to people's habitat. However, the larger-than-life authority delegated to it by the people allows it to emerge from among them as an empty space that can only be operated dialogically within the boundary of a collective.

For any resistance to globalization to be effective, this sort of public spirit must be recognized and respected.

Another example is the promotion of motherhood values in fostering solidarity within the community. The Wanli–Luxia Women's Credit Union–Cooperative in Baishui Township, Jiangxi Province was formed in 1994 as an alternative trade project in lily bulbs, supported by CSD, a voluntary group based in Hong Kong. With all the women of the two village communities of Wanli and Luxia voluntarily joining as members, the group has tried to organize itself along participatory lines to undertake community projects, such as contracting a piece of hill-land for collective organic farming, improving drinking water sources and operating labour-saving grain threshing machines, running literacy classes for its members and a kindergarten for the small children, organizing drawing and writing competitions for young people, and women's and children's health check-ups. In an uphill battle against the dominant trends of selfishness, individualism and calculation, the group has nonetheless managed to survive. One of its efforts has been to combat the malnutrition of children in this mountain area and, for three years, it has mobilized voluntary labour among the mothers to take turns to prepare breakfast for all the children of the community, so that each receives 10 buns and three eggs every week.[8] A simple three-storey building that the women's group managed to construct, largely with its own funds, bears witness to their persistence in carving out a space for women in a society dominated by male chauvinists.

This is another example of the contemporaneity of the people. Motherhood in Chinese tradition has always meant women's submissiveness in a patriarchal order, a woman's role as mother being confined within the house of her husband. But for the women of the credit union, motherhood is practised collectively outside their own homes. It becomes a public place for women to take part dialogically in inventing methods of co-operation and mutual help, an autonomous space for practices different from those dictated by the pursuit of wealth and success that are generally seen as the essence and promise of globalization.

Finally, I would like to cite an example in which resistance to the colonization of globalization processes is being carried out in more explicit terms.

Over recent years, the term 'rural reconstruction' has entered the arena of debate in China, indicating an acknowledgement of the critical situation in the rural world and the need to address it. In

2003, the James Yen Institute for Rural Reconstruction was set up to bring together efforts for rural reconstruction.[9] It aims at facilitating the study of rural development efforts in China over the last century, as well as practices of rural reconstruction in the world today. The institute will be running training programmes for peasants and other learners and conducting experiments in eco-farming, organic farming and appropriate technology. These activities will be carried out on its 30-acre campus close to Zhaicheng Village, Hebei Province, where James Yen first conducted his experiments in the 1920s.

These early efforts in rural reconstruction took place in the depth of the crisis created by China's political and social collapse, under the onslaught of the modern forces of the West. For many intellectuals, the task was to build a modern China and shape the population into citizens of a modern civilization. People like James Yen, Liang Suming and Tao Xingzhi were sufficiently rooted in the situations and sufferings of the people that they were not completely absorbed by the idea of building a new Chinese State, adequately armed to defend itself. Instead, their concern lay with the people and they saw their task as enabling them to engage in self-management activities and govern themselves at the local level, which means reviving the traditions that had been sundered by the invasion of campaigns from the West. In other words, they realized that the specific situation of China required that any meaningful transformation must be based at the local level, and that Western modernization could not be transferred to China. Today, efforts to reread their experience share the same insights: that the express train of globalization is not only undesirable but could be catastrophic for the majority of the peasant population of China.

The idea is to enable the rebuilding of rural communities ecologically to favour good relationships among the people themselves, as well as relationships between people and nature. It is recognized that the reconstruction of the rural world, where most Chinese people reside, is strategically important in order to rebuild the trust, mutual aid and co-operation that have been shattered by China's forced march towards modernization, to mitigate the polarization of society and to heal the wounds polarization has inflicted on people. Thus it takes a form of resistance that is not immediately engaging globalization – and may even be far away from the power house known as globalization – but rather takes the form of modest efforts to help the people manage their daily lives.

NOTES

1. Wen Tiejun (2001) 'Centenary reflections on the "three dimensional problems" of rural China', *Inter-Asia Cultural Studies*, vol. 2, no. 2, pp. 287–95.
2. See, for example, Wu Xiang (2001) *Zhongguo nongcun gaige shilu (True Record of the Rural Reform in China)* (Hangzhou: Zhejiang Renmin), pp. 131–8.
3. See David Lloyd (1995) 'Nationalisms against the state', *Gender and Colonialism* (Galway: Galway University), pp. 260–1.
4. Wen Tiejun (2000) *Study of the Basic Economic Institutions of Rural China* (Beijing: China Economic Press), pp. 301–3, 498–501. Seminar on Alternative Approaches to Rural Questions, *Resource Materials for the School on Sustainability*, January 2003, pp. 178–80.
5. Wen Tiejun (2003) 'The rise and demise of the Rural Cooperative Fund: 1984–1999', *China Reflected*, ed. Lau Kin Chi and Huang Ping (Hong Kong: ARENA), pp. 96–122.
6. Several books in China have been produced to present and discuss the Nanjie experience, and it has also been reported by the *New York Times, The Economist*, the BBC, etc.
7. Luo Hongguang (2000) *Exchange of Unequal Values: Wealth around work and consumption* (Hangzhou: Zhejiang People's Press), pp. 210–28, 255. Seminar on Alternative Approaches to Rural Questions, *Resource Materials for the School on Sustainability*, January 2003, pp. 183–5.
8. See Lau Kin Chi (2002) 'Pedagogical working on place: Women's economic activism in rural China', *Development*, vol. 45, no.1, March, pp. 84–7.
9. See website www.china-village.net

3

NGOs and Social Movements in Southeast Asia

Francis Loh

Rapid economic growth characterized the Southeast Asian countries during the 1980s and early 1990s. This growth was attributed to the role of the developmental State, which had adapted itself to the thrust of neoliberal globalization by adopting economic liberalization, deregulation and privatization policies. Following the 1997–98 financial crisis in the region, the role of the developmental State was attacked and rolled back, not least by means of the structural adjustment packages that some of the countries were forced to adopt in order to receive International Monetary Fund (IMF) aid. Meanwhile, as a result of growth prior to the financial meltdown, Southeast Asian societies were transformed, resulting in the consolidation of the middle classes and considerable political ferment. In spite of controls on civil liberties and reluctance to share power with civil society, democratic politics had emerged (or re-emerged) prior to, as well as following the 1997–98 crisis.

This chapter first discusses the rise and evolution of the non-governmental organizations and social movements in four Southeast Asian countries, namely, Philippines, Thailand, Indonesia and Malaysia, and evaluates their contributions towards deepening democratization and promoting equitable development. Co-operation with their governments, as well as networking with other regional NGOs and movements to facilitate changes to the global economic and political order will then be discussed. The last section elaborates on developments in Southeast Asia in the wake of the 11 September tragedy and increasing US unilateralism in world affairs, and how the NGOs and social movements have recently assessed their roles.

THE RISE OF NGOs IN SOUTHEAST ASIA

NGOs first came to attention in the Philippines, Indonesia and Thailand in the 1970s when relatively democratic governments were replaced by martial law or military rule. With the suspension of elections and parliamentary rule, the proscription of political parties, trade unions and student movements, and detention of the opposition and activists, critical groups of the middle classes turned to NGOs to sustain their involvement in alternative development as well as in civil liberty activities. In Malaysia, a certain group of the middle class formed NGOs as an alternative to communal-based political parties.

Another impetus for the formation of NGOs came from the 'new social movements' in the West. These included the women's, environmental, minority rights and peace movements, and neighbourhood-based 'direct action' groups. Subsequent growth of the NGOs was then spurred on by the consolidation of the educated middle classes resulting from the economic growth of the past twenty to thirty years.[1]

The NGOs may be categorized into four major types:

- charitable, providing welfare services;
- reformist or 'alternative development', promoting projects that emphasize self-reliance;
- more overtly political and human rights advocacy, stressing empowerment of the people and transformation of the political system;
- support, involving discursive work – researching, publishing and debating – to promote alternative views and contest official narratives and dominant discourses.

However, only a minority of the middle classes sought democratization. The larger group were imbued with 'developmentalism', a new political culture that promotes consumerist habits dependent on rapid growth, in turn dependent on political stability, even if authoritarian means are resorted to. In other words, the new discourse of developmentalism is the cultural by-product of an economic *dirigisme* successfully undertaken by the developmental State during the 1980s and early 1990s.[2] Even during the financial crisis, a majority of the middle classes in Malaysia and Singapore, for instance, shied away from demanding democratic reform. Restoring economic growth was considered more important. It was only in Indonesia and Thailand, which were less developed and more authoritarian (and earlier, in the mid-1980s in the Philippines as well), that a critical mass of the middle classes demanded political reform and regime change. In the latter three countries, NGOs and social movements were already very active prior to the 1997–98 crisis.

A review of the circumstances in each of the four Southeast Asian countries enables us to compare the roles played by the NGOs and social movements.

Philippines

According to one estimate, in 1995 there were about 70,000 NGOs of all types in the Philippines.[3] Most are involved in providing health, educational, physical and financial infrastructure assistance to poor rural villages as well as to urban slums. Some also help to organize co-operatives. Many of the NGOs involved in such welfare work are linked to the Catholic Church.

Civil liberties and human rights, women and peace, cultural and theatre, environmental and indigenous peoples' groups are numerous and active. Still other NGOs conduct research and publish pamphlets, books and journals, as well as organize forums.

There are also coalitions and networks of NGOs. Some of the mass-based sectoral coalitions are: the Congress for a People's Agrarian Reform, National Council for Fisherfolk and Aquatic Reform, Labour Centres in certain areas, the Urban Poor Coordinating Network, the National Confederation of Cooperatives and the People's Media Network. Through such networks, NGOs have also developed close ties with the working class, and sometimes worked closely with the trade unions, which, after the Marcos regime was ousted in 1986, have consolidated themselves.

Multi-sectoral issue-based coalitions include the Freedom from Debt Coalition and the Coalition for Peace; and the Caucus of Development NGO Networks, comprises some of the largest NGO networks in the country. In the Philippines, these coalitions, networks and caucuses of NGOs are usually distinguished from the 'people's organizations' (POs) which are involved in grassroots work. Together, they have mobilized large sections of the people through different types of mass action and played important roles in the overthrow of Marcos and subsequent democratization.

In conducting various socio-economic programmes, these NGOs have often assumed the functions of government in providing amenities and services to the poor majority. In fact, the 1987 Constitution adopted by Aquino's government commends the roles played by NGOs and POs. The Local Government Code 1991, also passed during Aquino's presidency, furthers the role of the NGOs in local affairs. There are provisions for the representatives of women, farmers, fishermen, workers and other special groups (including ethnic minorities and urban squatters) to sit on local councils at the municipality, city and provincial levels. Indeed, the 1991 Code specifies that at least one-quarter of the total membership of the Local Development Councils from the *barangay* to the provincial levels should come from the NGOs. NGOs are further represented on the Local School Boards, Local Health Boards, Local Peace and Order Councils, as well as the tender boards of the councils so as to monitor corruption.

Recently, NGOs and POs have ventured into electoral politics either by setting up alliances in support of particular candidates or launching their own political parties. The translation of the influence and support that the NGOs enjoy into more effective means of influencing government policies and political transformation is a current critical issue.

Thailand

A directory of NGOs listed at least 465 NGOs in Thailand in 1997.[4] Many of them were first established in the 1973–76 democracy period. After the military coup d'état, some of these NGOs were silenced but resurfaced during the 1980s.

One of the most prominent NGOs today is the NGO-Coordinating Committee on Rural Development (NGO-CORD), based in Bangkok, with some 200 development NGOs affiliated to it. In general they have advocated alternative, people-friendly development strategies. A prominent NGO associated with NGO-CORD is the Thai Development Support Committee, which conducts research and publishes the *Thai Development Newsletter*.

There are also NGOs concerned with the plights of hill tribe minorities, women, workers and children. Several NGOs have also taken up issues like sex tourism, the exploitation of prostitutes, sourcing alternative employment for sex-industry women, and AIDS education. In Bangkok, the NGO Co-ordinating Committee on Slums networks about ten grassroots NGOs, which focus on housing security and providing basic services for urban slum dwellers. Through the Co-ordinating Committee for Primary Health Care of Thai NGOs, some 20 small NGOs co-operate with one another.

Civil rights groups have also been formed, drawing support from lawyers, law students and lecturers in local universities. In 1979, many NGOs and NGO co-ordinating committees, led by the human rights NGOs, launched the Campaign for Popular Democracy (CPD) and drew in political parties, trade unions and religious groups including the Thai Inter-religious Commission for Development and the Coordinating Group on Religion for Society, both linked to the highly respected activist Sulak Sivaraksa. Thus when the military attempted to seize power in 1992, causing the incident of Black May 1992, it was opposed by a huge protest movement in Bangkok and other towns.

This successful campaign to restore democratic rule instilled a new sense of confidence and unity in Thai NGOs. The challenge for the NGOs today appears to be the deepening of democratic reform as well as the promotion of more culturally appropriate ways to achieve development. The Local Development Institute led by Dr Prawet Wasi has argued for 'a more moral capitalist ethic' wherein a balance is reached between promoting agricultural development and business activities that are beneficial to the majority.

Thai NGOs played a crucial role in forging the pro-democracy coalition that pushed for the drafting of a new constitution (Thailand's 15th!) in 1997, even when the country was severely hit by the financial crisis. After parliament passed the Constitution in September 1997, Prime Minister Chaovalit, who had sided with the conservatives to oppose the constitutional reforms, was forced to step aside. Among the new provisions are: elections to both houses of parliament as well as to local government; the establishment of an independent election commission, an independent constitutional court and a national counter-corruption commission and the guarantee of press freedom. While it is clear that economic problems continue to plague post-crisis Thai society, Thai democracy appears to have been consolidated by the promulgation of the most democratic constitutional changes in its history.

Malaysia

NGOs in Malaysia are limited to a few hundred. Compared to the Philippines and Thailand, Malaysian NGOs have made only modest gains. Strict laws *per se* do not explain the difference, but rather the hegemony of the dominant ruling party (United Malays National Organisation) over rural Malays. In turn, UMNO's hegemony depends on two factors: the multi-ethnic situation, which has led to communal politics, and the relatively successful rural development programmes, which have improved conditions for UMNO's Malay supporters. Consequently few NGOs are involved in rural development areas. Instead, the major Malaysian NGOs are urban-based and generally address middle-class concerns. Also, until the late 1990s, most NGO activists as well as those who supported them were non-Malays.

Malaysia has a number of successful consumer organizations. The most important of these is the Consumers Association of Penang (CAP), which has been active since the 1970s and has conducted campaigns on behalf of poor farmers, fisherfolk and estate workers. There are also environmental groups like Sahabat Alam Malaysia, the Malayan Nature Society and the Environmental Protection Society, which have lobbied with some success. On several occasions, environmentalists have also gone to court, on one occasion to challenge the government's hastiness in launching the massive Bakun Dam Hydro-Electric Project in Sarawak state, without conducting a proper environmental impact assessment.

Women's NGOs include AWAM (All Women's Action Society), Sisters-in-Islam, the Women's Aid Organisation and the Women's Centre for Change. Largely through their efforts, and co-operation with women's wings of the ruling parties, a Domestic Violence Act was introduced in 1996, and several laws that discriminated against women were amended.

Human rights groups include Aliran, formed in 1977, and Suaram and Hakam, formed in the 1990s. They have led the campaign, supported by opposition parties and unions, for the repeal of coercive laws, especially the obnoxious Internal Security Act (ISA), which allows for detention without trial. Legal support has also been provided to ISA and other political detainees, and a general educational campaign to make people more aware of their rights is ongoing. The Estate Workers' Support Committees have struggled for the introduction of a monthly wage scheme while other NGOs have protested alongside the Peneroka Bandar (urban pioneers) facing eviction by developers. Several NGOs also campaign for the rights of indigenous groups in the peninsula, in Sarawak and Sabah.

The NGO movement received a fillip in the late 1990s following the 'dual crisis' – the 1997 financial crisis and the 1998 political crisis, which developed after Deputy Premier Anwar Ibrahim was first sacked from the ruling party and then detained. Anwar's supporters, who initially fought for his well-being, quickly moved beyond that to campaign for 'rule of law', 'justice for all', for the repeal of the ISA and other coercive laws, and for curbs on 'corruption, cronyism and nepotism'. The result was the coming together of Anwar's supporters and the NGOs in a *reformasi* movement, and ultimately the establishment of a new multi-ethnic political party, which spearheaded the formation of a new multi-party opposition coalition called Barisan Alternatif (BA).

However, the *reformasi* movement as well as the BA has very little contact with the working class, which is generally pro-status quo. In fact, organized labour has been tamed by the State since the 1950s after the left-leaning independent unions were smashed, and a separation of trade unionism and political activism strictly enforced.[5] The Malaysian Trade Union Congress has been kept pliant through government support for a separate major organization for State employees, as well as the formation of Japanese-style in-house unions. In contrast, Islamic movements such as Abim and Jemaah Islah Malaysia have become increasingly critical of the ruling coalition. Compared to the past, the NGO movement is now more multi-ethnic and multi-religious, which augurs well for the future.

Indonesia

The *reformasi* movement in Indonesia also followed on the heels of the 1997 financial crisis. However, Indonesian NGOs had also contributed to the political ferment during Suharto's New Order period (1967–98), but became more overtly political and increasingly critical during the 1990s.

Most of Indonesia's several thousand NGOs are principally engaged in providing services to marginalized groups in the rural areas. Their projects include delivering drinking water, health services and community education. There are also NGOs like Dian Desa and *Bina Swadaya*, which promote self-reliance and co-operative efforts and the use of appropriate technology. Some of these NGOs, including the high-profile Lembaga Studi Pembangunan, have also been involved in mobilizing local communities to protest against specific grievances.

There are a number of human rights groups. The most well-known is the Legal Aid Institute, based in Jakarta, which monitors and publishes a report on the human rights situation, and provides legal services to victims of injustice. Prior to *reformasi,* other prominent NGOs included the LP3ES or the Institute for Social and Economic Research, Education and Information, which publishes *Prisma*; the Indonesian Consumer Forum; and *Walhi*, or the Indonesian Environmental Forum made up of several hundred smaller NGOs. Another group, established in 1990, is ICMI or the Association of Indonesian Muslim Intellectuals whose original aim was to defend the interests of Muslims sidelined by capitalist growth during the New Order regime. But the largest Muslim groups are Nahdatul Ulama, headed by Abdurachman Wahid and Muhammadiyya, headed by Amien Rais, both well-known intellectual activists. All these organizations were well-funded and though critical of various aspects of government policy they were nonetheless tolerated, probably owing to personal relations between leaders of these NGOs and particular ministers or generals.

There also existed thousands of smaller, poorly funded, less institutionalized NGOs, which maintained a low profile during the New Order days. They were also more overtly political and critical, and were engaged in empowering and mobilizing urban workers, squatters and hawkers, people evicted by dam construction and other development projects, and landless peasants. It was this group of NGOs that first organized alternative political parties like the People's Democratic Party, and independent trade unions like the Seikat Buruh Sejahtera Indonesia, founded by the lawyer Muchtar Pakpahan in 1992. Understandably, these efforts were subjected to harsh repression by the Suharto regime.[6]

Egged on by these radical NGOs, the established NGOs became more critical in the 1990s. For instance, prominent dignitaries supported by the established NGOs called for the establishment of a *negara hukum* (or constitutional government), in essence a criticism of the official 'dual policy' that sanctioned the military's role in politics. The formation of Forum Demokrasi in 1991, led by Abdurachman Wahid and other prominent personalities, was also a significant step towards democratization. The PIJAR (Centre for Information and Action Network), formed in 1994, brought together various groups seeking to introduce constitutional reforms in the country. Yet another political NGO was KIPP (Indonesian Election Watch Committee), formed in 1996 in anticipation of the 1997 election. AJI or the Alliance of Independent Journalists was set up to bypass the official Indonesian Journalists Union. There were also some ties established between the NGOs, workers and students in the wake of the 1997 financial crisis.[7]

Rapid changes have occurred on the NGO front since Suharto was removed in May 1998. Most dramatic, perhaps, was the appointment of Abdurachman Wahid, leader of Nadhatul Ulama and Forum Demokrasi as Indonesia's president; Muhammadiyya's Amien Rais as chairperson of the People's Assembly; and several other former NGO activists to other prominent positions in government.

These leaders were partly responsible for introducing a series of laws to enhance parliamentary rule while curbing the military's role: to decentralize power to the regions and villages; to restore citizens' right to establish parties, unions and other organizations of their choice, etc. However, given the continued poor performance of the economy, progress towards social justice has been slow. For instance, the independent unions have found it difficult to consolidate themselves as workers remain more concerned about keeping their jobs despite low wages and appalling working conditions.[8]

Moreover, after more than thirty years of authoritarianism, democratic institutions and practices remain weak. Not only have elements in the military attempted to reverse democratization, the country has also been threatened by separatist movements and Muslim extremists, some of whom, allegedly, were involved in the 2002 Bali and 2003 Jakarta bombings. The NGOs, including the more moderate Islamic groups, now find themselves hard pressed with the reintroduction of coercive laws to curb those extremist elements.

The NGOs and social movements have consolidated throughout the region. However, their influence upon their respective societies has been mixed. They have certainly been more successful in the Philippines and Thailand than in Indonesia and Malaysia. At any rate, the State still clearly dominates civil society in all the Southeast Asian countries. This is so even though much of the developmental State has been dismantled after the 1997 financial crisis. Consequently, the welfare of the majority has also been affected, especially in Thailand and Indonesia, which were forced to adopt IMF structural adjustment packages. Hence, deepening democracy and achieving equitable development have become urgent goals again. However, neoliberal globalization has made the goal of equitable development even more difficult than ever. In the circumstances, two tendencies may be noted: co-operation with their governments in dealing with the global system, and networking with other NGOs regionally.

STATE–NGO CONVERGENCE

A conflict emerged between the Western and Asian countries over the question of the universality of human rights during the UN World Conference on Human Rights (UN-WCHR) in Vienna in July 1993. In fact, there were two other issues raised by the Asian governments. The first concerned 'the right to development as a universal and inalienable right and [as] an integral part of fundamental human rights'. They argued that 'the creation of uniform international human rights norms must go hand in hand with endeavours to work towards a just and fair world economic order'. The second concerned an 'urgent need to democratize the United Nations system' ('The Bangkok Declaration 1993').[9] These concerns had earlier been expressed at the Asian Regional Intergovernmental Meeting held in Bangkok in March 1993. While critical of their governments' human rights record, the Asian NGOs supported their governments in their criticism of the unjust features of the global order. In Bangkok, the 240 participants from Asian NGOs declared, among other things:

We, representatives of NGOs, urge the following:

> 1. Industrial powers and global financial agencies in the North to write off the external debts of poverty-stricken nations in the South. 'Adjustments with economic growth' must be altered to espouse 'adjustments with a human face'.
> 2. The global community should democratise the structure of the UN so as to ensure greater participation of developing countries in the Security Council and greater efficacy of the General Assembly.... [10]

The Asian NGOs' insistence that these items be included on the agenda of the 'non-official' Forum of some 2,000 NGOs in Vienna caused some friction with their Northern counterparts.

There were also tensions between Asian and Northern NGOs at the UN Conference on Environment and Development held in Rio de Janeiro in June 1992. The North–South conflict between the governments that developed at the 'Earth Summit' was reproduced to some extent at the 'Global Forum' of some 17,000 people from NGOs and other organizations held in conjunction with the Summit. The Asian NGOs, like their governments, had submitted the need to link the question of 'sustainable development' to Northern domination of the global system.[11]

There have been other convergences on global issues adopted by Asian NGOs and their governments. It is in this regard that the recent anti-globalization movement marks a break from the past. For after Seattle, but especially after the World Social Forum 2001, held in Porto Allegre, more attention has been given to the development woes of the developing countries. Consequently, another convergence between Asian NGOs and their Western counterparts has also developed.

NETWORKING REGIONALLY

Before this convergence became evident, the Southeast Asian NGOs had largely networked regionally. Beginning from the mid-1980s, several coalitions concerned with both human rights and social issues were set up. These included the Asian Cultural Forum on Human Rights and Development (Bangkok, and publisher of *Asian Action*) and the Third World Network (Penang, and publisher of *Third World Resurgence*). The Asian NGO Coalition for Agrarian Reform and Rural Development (ANGOC, Manila, and publisher of *Lokniti*) and the Asian Centre for the Progress of Peoples (Hong Kong, and publisher of *Asia Link*) regularly scrutinized Asian Development Bank projects while ARENA (the Asian Regional Exchange for New Alternatives, based in Hong Kong, and publisher of *Asian Exchange*) has campaigned against globalization and its inimical impact on Asian people, in addition to formulating alternative development perspectives.

Human rights networks include the Asian Human Rights Commission (Hong Kong, and publisher of the *AHRC Newsletter*) and the Regional Council on Human Rights. Labour coalitions include the Asian Migrant Centre and the Asia Monitor Resource Centre.

Women's groups include the Committee for Asian Women (Hong Kong, and publisher of *Asian Women Workers Newsletter*), the Asia Pacific Forum on Women, Law and Development (Kuala Lumpur), and many more. Youth and student issues are co-ordinated by the Asian Students Association (Bangkok) and the International Movement of Catholic Students (Hong Kong).

Joint protests against globalism have been organized. In 1995, the Manila People's Forum Assembly (MPFA) was set up to protest against the meeting of leaders of the Asia Pacific Economic Cooperation (APEC) forum. The MPFA brought together about 500 social movements and NGO participants from APEC member countries, and in a parallel effort, the International Conference Against Imperialist Globalization was organized. Anti-globalization activists also waged protest actions during the UN Conference on Trade and Development (UNCTAD) meeting held in Bangkok in February 1999, and again when the Asian Development Bank met in Chiengmai in Thailand.

PEACE WITH SOCIAL JUSTICE

Two important regional meetings were held during 2002 and 2003. The larger of these was the Asian Social Forum in Hyderabad, in January 2003. The other was the inaugural assembly of the Asian Peace Alliance in Manila in late August 2002. On both occasions, there was an opportunity to reassess the roles of NGOs in the wake of recent developments in international security.

When the US launched its air strikes on Afghanistan on 7 October 2001, Asian NGOs, like their counterparts elsewhere, protested. Several Asian governments did so too. However, with the US declaring a global war against terrorism and introducing the Patriot Act to safeguard US security, many of the Southeast Asian governments also resorted to the use of coercive laws.

In Indonesia, Megawati's government introduced two repressive Perpu or 'Government Regulations in Lieu of Law'. Perpu No. 1/2002 on the Eradication of Criminal Acts of Terrorism empowers the police to search and arrest suspected terrorists for seven days, and to detain them for six months without being charged. The same law also allows telephone conversations, mail surveillance and intelligence reports to be used as evidence. Perpu No. 2/2002, passed after the Bali bomb explosion, provides the government with further sweeping powers. The sanctions under these Perpu are severe and include the death penalty or life imprisonment. (In March 2003, an Anti-Terrorism Bill, based on both Perpu, was passed in Parliament.)

In Thailand, the Thaksin government also introduced curbs after several explosions rocked a town in the south of the country in 2001. Some Thai Muslims were subsequently arrested. An attempt to introduce an anti-terrorism act was rejected by opposition parliamentarians, law lecturers and NGOs. However, on 5 August 2003, Thaksin announced a new anti-terrorism law by executive decree, without parliament's approval.

In Malaysia and Singapore, there already existed an anti-terrorism law, the ISA. First introduced by the British to combat communism some forty years ago, the ISA has been systematically abused to detain activists, unionists, student leaders, opposition politicians and even forgers, apart from alleged terrorists. When the US introduced its Patriot Act, these two governments proudly proclaimed that their use of the ISA had been vindicated, and quickly used it to detain Muslim radicals, some of whom were allegedly allied to *Jemaah Islamiyya*, the so-called proxy for al-Qaida in the region.

In the Philippines, the war against terrorism has built upon anti-Muslim jingoism and used as the pretext to stage a war against the Moro Islamic Liberation Front (MILF), which is seeking self-determination. Consequently, the Muslims in Mindanao have been subjected to unprecedented harassment, including torture, arbitrary detention, discrimination and displacement owing to the war. (An anti-terrorism law that will allow for prolonged detention is now in the offing.) Ominously, US military forces returned to the Philippines and began participating in 'joint military operations' under the pretext of providing training to their Filipino counterparts.

It was because of heightened US military adventurism as well as the erosion of democracy in the region that 12 organizations working on peace issues in Asia proposed the formation of the Asian Peace Alliance (APA) and held an inaugural assembly in Manila,[12] which brought together more than a hundred peace activists from all over Asia: Bangladesh, Cambodia, Hong Kong, India, Indonesia, Japan, Korea, Malaysia, Nepal, Pakistan, the Philippines, Sri Lanka, Thailand, and from Australia, Canada, UK and the US. The theme of the APA Assembly was *Kalinaw*, a Visayan word meaning peace and solidarity. The global war on terrorism and its anti-democratic implications for the region was the most pressing topic debated. But the Assembly also explored issues of human security, multi-ethnic and multi-religious conflict, gender and violence and the role of social movements. Strategies to pursue social justice and democratization via alternative pacifist and people-centred notions of security, as well as citizen-initiated peace actions in Burma, Acheh, Sri Lanka and Mindanao, were also discussed. These concerns are expressed in the Founding Declaration and the Program for Action adopted by the Assembly.

Several joint activities have been conducted since the Manila Assembly. Perhaps the most significant of these was its coordination of organizations and movements in the region to join with the rest of the world to observe the International Day of Protest against the US war on Iraq on 15 February 2003.[13]

The APA Assembly and the Hyderabad Social Forum were efforts by Asian groups and movements to network and co-operate with one another on a regional basis in order to further sustainable and equitable development and promote democratization. With neoliberal globalization impacting upon the region so severely, as in 1997, it has become necessary for the NGOs and social movements to mount trans-border efforts too. Indeed, the latest concerns about US unilateralism and its global war against terrorism have reconfirmed not only that social justice and democratic participation must underscore any sense of preserving the region's security: it further confirms the need to mount trans-border actions.

CONCLUSION

The real world is one of domination of the world economy and its geopolitics by the US and other Western powers. This is ever more evident in the age of globalization. In trying to bring about alternative development, the NGOs and movements have joined with their own governments in international forums where Southern NGOs hardly ever get a hearing. However, such co-operation with their governments is clearly circumscribed. For these governments are ultimately against participatory democracy. Nor are they inclined to promote equitable development domestically. In fact, in the wake of the US's war against terrorism, they have seized the opportunity to reintroduce anti-democratic laws and to jail critics, quite apart from alleged terrorists.

Hence, the regional networking of the NGOs and social movements has become especially urgent and pertinent. There is also a need to consolidate ties with their counterparts in the West provided that the latter are prepared to support the twin goals of deepening democracy and achieving equitable and sustainable development. The emergence of the anti-globalization movement these past years augurs well for consolidating these North–South ties.

NOTES

1. Abdul Rahman Embong (2001).
2. Loh (2002).
3. Clarke (1998), p. 70.
4. Shigetomi (2003), p. 130.
5. Jomo and Todd (1994), p. 172.
6. Hadiz (2003), pp. 101–4.
7. Hadiz (2003), p. 105.
8. Hadiz (2003), pp. 108–12.
9. Cited in Loh (1996).
10. Loh (1996).
11. Loh (1996). In the 'Kanagawa Declaration 1992' submitted by Asian NGOs to the Earth Summit, it was declared that 'Restoration of the global environment ... requires first and foremost, the solution of the North–South problem, the bridging of the social gap between the materially rich and poor and the restoration of the connections between them.' Like their governments, the NGOs condemned the wastage of energy and resources by the developed countries and stressed that 'third world debts should be cancelled and their economic independence should be promoted'. Another issue raised in the Kanagawa Declaration was reform of the UN. In Malaysia, the Philippines and Indonesia joint meetings of officials and NGO representatives were held to prepare for the Rio summit.
12. The organizations involved in the APA Steering Committee were: ARENA (Hong Kong); ASR Resource Centre (Pakistan); Bharat Gyan Vigyan Samithi (India); Committee for Peace Not War (Hong Kong); Focus on the Global South (Thailand); Forum Asia (Thailand); Nuclear-Free Philippine Coalition; Peace Camp (Philippines); Pakistan Peace

Coalition; People's Plan Study Group (Japan); People's Security Forum (Japan); and Women Making Peace (Korea). ARENA was appointed to act as the Secretariat of the Assembly and subsequently coordinated the documentation and compilation of the Assembly's proceedings. Seven Filipino organizations, coalitions and institutions dedicated to peace acted as the Host Committee. They were: Akbayan Citizens' Action Party; the Third World Studies Centre of the University of the Philippines; the Ateneo Human Rights Centre; FOCUS Philippines; Gathering for Peace; Nuclear Free Philippines Coalition; and Peace Camp.

13. For details on the demonstrations in the Philippines, Thailand, Malaysia and Indonesia, as well as in Japan, Korea, Pakistan and India, see the *Aliran Monthly* (2003), vol. 23, no. 2, special issue on 'Invasion and Occupation'.

BIBLIOGRAPHY

Abdul Rahman Embong (ed.) (2001) *Southeast Asian Middle Classes: Prospects for social change and democratisation* (Bangi: Penerbit Universiti Kebangsaan Malaysia)

Aliran Monthly (2003), vol. 23, no. 2, special issue on 'Invasion and Occupation'

Asian Peace Alliance (2002) *Kalinaw Asian People Speak Up for Peace: Proceedings of the Asian Peace Alliance Inaugural Assembly* (Hong Kong: APA Secretariat)

Clarke, G. (1998) *The Politics of NGOs in Southeast Asia: Participation and protest in the Philippines* (London: Routledge)

Hadiz, Vedi (2003) 'Changing State–Labour Relations in Indonesia and Malaysia and the 1997 crisis', in A. Heryanto and S. Mandal (eds) *Challenging Authoritarianism in Southeast Asia* (London: Routledge Curzon), pp. 90–116

Jomo, K.S. and P. Todd (1994) *Trade Unions and the State in Peninsular Malaysia* (Kuala Lumpur: Oxford University Press)

Loh, F.K.W. (1996) 'ASEAN NGOs in the Post-Cold War World', in J. Lele and W. Tettey (eds) *Asia – Who Pays for Growth? Women, environment and popular movements* (Aldershot: Dartmouth Publishing), pp. 41–61

Loh, F.K.W. (2002) 'Developmentalism and the Limits of Democratic Discourse', in F. K.W. Loh and Khoo Boo Teik (eds) *Democracy in Malaysia: Discourses and practices* (Richmond, Surrey: Curzon), pp.19–50

Shigetomi, Shinichi (2002) 'Thailand – A Crossing of Critical Parallel Relationships', in Shinichi Shigetomi (ed.) *The State and NGOs* (Singapore: Institute of Southeast Asian Studies), pp. 125–44

Siliman, G.S. and L.G. Noble (1998) 'Citizen Movements and Philippine Democracy', in G.S. Siliman and L.G. Noble (eds) *Organising for Democracy: NGOs, civil society and the Philippine State* (Manila: Ateneo de Manila University Press), pp. 280–310

4
Central Asia and the Southern Caucasus: US Rearguard Bases?

Bernard Dreano

The Caucasus and Central Asia once again find themselves at the heart of the Great Game for world domination, reminiscent of the way in which Rudyard Kipling, at the turn of the twentieth century, wrote about Afghanistan, then coveted by Russian and British imperialism. This time it is the United States that leads the dance. After the wars in Afghanistan and (especially) Iraq, with Iran still labelled a member of the Axis of Evil by George W. Bush, this whole region, from the Black Sea to the Caspian and up to the celestial mountains of Tien Chan and Pamir on the Chinese border, is considered strategically decisive. It has great energy resources, close to the oil eldorado of the Arabian/Persian Gulf, but is also a central platform of Eurasia, from which Moscow, Beijing, Teheran, Mecca and Istanbul can be kept under observation.

Unfortunately for the people who live in this region, it does not attract much attention from the international media, or enough solidarity from the alternative world militants. And yet what is going on there cannot be reduced to the calculations and manoeuvres of the geopoliticians of empire.

CENTRAL ASIA AND THE 'ANTI-TERRORIST' ALLIANCE

Central Asia is becoming increasingly a 'US rearguard base': this is the opinion of Vicken Chetarian, a close observer of the region.[1] Since the Afghan war, American troops have taken up a permanent position, in Kyrgyzstan (at the airport of Manas, where the French are also to be found); in Uzbekistan (air base of Khanabad); and in Tajikistan. Kazakhstan, which is rich in oil, does not have any US military, but is glad to receive American aid.

The indigenous population in each of these republics has, on the whole, welcomed the US presence. The Kyrgyz, whose country is poor and landlocked, hope for economic benefits, the inhabitants of the Fergana valley look forward to some peace and stability for their region, which is divided between Uzbekistan, Kyrgyzstan and Tajikistan and a centre of conflict, young students seek scholarships to go to the US, intellectuals hope for progress towards democracy.

As far as democratic progress is concerned, not to speak of prosperity and peace, it is very disappointing. True, the reinforced presence in the region of NGOs (mostly American) can sometimes act as a lever for those defending human rights. But dictatorial leaders, like the Uzbek Islam Karimov, and corrupt rulers like the present Kyrgyz government,[2] have other priorities. The American influence helps them to free themselves a little more from Russian tutelage, which, even so, is still considerable, with a substantial military presence in Kazakhstan, Tajikistan and Kyrgyzstan and numerous Russian minorities in Kazakhstan, Kyrgyzstan and elsewhere.

The NATO 'Peace Partnership' had envisaged the setting up of a common 'security battalion' in Kazakhstan, Kyrgyzstan and Uzbekistan: the 'CentrAsBats'. This never materialized, no doubt because it gave too many opportunities to each of them to oversee the others. Parallel with the Western military presence, there has been the institutionalization, in 2002, of the 'collective security treaty' of members of the ex-USSR in CSTO, a treaty organization. For the moment this has not been opposed by the US military presence, but it remains to be seen whether this will be a complement or a counterweight to NATO.

As for security, it is the 'war against terrorism' that seems to be the key concept. For Moscow this evidently means having a free hand in Chechnya and, for Washington, the right to permanent intervention. For the rulers of the Central Asian republics, the great merit of the post-11 September 'anti-terrorist' alliance is that it allows them to repress internal opposition by calling it 'Islamic'. Radical Islamic groups exist in the region and some *mujahidin*, Uzbeks and Tajiks from the ex-Soviet republics, fought in Afghanistan. However, the main regional Islamic movement, the Hizb-ut-Tahir-al-Islami (the Islamic Liberation Party), officially rejects terrorism, as does the Party for the Islamic Renaissance of Tajikistan (which experienced a bloody ethnic–religious civil war at the beginning of the 1990s in which Islamists were involved).

The Islamic spectre is useful for the rulers, particularly for Karimov in Uzbekistan, in discrediting all opposition, that is political parties that are not radical Islamists at all, such as Erk and Birlik, which are combating the Islamic threat. The democratic party Erk was founded by Muhammad Solih, former candidate for the presidency against Karimov and now living in exile in Norway. This party, which is banned, held a meeting in Tashkent in June 2003 for the first time since 1993. Among the participants were members of the Uzbek nationalist party Birlik (Unity): was this a sign of flexibility on the part of the government? Unfortunately, Karimov whistled the end of the game in spring 2004, after attacks by reported Islamists.

The American tolerance of the Ubuesque dictatorship of President Saparmurat 'Turkmenbashi' Niyazov [3] of Turkmenistan, whose personality cult is comparable to that of the North Korean leader, shows that democracy is no precondition for the US when it wants to profit from the huge gas reserves in the Turkomen territory.

In the short term, as has been remarked by Jonathan Feiser, the American observer, the US presence in Iraq 'requires sufficient regional support and the bases in central Asia make this possible'.[4] In the longer term, this installation helps to contain Russia, reduced to a medium-sized regional power, and to keep a check on China. To counterbalance this danger, the Russians and Chinese have set up, with the republics of Central Asia, a regional body, the Shanghai Forum. This body has aspired to being an organization of genuine regional co-operation following its meeting in the Tajik capital, Dusanbe, in June 2003 (with the participation of China, Kazakhstan, Uzbekistan, Kyrgyzstan, Tajikistan ... and Russia).

Nevertheless, Kazakhstan competes for regional hegemony with Uzbekistan, whose capital, Tashkent, was planned by the Tsars to be the capital of Central Asian 'Turkestan' (which used to be Russian and then Soviet). Noursoultan Nazarbaiev, the inveterate Kazakh president since well before the collapse of the USSR, has moved his capital from Almaty (formerly Alma Ata), considered to be too close to Tashkent, to Astana, a 'Brasilia of the steppes', in the middle of the country.

There are also problems with China, as the route from Almaty to Urumchi abuts the Chinese Xin Jiang province. Here the Uighur are no longer a majority in their own country because of the colonization and hegemonic policy of the Han, the Chinese majority ethnic group. Beijing regularly accuses the Kazakhs of serving as a rearguard base for Uighur nationalists (certain groups, sometimes under Islamic influence, have carried out attacks). Kazakhstan remains closely tied economically to Moscow (and the main Russian aerospace base is in its territory, at Baikonur). Uzbekistan thus finds itself in the political centre of the region, but its chaotic economic situation, aggravated by the ecological disaster of the drying up of the Aral Sea, hardly helps further its ambitions. Tajikistan is fragile, having barely recovered from a bloody civil war, and it carefully follows the situation in Afghanistan, where the Tajiks of the Northern Alliance control Kabul. As for little Kyrgyzstan, once considered the 'Switzerland of Central Asia' and the most democratic of the countries in the region, it has been unable to maintain this enviable reputation, fearing the appetite of its more powerful neighbours. The dictatorship of Turkmenistan remains in the wings.

Regional co-operation involving the two giants Russia and China – not to mention the Japanese who are economically very active – is, for the time being, very far from creating a zone of shared peace and prosperity.

THE SOUTHERN CAUCASUS

The Southern Caucasus (Armenia, Azerbaijan, Georgia) is, in certain respects, in a similar situation as it suffers from both the wounds of yesterday's wars and today's conflicts. To the north of the Caucasus mountains, the Chechnya war tragically continues and it has caused hundreds of thousands of deaths and refugees, contributing to the destabilization of the whole region. To the south, two major wars are frozen for the moment: Abkhazia in Georgia, a territory where the Muslim Abkhazian minority has expelled the Georgian majority of the population, and Nagorno-Karabakh, an enclave peopled mostly by Armenians, but included in Azerbaijan by Stalin and where the Armenians are in opposition to the Azerbaijanis. Other conflicts are latent (in Southern Ossetia and among the various minorities almost everywhere in Northern and Southern Caucasus). All these states are riddled with corruption and growing inequalities. Social questions and respect for elementary human rights are inextricably entwined.

The Americans are now firmly implanted in this area, and they try to increase their influence without overly upsetting the Russian Bear. Azerbaijan is rich in hydrocarbons and remains strategic for Russia, as indeed is Central Asia as a whole. The region is also important for the Pentagon because it is close to Turkey, Iran and Iraq.

Washington has benefited from the fact that Georgia has been trying to escape Moscow's constant pressure since declaring its independence in 1991. The Kremlin keeps up this pressure, mainly through the Abkhaz conflict and the Ossetian problem. In Abkhazia, the separatists are openly supported by Russian troops, although they are meant to be mediators. While there is no actual war in Southern Ossetia, this Georgian province is not controlled by the government in Tbilisi. The Ossetians are Christians whose language belongs to the Persian family. They are also to be found in the Northern Caucasus: Northern Ossetia is part of the Russian Federation, while the pass of the Cross, linking the two Ossetias, is the main passageway through the heart of the Caucasian mountains.

The Chechnya war is also a Russian excuse for intervention. Moscow accuses Tbilisi of allowing Chechen fighters to operate from Georgian territory, particularly the gorges of Pankisi, while Washington sees the traces of Al-Qaida there – a pretext for sending in military counsellors. This small Pankisi valley, which is a Georgian enclave on the northern flank of the Caucasus and hence gives access to Chechnya, was, for its sins, front page news when, at the end of August 2002, the Russians bombarded villages and then openly deployed elite troops on Georgian territory in pursuit of *boivickis* (Chechen fighters). It is a hot spot that the Russians utilize less for local military reasons than to justify 'external aggression' when needed. This is also a way of putting pressure on Georgia and testing the Americans. As a reaction, the Georgian Parliament voted to withdraw the country from the Community of Independent States (CIS) and to get rid of the last Russian bases still on Georgian soil. It also demanded that the country become a member of NATO. Former President Eduard Shevardnadze immediately declared such measures inapplicable and premature. Impoverished Georgia has thus been convulsed and also weakened through corruption, and this explains the collapse of Shevardnadze regime after the 'rose revolution' of November 2003.

In Azerbaijan the Americans are now firmly installed, in spite of an initial frostiness towards the US because of Congress's support of the Armenians at the beginning of the Armenian/Azerbaijan war over Nagorno-Karabakh. James MacDougall of the Swedish Centre for Social and Political Studies regards 1997 as the turning point of US strategy in the region: 'the year when the United States realized the geostrategic importance of the Caspian basin and started to conduct their foreign policy accordingly'.[5] Their oil companies are already there and are second in influence only to the British oil giant BP, while the other companies (Norwegian, French, Russian and Iranian) get only crumbs from the oil cake. In spite of the curious relations between the late Haydar Aliyev, the former chief of the KGB for the whole of the USSR, and Azerbaijan's president until his death in December 2003, and Vladimir Putin, who was once one of his subordinates, the latter has not been able to reverse the trend for Russian power to decline and give way to American influence in Baku.

The transportation of hydrocarbons from the Caspian Sea and beyond it, from Central Asia (Kazakhstan, Turkmenistan) to the consumer markets is responsible for large-scale manoeuvres. The Russians would like oil and gas to flow, as in the past, through the pipelines to the north of the Caucasus, through territory of the Russian Federation to the port of Novorossyisk on the Black Sea or through the Russian gas pipelines linked to Europe. But that would mean renovating the whole system. Other obstacles are the war in Chechnya and the disturbances in Ingush and Daghestan. The Americans benefit from the quarrels between the Russians and their former colonies, and they propose an oil pipeline through the Southern Caucasus, Baku–Ceyhan (a Turkish port on the Mediterranean), as well as a gas pipeline from Baku to Erzerum (this Turkish town being linked to the European gas distribution system). The construction of the famous oil pipeline is thus a strategic aim, which is to prevent the Russians from controlling the exports of hydrocarbons from Central Asia and discourage Iran from entertaining any desire to do so (a Caspian–Persian Gulf oil pipeline would be more logical economically). On the political horizon there is also the intergovernmental co-operation called GUUAM (between Moldavia, Ukraine, Georgia, Azerbaijan and Uzbekistan), an east–west axis being encouraged by the Americans to short-circuit the Russians.

However, the situation is far from being stable in the Americans' two favourite states, Georgia and Azerbaijan. In Georgia the new pro-Western leader, Michael Sakashvili, has been able to resolve peacefully the secession of the southern province of Adjaria, which the Russians were tempted to use to blackmail the new regime. But the economic situation remains disastrous. In Azerbaijan, questions are being asked about the successor to Haydar Aliyev, his son Ilham Aliyev, who has neither the charisma nor the experience of his father.

As for Armenia, it continues to be faithful to the Russian alliance and keeps good relations with Teheran. It thus forms a sort of north–south Russia/Armenia/Iran axis that tries to counter-balance the pro-American east–west axis. But this stance could turn out to be a liability for the Armenians, subject as they are to the pressure of the Russians, who have no interest in settling the question of Nagorno-Karabakh and the normalizing of Armenia's relations with Azerbaijan and Turkey, which deprives them of their main means of putting pressure on Erevan. Moreover, the negotiations on the status of Karabakh, carried out in recent years under the auspices of the OSCE (Organization for Security and Co-operation in Europe) through the Minsk Group, or under those of the Americans (the Key West meetings) have produced no results, a fact that does not displease Vladimir Putin.

This could also be in the short-term interests of Robert Kotcharian, the present Armenian president, who was the former leader of the self-proclaimed Nagorno-Karabakh during the war. The Azer minority in Karabagh have been got rid of and Armenia occupies strategic Azerbaijan territories that ensure continuity between Armenia and Karabagh as well as control over the northern bank of the river Araks (on the Iranian border). But an agreement could once again call this situation into question. Over recent months, for the first time in years, there has been an increasing number of incidents along the front line of Karabakh, as Aliyev, the only Azeri capable of imposing a peaceful compromise on his country, seemed likely to depart from the scene. Robert Kotcharian certainly considers that the status quo is in his favour. But in the long term Armenia's position could worsen considerably: the economic situation is worrying, the country is impoverished and its elites are leaving. And, in the huge redistribution of playing-cards in the region after the Iraq war, Erevan lacks trumps.

In terms of internal politics the Armenian State seems to be holding up better than its two neighbouring countries, but this is deceptive. It is true that Kotcharian has succeeded (with Russian support?) in marginalizing his predecessor, Levon Ter Petrossian, the father of independence. It is also true that the presidential and legislative elections, although contested, were won by Kotcharian's party, supported by the historic nationalists of Dachnaksoutioun (the old 'Armenian revolutionary federation', created in 1880). But Armenia is not immune from violent events, as could be seen when the prime minister and the president of the Parliament were assassinated in October 1999, in full parliamentary session. Nor is the small 'mountain republic' of Nagorno-Karabakh where Kotcharian's successor Arkady Gukassian has thrown General Samuel Babauan into prison. 'Unachieved self-determination' is how the situation was described by the International Federation of Human Rights Leagues. It does not seem to go with the development of the rights of individuals.[6]

OBSTACLES PREVENTING THE EMERGENCE OF CIVIL SOCIETY

The social and political conditions are hardly favourable, either in Central Asia or in the Southern Caucasus, for the development of a vigorous and democratic civil society. The NGOs that have been created to attract Western aid are often GONGOs (governmental or para-governmental NGOs) in disguise, or FONGOs (foreign-organized NGOs, i.e. NGOs organized from outside by funding agencies, very often in this region USAID). It is true that some European and American funding agencies (like the Soros foundations) try to support initiatives that meet genuine needs in the field, but on the whole genuinely autonomous and indigenous movements find it very difficult to organize themselves. This is particularly true in Central Asia, even if, particularly in Tajikistan, various movements to defend civic rights, the rights of women, etc. are gradually being set up.

The situation is better, from this point of view, in the countries of the Southern Caucasus. In Azerbaijan, small human rights movements are active in various fields (the rights of refugees, of soldiers, of prisoners, of national minorities, etc.). This was seen in 2002 when they intervened in Nardaran, on the periphery of Baku, where the police ferociously repressed a social movement, killing a demonstrator and arresting the local leaders, who were presented, once again, as Islamic terrorists. In this particularly impoverished district of the town, religious fervour has developed in recent years as a kind of refuge. Was it a provocation? The Center of Religious Faith and Protection of Freedom of Conscience, close to moderate Islamic circles, tends to believe so: 'It is interesting that Nardaran is a sensitive area for all those who want to stress the existence of an Islamic fundamentalist danger and who want the West to close their eyes to the pyramid of corruption supported by an illegitimate government. In this case, it is only too easy to provoke peoples' religious feelings and work them up, creating disorder.'[7]

Because of the shortcomings of the State, various forms of social self-management have sprung up, especially in Georgia, but also in Armenia and Azerbaijan. Groups of young people, ecological initiatives, co-operatives and other alternative economic activities have been trying to develop.

Another important field of activity is the problem of refugees and their civic and economic rights, as well as their resistance to the manipulation of which they are victims. This is particularly the case for the 300,000 refugees from Abkhazia in Georgia and the 600,000 refugees from Karabakh in Azerbaijan, but there are others (Armenian refugees from Azerbaijan in Armenia, Kurds in Armenia and Azerbaijan, Chechens in Azerbaijan and Georgia, and so on).

The three countries of the Southern Caucasus (four, if one counts the self-proclaimed republic of Nagorno-Karabakh) can certainly be considered in that category that the Croat writer Pedrag Matvejevitch describes as 'democratures', something between a dictatorship that tolerates a certain pluralism and an aberrant democracy. There are opposition parties and the media have a certain freedom, but there are few progressive left-wing political forces in the European sense. However, there are some genuine fighters for democracy. Citizens are trying to counter fraudulent elections everywhere (for example, during the last Armenian presidential elections, in the town of Vanadzor in the north of the country) and during the Azerbaijan presidential campaign, in spite of the 'locking up' of civil society and of the judicial system by the Alyev regime, as observed by the International Federation of the Human Rights Leagues.[8] In Georgia, Armenia, Nagorno-Karabakh and Azerbaijan, small groups are trying to push for free expression and independent media and to challenge local authority, etc.

Even more important are the initiatives for peace and dialogue between Armenians and Azerbaijanis in Georgia *à propos* of Abkhazia as militants in the countries of the Southern Caucasus are trying to come together to envisage their common future.[9] For example, the international network Helsinki Citizens' Assembly met at Baku in November 2000 and attracted a strong delegation of Armenians from Armenia and Nagorno-Karabakh, while there were meetings of Armenian and Azerbaijani families of people who had disappeared (widows, refugees, young people and women from the three countries), as well as encounters between children from the 'countries of the Silk Route'.[10] Despite the presence of some external activists, who had come from Western Europe, Russia and Canada, these extraordinary initiatives had no follow-up. Isolated as they are, the NGOs have few interlocutors apart from the North American foundations – for better and, all too often, for worse. In spite of the presence of Arzu Abdullayeva, an Azer militant for peace and human rights, at the Third World Social Forum of Porto Alegre, the linkages between the civic movements of the Caucasus (and even more so, of Central Asia) and the world citizens' movement have yet to be built.

NOTES

1. Vicken Chetarian (2003) 'L'Asie centrale, base arrière américaine', *Le Monde Diplomatique*, February.

2. Not long ago these Kyrgyz rulers even sold part of the national territory to the Chinese, 'forgetting' to inform Parliament!

3. President Saparmurat Niyazov calls himself 'Turkmenbashi', which means the greatest of the Turkomen.

4. Jonathan Feiser (2003) 'Finding a new Central Asian doctrine of lucid flexibility', *Eurasia Insight*, 30 July.

5. James MacDougall (1997) 'A new stage in the Caspian Sea basin relationships?', *Central Asia*, no. 5 (11) (CSPS, Stockholm).

6. International Federation of Human Rights Leagues (2003) *Unachieved Self-determination and the Impact on Human Rights*, Mission Report, Paris, April.

7. Communication of the Center of Religious Faith and Protection of Freedom of Conscience (CRFPFW), distributed by the HCA, Azerbaijan, 2 August 2002.

8. International Federation of Human Rights Leagues (2002) *Azerbaijan, Civil Society and Justice Locked by the Aliyev System*. Report by the Juridical Observation Mission, Paris, November.

9. For information on the citizens' movements in the Southern Caucasus, particularly the Helsinki Citizens' Assembly network, see Bernard Dreano (2003) *Dépression sur le Sud-Caucase, voyages entre guerres et paix* (Paris: Editions Paris Méditerranée).

10. See, for example, *Through Women's Eyes* (2002), a collection of Armenian, Azerbaijani and Georgian testimonies, published by the Association of Displaced Women (AIDPW) of Georgia and Feed the Children (CFTC), a Canadian NGO, Tbilisi.

5

Resistance to Neoliberalism in Australia and Oceania

Verity Burgmann and Andrew Ure

In Australia, social struggles against neoliberal globalization received new impetus with the three days of protest against and blockade of the World Economic Forum's Asia Pacific Economic Summit in Melbourne in September 2000, popularly known as 'S11' after the date – September 11 – on which the Summit and protest began. This protest, notable both for its size (attracting some 30,000 people to the streets of Melbourne) and its militancy – in the words of *The Australian*, protesters had 'laid violent siege to' the Summit[1] – may have marked a turning-point in contemporary Australian politics.[2] But whether this in many ways remarkable event may be better understood as evidence for the emergence of a radical challenge to the neoliberal project in Australia, or merely a temporary aberration in its otherwise implacable progress, is yet to be decided.

For, on the other side of the world and precisely one year later, the terrorist attacks on the United States brought in their wake a fracturing of this opposition[3] and forced the movement to abandon (temporarily) its fight against neoliberalism to concentrate on fighting a government engaged in a deeply unpopular 'War on Terror', first in Afghanistan and now in Iraq,[4] and whose Prime Minister John Howard has described Australia as the United States' deputy in the Asian region;[5] it is a government that is at the same time even more committed to furthering the neoliberal agenda (first advanced by its social democratic opposition in the 1980s and 1990s).[6]

In a context of war, new, highly repressive anti-terrorist legislation, the continuing rollback of the welfare state, sharpening inequality, continued environmental degradation, the creation of a bilateral 'free trade' agreement with the US[7] and a political Opposition almost indistinguishable from the Government in its central policies and platforms, the immediate prospects for change might seem grim. And yet 'S11', the anti-war movement, the various campaigns that have sprung up in defence of civil liberties, refugee and workers' rights, the continuing popularity of the Australian Greens[8] and, perhaps most importantly, the (re-)emergence and popularity of a critique of neoliberalism that recognizes it as being fundamentally at odds with egalitarian and democratic values: all these point towards a period of renewed political and cultural contestation, one that may not only bring increasing pressure upon neoliberalism but also open up a space for a renewed assault upon its foundations in contemporary Australian capitalism.

This chapter examines the history of the 'anti-globalization'[9] movement in Australia since these pivotal events, and attempts to pinpoint some of the more significant moments in its development in the context of the so-called 'War on Terror', a war that the Australian Government has not only joined with great enthusiasm, but whose Prime Minister has declared is likely to 'go on for some years'.[10] For the first time since the Vietnam War and despite equally massive opposition, the Australian Government has found itself not dragged but enthusiastically venturing into a (real) war, this time in Afghanistan and Iraq. For those involved in social struggles against neoliberalism, this War on Terror has created tremendous uncertainty and served to derail, if only temporarily, many of these struggles. This has been achieved both through the introduction of draconian anti-terrorist legislation (ostensibly aimed at giving the State increased powers to combat the terrorist threat such countries are considered to represent) and the fostering of a political climate in which loyalty to the State and its programmes has become a powerful tool for taming movements that aim to bring the central dynamics of the Australian State and economy into question.

While it is not possible here to delineate the full range of issues confronting oppositional movements in contemporary Australia and the region, the following are argued to be of particular significance:

- first, the Australian Government's repressive response to the plight of asylum seekers – one conditioned by the movements against border control that have fought the creation of concentration camps for these 'unlawful non-citizens';
- secondly, a labour movement that is still reeling from the fragmentation brought about by structural changes to the Australian economy and whose Government is committed to 'reining in' those elements[11] that might create the most fertile

grounds for radically undermining neoliberal doctrines and explicating alternatives to it;

- finally, the cultural struggle to maintain critical public spaces from which (once again) to marshal those social forces that have the most to gain from any successful confrontation with neoliberal programmes.

FORTRESS AUSTRALIA (AND OTHER REFUGES FOR SCOUNDRELS)

Founded upon an explicit commitment to the propagation of a White Australia – a doctrine officially abandoned only in 1972[12] – the Australian Government has been able to draw upon a long history of xenophobic sentiment in its more recent attempts to isolate and contain the threat to Australia's territorial integrity that refugees from predominantly Middle Eastern countries are said to represent.[13] This desire to protect Australia's 'territorial integrity' was expressed most clearly in a speech given by Prime Minister Howard in Parliament in June 2001. In attempting to justify the actions of Australian troops in boarding and seizing command of the Norwegian freighter MS *Tampa* carrying over 400 mostly Afghani refugees (picked up from the sinking fishing boat carrying them to Australia) – an event widely referred to as 'the Tampa incident' – Howard remarked that 'Every nation has the right to effectively control its borders and decide who comes here and under what circumstances, and Australia has no intention of surrendering or compromising that right.'[14] Whatever misgivings some critics of globalization may have concerning the erosion of State power, for the Australian Prime Minister at least, the right of the (Australian) State to determine entry to its territory is absolute.

While the policy of 'mandatory detention' for asylum seekers was – like the neoliberal economic doctrines perversely described in much Australia political literature as economic rationalism – first implemented by an Australian labour government,[15] it is under the current coalition government that this policy has, perhaps, reached its apogee.

The widespread recognition by numerous international networks that neoliberal globalization embodies the increased freedom of movement of capital while simultaneously restricting the freedom of movement of people – and that, rather than constituting a contradiction, the successful implementation of neoliberalism *requires* the establishment of strong(er) border policing and hence a strong(er)

State[16] – has not been lost on the thousands who have gathered at the gates of Australia's detention centres... nor those unfortunate enough to be locked behind them. (Indeed, the Australian government's 'Pacific Solution' – the imprisoning of asylum seekers on Pacific islands – may be understood as evidence of its own implied recognition that the establishment of a new order requires a new settlement for the distribution of a new, racially segmented division of labour.[17])

Thus the struggle against the camps – most notably in the form of Woomera 2002 and Baxter 2003[18] – has assumed central importance in the struggle against neoliberalism, and draws upon much the same networks of opposition and dissent as has the broader struggle against its other, ostensibly 'domestic' forms.[19] It is ironic, perhaps, that 'the movement' that had previously encircled members of a new transnational ruling class outside of Crown Casino[20] – placing real physical constraints upon the free movement of one of its leading intellectual and political exponents in the shape of the World Economic Forum – finds itself encircled by the State as a whole in the form of 'border protection'. Or perhaps it would be more accurate to suggest that, in attempting to question or subvert the State's authority to determine who it is that is allowed to enter this (or any other) country, movements opposed to neoliberalism have come up against one of the strongest obstacles yet to be placed in their path: nationalism.[21] And while nationalism is hardly a new phenomenon, if the struggles engaged in by the shifting networks that constitute this movement are to transcend this barrier, it would seem that the slogan emphasizing that 'our struggle must be as transnational as capital' must necessarily become a reality grounded in more than rhetoric; indeed, an altogether new, transnational community must not only be imagined but placed at the centre of this project.

In summary, then, the terrain upon which neoliberalism is being fought has been broadened by the war on refugees no less than the 'War on Terror', and in so doing exposed the relative weakness of the 'anti-globalization' movement. On the other hand, social struggles against neoliberalism have also demonstrated the ability of forces opposed to current economic and political arrangements to force the State to resort to ever greater and more desperate measures to contain the multitudes that threaten its political and territorial integrity. Thus the social struggles against neoliberalism in Australia have taken important new forms in the last few years, developments that are reflected in the debates and divisions arising within the disparate forces that form its constituency.

In the political realm, these divisions are evident in the limited, though nevertheless real decline in popular support for the Australian Labor Party (ALP) and a significant rise in electoral support for the Greens.[22] While the ALP has undergone similar ideological crises in the past, it appears that in this instance there is a real danger of the party losing its grip upon the progressive forces that have previously given it considerable support.[23] The industrial wing of the labour movement is also undergoing something of a crisis, having to combat steadily declining rates of union membership and, given the ALP's commitment to neoliberalism and a hostile coalition government, having to develop effective forms of action outside the parliamentary realm. As such, the relationship between the labour and other social movements, especially the environmental movement, has been brought into much clearer focus, as has the question of how to combat most effectively the steady erosion of the proportion of social wealth accruing to workers and the ever-increasing likelihood of ecological collapse.

'BRINGING IT ALL BACK HOME': NEOLIBERALISM AND/AS NEOCOLONIALISM

In this respect, the case of Aotearoa/New Zealand[24] provides a useful counterpoint to the Australian one. In many ways, Aotearoa/New Zealand has been at the forefront of opposition to neoliberal globalization – unsurprisingly perhaps, given the somewhat earlier and more savage implementation of such policies (again, spearheaded by a social democratic party).[25] Further, as a 'post-colonial' society, 'globalization' is understood by many indigenous (Maori) peoples as an extension of the colonialist project, and the struggle against domination by multinational corporations represented by processes of neoliberal globalization is understood as a continuation of the struggle against colonialism and *for* 'Tino Rangatiratanga'. (Indeed, the *positive* dimension of such struggles is often best expressed precisely by those social groups that have been most victimized by them.) The 'closest English translation' of *Tino Rangatiratanga*, according to the group Aotearoa Educators, 'is self-determination, although many also refer to it as "absolute sovereignty" or Maori independence. Such a concept embraces the spiritual link Maori have with "Papatuanuku" (Earthmother) and is a part of the international drive by indigenous people for self determination.'[26]

It is no coincidence that this desire for self-determination often finds its most intense expression in indigenous struggles and that, as such, the role of indigenous peoples in struggles against neoliberalism has been crucially significant to its spread to other sectors of global society.[27] Further, the practical critique of neoliberalism embodied in indigenous people's resistance to their incorporation into the global market is one informed by an often acute recognition of not only the global dimensions of such resistance but also an acknowledgement of anti-imperialist struggles stretching back over many hundreds of years. Aside from any legal ruling,[28] in Australia, the fiction of 'terra nullius' – the absurd claim that Australia was a continent unoccupied by human beings and could therefore be claimed as part of the British Empire without regard for the rights of its supposedly fictitious inhabitants – has been exploded by the determined struggles of indigenous Australians for recognition of such rights.

As elsewhere, strategies intended to lessen the political impact of Australian opposition to neoliberal globalization have focused upon critics' supposed inability to theorize a convincing alternative. A common criticism of this movement is that, as the name 'anti-capitalist' suggests, it lacks a coherent vision of a dramatically different world order. It is a movement that is clear about what it is against, but less clear about what the alternative should be. Here the contributions of indigenous struggles for self-determination have been particularly useful. For one, they have enabled non-indigenous groups and movements to root their critique in an anti-capitalist perspective that emanates from non-Western sources. In Australia, Aboriginal societies developed a precise, although complex, concept of landholding, in which individual men and women hold particular relationships to land, inherited from parents and arising from their own conceptions and birth sites. These relationships entail obligations and responsibilities to protect the land, its species and people from damage and unauthorized use; and to husband the land, use it, harvest it and do what needs to be done to maintain its productivity. As Heather Goodall explains, the Aboriginal concept of landholding is very different from the European concept of land as individually owned private property, a commodity to be bought, sold and used to generate profit.[29] Further, despite a history of attempted genocide and continued racism and dispossession, the Aboriginal response to white control – the development of an autonomous social movement that embraces tactics of self-help or self-management and the political principles of self-determination – both mirrors and in some, both developed and yet-to-be developed ways, reinforces the development of a nascent movement within the broader white society.

Aziz Choudry has argued convincingly that, particularly for people living in colonial settler states such as Australia and Aotearoa/New Zealand, contemporary opposition to 'globalization' (neoliberalism) must first come to terms with this legacy:

> We cannot ignore the centuries of resistance by many indigenous nations against incorporation into the colonial state. We cannot ignore the colonial foundations of the countries in which we live. To do so is to mask the true nature of our societies, and the extent to which they are built on colonisation and exploitation.[30]

Of course, the process of unmasking this reality is being pursued by a range of groups and in a number of struggles.

'ANTI-GLOBALIZATION' AS A RADICAL ALTERNATIVE TO THE RULE OF STATE AND CAPITAL

As Aggy Kelly and Andrew Blussat have noted,[31] '[r]ecent years have seen the large growth of northern social movements resisting capital and corporate globalisation' and within these movements there has been a 'shift ... from hierarchical and bureaucratic methods of organization to more decentralised and participatory models'. Australia and Aotearoa/New Zealand are no exception to this trend, as the existence of 'S11–AWOL' and the establishment of PGA–Pacifika attests.[32] The attempt to create movements that, in the words of George Katsiaficas, 'aim to transcend nation states rather than capture them',[33] finds increasing resonance among a newer generation of activists, and as such it may be that contemporary neoliberalism, and in much the same manner as earlier forms of capitalist dominion, is creating its own gravediggers. Nor is this trend towards increasing autonomy from governing political structures confined to 'anti-globalization' protest.

NEOLIBERALISM AND THE LABOUR MOVEMENT

For the labour movement, the struggle against neoliberalism has until recently been a battle conducted on largely defensive terms. Thus, while the 1998 maritime dispute[34] may be regarded as having been a qualified success for workers (in the sense that it prevented the de-unionization of a critical industry), it was essentially concerned with maintaining rather than extending union influence. Further, as the example of Seattle attests, relations between trade union officialdom and activists from other social movements are just as often characterized by conflict as co-operation. During S11, for example, one local official boasted of the capacity of trade unions to 'impose working-class discipline' upon protesters.[35]

Exactly what was meant by such rhetoric was illustrated not only by the refusal of the local peak trade union body to endorse a blockade but also – as in Seattle[36] – the careful distance trade union officials kept from allowing direct worker involvement; it was a neat reversal of the example of the maritime dispute, in which officials called for public participation in a 'community picket' in support of locked-out workers.[37] The Victorian Trades Hall Council supported rally of 12 September was explicitly intended to fulfil this aim,[38] but again, in Melbourne, just as in Seattle, small groups of determined unionists were able to circumvent official union policing ('working-class discipline') in order to join the blockade. Neoliberalism, then, would appear to be an issue that agitates union activists, and the example of S11 suggests that relations between the industrial and political wings of the Australian labour movement are becoming more strained than has historically been the case, a development that provides important new possibilities for the (re-)establishment of an 'autonomous' union movement.[39]

CREATING AND SUSTAINING A CULTURE OF DISSENT

The need to 'defend and extend' critical public spaces – both 'real' and 'virtual' – from which to reinvigorate social struggles against neoliberalism[40] is under threat from a number of different directions. For an international audience, the increasingly violent police response to anti-Summit protest may well call to mind the police shootings in Gothenburg in June 2001, or perhaps the police murder of Carlo Giuliani in Genoa in July 2001,[41] but in Papua New Guinea a month earlier at least three and possibly as many as six unarmed students were shot dead protesting against the IMF and World Bank.[42] While Australian protesters have thus far been spared such a fate,[43] the State has followed the example of governments in other countries in introducing punitive legal measures.

In Australia, as elsewhere, new legislation has made it easier for citizens to be spied upon and for the government to call out the defence forces against protesting citizens, to ban any organization considered 'likely to endanger the security and integrity of the

Commonwealth or another country', to let ASIO detain people incommunicado, and to allow the government to label some union activity as civil disobedience and other activism as terrorist, with life imprisonment as potential punishment.[44] Jenny Hocking has shown recently how counter-terrorism developments such as the Security Legislation Amendment (Terrorism) Act allow for the pre-emptive control of political dissent, which may or may not protect individual citizens but which certainly protect the State itself.[45] While such measures have hardly gone unnoticed or unopposed by a wide range of organizations,[46] the ALP has once again distinguished itself by the very partial nature of its own opposition.

On another level, the battle of ideas – in Gramsci's phrase, the battle for cultural hegemony – continues to be fought in a context of government attacks upon the public education system and in a mediascape increasingly hostile to the articulation of not only radical but even mildly reformist alternatives to current economic, social and political structures. The proliferation of well-funded neoconservative think-tanks with strong links to US institutions and corporate funding has had a sizable impact upon Australian political discourse,[47] from debates surrounding issues of indigenous struggles and the history of black–white relations[48] to those surrounding environmental crises such as global warming[49] to the restructuring of workplace relations and the diminishing share of social wealth accruing to workers (as well as those unable to find jobs in an increasingly competitive labour market).

Such attempts may well be subverted, however, by the strategic use of the Internet as a tool of international networking. In this respect, it is worth noting that the software that has allowed for the establishment of a global network of Indymedia sites was developed by Australian activists working for the Sydney-based Community Active Technology: 'Active is behind most of the indymedia.org network and all of active.org.au. Active has helped identify the concept of open publishing. It is free software, and *copyleft*. It can be run on an entirely free software server...'[50] Since its debut in Seattle in 1999, the Indymedia network has blossomed into a truly global network, one with active centres on all continents and well over one hundred different cities. The importance of computer-linked social movements has never been greater.[51] It demonstrates both the resourcefulness of new social movements and puts paid to the lie that movements opposed to neoliberal globalization are somehow opposed to the internationalization of culture and, of course, struggle.

OTHER ISLANDS

Elsewhere in Oceania, struggles against neoliberalism have focused among other things on combating its environmental effects, particularly the devastating impact of rising sea levels on island groups. This is one battle that Islander peoples in particular simply cannot afford to lose. However, barring a sudden and dramatic reversal in greenhouse gas emission levels – an unlikely occurrence given the refusal of the US and Australian governments to ratify even the Kyoto Protocol – it seems, unfortunately, that in most cases they will lose out.[52] Australian military intervention in the Solomon Islands in July 2003 – after a prolonged period of civil unrest – has been depicted as being in the same vein as East Timor and, like East Timor but *un*like the war in Iraq, has met with little public opposition.[53] According to Ellie Wainwright of the Australian Strategic Policy Institute in an interview of October 2002, given the 'state of virtual lawlessness', 'parlous' economic situation, 'weak security infrastructure' and limited 'capacity to regulate people flows' prior to intervention, the Solomon Islands provided a fertile breeding ground for potential terrorists, especially those who might want to target Australia.[54] According to Doug Lorimer, however, '[s]ince December 1997, under blackmail from Canberra and the US-dominated International Monetary Fund, the Solomons government has implemented a neoliberal "structural reform program" involving privatisation of government services... substantial cuts in public sector jobs and the introduction of high fees for education and health care'.[55]

In other words, in a pattern familiar to many who have studied its history, the imposition of neoliberal globalization through the 'stabilization' and 'structural adjustment' programmes of the IMF and World Bank lead to increasing economic, political and social instability: developments 'necessitating' some form of military intervention.[56] Elsewhere, while East Timor may have won independence from Indonesian control, a bloody struggle continues in the former Dutch colony of West Papua.[57] The ironically named 'Act of Free Choice' – dubbed the 'Act of No Choice' by West Papuan dissidents – which gave control of the territory to Indonesia in 1963 continues to be fought by independence groups within the province, largely to the indifference of Australian authorities but of growing interest to both local, regional and global networks.[58]

CONCLUSION

As suggested at the beginning of this chapter, current struggles against neoliberal globalization in Australia and the Oceania region face numerous additional obstacles as a result of war: whether understood as being of a traditionally military nature, a war on refugees/displaced labour or a 'war on terror'/dissent. Only time will tell whether the extra room for authoritarian manoeuvre provided to the Australian State by the events of 11 September resolves the problem of how to contain such struggles within acceptable limits. For while the attacks on the Pentagon and the World Trade Center have provided the State with a pretext for tightening its grasp upon the social terrain in which they take place, dependent as globalizing capital is upon labour for profit-making, struggles against neoliberal globalization are likely to 'go on for some years' yet.

NOTES

1. 'Melbourne under siege', *The Australian*, 12 September 2000.
2. For a general overview of S11, see Verity Burgmann (2003), *Power, Profit and Protest: Australian social movements and globalisation* (Crows Nest: Allen & Unwin), esp. pp. 276–326. Also *Overland*, no. 161, Summer 2000, esp. Kurt Iveson and Sean Scalmer, 'Contesting the "Inevitable": Notes on S11', pp. 4–12; *Arena Magazine*, no. 49, October–November 2003, pp. 2–3, 8–11; Owen Gager, 'From Seattle to South Melbourne, and After', *Red & Black*, no. 29, Autumn 2001, pp. 31–7. An engaging personal account may be found in Led Pup (2001) 'S11: Make Crown a prison, the criminals are already inside', *This Is Not A Commodity*, issue 0, no. 1, February, pp. 16–20 (available online at http://ledpup.dyns.net/Treason/TINAC/Pup_S11.html). SKA TV's documentary video *Melbourne Rising* is one of a number of independent films produced in the aftermath of S11 (for more information, see www.skatv.org.au). Also of interest is the Victorian Government Ombudsman's Report, an *Investigation of police action at the World Economic Forum demonstrations September 2000*, June 2001 – police action that is currently (mid-October 2003) being 'investigated' by the legal system.
3. The movement from 'S11' to '9/11' and its impact is explored in Kevin McDonald (2002) 'From S11 to September 11 – implications for sociology', *Journal of Sociology*, vol. 38, no. 3, pp. 229–36.
4. The war in Iraq attracted some of the largest demonstrations in Australian history; in Melbourne, on 14 February 2003, up to a quarter of a million people marched to protest the war ('Peace rally draws more than 100,000 to heart of Melbourne', *The Age*, 15 February 2003).
5. Originally appearing in an article by the journalist Fred Brenchley (*The Bulletin*, 29 September 1999) and based on an interview with the Prime Minister, Howard has since moved to distance himself from the

appellation of 'deputy', and denies ever having described the relationship between the Australian and United States' Governments in these terms. Nevertheless, and for obvious reasons, the term has stuck. For further discussion, see Gerard Henderson, 'Shooting from the lip has been costly', *The Sydney Morning Herald*, 3 June 2003.

6. On the Hawke and Keating Government's 'love affair' with neoliberalism, see Tom Conley (2001) 'The Domestic Politics of Globalisation', *Australian Journal of Political Science*, vol. 36, no. 2, July, pp. 223–46.

7. Described by the Department of Foreign Affairs and Trade http://www.dfat.gov.au/trade/negotiations/us.html as representing 'a unique opportunity to advance the interests of Australia's exporters', one 'offer[ing] significant benefits to the nation in terms of economic growth and employment'; Susan Hawthorne, on the other hand, argues that 'the Australia–United States Free Trade Agreement leaves Australia as a party to aggression in an agreement that will not benefit the Australian people, especially women, Indigenous peoples and the poor': http://globalresearch.ca/articles/HAW308A.html.

8. As documented in Amanda Lohrey (2002) *Groundswell: The Rise of the Greens*, *Quarterly Essay*, no. 8.

9. As in the US, and to a lesser extent elsewhere, the diverse range of actions and groups opposing neoliberal forums, processes and policies have been dubbed 'anti-globalisation' by the Australian media. However, such attributions, and the false dichotomy between 'forward-looking globalisation' and 'backward-looking nationalism' that the use of such terminology generates, are widely rejected by those opposed to neoliberal globalisation. For further discussion, see Burgmann (2003), esp. pp. 242–55.

10. 'Endless War', *The Bulletin*, 10 September 2003. For the Prime Minister as for others then, *la lucha continua*.

11. The Cole Royal Commission into the Building and Construction Industry (2001/2) was criticized by construction unions as being a politically motivated attack upon one of the largest, militant and progressive unions in the country; its findings were described by one official as 'no more than a list of technical industrial breaches' against a small number of union members (http://www.cfmeu.asn.au/construction/press/nat/20030326_RCreport2.html).

12. Laksiri Jayasuriya and Jenni Cook (1988) 'A Struggle for Equality', in Verity Burgmann and Jenny Lee (eds), *Making a Life* (Melbourne: McPhee Gribble/Penguin), p. 171. See also A.T. Yarwood and M.J. Knowling (1982) *Race Relations in Australia: A History* (North Ryde: Methuen).

13. See Mungo MacCallum (2002) *Girt By Sea: Australia, refugees and the politics of fear*, *Quarterly Essay*, no. 5; also Peter Mares (2001) *Borderline: Australia's treatment of refugees and asylum seekers* (Sydney: UNSW Press).

14. 'Howard's speech', *The Sydney Morning Herald*, 29 August 2001.

15. 'In 1992 Immigration Minister Gerry Hand introduced laws that made Australia only the fourth Western nation to ensure mandatory detention for all unauthorised arrivals ... the only complaint from the then opposition spokesman on Immigration, Phillip Ruddock, was that they didn't go far enough': MacCallum (2002), pp. 23–4.

16. For further discussion, see Angela Mitropoulos (2001) 'Habeas Corpus', *Arena Magazine*, no. 55, October–November, pp. 52–4.
17. Stuart Rosewarne (2001) 'Globalisation: The new migration', *Overland*, no. 164, Spring, pp. 29–33.
18. Woomera 2002: variously described as 'a kaleidoscope of cascading autonomous actions, media streams and screenings, workshops, discussions and happenings [embracing] a diversity of tactics to disrupt the present and create the future' and an 'Autonomadic Caravan & Festival of Freedoms'; an 'event that brought together a diverse range of people and groups – around the remote migrant internment camp in Woomera, South Australia – seeking to create new ways of connecting the struggles around indigenous land rights, new world borders, toxic waste, uranium mining and the not-so-new warlords' (http://woomera2002.antimedia. net/). A critical review of the Baxter protest may be found in Anna Trembath and Damian Grenfell (2003) 'No Horizons', *Arena Magazine*, no. 65, June–July, pp. 9–10. On Woomera, see Andrea Maksimovic (2002) 'Beyond North and South – Woomera 2002', *Arena Magazine*, June–July, pp. 11–12.
19. This is in addition to the 'unlawful non-citizens' engaged in their own bitter struggle against imprisonment in Australia's camps; sometimes in co-operation with 'lawful citizens' outside of them, but more often in relative isolation.
20. James Goodman (2002) 'Capital's First International? The World Economic Forum is coming to town', *Arena Magazine*, no. 47, June–July, pp. 45–7.
21. For further discussion on the subject of nationalism and the (Australian) labour movement, see Damien Lawson (2001) 'The movement of Labour', *Overland*, no. 164, Spring, pp. 46–94.
22. On election results for 2002 Federal election, see http://www.roymorgan. com/news/polls/2003/3646/.
23. Lohrey (2002).
24. 'Aotearoa', meaning 'land of the long white cloud', is the (indigenous) Maori term for New Zealand, and is used here as elsewhere in recognition of the fact of Maori (dis-)possession.
25. See Jane Kelsey (1995) *Economic Fundamentalism: The New Zealand experiment – A world model for Structural Adjustment?* (London: Pluto Press).
26. 'Neo-liberal Globalisation and the Tino Rangatiratanga movement', http://aotearoa.wellington.net.nz/he/global.htm.
27. Of obvious and much noted significance here is the struggle of the EZLN or Zapatista movement in Chiapas, Mexico: Midnight Notes (2001) *Auroras of the Zapatistas: Local and global struggles of the Fourth World War*, 2nd edn (New York: Autonomedia).
28. *Terra nullius*: 'uninhabited land'. The June 1992 Australian High Court ruling, widely referred to as 'the Mabo judgment' after Eddie Mabo, who led the case for and on the behalf of the Murray Islanders of northern Queensland, overturned the long-standing legal fiction that Australia was uninhabited when the British arrived in 1788. Henry Reynolds (1991) 'For Seven Judges, Two Hundred Years of Questions', *Australian Society*, January–February, pp. 12–13.

29. Heather Goodall (1996) *Invasion to Embassy: Land in Aboriginal politics in New South Wales, 1770–1972* (Sydney: Allen & Unwin in association with Black Books), p. 9.

30. 'Bringing It All Back Home: Anti-globalisation Activism Cannot Ignore Colonial Realities', http://www.voiceoftheturtle.org/show_article.php?aid=7.

31. Aggy Kelly and Andrew Blussat (2002) 'Autonomy and the New Global Social Movements', *Arena Magazine*, no. 58, April–May, p. 48. Significant by its absence is any mention of the influence of anarchism upon the development of 'autonomous' social movements; a situation that various articles in vol. 11, no. 1 of the journal *Anarchist Studies* goes some way towards rectifying. Evidence for this in the Australian context in particular may be found in numerous events, groups and projects. Of particular significance is the intervention of anarcho-syndicalist public transport workers in the 1990 Melbourne tram dispute, in which locked-out tram workers placed the industry for a relatively brief period under workers' self-management (as documented in, for example, Dick Curlewis (1997) *The Melbourne Tram Dispute* (Sydney: Jura Media). See also http://www.takver.com/history/tram1990.htm). The widespread adoption of 'direct action' in the peace and environmental movements is also attributable in part to the influence of anarchist discourses on (radical) social change.

32. On S11–AWOL, see http://www.antimedia.net/s11awol/main.html; on PGA–Pacifika, see http://www.nadir.org/nadir/initiativ/agp/pgapacific/.

33. Kelly and Blussat (2002).

34. Tom Bramble (1998) *War On The Waterfront* (Brisbane: Brisbane Defend Our Unions Committee); also http://www.takver.com/wharfie/index.htm.

35. The World Today Archive – Police face difficult task during World Economic Forum: http://www.abc.net.au/worldtoday/s172710.htm.

36. See Alexander Cockburn, Jeffrey St Clair and Allan Sekula (2000) *5 Days That Shook the World: Seattle and Beyond* (London: Verso), esp. pp. 22, 29.

37. Leigh Hubbard (2000) 'The MUA Dispute: Turning industrial relations into community relations', *Just Policy*, nos 19–20, September, pp. 134–44.

38. Paul Robinson, 'Union head blasts S11 organisers', *The Age*, 5 September 2000; Michael Bachelard, 'Unions lend S11 a pacifying hand', *The Australian*, 9 September 2000.

39. Under the impact of 'globalization' and the retreat of social democracy, the need for reform of the labour movement is becoming an increasingly pressing concern for workers, which is reflected in the growing influence of anarchist and syndicalist ideas. Such developments are coming under increasing scrutiny, as evidenced by the recent (October 2003) Workers' Control Conference in Sydney, involving both academics, activists, and union officials: see http://www.jura.org.au/workerscontrol/. In this regard, the experience of the NSW Builders' Labourers Federation is informative (see Meredith Burgmann and Verity Burgmann (1998) *Green Bans, Red Union: Environmental activism and the New South Wales Builders' Labourers Federation* (Sydney: UNSW Press). (In the attenuated form of employee

consultation 'works councils' – which seeks to harness workers' desire for self-management to increased productivity – see Greg Combet (2002/3) 'From Wise Counsel Good Works Shall Come', *Arena Magazine*, no. 62, December–January, pp. 38–40.)

40. Anita Lacey, in 'A Shared Space for Activism' (*Arena Magazine*, no. 43, October–November, pp. 22–3), provides an interesting account of the new possibilities presenting themselves in the occupation of public spaces by dissenting groups.

41. *On Fire: The battle of Genoa and the anti-capitalist movement* (One Off Press).

42. Which in the manner of IMF and World Bank schemes elsewhere, is forcing a harsh privatisation regime on the country: see http://www.nadir.org/nadir/initiativ/agp/free/imf/asia/pngprotest.htm for details of this and accounts of the associated protests and murders.

43. Despite increasingly harsh police responses to protest; see Jude McCulloch, (2001) 'Paramilitary Policing and Protesters', *Forum*, no. 27, p. 3. The increasingly violent police response to protest is evident, for example, in the Sydney May Day and anti-WTO protests of 2002.

44. See Burgmann (2003), p. 325.

45. Jenny Hocking (2003) 'Counter-Terrorism and the Criminalisation of Politics: Australia's new security powers of detention, proscription and control', *Australian Journal of Politics and History*, vol. 49, no. 3, pp. 355–71, at p. 371.

46. See Damien Lawson (2002) 'Fighting A New Terror', *Arena Magazine*, no. 59, June–July, pp. 16–17.

47. Alex Carey (1995), in *Taking the Risk Out of Democracy: Propaganda in the US and Australia*, ed. Andrew Lohrey (Sydney: UNSW Press), provides a useful history from the pre-1914 era to the 1980s of the shaping of the public mind by corporate propaganda – memorably described by Walter Lippmann as the 'manufacture of consent'.

48. Robert Manne (2001) *In Denial: The stolen generations and the right*, Quarterly Essay, no. 1; Stuart Macintyre with Anna Clark (2003) *The History Wars* (Melbourne: Melbourne University Press).

49. Sharon Beder (2000) *Global Spin: The corporate assault on environmentalism*, rev. edn (Melbourne: Scribe Publications).

50. http://www.active.org.au/doc/.

51. Harry Cleaver, 'Computer-linked Social Movements and the Global Threat to Capitalism': http://www.eco.utexas.edu/homepages/faculty/Cleaver/polnet.html.

52. The World Today Archive – Pacific islands issue plea for greenhouse gas reduction: http://www.abc.net.au/worldtoday/s649781.htm.

53. Hugh White, 'Why we still have to be ready to fight', *The Age*, 30 July 2003.

54. Also mentioned as possible havens for 'terrorists' are Papua New Guinea and Vanuatu: http://www.aspi.org.au/newsroom.cfm?t=releases&presspath=press/10-02/pacific_base.html.

55. Doug Lorimer, 'Solomons intervention serves Australian big business', *Green Left Weekly*, no. 547, 30 July 2003.

56. John Walton and David Seddon (1994) *Free Markets and Food Riots: The politics of global adjustment* (Oxford: Blackwell).
57. Or 'Irian Jaya' as it is termed by Indonesian authorities.
58. 'Mamberano Madness: Progress and Resistance in West Papua' and 'Rumble in the Jungle: Fighting for Freedom in West Papua', *Do or Die: Voices from the ecological resistance*, no. 8, 1999, pp. 225–41.

6

Social Movements in the Arab World

Azza Abd al-Mohsen Khalil

It is widely accepted that neoliberalism often overtly affects the interests of broad segments of the population, especially the most impoverished and marginalized in the global order. This raises the question of whether this encroachment positively or adversely affects the ability of these populations to resist and defend their interests. Today, most of the population in the Arab world is subjected to increasing pressures on economic, social, political and cultural fronts, and the social context allows them no space from which to defend themselves effectively. Careful examination of social movements in Arab societies would initially seek to define the characteristics acquired by social movements as the social structure in the Arab world evolved. It necessitates focusing on the emergence of these movements, their modes of expression, the dynamics of their interactions with their environment, the prospects they offer for change, their potential and the extent to which they are influenced by external, global conditions.

This chapter is divided into three parts. The first examines briefly the social, economic and political background against which the social movements operate in post-independence states. The second is mostly concerned with the main social movements in the region. The third part discusses the potential of social movements and their challenges in resisting neoliberalism.

SOCIAL MOVEMENTS IN CRISIS IN POST-INDEPENDENCE STATES

After Arab liberation movements achieved their objective of independence, a new type of state was established in the region, known as the independence state. Its priorities were reinforcing independence and cementing the state as the symbol of national identity and unity, while at the same time promoting economic and social development to overcome backwardness and accommodate the needs and aspirations of social segments mobilized in the struggle for independence.

Nations thus favoured the strict centralization of power, seen as the means to maintain independence, confront external challenges, contain domestic social and class cleavages and reduce sources of conflict. The ruling elite (composed of technocrats, senior civil servants, plus military and nationalist elements) saw the key to overcoming historical backwardness in economic structures and building an industrialized, nationalized economy. This required a centralized state to plan the modernization of society and mobilize the public for carrying out radical changes in a very short time. Building the state was given priority over building democracy and unity favoured over pluralism. This ultimately degenerated into an authoritarian state jealous of its autocratic power.[1] Constitutions in most Arab countries secured autocratic rule based on the imbalance of powers, privileging the executive and centralizing power in the hands of the president. Social and economic institutions were weak and relatively ineffective, especially considering the role played by the military elite.[2] This only strengthened the patriarchal system in the economic and political sphere and cemented the personalization of power – though the degree to which the masses benefited from this system varied.

The independence states launched agricultural reforms to achieve a base of capital investment required for industrialization and the expansion of infrastructure and education, using the strategy of import substitution and central planning. Although industrialization and development were successful in the early years, crises began to erode their real achievements. Financing became a problem. The state either tried to fund the deficit through inflation, which led to price rises, or cut back on public expenditure by decreasing the quality of services, which lowered the standard of living. Or else it borrowed, which only added to the problem of servicing the debt. The shock of military defeat reinforced the systematic erosion of the state's popular legitimacy, the population experiencing neither development nor independence.

Opposition thus emerged in the form of social movements, whether student, labour or democracy movements. As Samir Amin argues, the bourgeois enterprise demonstrated that the independence on which it had relied to legitimize its dictatorship was impossible.[3] Given these crises, many countries sought alliance with the West and were impelled to implement neoliberal policies dictated by the international donor institutions. In turn, this new alliance and these new policies necessitated a new form of legitimacy based on political liberalism.

This emerged under the influence of the patriarchal tradition and centralized authority, and these states continued to derive their legitimacy from Islamic, monarchical and tribal traditions.[4]

With the leaning towards a market economy, privatization saw the sale of a significant sector of state enterprises and the expansion of the private sector, initially and notably in contracting, followed by the banking and service sectors and, to a lesser degree, agriculture and light industry. The private sector also started obtaining franchises for foreign companies, particularly multinationals. This rapid expansion brought parasitic practices in its train, the most important being property speculation, forms of brokerage and commissions, which induced the growth of the informal sector among the upper classes. Moreover, high-ranking civil servants, army officers and security personnel started to engage covertly in private sector activity before they retired and afterwards did so openly. Kinship relations strengthened the bond between the economic and political elite and political power started to play a key role in economic activities. Termed by some speculative, or unproductive capitalism, such economies prioritize distributional relations, giving rise to a distributional, rather than productive economy.[5]

In addition to the relationship between business and politics, which already undermines the authenticity of liberalism in Arab societies, the economic elite in this kind of economy are not independent, as their existence depends on the direct or indirect services they offer to the global market. For them, the national market is a means of accumulating the capital necessary to become a part of global capitalism. The bourgeoisie have become isolated from their surrounding environment, in which the majority lives in poverty with simple distribution patterns and a burgeoning informal economy. This class was never likely to welcome democratic freedoms to accompany the economic freedoms to which they owed their very existence; nor are they interested in finding a domestic social basis to endorse their liberal enterprise, relying on pressures exerted by international institutions on the state. The alliance with foreign powers, coupled with the creation of a despotic authority, are the two primary reasons for the persistence of dependent capitalism, despite continuous social opposition.[6]

Arab regimes were then under pressure from Western allies and debtor institutions to implement a form of democracy that reduced the social and economic role of the state in the interests of the economic and cultural elite, promoting the merits of liberal enterprise and the inevitability of globalization. This of course did not increase opportunities for popular groups and organizations to affect political and economic decision-making. In this context, political pluralism, especially in ostensibly democratic countries, was a gift from above that could be retracted if misused. The authoritarian nature of the state has thus persisted with a minor reorientation involving a shift from an absolutist form to a supervisory one.[7] Indeed, this form of political pluralism represented a huge step backwards to the Mameluke autocratic systems, as the ability of popular forces to organize independently was severely curtailed.[8] In Egypt, for example, in the late 1970s restrictive legislation (known locally as 'the disreputable laws') was enacted, allowing life imprisonment for political offences. In addition, emergency law became a permanent feature of the political landscape.

The authoritarian climate was a significant factor undermining diverse political and intellectual currents of thought. In addition, the crisis of liberalism was exacerbated for lack of a social basis, resulting from the nature of the economic elite. The crisis of the left intensified with the collapse of the Soviet Union. In spite of increased security confrontations with various stripes of political Islam, some of these trends carried political weight, which afforded considerable negotiating power. Political parties found a role within the game of politics, the rules of which, however, they did not set. With time, they became experienced in adjusting to the margins of opposition allowed them, participating in parliaments with no actual role in decision-making. There is also a notable similarity between the political regime and party practices: despite demands for freedom and the democratic practices enshrined in party regulations, the reality differs radically. Most party leaders have consolidated the decision-making process in their own hands and restricted the participation of the base and intermediate levels.[9]

Thus, elites of all kinds have realized that change comes exclusively through the central power itself, and then only when dictated by external pressures. The strategy of change adopted by elites thus attempts to encroach upon the patriarchal system by provoking global public opinion and foreign power centres. This was the path of resistance taken by leaders of NGOs, whose numbers increased dramatically in the 1990s through the support of donor institutions and international organizations in order to reinforce the transformation to neoliberalism.

But can social movements move towards change in a way that meets the interests of the masses? This is the question addressed in the rest of the chapter.

THE MAIN SOCIAL MOVEMENTS IN ARAB SOCIETIES

The advent of neoliberalism in Arab societies raises several questions about the possibility of correcting long-standing imbalances in the Arab world, especially given the frequent occurrence of violence. Observers sense that the region is on the brink of change, although these changes are often difficult to measure or predict. Will political and social powers be content to continue to play the role defined for them? And will the popular masses be able to hold out much longer in present conditions?[10] Let us look at the more important social movements and their situation in the overall context outlined above.

Labour movements

The attention given by many countries to industrialization in the early post-independence period gave rise to a new working class both qualitatively and quantitatively different from that of the pre-independence era. This shift has been reflected in labour movements. While colonization had endowed the labour movement with nationalist sentiments, the existence of a nationalist state as the largest employer influenced the debate between politics and economics and the relationship between the state and trade unions.

Arab countries adopted policies granting some gains to workers, while at the same time restricting their independence of action by other means, including legislation that restricts or bans the right to form independent organizations, the prohibition of all means of resistance, and the use of the security system and violence if necessary. The obvious examples are Syria and Egypt, although the policies had varying effects in each country. In Egypt, they led the labour leadership to attempt to escape from state hegemony, with the labour movement ultimately emerging outside the framework of the official union. In Syria, on the other hand, workers tended to exert pressure through official channels.

The large post-independence labour movements in Egypt began their activities in 1968, operating outside the framework of the official union and against the government. Public sector workers played a leading role, many having come of age in communist movements in the 1940s. The workers' negative views of the official union became obvious when union representatives were dismissed and workers refused to deal with them during a strike in Shoubra El-Kheima in 1975.

In Syria, the workers' union became a political syndicate after the rise of the Baath party in 1963, and the working class in effect became a partner to the government. The Union of Labour Syndicates still represents a major force through pressures from the worker base, its active participation in the International Union of Labor Syndicates and the vitality of certain left-wing elements, such as Dr Shebel Marzouk. However, there remain questions regarding the sustainability of this movement as the government takes further steps towards economic and political reform.[11]

The Tunisian experience illustrates a different relationship between the labour movement and the state. The absorption of the General Labour Union by the state exposed the movement to other political agents. Thus the movement was an actor in the political system, even while it suffered from the contradictions inherent in the system. In the 1970s the Tunisian Labour Union acted as an umbrella for the most important opposition forces and represented the most powerful popular organization in the country. This allowed syndicate movements to impose a social programme compatible with the interests of the popular masses and supportive of the democratization of state systems. Nonetheless, the involvement of Habib Ashour (the leader of the union at that time) in a struggle for the succession to Bourguiba kept him focused on his personal interests. In turn, conservative forces within the union favoured certain confrontations for their own interests, which ultimately undermined the union and transformed it into a 'partnership syndicate' with the new government in 1987.[12]

Another vivid example is Sudan. The alternation between civil democratic rule and military rule engendered rapid transformation in syndicate and union organizations. At times, they led the push for change through public revolt and insurrection, as in the 1964 revolution and the 1985 uprising, while at others they resorted to covert operations, as after 1970 during the Numeiri administration.[13]

The relationship between leftist political forces and the labour movement played a central role in politicizing labour movements in most Arab countries. This aggravated the crisis of independence among labour activists and gave rise to factional differences, which undermined the natural cohesion of the labour movement. This was evident in Egypt, where the crisis coincided with the beginning of policies of structural adjustment, which put the working class on the defensive and debilitated it.[14]

These interactions revealed the patriarchal nature of Arab social institutions, which influenced the relationship between the nationalist state and workers, where certain gains were at the expense of a clampdown on independent action. It also allowed leftist forces to control the movement. Patriarchy was further manifested in the way certain individuals were able to determine the path of an entire social movement. In Tunisia, for example, Bourguiba's individualist policies imposed his control on the ruling party and the labour union, inspiring a vicious, personal conflict over succession among labour movement leaders, which may represent a lost historical opportunity.

As Arab regimes began to implement structural adjustment policies, workers were stripped of powers the state had granted to syndicates when it had adopted socialist policies and the defence of workers' rights. Consequently the labour movement encountered four counter-forces:

- first were employers, who tend to operate like contractors in the informal sector, paying little attention to laws or traditional employer–employee relationships. They are also closely connected with the ruling party through kinship and networks of mutual interests,[15] and are thus able to encroach on workers' rights and make them vulnerable;
- secondly, governments tend to oppose independent labour movements as their interests are at odds with current official policies, and labour movements are capable of building up social resistance to these policies;
- thirdly, labour movements have been influenced by the status of their allies, particularly leftist forces. The current weakness of the left, the erosion of their political power and their limited influence on society have also blunted the effectiveness of labour movements;
- finally, the composition of the labour force has been transformed through structural adjustment and shifts in the economic activities of Arab states.

The public sector labour force has declined dramatically, while the private sector has grown. New elements have also joined the labour force, for example, workers in the new Egyptian industrial cities. As a result, the number of workers with a marked nationalist consciousness has declined, to be replaced by workers who, having been raised on consumer values, have no links with the labour movement and its ideals. This is in addition to labourers who work without any legal protection in the informal sector, which often affects their capacity for unification and solidarity.[16]

All these obstacles have paralyzed the labour movement and turned its activities into a series of disconnected, scattered protests, largely of a random, transient nature. This raises issues for those concerned with labour affairs, e.g. the democratization of the movement's structure and the limits of working through official unions or attempting to increase the number of syndicates. Thus, while many Egyptian labour activists hope that increasing syndicate centres will free the labour movement – and indeed, they have tried to establish independent organizations within the official union – the government's keenness to dominate the Union of Labour Syndicates has prevented this.[17] In Algeria, the plurality of syndicates has not helped the labour movement move beyond its defensive position, as these syndicates were created when the movement was extremely weak. We must also consider the relationship of the political elites and intellectuals to the working-class movement, to resolve this complex equation of engendering solidarity and an independent leadership for the labour movement.

Recently some groups have emerged, bringing together labour activists, historical labour leaders and NGOs. For the most part, they focus on defending labour interests that have been eroded following implementation of neoliberal policies. Most of these groups in Arab countries co-operate and coordinate activities (for example, between Egypt and Algeria). Although quite active recently, their activities are always dependent on the influential intellectuals and human rights activists involved and they are constrained by the narrow democratic limits for such activities, particularly by the labour movement.

Peasant movements

In the post-independence era, most Arab countries implemented agricultural reform programmes as part of a nationalist, bourgeois enterprise seeking to eradicate the economic, political and social influence of large landowners and achieve a surplus for industrializing the country. Immediately after the July revolution in Egypt, in September 1952 the state passed a series of agricultural reform laws, which set a maximum limit on agricultural land ownership, and redistributed some land among small farmers. This law, however, only affected 7 per cent of agricultural land, which was redistributed to only 5 per cent of the households working in agriculture.

During this period in Egypt, a peasant movement emerged to resist the appropriation of surplus land by large landowners and to confront the attempts of the affluent in rural areas to control land. Many confrontations took place between peasants and large landowning families, and they left several victims in their wake, including Salah Hussein, Dessouki Ahmed Ali and Abdel Hamid Ghandour. The bureaucratic administrative authorities then conspired with large landowners and agents of the Socialist Union to eat away at the small gains made by farmers. The co-operatives were turned into institutions tailored to serve their interests. From 1960 to 1965, the government appropriated approximately 11 per cent of the agricultural surplus. As the development process stumbled in the 1960s and, with the advent of the Open Door Policy, in 1976 village banks started to replace the co-operatives. Credit, given at high interest rates, became a burden on farmers and led to a deterioration in living conditions. This spurred emigration from villages to cities and to the oil-rich countries of the Gulf.

The implementation of neoliberal policies was associated with the enactment of a law in 1992 that freed rents on agricultural land and stripped tenant farmers of their rights. Landlords were thus given the freedom to set the rental value and the tenure of the contract. As a result, many tenant farmers lost their land and joined the agricultural or manual labour force. Liberalization policies were also responsible for the abolition of subsidies on agricultural inputs, the liberalization of interest rates on agricultural loans, and the abolition of tax exemptions for small landowners. This allowed monopolistic forces to dominate agriculture, which led to an increase in rural unemployment and worsening conditions for agricultural labour. Thus, the relationship between impoverished peasants, on one hand, and the state and large landowners, on the other, became conflictual.

To resist these developments the Peasants' Union was established in 1983 within the nationalist, progressive Tagammu Party. Research centres, NGOs and political parties also started devoting attention to farmers' concerns. Their demands can be summarized as follows: the revival of the central co-operative union as a body capable of playing a real role in serving farmers' interests, the establishment of a co-operative bank for farmers, the formulation of responses to agreements concluded with the World Bank and USAID and a resistance to normalization with Israel.

The peasant resistance movement began in the 1990s by sending complaints to officials and the press. It then proceeded to collect thousands of signatures from wronged tenant farmers and convened at least 200 peasant conferences, largely organized by opposition parties. The movement then moved on to public demonstrations and sit-ins in front of the co-operative headquarters. Since late 1996, movements aiming at the repeal of the agricultural rental law have expanded to various parts of rural Egypt: the law has strongly affected peasants since it first came into operation in 1997, a year that witnessed several bouts of violence.

Other factors, however, have helped allay the tension and have facilitated farmers' acceptance of the new law. Some farmers were unaware of the impact the law would have on their income, while at the same time certain compromises were reached between tenants and landowners. Moreover, there has been a virtual press blackout on peasant movements. Despite disagreement among analysts about the size, effectiveness, and sustainability of these movements, they agree that they are an expression of the desires of impoverished peasants, especially agricultural labourers.[18]

In Sudan the first general union for Sudanese peasants was formed under the military regime of May 1967, though it was preceded by the peasant union led by prominent communist leader Muhammad Amin before independence. The first general union was set up to represent peasants in the Socialist Union, Sudan's sole political organization, but it did not fulfil its role. With the coming to power of the current government in 1992, the union was opened up to farmers all over Sudan. It had a direct membership of 560 members representing Sudan's various provinces in accordance with agricultural density.

Farmers in Sudan suffered from the drop in crop prices set by the government. This led many to give up farming and immigrate to Khartoum. Agricultural enterprises were also privatized in 1992. A total of twenty agricultural institutions were sold off and 492 of 2,229 workers were laid off. The peasant union was unable to take action.

THE ANTI-GLOBALIZATION MOVEMENT

Anti-globalization activities began in the Arab region through the efforts of various social movements. Non-governmental research centres have played an important role in promoting anti-globalization as have certain labour-oriented centres (the Centre for Syndicate Services), peasant-oriented centres (the Land Centre in Egypt), student movements (the General Federation for Students in Tunisia), and cultural, nationalist or advocacy movements (the Arab Research Centre, the Hisham Mubarak Law Centre, anti-normalization committees in Egypt, boycott committees, cultural forums and committees supporting Iraq and Palestine in Syria). Women's organizations have also played a role in raising awareness of anti-globalization activities.

Groups proposing economic and social alternatives to neoliberalism included certain nationalist intellectuals as well as advocates of democracy. One example was the Coalition of Egyptians, formed in 1979, which involved more than a hundred individuals belonging to different parties and syndicates, who critiqued the implementation of the Open Door policy. With the growth of the global anti-globalization discourse, some of these activities acquired an essentially socio-economic nature. This drew new generations into activism, alongside the old generation who had resumed their activities.

Some activities were mainly concerned with criticizing the globalization process, while others were more socialist in nature. Although many committees have been established calling for the boycott of Israeli and American goods and using anti-globalization rhetoric, the first explicitly anti-globalization organization, the Egyptian Group for Combating Globalization, was set up in 2002. The group is committed to fighting all forms of neoliberalism in the economic and social fields, as well as tackling the resulting poverty, unemployment, and state withdrawal from the public service and social sectors. It has held discussion groups and workshops in various regions of the country, publishing simplified pamphlets and coordinating campaigns.

Other research centres are involved, for example the Centre for Socialist Studies and Research in Egypt, established in 1999, with many young people as members. In Syria, the National Committee for Boycotting Imperialist Goods and Interests was established after a statement made by several intellectuals in 2000.[19]

In recent years, attempts have been made to coordinate these disparate anti-globalization efforts. A number of organizations participated in a pan-Arab conference in Cairo in October 2001, held in response to the World Trade Organization conference held in Doha at the same time. The conference included representatives from organizations from Syria, Palestine, Lebanon, and Jordan, Senegal,

Nigeria and other African and Asian countries. With the participation of representatives from Arab organizations in the African Social Forum, the Asian Social Forum and the World Social Forum, more attention has been paid to formulating national and regional social forums across the Arab world. It is important to note, however, that many of these activities are limited to a tiny number of intellectuals and civil society activists.

CHALLENGES FACING SOCIAL MOVEMENTS IN RESISTING GLOBALIZATION

Social movements between the old and the new

The preceding analysis suggests that the so-called 'old' social movements or class movements are represented today by labour and peasant movements. Given the conditions in the Arab world, these movements today make only sporadic protests, or carry out dispersed, reactive, spontaneous actions that prevent them from developing into a strong resistance. On the other hand, advocacy groups, religious organizations and women's groups can be described as new social movements insofar as they are not based on any class identity (with the exception of advocacy organizations working with labour and peasant issues and anti-globalization committees of a leftist stamp). These new movements have a different configuration. Most attempt to achieve their demands from above by dealing with various decision-making authorities, rather than attempting to bring about change through social and cultural hegemony or changing social patterns. Only a very few organizations are operating in this sense, including some women's organizations, religious organizations and human rights centres.[20]

The patriarchal system and its relationship to the state and authority

The hegemony of the state over social action varies throughout the Arab world. It can be direct, as in the case of labour syndicates, where state acceptance of pluralism is impossible, or indirect, as in some advocacy organizations, where the hegemony is only visible in conflict. The relationship between the state and social movements is often a zero-sum game, with the increase of one player's share necessarily creating a decrease in the other player's share. When the state is weak, civil society becomes stronger and more prosperous, as was seen in Egypt from the advent of Mohamed Ali until the 1919 Revolution, or after the 1967 defeat.[21] Although state power has varied at different historical stages, the relationship of conflict has remained constant. When civil society attempts to outsmart or negotiate with the state to achieve its demands, this does not signal the absence of conflict. Rather, it merely reflects the balance of power, in which civil society is even weaker than the weak, but still hegemonic state.

Social action is not concerned with the accumulation of power. Given patriarchal hegemony and the relationship of conflict, new social movements are primarily concerned with guaranteeing their own survival. They do this by dealing with the political authority in order to induce change, or by clashing with it by allying themselves to influential power centres abroad. These organizational frameworks seldom attempt to acquire more social power by cultivating popular legitimacy, which is crystallized by mobilizing its supporters to defend their own distinctive identity.[22] The main challenge to social movements today is to break the patriarchal framework and become self-sufficient through reinforcing a climate of civil democracy that will be reflected in interactions with the government, foreign partners and other political forces. This is a basic step for the labour movement, which is searching for a pluralistic model that can strengthen and improve the nature of its protests, its fragmentation and the lack of solidarity. Self-sufficiency requires a certain level of self-confidence and confidence in the abilities of the masses to induce change and defend their interests.

Defining an identity

As the frameworks for social action seek to define their identity, a number of important issues arise, for example the way they feel about what separates them from each other and their position as a part of the whole. This requires a certain amount of independence. Here, then, it is possible to discern another challenge, insofar as the various relationships of hegemony make it difficult to distinguish between these movements and the government, on one hand, and between these movements and political activists, on the other.

Another question arises concerning the extent to which these frameworks have secured the involvement of their target group to defend their own interests. That is, should a movement be described as a peasant or labour movement based on the identity of the people affiliated to it, or can it be a movement of interested parties who advocate for labour or peasant interests, without being affected by them? This, then, is the challenge: correlating the identity of the movement's framework with the people belonging to it, and supporting the capabilities of the masses to organize themselves. The debate between professionalism and voluntarism is also relevant: although professional activists are an asset, they often prevent these organizations from becoming an active resistance movement, particularly as professionals slowly become employees.

The issue of identity also raises the issue of a national versus a global identity. It should be noted that considering local frameworks for action as part of a global social movement does not necessarily negate their ability to represent a national identity. Rather, this national identity allows the local organization to interact as equals with the global movement. This, in turn, helps to break with the tendency to transfer models of external interactions and graft them on to the local scene.

The political content of social action

This issue is linked to the debate about the strategies of the social movements for change. Various studies on global social movements point out that movements formulate their opinions and positions in the course of action itself. Strategies and tactics imported from abroad are worthless.[23] The alternatives proposed by the movements are intimately related to the quest to defend their identity. In the Arab region, the ideological vacuum resulting from the erosion, then collapse of first the populist, nationalist enterprise, then socialism, prevented existing political and social conflicts from giving rise to possible alternatives.[24] As a result, political parties cannot offer alternatives that would enrich the struggle of social movements or affect their horizons. Instead, political activists demand that social action frameworks do their job as well. This represents a challenge for both politicians and social action frameworks.

Organizational frameworks and the elitist nature of social action frameworks

The social heritage in the Arab world includes spontaneous movements, particularly among peasants and, to a lesser degree, labourers, characterized by their reactive, temporary and effervescent nature. In contrast, most forms of social activity are based on a strict hierarchy in which the individual plays a fundamental role, replacing internal codes within the movement. The authority of the individual is prevalent, and the relationship between the leader and the base is patriarchal. Competition is strong on the horizontal level, and is ultimately dependent on vertical relationships. In this climate, acceptance of the Other and collective action are rare, which have been critical factors in aborting experiments in public social action. Indeed, this deference to authority poses a major obstacle to changing power relations at the base. Some believe the involvement in social movements of activists with experience in political organizations (either present or in the past) has played a vital role in transferring this autocratic legacy to social action frameworks. This poses the challenge of breaking with this legacy and other endemic features in the socio-political system and relationships.

Yet, the persistence of a certain legacy over an extended period of time does not mean that society has acquired certain unalterable cultural characteristics. It simply means that Arab societies have not yet broken with old frameworks and relations in order to create new ones in their place. In the Arab world, both exist side by side, each waxing and waning in ways that have hindered real progress in society.

With the growing desire of certain segments of the population – including the intellectual elite – to break free from this system, the time is ripe to foster democratic relationships, which would pave the way for collective action, dialogue and acceptance of the Other. This would break with a constraining legacy and allow a role for social activists willing to face the challenges. At this point, it is not important whether we call such collective social action a social movement or some other name: what is important is to open horizons for solidarity among those who are marginalized in the global order at both local and global levels.

NOTES

1. Ali Aoumleel, in Saad El-Din Ibrahim (1998), pp. 175–6.
2. Amany Kandeel (1995), pp. 184–6
3. Samir Amin (1991), p. 136.
4. Samir Amin (2003).
5. Bourhan Ghaliouen (1994), p. 127; Saad El-Din Ibrahim (1998), pp. 275–7.
6. Bourhan Ghaliouen (1994), p. 128; Ali Omleel (1999); Samir Amin (2003).
7. Amany Kandeel (1995), p. 51.
8. Samir Amin (2003).
9. Amany Kandeel (1995), p. 134.
10. Mohsen Marzouk (2003).
11. Saber Barakat (1998); Kamal Abbas (1998); Moustafa Magdy El-Gamal (2003); Sawsan Zukzuk (2003).

12. Mohsen Marzouk (2003).
13. Othman Serag El-Din & Akram Abd al-Qayum Abbas (2002).
14. Saber Barakat (1998); Nasser Gaby (2003).
15. Ahmed Thabet (2002).
16. Kamal Abbas (1998).
17. Saber Barakat (1998).
18. Hanan Ramadan (2003).
19. Mohamed Ismail (2003); Sawsan Zukzuk (2003).
20. Alan Scott (1990), p. 18.
21. Mohamed El-Sayyed Saeed, p. 9.
22. André Gunder Frank and Marta Fuentes (1991), p. 148.
23. André Gunder Frank and Marta Fuentes (1991), p. 149.
24. Samir Amin (1991).

BIBLIOGRAPHY

Abbas, Kamal (1998) 'The Egyptian Labor Movement Now: Primary Questions', unpublished paper presented to the Alternative Research Development Program

Abd al-Malak, Anwar (1983) *The Renaissance of Egypt: Thought and ideology in Egypt's national renaissance (1805–1892)* (Cairo: General Egyptian Book Organization)

Abd al-Megid, Youssri (2003) 'The Egyptian Human Rights Movement Between the Local and the Global', unpublished research paper, Arab Research Center

Amin, Samir (1991) 'On the Periphery of the Global Order: The end of national liberation', in *The Great Chaos*, ed. Immanuel Wallerstein *et al.*, trans. Essam Khafaji and Adib Ni'ma (Beirut: Farabi Press)

Amin, Samir (2003) 'Grassroots Organizations in the Arab World', in *Anti-Globalization: The global movement of grassroots organizations*, ed. Samir Amin and Francois Houtart (Cairo: Arab Research Center and the World Forum for Alternatives)

Barakat, Saber (1998) 'The Student and Labor Movement After 1946', in *Workers and Students in the Egyptian Nationalist Movement*, ed. Essam al-Dessouqi (Cairo: Mahrusa Press)

El-Beshery, Tarek (1983) *The Political Movement in Egypt: (1945–1952)* (Cairo: Shurouq Press)

El-Gabry, Mohammed Abed (1984) 'Authenticity and Contemporaneity in Modern Arab Thought: Class struggle or cultural problematic?', in *The Arab Future* (Beirut: Center for Arab Unity Studies)

Gaby, Nasser (2003) 'Social Movements in Algeria Between the Crisis of the Nationalist State and Social Cleavages', unpublished research paper, Arab Research Center

El-Gamal, Moustafa Magdy (2003) 'The Labor Movement in Egypt', unpublished research paper, Arab Research Center

Fernandez, Cesar (1995) 'Private But Public: The third sector in Latin America', in *The Global Alliance for Citizen Participation: Supporting global civil society* (Cairo: Publications of the Global Coalition)

Ghaliouen, Bourhan (1994) 'Arab Democracy: Roots of the Crisis and Horizons for Growth', in *On Democratic Choice: Critical Studies*, ed. Burhan Ghalyoun *et al.* (Beirut: Center for Arab Unity Studies)

Gunder Frank, André and Marta Fuentes (1991) 'Social Movements in Contemporary Global History', in *The Great Chaos*, ed. Immanuel Wallerstein *et al.*, trans. Essam Khafaji and Adib Ni'ma (Beirut: Farabi Press)

Hannah, Abdullah (2002) *Civil Society in the Contemporary Arab State* (Damascus: al-Mada Press)

Ibrahim, Saad El-Din, ed. (1998) *Society and the State in the Arab World* (Beirut: Center for Arab Unity Studies)

Ismail, Muhammad (2003) 'The Egyptian Intellectuals' Movement in the Framework of Nationalist and Social Protest', unpublished study, Arab Research Center

Kandeel, Amany (1995) *Democratic Transformation in Egypt: 1981–1993* (Cairo: Ibn Khaldun Press)

Karam, Azza (2001) 'The Life of Shuhrat al-Alam: Women Against Women', in *Women, Islamist Movements, and the State* (Cairo: Kitab Sutur)

Marzouk, Mohsen (2003) 'Social Movements in Tunisia: Searching for the Absent', unpublished research paper, Arab Research Center

Memdani, Mahmoud (forthcoming) Introduction to *Studies in Social and Democracy Movements in Africa*, ed. Mahmoud Memdani, trans. Helmy Shaarawy *et al.* (Cairo: Supreme Council for Culture)

Mohey El-Din, Abdullah (2003) 'Social Movements in Lebanon', unpublished research paper, Arab Research Center

Omleel, Ali (1999) 'The Concept of Partnership', unpublished study

Ramadan, Hanan (2003) 'Peasant Movements in Egypt', unpublished research paper, Arab Research Center

Scott, Alan (1990) *Ideology and the New Social Movement* (London: Unwin Hyman)

Serag El-Din, Othman and Akram Abd al-Qayum Abbas (2002) 'Social Movements in Sudan: A documentary and analytical study', unpublished research paper, Arab Research Center

Shaarawy, Helmy (1999) 'Civil Society in North Africa', unpublished research paper, Arab Research Center

Sharaby, Hesham (1993) *Patriarchy and the Backwardness of Arab Society* (Beirut: Center for Arab Unity Studies)

El-Shenawy, Abd El-Aziz Mohammed (1967) *Omar Makram: Hero of the popular resistance*, no. 68 in the Great Arabs Series (Cairo: The Arab Writer Press)

Seyyam, Emad (2003) 'Social Movements in Egypt: Between religious roots and democratic inroads', unpublished research paper, Arab Research Center

Thabet, Ahmed (2002) 'Elite Businessmen in Egypt', paper presented to Elite and Society in the Arab World seminar, Arab Research Center and the Center for Applied Economics for Development, 23–25 March, Algeria

Zayed, Ahmed (2002) 'The Political and Social Elite: Theoretical Introduction with special reference to Egyptian Society', paper presented to Elite and Society in the Arab World seminar, Arab Research Center and the Center for Applied Economics for Development, 23–25 March, Algeria

Zukzuk, Sawsan (2003) 'Social Movements in Syria', unpublished study, Arab Research Center

7
Struggling and Surviving in the Democratic Republic of the Congo

François L'Écuyer

The Congo had hardly been liberated from the Mobutu dictatorship when, in 1998, it was caught up in a number of murderous conflicts. Aware of the many internal divisions in the eastern part of the country, regional and international powers took advantage of the chaos to plunder the country's resources and to commit rape and murder. In spite of three peace agreements, a transitional government and the 'official' withdrawal of the Ugandan and Rwandan troops, conflict has broken out again in the east of the country, bringing the death toll at the time of writing to almost four million people since the fall of the Mobutu regime. The Congolese people, demobilized and demoralized, look on helplessly at what looks like the dismantling of their country.

MOBUTU AND THE KABILAS

Mobutu's dictatorship lasted, with the support of Belgium, France and the United States, for thirty terrible years. At the end of the 1970s, faced with the offensive of the Congolese National Liberation Front (dissidents of the Congolese army who had taken refuge in Angola and who had the support of their host country), the dictator was able to save his skin thanks to the military support of France. Later, in the 1980s, Mobutu was commissioned by the US with the task of isolating Angola and putting spokes in the wheels of the liberation movements of Namibia, Zimbabwe and South Africa. During this period, however, a movement developed against the dictator, particularly among the students in Kinshasa and in rebel provinces like Kasai, Shaba and the two Kivus. These movements were sometimes supported by the Catholic Church and they also elicited a certain response among the politicians, who created the Union for Democracy and Social Progress (UDPS) in 1982.

In the early 1990s, in the face of mounting pressure, Mobutu finally agreed to negotiate a 'democratic transition' in the context of a national sovereign conference. But he sabotaged the process, playing on the contradictions in the political opposition and some sectors of the social opposition, particularly the church. Subsequently, the UDPS was weakened: the students failed to keep the population mobilized and various social movements, with the support of the church, took refuge in associations, creating a wide network of grassroots initiatives, which, in certain provinces, became a kind of state within the state. However, they were unable to carry out really decisive action against the dictatorship.

In the political vacuum, a revolt broke out in 1996 to the south of Kivu, among the Rwandan-speaking population known as the *bayamulenges*. From the start this movement was supported by Rwanda and the Rwandan Patriotic Front (FPR) who wanted both to punish Mobutu for having supported the military forces responsible for the 1994 genocide and to destroy the *Interhamwés* militia who had taken refuge in Zaire. The revolt was organized by a miscellaneous coalition, the Alliance of Democratic Forces for the Liberation of the Congo (ADFL), which had the support of several countries that had decided to root out the Mobutu cancer. At the end of 1997, the AFDL, officially led by Laurent Désiré Kabila and supported by Rwandan and Angolan officers, took over Kinshasa.

The anti-dictatorship political and social movements were more spectators than actors in this spectacular advance. Some supported the AFDL, but did not play a decisive role in what was essentially a military operation. Others declared themselves hostile to it, considering it to be an opportunistic movement, manipulated behind the scenes by foreign countries.

Once in power President Kabila sent out contradictory messages. He proclaimed the reorganization of the country on the basis of 'people's committees', set up for administrative purposes. The opposition parties, particularly the UDPS, as well as the social movements, were marginalized, without actually being outlawed. As from 1998 a new polarization developed between those who were close to Rwanda and Kabila, supported by Angola and Zimbabwe. Against a background of ethnic tensions (led by Rwandan-speaking and Tutsi communities), the pro-Rwandan elements revolted and soon after took over the east of the country. This gave rise to a new cycle of violence.

It was very soon apparent that the rebels, organized under the auspices of the Congolese Union for Democracy (RCD), were dependent on Rwanda. The first RCD president, Ernest Wamba di Wamba, was removed when he opposed the depredations of the Rwandan army. In fact, the militarization of the movement ended up in widespread plundering and killing in the eastern part of the country. Some elements in the RCD tried to get the support of Uganda in blocking the Rwandan onslaught, but in vain: the Ugandan army had also set to pillaging and massacring. In Kinshasa the Congolese president increased his authoritarian stance and the opposition leaders found themselves in prison. Demonstrations by students and women were suppressed. All the while, Kabila condoned and encouraged land theft, mainly because he wanted to keep his Zimbabwean allies in the country.

As a consequence, the social movement became still more fragmented. Some supported Kabila in the belief he was the only person who could 'defend the country' against the invaders. Others, for better or worse, supported the RCD and a new rebellion that flared up in the north under Jean-Pierre Bemba, leader of the National Movement for Congolese Liberation (MLNC). Nevertheless most associations refused to take sides. The ethnic factor was also responsible for poisoning the political scene: to a certain extent it had been dormant in the Congo but it was now partially imported from Rwanda. The RCD straightaway sought support from the Rwandan-speaking people who had resided in the Congo for a long time. To deal with this Kabila indulged in 'Tutsiphobia', negotiating a despicable alliance with the remnants of the Rwandan army and the genocidal militia (the *Interhamwés*).

During the transitional period between the end of the Mobutu regime and the taking over of power by Kabila, the US and France, the two leading imperialist powers involved, clung to their former positions. The US, through its Rwandan and South African allies, at the beginning supported the AFDL and then the RCD. France first tried to save Mobutu and stop the AFDL from taking power but later changed its strategy, associating itself with Laurent Kabila.

In 2000, a negotiation process got under way, which accelerated when, in the following year, Laurent Kabila was assassinated and replaced by his son Joseph. The protagonists, meeting in South Africa in February 2002, finally signed an agreement. This, however, was full of loopholes and the war continued. The imperialist powers, headed by the US and France, favoured ending the fighting as they feared the destabilization of the whole region. As for the RCD and Rwanda, they counted on economic and social collapse in Kinshasa. In sum, the situation became increasingly disastrous. But the opposition, both political and social, was too fragmented and weak to organize an uprising.

AN UNPRECEDENTED CRISIS

The political crisis that has been paralyzing the Congo for over a decade has accelerated the economic and social deterioration of the country, for example:

- As far as employment is concerned, the crisis completed the disorganization of the primary and tertiary sectors, destroyed industrial capacity and completely demolished essential infrastructure. In 2000 only 4 per cent of the active population was formally employed. From 1998 to 2003 more than 300,000 Congolese refugees fled into neighbouring countries to escape the fighting. The UN has calculated that there are 2 million displaced people in the country as a whole, and the number of victims is estimated at 4.7 million.
- The war has destroyed hospitals and health centres, as well as making access to health care and medicines prohibitively expensive.
- In many regions of the country rape is used as a tactic to prevent the women from going into the fields. Pillage and theft of the harvest by armed groups is common practice.
- The Ministry of Health puts the proportion of the population affected by HIV at 10 per cent.
- The daily income of a Congolese was estimated in 1998 at 30 US cents.
- Joseph Kabila hopes that the Rwandan presence can be ended in the Congo, partly through international pressures, partly through internal resistance from various militias known as the *mayi-mayi*. As for Uganda and its allies such as the MNLC, they hope for a pact that would enable the return to Kinshasa of former Mobutu supporters, some of whom are extremely wealthy. But this possibility does not inspire much confidence.

Against this desolate background, there is the prospect of the country being divided into 'spheres of interest' in which the political and social actors would be marginalized. At present the social movement is not strong enough to influence the main political actors. It has largely lost its power to mobilize people on a massive scale and to some extent has taken refuge in associations, being incapable of forcing the political opposition to adopt a clear position and to unite among themselves.

The groups defending human rights have, however, identified one of the important roles that can be played by civil society, which is to draw up weekly reports on the numerous violations committed by the different armies against the local population. The accounts of massacres, theft of livestock and pillage of natural resources, as well as rape, sexual slavery and forced labour carried out by foreign and local troops have been taken up by several international organizations, supporting the demand of the international community to reinforce the mandate of the UN mission to the Congo (MONUC). Despite this new mandate – which is strictly limited to the region of Ituri, while the fighting continues in other provinces – there are many who worry about its effectiveness as the numbers of the peace force elsewhere in the country have been reduced in order to strengthen the international presence in Ituri. The amateurish nature of MONUC is indicated by the declaration of its officials, responsible for peace in the Kivus, when they declared that there were no more Rwandans in the region, which provoked strong local protests.

A BRIEF ROUND-UP OF HUMAN RIGHTS VIOLATIONS IN THE DRC

- There are 3,500,000 deaths.
- More than 50 per cent of school-age children no longer go to school.
- Each season there are droughts in the conflict areas.
- The main public infrastructures have been destroyed.
- Freedom of expression has been muzzled, which has led, *inter alia*, to journalists being arrested.
- Women are subjected to violence of all kinds (rape, torture, forced prostitution, forced enrolment of young women as combat troops, mutilation). The women who consorted with foreign soldiers are abandoned when the troops withdraw, while others are kidnapped by the armies in the field.
- The Pygmy populations have been marginalized and destroyed.
- There has been concern and dismay about the death sentences pronounced by the Court d'Ordre Militaire (30

people condemned to death and others to receive various punishments).

- Those defending human rights go in danger of their lives.
- Inhumane prison conditions, for example, cells that are too narrow, lack of sanitary arrangements, selling off of the food to be distributed to prisoners, restriction of visits, the continued use of cells that are not part of the judicial system, in spite of a presidential decree to close them.
- Ineffective demobilization of child soldiers.

Congolese civil society is divided, falling back on associations concerned with human rights and social dialogue for peace, and has not been able to mediate between the state and the population, which, after thirty years of Mobutu, still suffers the horrors of war. The civilian population has been left to its own devices and lives in extreme poverty, which unfortunately makes for easy recruitment by the petty feudal chiefs. Today, in the Democratic Republic of Congo, taking up arms seems to be the easiest way to make oneself heard. The case of Thomas Lubanga in Ituri is an example: frustrated by having been marginalized by the agreements made at Sun City in February 2002, the head of the Union of Congolese Patriots (UPS) took advantage of the departure of the Ugandan forces – so long awaited – to take up arms and massacre the inhabitants of certain villages, thus obliging MONUC to redeploy its forces. As long as the situation makes social negotiation of this kind possible, it is to be feared that Congo will continue to be an inferno.

SOURCES

Réseau National des ONG des Droits de l'Homme de la République du Congo, Réseau des Organisations des Droits Humains et d'Education Civique d'inspiration Chrétienne, Réseau des Droits Humains au Congo, Collectif des Organisations des Jeunes Solidaires du Congo-Kinshasa, Réseau Action Femme, Coalition des ONGs des Droits de l'Enfant, Réseau National pour la Promotion des Droits de l'Enfant, Comité Droits de l'Homme Maintenant.

8

Social Movements: Experiences from East Africa

Opiyo Makoude

Social movements, according to Sydney Tarrow (1998),[1] emerge when ordinary people take advantage of 'changing political opportunities and constraints' to engage in sustained 'contentious collective action' through 'known repertoires of action' to confront powerful elites, using social networks and cultural frameworks. He contends further that contentious collective action may be 'brief or sustained, institutionalized or disruptive, humdrum or dramatic'. Tarrow's explanation in his ensuing chapters (see chapter 9, for instance), in my view, fails to explain convincingly why ordinary people suddenly rise up against powerful opponents, knowing very well that opportunities for mounting contentious collective action are limited, and that violent repression would most certainly be provoked.

Why, for instance, in March 1992, did a group of about fifty elderly women dare police brutality in the then repressive Daniel Arap Moi regime in Kenya? These women's sons and husbands had been imprisoned by the Kenyan government for alleged political crimes, and the women decided to fast and camp for several days at a public recreational stadium within Nairobi, to demand the release of the political prisoners. The government became irritated by the daily publicity the women were getting from both the broadcast and print media, and predictably used excessive force to evict them from the facility, Uhuru Park. Having no other recourse, the women stripped naked, and dared the police to beat them. Bizarre it might seem, but the elderly women were beaten unconscious and bundled into police lorries. Of course, this incident was one among many in a series of 'cycles of contention', but what is clear is that something other than opportunism compelled the women to brave police brutality. Many more such examples can be cited across East Africa and Africa in general.

At another level, Tarrow does not explain sufficiently the reasons behind civil disobedience that is less expressed violently but rather in violation of rules, cultural norms and so on, in defiance of established authority – the kind of street politics Asef Bayat finds in his study of Teheran and Cairo (as cited by Nederveen[2]) – what is referred to as 'quiet encroachment'. The 'informalization' of the economy and settlement patterns in much of East Africa could be said to be a livelihood strategy, but it is also a defiance of government laws that require citizens to pay taxes, obtain trading licences and live in demarcated areas. Violent confrontation only becomes evident when governments attempt to institute order – slum evictions have occasioned protracted street battles between government forces and traders in Kenya specifically, but in East Africa in general (see also Gibbon for similar examples of northern Tanzanian village associations during Nyerere's collectivization period [3]).

Anyang' Nyong'o, on the other hand, sees movements as emerging out of the contradictions between the 'legality of participation and rules of entry' as defined by powerful actors and institutions, and a desire by citizens to be fully involved in the affairs of their society. Nyong'o contends that powerful individuals and institutions set rules that determine who is allowed to participate, and the norms that govern participation. Most of the time, such rules are limiting and discriminatory, and leave out the concerns and input of large sections of the population. Since the political process can only handle a certain amount of public concerns at any one time, powerful groups have the wherewithal to push through their interests, leaving the less powerful ones disenchanted. It is this failure by the political process to handle all demands of certain sections of the population that gives rise to movements. To this can be added Peter Gibbon's contention that states 'play a constitutive role in the formation of transindividual identities'. By implication, the process of identity formation (along economic, political and socio-cultural dimensions) and the transindividual identities created by such processes may be sites of contentious politics, and such contestation may give birth to social movements.[4]

I shall argue that social movements are frequently mounted to challenge rules of entry and legality of participation or their consequences, at times beyond the confines of what is legally feasible, if citizens feel that the processes as they exist will not accommodate their concerns. Contentious politics need social networks, and they must be *sustained* against powerful opponents, if they are to qualify as social movements, as Tarrow (1998) aptly puts it. Whether or not a movement succeeds in its purpose, the fact of taking action against powerful opponents proves a point and sends a message, that is, that the system or processes on which it relies are unjust, and that the system needs to change to accommodate the concerns of citizens who feel disenfranchised (politically, socially, economically or at times, even culturally in terms of identity).

Not all social movements pursue social justice, and some movements may be unnecessarily violent and based on sectarian and parochial interests, a good example being the Lord's Resistance Army (LRA)[5] in Uganda, and the outlawed Mungiki[6] sect in Kenya. Thus, movements are neither good nor bad in themselves; it is the goals they pursue that matter.

One factor that has speeded up the reach and impact of social movements is the media. Real-time transmission of news and events, especially through television, means that even localized collective action can be broadcast as it unfolds, reaching millions of viewers simultaneously across the globe. This would hold true for incidents occurring in the North, but local-level action in East Africa also gets reported in national media, and occasionally, globally. Such repertoires of collective action inform, provide examples for and may influence similar contentious action in places geographically and temporally distant from them, the so-called *demonstration effect*.

Besides, the ease with which information can be conveyed through the Internet makes it easier for people who are separated by huge distances to organize and share information. A notable example is that of the Ogiek, a forest-dwelling indigenous community in Kenya, which was able to mobilize support internationally from rights and environmental lobby groups against their proposed eviction by the government (see below).

EXPERIENCES FROM EAST AFRICA

Social movements in present-day East Africa have taken three main forms: contentions over rights to citizenship and political participation, economic governance and localized community-based contention over citizenship rights and space. I will look at each of these in turn.

Democratization and citizenship

The three East African states lapsed into authoritarian (Kenya and Tanzania) or despotic and anarchic (Uganda) regimes barely a decade after independence. Political freedoms for which independence had been fought were subverted and tyranny became entrenched in various degrees across the region. Uganda teetered precariously on the verge of State collapse under the late Idi Amin Dada and Obote II regimes. Kenya under Moi and Tanzania under Julius Nyerere outlawed political competition and sanctioned single-party regimes.

In Tanzania, Nyerere dealt with his opponents by expelling them from the ruling Chama cha Mapinduzi (CCM) party. To unite a country as ethnically and geographically diverse as Tanzania, Nyerere relied on the party machinery, a single *lingua franca* (Kiswahili) and the Tanzanian brand of socialism, *ujamaa*. The forceful collectivization of economic activities under the *ujamaa* policy thwarted the rise and vibrancy of organized citizen action, and it was not until the first multi-party elections in 1995 that political organization began to develop in any meaningful way. Most visible have been political contestations by supporters of the Civic United Front (CUF), with its base in the island cities of Zanzibar and Pemba, around perceived malpractices in the electoral process. These protests reached a climax in the 2000 elections when several CUF supporters were injured in skirmishes with the Tanzanian security forces; many were arrested and hundreds sought refuge in Kenya. On mainland Tanzania, political agitation around the electoral process has generally been low-key.

In Kenya, the regime of Daniel arap Moi also relied on the party machinery to contain dissent but became increasingly authoritarian after an attempted coup d'état in August 1982. By the mid-1980s, State repression had become unbearable in Kenya. Inevitably, an underground movement, calling itself 'Mwakenya', was formed to wrest power from Moi. A number of other groups reportedly started receiving military training in Libya, Angola and Uganda, although to date these claims have not been verified. What is clear is that such reactions gave the regime a justification for cracking down on perceived or real dissent, and sowed the seeds for political struggle that peaked in the early 1990s.

Moi responded by detaining without trial people suspected of belonging to the clandestine movements. The more the regime became repressive, the more the opposition hardened, and the more the regime's paranoia mounted. Increasing numbers of people were detained and tortured in the infamous Nyayo House.[7] Political sycophancy became routine, and regime loyalists settled scores with their opponents under the pretext of fighting dissidence. By the early 1990s, the Church in Kenya became a vocal, persistent and irritating critic of the Moi regime, demanding respect for personal freedoms, liberty, the return to multi-party elections, and an unconditional release of political prisoners (see Sabar-Friedman[8] and Kanyinga[9]).

External factors and global trends also contributed to the democratization process in Kenya. Pressure from Kenya's bilateral and multilateral donors, and at times their tacit and indirect support to democratization efforts hardened the resolve of Kenyan activists agitating for change. Moreover, the early 1990s witnessed the unprecedented fall of Communist regimes across the globe, with widespread calls internationally for greater respect for human rights, pluralism, democracy and good governance. This further weakened the Kenyan government's resistance to pluralism and democracy. The movement for change became irreversible, and Kenya returned to a multi-party political system in 1992. However, multi-partyism did not signal an end to contentious politics, with President Moi's continued stay in power.

There was widespread perception that Moi's mandate was flawed, despite the fact that he won two consecutive elections, and many saw him as the greatest impediment to Kenya's democratization and development. A number of NGOs, religious groups, women's lobby groups, college and university students and their lecturers joined diverse movements to press for change. Certain days became symbolic, and 7 July, named *saba saba* (Kiswahili for *7 – 7*) assuming symbolic importance because it was the day (in 1990) on which the first political rally to demand political pluralism had been held. The Kamkunji grounds, the public stadium where this rally met, also became symbolic. Up to 2001, *saba saba* and Kamkunji were synonymous with political agitation for change in Kenya.

Another political process was the demand for a review of the Kenyan constitution. A loose network of social activists coalesced as the National Convention Executive Council (NCEC). These groups used to meet at Ufungamano House – the premises of the Anglican Church. The coalition developed and disseminated a draft constitution, and when the government officially launched a commission to review the process, the group demanded and got representation in it. This group, popularly known as the Ufungamano initiative, insisted on a people-driven constitution-drafting process, contrary to the government's position that parliament would do this. To mobilize popular support, the Ufungamano group developed the symbolism of *wanjiku* – a mythical village-born-and-bred Kikuyu woman whose interests must be met by the constitution.

Economic governance

The period from the mid-1980s to the 1990s was characterized by unprecedented phases of economic liberalization in East Africa. Tanzania was forced to dismantle state socialism and embrace free-market private sector-led growth. Kenya eventually bowed to international pressure and reluctantly embraced trade and economic liberalization reforms. Of the three countries, Uganda has been singled out as the most enthusiastic and steady liberalizer.

In this process of liberalization, urban-based civil society groups have been particularly persistent in their criticism both of their governments and the external multilateral supra-state institutions that drive the process. For instance, the Uganda Debt Network (UDN) has used the debt cancellation campaign, organized under the auspices of the Jubilee 2000 campaign, to demand transparency in government transactions, while simultaneously lobbying for the cancellation of Uganda's debt by international creditors. UDN was involved in the formulation of Uganda's Poverty Eradication Action Plan (PEAP), which was later adapted to form the country's Poverty Reduction Strategy Paper (PRSP), under the IMF/World Bank lending conditionality. UDN and other civil society groups in Uganda have also been involved in budget monitoring, anti-corruption crusades and reviewing the expenditure of the Poverty Action Fund, an initiative based on funds derived from debt relief savings.

Alongside the backdrop of economic restructuring has been the globalization of a regime of trade rules driven through the WTO and trade negotiations between the EU and ACP (Lomé) group of countries. Here, networks of civil society and trade unions have emerged to lobby regional governments on positions to take in the trade talks. These networks enjoy wide-ranging collaboration with international networks, and social movements. ActionAid, Oxfam, Heinrich Böll Foundation, Frederick Ebert Stiftung and EcoNews Africa as well as the trade unions from the three countries have been at the forefront of campaigns aimed at influencing the process, rules and outcome of trade negotiations.

Social movements in East Africa have engaged in training government teams for trade negotiations and in organizing public forums to debate issues related to trade, debt and economic governance. There has also been considerable publicity around these issues in the print and broadcast media. Such efforts have seen greater awareness among government teams, unlike the first Uruguay Round negotiations in 1994, in which East African governments were seen to have signed away safeguards they would have enjoyed under the WTO provisions for their agricultural and other development sectors.

Another interesting aspect of social movements organized around economic governance is their ability to link up with movements operating at the global level. East African activists maintain strong links with lobby groups organized around the WTO, the policies of the World Bank and IMF, and debt cancellation issues. By doing this, they have added to the millions of voices calling for a fairer and more equitable world, and have helped to sharpen perceptions of Africa and its development dilemmas. Interestingly, the demand by African movements has grown for transparency, equality and respect when dealing with movements from Europe, North America and, at times, Japan.

While East African social movements have achieved a lot, cynics have been quick to point to perceived weaknesses. The most damning criticism has been that urban-based movements are elitist, with no connection to the poor on whose behalf they purport to speak. For instance, in nearly all the PRSP processes in each country, governments, the press and trade unionists repeatedly questioned the mandate of NGOs. This has been called turf defence and a crude attempt to lock out social activists with their roots in NGOs from economic governance processes. A number of social activists are getting round this by establishing satellite networks beyond the capital cities, and supporting the work of more distant grassroots movements.

For example, according to the UDN annual report for 2001, the UDN had established Poverty Action Monitoring Committees (PAFPMCs) in 17 districts to monitor the implementation of the Poverty Action Fund. Similarly, the Social Development Network (SODNET) has 'Futa Magendo' (Wipe out Corruption) chapters in nearly all districts in Kenya. These chapters are linked to grassroots organizations, including community-based organizations (CBOs), farmers' associations, workers' unions and associations of petty traders. They report regularly to the umbrella network any incidents of economic corruption, monitor the budget of local county councils and regularly hold meetings around economic governance issues.

Another common criticism levelled against social activists working in NGOs is their dependency on foreign support. When governments' actions are questioned or criticized by NGOs, the NGOs are sometimes said to be acting at the behest of foreign donors. For instance, in early 2003, there were widespread riots in the Export Processing Zones (EPZ) in Kenya. The Central Organization of Trade Unions (COTU) and the government actually accused NGOs of fuelling the riots to get donor aid. These accusations were far-fetched. Workers in the EPZ had been subjected to appalling and subhuman working conditions but under the Moi regime they had no outlet for their grievances because of government collusion with employers in the EPZ. The advent of a popularly elected regime merely provided the opportunity for suppressed labour grievances to explode. With the government and trade unions unprepared for this sudden upsurge of labour unrest, NGOs became an easy scapegoat.

These negative views of NGOs are underpinned by what many see on the ground as the ostentatious lifestyles of the activists – big cars, big salaries, perpetual global travelling – all in the midst of appalling levels of poverty and tremendous inequality. Critics maintain this repudiates the claims by social activists of working for social justice, equality and development. At a workshop organized by the Agency for Cooperation and Research in Development (ACORD) in November 2002, Murtaza Jaffer, one of the key speakers, highlighted another accusation, namely an inordinate use of jargon to obscure meaning, in what has become derogatively known as NGO-speak: 'empowering the poor, mainstreaming gender, ring-fencing poverty, consulting all stakeholders', etc. Jaffer also argued that the *institutionalized structures* in which NGOs do their work are ill-suited for the spontaneity and innovation required of movement activity. In his view, NGO activists enjoy privileges that make it questionable whether they should be championing social justice, equity and human rights.

GRASSROOTS MOVEMENTS IN EAST AFRICA

Grassroots activism takes many forms, from Maasai pastoralists in Tanzania organizing to take their government to court to protest at encroachment on their communal land by Tanzanite (mineral) companies and large-scale farmers, to the Ogiek of Kenya fighting government eviction from the Mau forests, to religious leaders organizing to end the nearly twenty years of civil unrest in northern Uganda. Indeed, there are many instances concerning the environment, women's rights, land rights, farmers' rights, fisherfolk, but I will just cite the Ogiek and northern Uganda.

The Ogiek struggle

On 24 June 1999[10] a group of 5,000 Ogiek people caused a stir on the streets of Nairobi when they marched to the High Court in their traditional regalia of monkey skins. This community of about 20,000 people is perhaps the oldest in East Africa and has been struggling to keep its indigenous areas in the Tinet area of Mau Forest. Ogiek struggles over their right to live in the forest predate Kenya's independence, going back to the early 1930s under the British colonial government. However, things worsened by 1997 when the government sought to evict the community from the forest, ostensibly to protect the forest from further depletion. Its real intention is believed to have been to give access to commercial logging companies, which the Ogiek would resist because the forest not only gives them their habitat but is also the source of their honey, firewood and other necessities.

What made the events of 24 June dramatic was that this (until then) hardly known community suddenly stole the limelight, feeding the media in Kenya and around the world with headline stories and launching a legal struggle against a powerful government that had kept issuing official notices to the community to vacate the forest or risk forceable eviction. Also, the level of international support for the Ogiek cause was overwhelming – e-mail campaigns were circulated globally by Kenyan human rights, environmental and NGO networks, and internationally by such organizations as the World Rainforest Movement and Survival International. The Ogiek eventually managed to get a court order restraining the Kenyan government from evicting them from the forest. The government in turn kept ignoring the court order and issued further eviction orders. At one time, in 2001, the plight of the Ogiek was discussed in the Kenyan National Assembly. Currently, they are using the ongoing constitutional process to have their rights recognized by the new constitution.

Three aspects of the Ogiek case are worth noting:

- First is the manipulation of cultural symbols. The use of monkey skins made the Ogiek unique, attracting instant media and public attention, which the Ogiek used to promote their agenda, namely that they had rights under the constitution that were being violated by the Kenyan government.
- Second, careful planning and networking behind the scenes helped the Ogiek build clout and strength for their cause. Modern movements can use their numerical strength for solidarity, to share information and to demonstrate visible public sympathy.
- Third, existing rights under the constitution may be used to demand further rights: the use of the ongoing constitutional

review process has allowed the Ogiek to pursue other goals, especially education, health and political participation.

Struggles in northern Uganda

In northern Uganda, the Acholi Religious Leaders' Peace Initiative (ARLPI) finds itself locked between the Lord's Resistance Army and the Uganda government. The initiative brings together Muslim, Orthodox and Christian leaders seeking an end to the long war in the region. The leaders have been playing a mediation role between government and rebels, at times taking great personal risks to achieve their aim. For instance, two Catholic priests, Father Tarcisio Pazzaglia and Father Carlos Rodriguez, met with the LRA rebels in 2001 and 2002 respectively (see *Seventy Times Seven*, 2002, and *War of Words*, 2002[11]).

Both priests were detained at different times by the Uganda People's Defence Forces (UPDF, the army) for allegedly working with the rebels, while simultaneously being accused by the rebels of laying traps, after the UPDF attacked or ambushed the rebels whom the priests had met. In July 2003, Christian and Muslim leaders slept on cold verandas in Gulu town for several days to express their solidarity with the thousands of children forced to spend the night on verandas in the town for fear of abduction by the LRA. In the same month, during President George Bush's tour of Africa, the ARLPI sent a petition to the US President, asking him and the international community to end their silence and inaction on the plight of children in northern Uganda.

The ARLPI has relied on moral integrity and authority to weather suspicion, public scepticism and apathy by building solidarity with other religious groups around the world. In a conflict occurring several miles from the capital city and largely perceived as a 'northern' problem, personal risk-taking and a strong commitment to values have enabled the leaders to sustain their struggle against both the LRA and the Ugandan government.

The lesson from the ARLPI experience is that sustaining a struggle between two strong forces pushing in different directions can be difficult, especially in protracted conflicts far from mainstream media scrutiny. In such movements, moral authority and conviction, together with a strong commitment to values, is about the only thing that keeps the movement alive. While networks are important at both the local and global levels, movements working on the periphery may not always benefit from such networks.

CONCLUSION

Governments often try to restrict the space for citizen activity and organization. This limits the political and economic choices of citizens and inevitably creates identities – both of politically or economically powerful citizens, or powerless ones. Depending on how coordinated and thorough such restrictions are, citizens can react by acquiescing in them and thereby managing within the confines of such constructed identities; by passively resisting and extending the boundaries of what is normatively and legally feasible ('quiet encroachment'); or actively resisting and challenging the 'legalities of participation'.

If citizens choose to resist, ordinary events and objects may be reconstructed, re-energized and imbued with new and powerful symbolic meanings. Dense social networks can be built around the issue and external actors' support appropriated to expand the space for citizen engagement and to demonstrate significance, public support and mandate. In East Africa, the legalities of participation, the rules of entry created by powerful forces and the resultant identities, as well as the processes and outcomes these engender, have been and continue to be spaces for social movement activity. The availability of global networks, the media and spaces for organizing at various levels continue to shape movement activities in East Africa.

NOTES

1. Sydney Tarrow (1998) *Power in Movement: Social movements and contentious politics*, 2nd edn (Cambridge: Cambridge University Press).
2. J.P. Nederveen (1999) *Globalization and Collective Action*, Working Paper, Institute of Social Studies, The Hague, Netherlands.
3. P. Gibbon (2001) 'Civil Society, Locality and Globalization in Rural Tanzania: A forty-year perspective', in *Development and Change*, vol. 32 (London: Blackwell).
4. Prof. Peter Anyang' Nyong'o made these observations at a meeting organized by the Agency for Cooperation and Research in Development (ACORD) on African Social Movements, in Nairobi on 25 November 2002.
5. The Lord's Resistance Army (LRA), headed by rebel leader Joseph Kony, is a militant group operating in northern Uganda, with an operational base in southern Sudan. It seeks to rule Uganda on the basis of the ten commandments of the Bible. It has committed atrocities for many years, killing, abducting and maiming thousands of children and displacing an estimated 800,000 people.
6. 'Mungiki', literally meaning multitude, is an outlawed religious sect, which was formed in the early 1990s and sought to 'purify' the Kikuyu

culture of Western imperialism by forcefully circumcising women, encouraging its adherents to engage in cultic rituals like sniffing snuff, wearing dreadlocks and oath-taking. The group became notorious when it began controlling several public transport termini and engaged in indiscriminate ritual killing orgies. The government has since banned the group.

7. The secret bunkers of Nyayo House torture chambers were opened to the Kenyan public in early 2003 at the end of the Moi regime. Many human rights activists, lawyers, scholars and ordinary Kenyans were detained without trial and tortured in the underground cells, ostensibly constructed to be used as government stores and archives for stationery and documents. Among the tortures were spending the night with a corpse in an unlit and windowless room, drinking one's own urine and indiscriminate beatings including electric shocks to the genitals.

8. G. Sabar-Friedman (1997) 'Church and State in Kenya, 1986–1992', *African Affairs*, vol. 96 (London: Oxford University Press).

9. K. Kanyinga (1995) 'The Changing Development Space in Kenya', in P. Gibbon, *Markets, Civil Society and Democracy in Kenya* (Uppsala: Nordiska Afrikainstitutet).

10. See *Daily Nation*, 25 June 1999, available at: http://www.nationaudio. com.

11. Both are research publications produced by the ARLPI.

9

South Africa's New Social Movements

David Coetzee

At the International Labour Organization's annual congress in Geneva in 2003, South Africa's President Thabo Mbeki cited John Maynard Keynes approvingly in stressing that the market could not solve deep problems of underdevelopment. Mbeki sang the praises of the European Structural Fund, which supported development among EU members, called for a transfer of resources from the industrialized North to the South and spoke of the 'curse of the money merchant'.

It was a surprise for those who had expected from him a hard-nosed defence of free markets in general and South Africa's neoliberal Gear (Growth, Employment and Redistribution) plan in particular, which has broadly followed the path of adjustment plans urged on middle-income countries elsewhere in the world.

Since South Africa's first democratic election of 1994, neoliberal economic policies have massively increased job losses, instead of creating the thousands of jobs promised, and generated a widening gap between white and black, rich and poor. The share of the poorest two-thirds in the country has dropped about 15 per cent. The average income of African households fell around 19 per cent while the average white household rose 15 per cent. Unemployment doubled – South Africa now has around eight million unemployed.

Yet even with statistics like these the ruling ANC has retained overwhelming support, increasing its majority in the 2004 general election. In a sense the government does not have to try particularly hard to satisfy its constituency – a predominantly poor African one. A survey on political trends from March 1999 to March 2002 carried out for the liberal Helen Suzman Foundation found that the ANC could count on retaining up to 66 per cent of its support, even when voters are dissatisfied. Among African voters, 77 per cent of those who voted for the ANC in 1999 still supported the ANC – and this was despite a finding that three-quarters of ANC supporters believe the party neglects the poor and the unemployed.

So the government could soldier on without any active intervention while waiting for a trickle-down of benefits from a growing economy. But at the ILO Mbeki, in a speech that could be referring to South Africa, was hinting darkly at a revolt by the world's poor. His government had already changed tack, and in its annual budget in March 2003 allocated more resources to social programmes in a modest Keynesian way. The June 'Growth and Development Summit' agreed on job creation projects and infrastructure investment, and the government has announced an ambitious Black Economic Empowerment (BEE) programme to transfer resources from whites to blacks.

The Growth Summit committed government to public investment initiatives that would see capital investments by the national and provincial governments grow by 15 per cent per year in the following three years. Other objectives were the expansion of public works programmes to bring relief to the unemployed, and an increase of the number of jobless drawn into 'learnerships' to 72,000 by May 2004. The agreement would also seek to give the poorest households access to free general education.

The changes in policy seemed to indicate a shift back to some of the elements of the Reconstruction and Development Programme that had effectively been abandoned for Gear when the ANC government took power in 1994. Cosatu (the Congress of SA Trade Unions) says that this swing to social investment hardly represents a justification for Gear, and other critics labelled the budget timid in the face of the massive social reconstruction needed. The economic marginalization of millions has led to the growth of resistance to overall ANC policy, both within the Triple Alliance (the ANC, the unions and the SA Communist Party) and outside, among new and radically left-wing social movements.

The unions acknowledge that the Triple Alliance is losing its hegemony in civil society; the problem for Cosatu is how to remake links within civil society and show its relevance to on-the-ground struggles outside the workplace. Cosatu says it cannot work closely with the 'ultra left' who are so active in the new movements because the differences run too deep, but that it can work with other civil society organizations. However, when it does so, 'the authoritarian clique' in government accuses it of becoming part of the ultra left and of seeking a relationship with the rest of civil society in order to create a new workers' party.

CIVIL SOCIETY AND THE NEW SOCIAL GROUPS

Mbeki's strategy may have been all along to deliver the social benefit goods just before his re-election. But it may also have been a response to pressure from mass actions by Cosatu and from the 'new social movements'. These new groupings attracted international attention at the UN's World Summit on Sustainable Development (WSSD) in Johannesburg in September 2002, when they gathered together for the first time under the umbrella of the Social Movements Indaba, and when their protests outstripped demonstrations backed by the government. Their vociferous criticism of the government's policies found a ready response among many international delegates, who saw in the South African struggles a reflection of their own.

South African civil society is filled with organizations and groups dating back to the anti-apartheid struggle; there is therefore a culture of resistance to officialdom, and some of the new groups carry on traditions initiated by the broad-based United Democratic Movement of the 1980s and by non-governmental or church organizations.

But what is new is the development of radical groups mobilizing support around disaffection from government policies and around anti-globalization themes. These groups are winning support on land, housing, health and privatization issues in overtly political and confrontational actions against the government. Sometimes they are led by left-wing radicals, or former members of the ANC or the SACP, or members or adherents of various Trotskyist groupings. In other instances leaders are veteran dissidents from the broad anti-apartheid movement. The focus of the new social movements has been on HIV treatment, land reform, housing and privatization, especially the privatization of services.

Common cause with the 'old left' was most visible in the alliance struck between the Treatment Action Campaign and Cosatu, a breakthrough in the thinking of traditionalists. The TAC first led a legal campaign against the pharmaceutical giants and secured an out-of-court agreement that opened the way for the manufacture of generic anti-HIV drugs. Then it took on the government and successfully fought a case in the constitutional court obliging the State to provide treatment drugs to prevent mother-to-child transference of the HIV virus. The victory in the battle to force government to provide treatment in State facilities can largely be ascribed to its campaigning, in the view of local analysts. It was the combination of Mbeki's obstinacy on the issue of treatment and the urgency of the

AIDS situation that convinced Cosatu to pursue this alliance. But the ANC in government was deeply unhappy about the prospect of similar alliances, breaching the containment field it had placed around its constituency of the working class and poor black population.

The government's uncertain handling of the land issue opened the way for further inroads by radical groups into the constituency of the landless and homeless. The government has found it easier to move on land restitution, handing back land to communities driven off by apartheid laws, than to supply the need for houses, and inevitably its police have been engaged in highly visible evictions of squatters, mobilized by the new radical groups, on the outskirts of cities. On land reform its strategic aim has been uncertain and its tactics unsure, and again this has allowed mobilization by the far left. Here the lead has been taken by the National Land Committee (NLC), formed in the last years of apartheid to oppose forced removals. It overlaps with the Landless People's Movement (LPM), the largest of the social movements, formed in 2001 to speed the pace of reform.

Another area of mobilization concerns the privatization of parastatals, at the centre of the government's macro-economic strategy. Battle has been waged on this front since the inception of Gear in 1995. The Anti-Privatization Forum (APF), an umbrella for 16 smaller organizations, was formed in early 2000 in response to municipal services privatization, and there has been widespread publicity for the actions of its affiliated Soweto Electricity Crisis Committee (SECC), also set up in 2000 in response to power cut-offs in the East Rand, Vaal Triangle and Soweto. Its campaign involves the illegal reconnection of residents' electricity, but it also campaigns against water cut-offs and privatization and the eviction of township residents.

Characteristically, the unions do not reject the concept of privatization out of hand but remould it as 'restructuring' and seek to install guarantees of black staff empowerment through worker shares in the newly privatized companies and job guarantees. Typically the government seeks to restructure the parastatals to make them saleable in chunks and – according to critics – by boosting their profitability through expelling workers and squeezing consumers. Sometimes the demands of government and unions overlap on contested ground – as over BEE considerations. Mostly they are at odds.

The unions have concentrated on job losses through privatization. The new social groups are focusing on the privatization of services such as water and electricity. For every government announcement of successes in social provision the new groups produce more data on water and electricity cut-offs as a result of the privatization process. The issue was highlighted at the World Trade Organization meeting in Cancún, Mexico in September 2003, which discussed the General Agreement on Trade in Services (GATS); South Africa's new social groups were active as part of an activist groundswell against the privatization of basic services.

Privatization, for the unions, is primarily a workplace issue related to unemployment. In the wider context of the 'National Democratic Revolution', to which Cosatu and the SACP subscribe, it also relates to working-class economic power and State influence. For the radical new social movements, who reject the notion of the NDR, the central issue is the privatization of services because of its effect on the marginalized poor.

The new social movements are not only filling in the spaces left by trade union organization and mobilization. They are also covering ground not occupied by existing political parties; on the left, the SACP is also in the Alliance, muting its public voice in opposition. Some in the new groups are starting to wage a political campaign inside the labour movement to end its alliance with the government and to foster the formation of an independent workers' party.

On these and other issues – from apartheid reparations to 'odious debt' – the new social movements have become well known as part of a fluid international anti-globalization movement. But Cosatu recently reminded its members that it is still by far the largest – with 1.7 million members – and best organized of South Africa's civil society institutions. In many ways the new groups respond to its actions (or lack of action) as much as they do to those of the government. It is therefore important to assess the future of the trade unions.

THE TRADE UNION MOVEMENT AND THE ALLIANCE

The Congress of SA Trade Unions acknowledges it is in crisis. It is not an unfamiliar crisis for the labour movements of relatively advanced, modern capitalist states, and it relates in the country's 'formal' sector to structural changes in industry in response to increased international competition. Workforces have been cut as industry moves to more capital- intensive operations. As a result of this and relatively low growth, as well as the depletion of the workforce through privatization, there has been a massive loss of jobs (the current unemployment rate is 30–40 per cent) and therefore of paying members of the unions. Even among the employed only about half of South Africa's workforce belongs to unions.

In some ways the same forces at work earlier in the more developed capitalist economies are at play in South Africa; in other ways the situation of the unions and the new social movements is very different. A large part of the potential workforce is in the unenumerated 'informal' sector, and Cosatu is trying to organize in this notoriously difficult sector of the unemployed and the economically marginal. This is where the new social movements have mobilized, primarily around issues of living conditions in the townships and the rural areas, and not in the workplace.

The unions, struggling to stay relevant and influential on government, are in a contentious relationship with the new social movements' far left positions. The intra-ANC left hold instead to a continuing 'National Democratic Revolution' (somewhat variously defined, depending on the interests of the speaker), while many of the new social movements' leaders see the active polarization of the classes as the route to social revolution.

There has a been a good deal of fluidity in party politics in South Africa, with the New National Party moving into alliance with the ruling ANC and the much-reduced Inkatha Freedom Party, and the IFP itself moving closer to the Democratic Alliance. A number of small parties have also been formed in recent months. Nothing, however, is denting the hegemony of the ANC, which still maintains its credibility as a national liberation movement. The ANC's Alliance partners have been remaining under its wing to retain influence on policy. If the new movements and rebellious memberships succeed in driving them out to form a workers' party there seems little chance that it will have the same measure of influence.

So the current Cosatu leadership is caught between a rock and a hard place. The government wants to unseat it and to replace it with more amenable leaders. The ultra left wants to unseat it to replace it with leaders who will break the Alliance.

LABOUR MOVEMENT FRAGMENTATION

Cosatu's problems are not only with the radical left groups and the government – the enemy is capital, not the 'ultra left', says its leadership. Its crisis is also a consequence of its internal organization and to challenges from rival union organizations, all stemming from the radical restructuring of the economy and rocketing unemployment. Cosatu president Willy Madisha told his central committee in May 2003 that Cosatu was at a 'turning point' in its history. Since 1995, when government began to collect the data, unemployment soared from 15 per cent to over 30 per cent as of September 2002 (in the narrow definition of unemployment). If discouraged workers are included, the figure rose to over 40 per cent or close to 8 million people. The unions are increasingly describing this as a 'jobs bloodbath'.

'No other country has experienced such growth in unemployment unless there was an economic catastrophe underway,' Madisha added. Almost three-quarters of the currently unemployed are aged under 30, and almost half of all African youth are unemployed.

After a couple of national stay-aways that failed to sway the government, Cosatu seems, for the time being, to have turned away from seeking the basic shift in industrial policy that it has long sought. Instead, as at the Growth Summit, it is trying to improve the government's offers. Gear is based on export-led growth and involves the opening of the formal economy to competition, and therefore constant modernization, mechanization and cuts in payrolls. But the unions are now firing off broadsides at companies who are replacing workers with machinery, or are choosing casual or part-time workers. Without full backing from the State and industry – support only weakly signalled at the Growth Summit – this seems like Canute ordering back the tide.

Even within the labour movement Cosatu is facing significant inroads into its dominance as new unions emerge. A new giant labour federation, the Confederation of South African Workers Union (Consawu), claiming to represent 400,000 workers, was launched in May 2003. It is aligned with the Christian World Confederation of Labour based in Brussels and aims to provide a platform for independent and non-aligned unions in South Africa.

It is opposed by the other major federations, the National Council of Trade Unions (Nactu) and the Federation of Unions of SA (Fedusa), but it will add a further layer of competition to Cosatu's drive for membership to make up for its own lost members. Consawu said it wanted to attract non-unionized workers. Its 20 affiliates include unions from the fishing, mining, trade, clothing and construction sectors.

Challenges to Cosatu are coming from other quarters, too. Fedusa, formed in 1997, is a largely white-collar union that has eclipsed Nactu as the second-largest federation. It favours co-operative agreements between labour, business and the state. Its membership is around 540,000 and it is on a membership drive for youth, women and retirees.

The one growing union is Solidarity, formerly the Mynwerkersunie (Mineworkers' Union), which is 90 per cent white and is strongest in the parastatals, the mining industry and at steelmaker Iscor, but is now seeking to diversify racially, mainly among Coloured workers in the Western Cape. It has 130,000 members, and is growing primarily because of its campaign against BEE, which is particularly threatening to white male State employees. It wants an alternative modelled on the Malaysian empowerment programme.

It is not just white workers who are concerned about BEE; many in Cosatu's ranks are deeply suspicious of the enrichment of the new black bourgeoisie. This suspicion may increase as the mounting influence of the new elite on the ANC itself becomes apparent – according to Wits academic and independent ANC watcher Tom Lodge, this group is now becoming a major contributor to the party's coffers.

So the labour movement is likely to see a significant dilution of Cosatu's power and perhaps alliances on specific issues with other unions, and with some of the new social groups.

CONCLUSION

The difference between South Africa's route and that of modern industrialized countries lies in the heightened inequity that is the downside to growth and trickle-down policies. The political effects of this in other countries may not be as extreme as in South Africa, a country where memories of organization against an oppressive state are recent, and where populist mobilization holds perils for social stability.

The government is in a quandary – as the unions weaken so do maverick groups increase in influence. Hitherto it has chosen to play the two against each other to weaken both – notably tarring the unions and the SACP with the same 'ultra left' brush as it uses against the smaller radical groups.

With the weakening of Cosatu, which views its role as embracing the concerns of all the marginalized, it is the radical new groups who are mobilizing around their interests. The State's reaction has been antagonistic and sometimes repressive. The Freedom of Expression Institute reported that there were very few cases in the recent past involving traditional forms of censorship, such as jailing journalists or muzzling media outlets. Instead most of the cases it listed involved the shutting down of public assemblies and mass demonstrations or restrictions on public graffiti and leafleting. These are being perpetrated not only by the State but by private corporations. The rise of the new social movements and the State's reaction to them is therefore having an impact on the country's developing and still tentative democratic culture.

The government has chosen to live within the international capitalist system, seeking the goodwill of transnational corporations and of the Bretton Woods financial establishment. It occupies the schizophrenic territory most developing states find themselves in – until recently effectively accepting a trickle-down 'solution' to deepening poverty while keeping the lid on domestic instability. To many its policies – even with a Keynesian tinge – still appear little more than promises of 'jam tomorrow'.

The radical social groups' confrontational solutions are no doubt bringing pressure to bear on government and may ameliorate its policies for many, but are unlikely to effect core changes. Critics of their radical line say that the problem is not State funding of social provision but lack of institutional capacity to disburse the funds. This is not going to be resolved quickly by militant action.

They may be a focus for anti-globalization protest and a spearhead of international attack against the Washington Consensus. But the government hopes they will be a busted flush as the programme of social benefits kicks in. Their supporters say that poverty and unemployment is bound to increase and that a radical change is needed. Yet the government knows that its voter support base will not go away. Changes will have to come from inside the ANC. The question then is how successful the new social groups will be in securing this change.

10

Neoliberalism and Social Conflict: The Popular Movements in Latin America

Clara Algranati, José Seoane and Emilio Taddei

The second half of the 1990s in Latin America saw a continual increase in social protest and the emergence and consolidation of social and popular movements of national and international significance. These formed part of the struggles against the regressive structural transformations brought about by the introduction of neoliberalism.

The 1990s had opened the way for a renewal of the globalization of capital in its neoliberal form. This built on a process started in previous decades and, through the 'Washington Consensus', the adoption of neoliberal policies seemed to be unstoppable. The application of these policies met with some resistance and protests. Two Latin American presidents (Collor de Melo in Brazil and Carlos Andrés Pérez in Venezuela) were 'unexpectedly' forced from office, although resistance to the application of neoliberal prescriptions in the first half of the 1990s was then more fragmented socially and more localized sectorially and territorially than before. At the same time intellectually the problem of conflict and social movements was displaced from a relatively central position to an almost marginal status.

During the second half of the decade a new cycle of social protest spread throughout the continent questioning the neoliberal model. The opening of this period, it should be noted, coincided with the Zapatista uprising at the beginning of 1994. This protest was recorded by the Latin American Social Observatory (OSAL-CLACSO) in 19 countries in Latin America. In the May–August period of 2000, 2001 and 2002, the number of conflicts increased over the first annual period by 180 per cent and by 11 per cent for the second. This deepening of social conflict was the expression of a double crisis challenging the neoliberal regime: economic crisis, caused by a recession that appeared to be spreading at both regional and international level; and a crisis of legitimacy that it seemed to have imposed successfully in the first half of the decade.

However, this cycle of protest cannot be seen only in quantitative terms. In the later 1990s the Latin American region experienced various social confrontations of national significance. These included, in Bolivia, the 'water war' of Cochabamba and the struggles of the coca farmers' movement in the Chapare; the indigenous uprisings led by CONAIE in Ecuador in 1996 and 2000, which both ended in the fall of the government; the emergence and expansion of employed workers' movements in Argentina and the mobilizations and protests that brought down the government in 2001; the determined occupation of land on a massive scale, led by the Landless Rural Workers Movement (MST) in Brazil; the peasant mobilizations in Paraguay that played an important role in dislodging President Cubas Grau; the intense social protest in Peru (particularly among the Regional Civic Fronts, Frentes Cívicos regionales), which marked the end of the Fujimori regime; and the Zapatista movement.

This chapter analyzes the range of oppositional struggles in Latin America. It briefly describes some of the salient characteristics of this cycle of protests, as well as the themes and social movements that developed. The dimensions of the crisis of the neoliberal model in the region, which gave birth to the cycle of protests, are outlined. We then look at the typical features of these social and popular movements, and the dynamic of the conflicts they have generated. The major conflicts during 2002 and 2003 in Latin America are then examined. Lastly, we analyze the process of social militarization spreading throughout the region in support of the neoliberal course, as well as the continental convergences that emerged to confront this policy.

DIMENSIONS OF THE NEOLIBERALISM CRISIS

Since the mid-1990s Latin America has been experiencing a new cycle of protests challenging neoliberal policies. This renewed dynamism of social conflict, also connected at the international level with the emergence of the anti-globalization movement, shook up the regional political scene and controverted the more optimistic predictions of 'social peace' coming from the market economy.

These ongoing social struggles express the deep crisis of political legitimacy facing neoliberal institutions, including the International Monetary Fund, World Bank, World Trade Organization and Interamerican Development Bank, which have been promoting globalization policies and are mainly responsible for implementing the guiding principles of the 'Washington Consensus' and have disseminated the regime of financial accumulation in Latin America.

Persisting protest shows how the model of neoliberal capitalism adopted in the early 1990s has played itself out. This second dimension of the crisis is related to the successive financial tremors in many parts of the world from 1997 and which still continue under the effect of growing economic recession.

During previous crises in the region (e.g. Mexico in 1994 and Brazil in 1999) the effects could partly be offset by massive injection of IMF loans. The dynamism of the international economy still prevalent in those years made it possible to salvage the two most important economies in Latin America – as also Russia, Turkey and Southeast Asia – although at the price of accepting still more stringent orthodox economic policies. The result was modest or negative growth for 2001 and 2002 in the Latin American economies and a new cycle of social protest that concerns us here.

The promises of the 'market culture' played a decisive role in legitimizing market economy policies from the early 1980s and were a godsend to powerful property owners who could legitimize, among other things, successive waves of privatization over the continent. The exaltation of private property to the detriment of social and/or public property and the commodification of life (natural resources, health, pensions, education, environment, housing, free time and leisure, etc.) were all fields in which the guiding principles of the vast neoliberal consensus were put into practice.

Today, after the notorious failure of the market as the 'natural' and 'universal' distributor of resources, this consensus seems to have collapsed because of the drastic social polarization brought about by the concentration of wealth in Latin America. Many of the social movements emerging in recent years in the region learned from the dynamic of conflict to organize effectively and recreate spaces for solidarity.

MAIN CHARACTERISTICS OF THE CONFLICTS
AND OF THE SOCIAL MOVEMENTS

The new cycle of protests from the mid-1990s was new for several reasons. First, the organizations were themselves relatively novel. Then, they were frequently the results of the consolidation and extension of previous social movements, which had different organizational methods, forms of struggle, self-awareness, conceptions of collective action and understandings of power, politics and the state.

Until the end of the 1980s, the conflict of the Keynesian–Fordist wage-earners (and particularly industrial conflict) had been central to social conflict in the region, but the structural transformation and its impact on the labour market seems to have diminished (although not eliminated) the relative weight of the trade unions of wage-earners as major protagonists in the conflict. The model of prioritizing the economy, and the central role it played in agrarian restructuring in the region, meant that the qualitative importance of indigenous and peasant movements was revived. This is a distinctive characteristic of the new phase and it merits special attention. While it is true that, in absolute terms, the number of conflicts in which wage-earners were protagonists was greater than in the actions of the peasant and indigenous movements, the latter were particularly active in Bolivia and Ecuador; in the latter case, their struggles for the recognition of a multi-nation state brought together different indigenous nationalities.

Other examples of this kind of struggle are the Zapatista campaign for constitutional recognition of the rights of indigenous peoples (the March for Dignity in early 2001), and the prolonged action of the Mapuche Indians of southern Chile (Coordinador Arauco-Malleco) against the loss of their land and over-exploitation of natural resources. There was also the dispute of the Aymara peasants of Chapare and the region of the Yungas in Bolivia against policies to eradicate crops and 'zero coca' as required by the US Government. Another example is the movement, starting in 2002, of the original peoples of Mesoamerica against the Plan Puebla Panamá, which aims to accelerate the penetration of capital and transnational investment in Central America.

The consolidation of the successful Movimento dos Trabalhadores Rurais sem Terra (MST) in Brazil can be highlighted. Its sustained occupation of land and public buildings while demanding progressive and comprehensive agrarian reform, its actions against the spreading of transgenetic agriculture and its rich community and productive experience in rural settlements have turned the MST into one of the most politically relevant social movements in the region.

As for protests and movements among urban workers, these are particularly strong in the public sector, in response to the reform and privatization policies of orthodox neoliberal policies, particularly the imposition of fiscal adjustment packages. The dynamic movement of teachers deserves special mention: their claims were basically for an increase of salary, payment of overdue salaries, an expansion of the education budget and rejection of proposals for educational reform (in particular flexibility of working conditions). In some countries actions opposing the privatization of public education have fostered convergence with university students and/or with other sectors of the education community that support the teachers' demands.

There are also strong demands by administrative employees who mobilized for wage increases and adequate remuneration and against lay-offs and state reforms. In the public sector, too, health workers in many countries have been involved in wage conflicts, calling for budget increases for public hospitals, as well as improved working conditions. It is interesting that protest in these sectors has taken the form of recurrent and prolonged strikes (including indefinite strikes) and have been mobilized by trade union confederations, as have street protests.

The structural effects of unemployment resulting from neoliberal policies have led to consolidation of movements of the jobless. In Argentina this movement has a high level of women and young people in a central role, and this became decisive in accelerating the political and social crisis that culminated in President Fernando de la Rua standing down in December 2001.

The first-generation privatizing wave, undertaken early in the 1990s by some governments in the region, met with social resistance orchestrated by trade unions and workers in the sectors affected. Where resistance remained limited to these sectors and was unable to develop into broader social fronts transcending specific demands, the struggles were defeated. The new social protests are quite different in this sense.

Struggles against second-generation privatization constituted a social aggregation of protest through wide-ranging political and social convergence. Some recent examples include the formation of the Frentes Civicos in Peru (the struggle in Arequipa against the sale of two public electricity services) and the Congreso Democratico del Pueblo in Paraguay (which demanded abolition of the law authorizing privatization of state enterprises). They both illustrate the broad convergence of social sectors against the privatizations (peasant federations, trade unions, students, NGOs and political parties), which has been successful and obliged the governments to retreat on this issue. This kind of protest often takes on a confrontational radical form (urban uprisings, huge processions, the occupation of company plants).

Additionally, Latin American cities have undergone great spatial and social changes as a result of liberal policies. The process of 'municipal decentralization' has had an enormous impact on the urban landscape and daily lives of city-dwellers. Fragmentation and polarization in urban areas, the abandonment of public spaces, the deterioration of services and spreading urban violence are only some of the more visible consequences. The recent urban conflicts seem to typify the problems of the social polarization of the market. The struggles for access to and improvement of services and against high charges, in defence of the public school system and in opposition to decentralization policies also often bring different social sectors together. Disasters created by natural catastrophes (earthquakes, cyclones, floods) and the neglect of urban populations needing official assistance and investment in infrastructures are also the cause of numerous mobilizations demanding aid from local and national governments.

In past decades the participation and mobilization of young people in Latin America was for the most part represented by a strong presence of the university student movement. Currently protest by young people seems to be taking on new forms and be expressed through new channels. The drop in school attendance, resulting from the combined effects of the privatization of education, the concentration of wealth and the growth of poverty, is one explanation for the relative loss of student influence. While students are still a dynamic force in social conflict, the discontent of young people is channelled into active involvement in unemployed movements, on behalf of the young *favela* (slum) dwellers in Brazil, in alternative cultural collectives of various kinds, human rights movements, protests by indigenous peoples and peasants, and trade union collectives of young people whose jobs are precarious. The new generation of youth played an active and prominent role in the massive political protests that forced the presidents of Peru and Argentina to step down, and they radically question the imposition of structural adjustment and privatization.

Particularly relevant in current Latin American social protest is the emergence of regional and transnational convergence, which has created enormous impetus and constitutes an unprecedented experience for the continent, through its geographical extension and broad-based capacity to call on social and collective movements.

In the past, massive trade union movements and the inclusion of university students were the most prominent form of coordination and articulation at the regional level. But these convergences were centred on the defence of sectorial and/or professional interests and seldom moved beyond their specific demands. Now, problems of continental import (the FTAA, free trade, militarization, etc.), very often linked to the penetration of transnational, particularly US capital, erupt on the political scene and stimulate consolidated responses in the region. Trade union, women and student movements, NGOs, political parties, anti-military collectives, environment protection groups and peasant and agrarian organizations (CLOC and Vía Campesina) have all moved closer. The Continental Campaign against the FTAA, promoted by the Continental Social Alliance and other networks and collectives, is one of the most remarkable examples, bringing together a huge number of regional and continental meetings (which also include movements from North America) against the Plan Puebla Panamá, militarization, the Plan Andino and other issues. The Social Forum of Porto Alegre is in this sense the most outstanding experience of these convergences, not only at continental but also at international level.

Finally, we should mention the alarming growth in repression, criminalization and militarization of the conflict. Draconian measures are frequently the response of the political regimes and elites, confronted with the increase of social protest over the whole continent. This reactionary position poses a huge challenge to popular movements and, in some countries, has stimulated a renewal of the human rights movements in campaigns against the repression of social militants and activists.

Overall, there are two distinct characteristics of this new cycle of protests. First is the displacement of wage-earner conflict to the public sector. In general, the demands of the public sector workers attract the participation of other social sectors in defence of the universal right to education, health, etc. (guaranteed constitutionally in many countries of the region). In the most recent struggles against privatization, the drive towards convergence does not necessarily depend upon the wage-earner trade unions, as other organizations (movements of peasants, indigenous peoples, the unemployed, students and urban dwellers, among others) have played a key role in creating 'broad social coalitions'.

The second characteristic is the consolidation of rural movements – indigenous people and peasants – which now have national and regional impact. They have developed a remarkable ability to articulate with urban social sectors, managing successfully to link the struggle against neoliberalism with a broader questioning of the legitimacy of political systems in the region. There is also a greater diversification in the issues in the protests than when the struggles of the waged workers' trade unions predominated in previous decades. The convergence of different social sectors around many conflicts provides perhaps the clue to understanding these transformations.

It is important to emphasize the trend, increasing over recent years, towards a greater radicalization of the forms of struggle, evident from the duration of the protests (prolonged or indefinite action). Also there has been a growth in confrontational forms of struggle as opposed to demonstrations, and an expansion, at regional level, of certain kinds of protest and organization, such as street processions and *cacerolazos* (demonstrations in which saucepans are banged in protest), some of which have received massive support and been highly political. Huge marches and demonstrations that last days and weeks, crossing regional and national territories, seem to counteract the dynamics of territorial separation promoted by neoliberalism. The processions of lorries and blockades indicate strategies that aim at reappropriating space collectively and recovering the collective visibility denied by the mechanisms of power.

Many of these movements and experiences in social organization take on a socio-territorial pattern. The concept of 'social territoriality' is not limited to a physical concept of space, but refers more to a crystallization of social, productive and reproductive relationships. Any social appropriation of territory means modifying it and constituting a 'new social territoriality' linked to the social practices employed. These practices have included: the setting up of social self-management; assembly and/or participatory forms of organization; productive self-management practices; and forms of community management. Some of the more visible examples of this process of social territoriality include the land occupations and settlements of the Brazilian MST and, in Argentina, the production enterprises of various unemployed movements, experiments in solidarity production and trade of occupied factories.

Finally, one of the recurring questions within the movements is that of broadening the democratic mechanisms of participation, the promotion of more horizontal and open participatory forms, and working to limit tendencies towards the bureaucratization and manipulation in the movements. This concern usually accompanies a questioning of traditional models of representative and delegatory democracy, a questioning that is supported by recent experiences in direct democracy and social self-management.

THE DYNAMIC OF THE STRUGGLES IN 2002 AND 2003

Latin America traversed a deep crisis during 2002, the social, political and economic impact of which was protracted into 2003 and will certainly mark the region over coming years. The deepening of the recession and economic instability dealt a severe blow to the political and ideological legitimacy neoliberalism had enjoyed in the previous decade. The debacle of these policies in Argentina was the most striking example of the failure of the market utopia to act as the main regulator of the social order. The bankruptcy of neoliberal legitimacy and the growing difficulty of reconstituting it typified these two years.

A second characteristic of the Latin American political and social conjuncture during this period was a deepening of social protest, as recorded in the OSAL-CLACSO data on increasing social conflicts mentioned earlier. This appears to be related to an intensification of the crisis and the efforts to push through adjustment plans and privatizing policies by governments in the region, who continue to apply only one formula, which now lacks all social credibility.

This increase in social conflict suggests the growing maturity of certain social movements and the emergence and consolidation of experience in social convergence vis-à-vis neoliberal policies, also seen in the qualitative increase in the politicization of the struggles. Many of the conflicts of 2002 and 2003 – which succeeded in limiting, if only temporarily, the privatizing intentions of governments – took the form of heterogeneous convergences, broad social fronts, national and regional multi-sectorial coordination. This contrasts with the previous first-generation struggles against adjustment and privatization, the failure of which made way for the hegemony of the neoliberal order in Latin America during the early 1990s.

Confronted by this legitimacy crisis, the regimes, instead of making political changes, continued with the neoliberal course, combined with increasingly authoritarian and repressive policies. This could be considered a fourth tendency of the period. Legitimized by the anti-terrorist crusade launched by the Bush government after 11 September and inextricably linked to US strategies to impose economic and military subordination on the region, 'armed neoliberalism' has increasingly served as a juridical and ideological suppport for growing repression and the persecution of social leaders. The militarization of Colombian political life promoted by the neoliberal government of Uribe is, in this context, the region's most evident and tragic example.

The rich content of the demands that have spread throughout Latin America makes it difficult to offer a detailed analysis of the conflicts recorded in 2002 and 2003. We make no claim to be exhaustive, but highlight some of the most significant instances of social protest to illustrate the characteristics mentioned earlier.

2002: NEOLIBERAL DEFEAT IN ARGENTINA AND STRUGGLES AGAINST PRIVATIZATION IN PERU AND PARAGUAY

The first quarter of 2002 was marked in the region by the national and international repercussions of the economic crisis of Argentina, where the failure of the neoliberal model inaugurated a new cycle of economic crises with devastating social effects. On 19 and 20 December 2001 an immense popular mobilization led to the fall of President Fernando de la Rua and, beyond the collapse of the Alliance government, questioned the very basis of the neoliberal regime. In the heat of this crisis there were numerous experiments in social self-management linked to assembly forms of organization. These were characteristic of the emerging movement of the unemployed and the townships in the years before 2001. Such activities underpinned the popular assemblies, particularly in Buenos Aires and the urban belt around it, as also in the movement to occupy and run bankrupt factories, which intensified during 2002. Self-management and autonomous subsistence production typified working practices in the micro-enterprises and productive workshops of the unemployed movement.

This intense experimentation, from the end of 2001, despite its limitations and weaknesses, was a process of social reappropriation of territory. It proposed and developed a distinctive form of management that accompanied a radical democratization of social relationships. Not only did this involve questioning and destructuring the employer–employee relationship, but it expressed a dynamic that transcended gender and generational relationships. The dominance of women and young people in the pickets and assemblies is an example of the 'earthquake' that challenged the existing social tissue of hierarchy and oppression.

The victorious mobilizations against the privatizations in Peru and Paraguay were among the most significant social struggles of the second quarter of 2002. These mobilizations managed to build on the growing experience in multi-sectorial coordination in the Frente Amplio Cívico of Arequipa in Peru and the Congreso Democrático del Pueblo in Paraguay. They were remarkable for the massive popular participation and for their demonstrated capacity to halt the privatization offensives of both governments. They were also representative of a more general process developing in other countries of the region.

In Peru there was a two-day regional strike in the southern *departamentos*, with its epicentre in Arequipa, called by the Frente Amplio Cívico against the announced privatization of electricity production, EGASA and EGESUR. The 'battle of Arequipa' and the significant participation of the town's Frente Amplio Cívico were echoed by actions of other fronts over southern Peru and other regions of the country.

These urban strikes and the existence of a National Coordination of Regional Fronts illustrate the methods of struggle characteristic of this movement, which at its height involved the virtual occupation of towns, as well as showing how national articulation had consolidated. There was a striking similarity of the Arequipa conflict with the so-called 'water war' in Cochabamba against the privatization of the local water company in Bolivia in April 2000. As in Peru, urban mobilization managed to paralyze and occupy the town for days and halt the privatizing process.

The process in Paraguay was somewhat different. Here the coordination was national – and not local – but also because it was multi-sectorial following an agreement between many social and political movements. The Congreso Democrático del Pueblo emerged from the convergence of two previous platforms (el Frente en Defensa de los Bienes Públicos and the Plenaria Popular contra el Terrorismo de Estado), which had recently developed. This convergence combined the most important social organizations of Paraguay and had strong ties to the main peasant organizations, the Federación Nacional Campesina (FNC) and the Mesa Coordinadora Nacional de Organizaciones Campesinas (MCNOC).

In Uruguay the privatization policies in the 1990s were also unsuccessful in establishing themselves, although for different reasons. Here the national coordination, led mainly by the PIT-CNT, included various social organizations and was linked with the FA-EP (Frente

Amplio-Encuentro Progresista). Protest against the new privatizing offensive of President Battle was also repeated in the second quarter of 2002, although it seemed to take second place to deepening economic crisis. It obtained a partial victory, however, with parliament abrogating legislation supporting the privatization of two companies ANTEL (telephones) and ANCEL (mobile phones).

During the last-quarter of 2002 the IMF and the World Bank persisted with pressure to increase fiscal adjustment, deregulation and privatization, despite deepening economic crisis in the region and the diversity of the various national situations. These measures were aimed essentially at guaranteeing the strengthening of the governing rules of the neoliberal regime. Accordingly, in the last four months of 2002, many governments prepared fiscal budgets for the next period, as well as pursuing legislative projects to approve the adjustment of public accounts. Examples included laws regulating economic transition in Paraguay, laws to revive the economy in Uruguay, reform of the health sector in Chile, laws concerning drinking water and sewerage systems in Honduras, and labour and tax reform in Colombia.

These measures explain the relative growth, between September and December 2002, of the conflicts in which public sector employees were the chief protagonists. There was also a strengthening of the territorial movements, of convergence and multi-sectorial processes at local and national levels. Two such actions were led by the Frente Nacional contra la Privatización de la Industria Eléctrica en México and the Coordinadora por la Defensa del Gas en Bolivia. Thus the neoliberal counter-reforms encountered a growing resistance on socio-territorial patterns which, apart from rejecting these policies, in many cases proposed and promoted the debate on alternative ways of managing public affairs.

These struggles against the privatization of public enterprises – and in some cases the claims for renationalization, such as in Bolivia of certain mining companies – combined with huge protests against the restructuring, privatizing and decrease in funding of health and education. Mention should be made here of the intense, protracted conflict in El Salvador against the privatization of the Social Security Institute, the many protests in Honduras rejecting a proposed law on drinking water and the sewerage system and claims that municipalization of the service constituted a step towards privatization of the sector, as required by the Plan Puebla Panamá, and the long-drawn-out conflict led by doctors and health workers in Chile against a proposed law to reform the sector.

All these conflicts came together, leading to multi-sectorial mobilizations and questioning of the political economies and governments in many countries of the region: in early September, in Uruguay, against the fiscal adjustment laws; towards the end of the same month, in Colombia, the trade union strike, peasant blockages and student mobilization against labour reform and the FTAA; also in September, in Paraguay, worker and farmer protests against the rise in rates and the law for economic transition; the demonstrations in Bolivia up to the end of the quarter; and the mobilizations in Argentina on the first anniversary of the protests on 19/20 December 2001 in which the unemployed were the main protagonists.

These experiences enhanced, from an organizational viewpoint, the setting up of spaces for political convergence in the last quarter of 2002. This was evident in the mobilizations called by the 'anti-neoliberal bloc' in Bolivia and the formation of the Frente Nacional por la Defensa de la Soberanía y los Derechos de los Pueblos, established in Salvador Atenco, Mexico, in November. The results of these struggles against privatization policies were, however, unequal. The failure of the privatization offensives in Peru and Paraguay and the Mexican government's abortive attempts to privatize electricity have to be set against the approval – although with modifications – of many laws questioned by popular movements, with the resolution, in some cases, still pending.

In any political and social review of 2002, it is impossible to overlook the importance of the presidential elections in Brazil and Ecuador towards the end of the year. The electoral victory of parties and/or political coalitions that started and developed in confrontation with the neoliberal model was an unprecedented event in the recent political history of the region. These triumphs were the result, not only of mounting social discontent vis-à-vis the model, but of pre-existing struggles and the constitution of social movements and organizations that in different ways were articulated with the politics expressed in the electoral victory. This creates huge new challenges for the future of the continent. The triumph of the MST was, in this sense, the most important event of all – politically, socially and regionally – for the advent of Lula's government was the result of a sustained convergence and common struggle with massive social sectors over the previous two decades.

Then there was the triumph of the political coalition headed by Lucio Gutiérrez in Ecuador, including the Movimiento Pachakutik, an expression of the social and political struggles led over recent years by

Ecuadorean indigenous movement. This electoral victory, in which the Movimiento's support for the elected candidate was decisive, was preceded by a national, multi-sectorial two-day strike, convened in mid-February by the Confederación de Nacionalidades Indígenes del Ecuador (CONAIE) and social and trade union organizations. The aim of this protest, which included road blocks and demonstrations in Quito and other towns, was the rejection of government policies. Nevertheless, the great expectations of change the new government had generated were soon dashed when the adjustment policies were continued (at least in some cases). In August 2003, this provoked the rupture between the Sociedad Patriotica and the Movimiento Pachakutik within the government alliance.

In Bolivia, the surprise of the electoral performance of the Movimiento al Socialismo and its candidate Evo Morales cannot be understood without reference to the political legitimacy of the struggle of the Bolivian coca producers and the social recognition of the struggle against water privatization in Cochabamba. Even the electoral defeat of President Toledo in the regional elections of Peru, demonstrating the weakness of a government that rapidly disappointed popular expectation of change, seems related to the intense regional protests against privatizations – headed by the Frentes Civicos – particularly in the southern part of the country.

To conclude this brief survey of the most important conflicts of 2002, it is important to include the prolongation, until the end of the year, of the Venezuelan political crisis, after the failed coup d'état against President Chávez in April 2002, perpetrated by representatives of the 'Triple Alliance' (business, church and army). The break in the constitutional order had among its main objectives privatization of the state company Petróleos de Venezuela SA (PDVSA) to the benefit of transnational interests and the proposal to terminate the autonomous oil policies of Chávez's government. The political tensions that followed this abortive attempt intensified until early December, with the so-called 'civic strike' convened by a collection of business, unions and political and social organizations, demanding first elections and then the dismissal of Chávez. This new offensive of the Venezuelan economic elites against the Chávez government organized street mobilizations, attacks in the media, lock-outs by employers, an oil coup and an invitation to military disobedience – which could only be interpreted as a call to repeat the failed military coup – and to fiscal non-compliance. But it did not bring down the constitutional government or seriously destabilize it.

2003: ANDEAN CRISIS AND POPULAR MOBILIZATION

For the first four months of 2003 the OSAL statistics show a large increase in 'multi-sectorial' protests. Political demands were made in more than half of the cases. These articulations produced a situation in which there was a radical withdrawal from passive support for governments elected democratically when they adopted the neoliberal agenda and started preparing to squander their political capital, against a background of popular demonstrations.

In February 2003 there was a huge political crisis throughout the Andean territory of Bolivia when different social sectors organized their opposition to the presidential decree on the reform of the General Budget of the Nation. The decree imposed a tax of 12.5 per cent on employees, adhering to the IMF requirement to reduce the fiscal deficit. There was an immediate popular reaction to this measure. After days of growing support for the conflict from different social sectors there was a rising of the main police units in the country. A massively backed demand was made for the president to resign while confrontations occurred between the police and army. The savage repression unleashed by the government, which placed snipers on the top of public buildings, resulted in 35 deaths and over 200 wounded.

President Toledo of Peru also had difficulties in trying to differentiate himself from 'fujimorismo' without changing the course of the economic policies his government was promoting. This was similar to what happened to President de la Rua in Argentina who – having won the elections on an 'anti-Menem' stance – continued, once he was in government, in the steps of his predecessor, carrying his policies still further. The similarity of these two cases indicates that these processes tend to develop rapidly when the news in the press and on television can no longer hide the practical negative results of the policies.

This brief summary of events in Boliva and Peru shows that, while a political accommodation within the national states is possible even if the neoliberal model is continued, popular discontent rapidly breaks out again. This makes 'neoliberal governability' increasingly difficult and unstable. At the same time, the more dynamic social movements in the region have drawn up a critical balance sheet on the social consequences of the application of neoliberal prescriptions and their negative impact on the majority of the population. In fact, this social experiment shows there is a limit that cannot easily be exceeded when the intention is to reinforce measures against the will of the people.

The new regional scene in 2003 saw leaders from the social movements participating in electoral alliances that brought them into power, with considerable political heterogeneity. This created tensions among the movements themselves, driving them into crucial debates about governmental policies and their own position towards the state. In the first quarter of 2003 social conflict in countries like Brazil and Ecuador, far from diminishing, increased 50 per cent in Brazil and 98 per cent in Ecuador, compared with the last quarter of 2002. We should therefore look carefully at how, in these situations, relationships were forged between the social movement and the government concerning politics, autonomy and the creation of alternatives.

In Ecuador this issue was seen in the escalation of the debate of the indigenous movements regarding the new government of which they form part. An early result was the breaking away of the Ecuarunari (la Confederación de Pueblos de la Nacionalidad Kichwa del Ecuador) from the government, which finally took place on 24 April 2003. Later, in August, there was the failure of the governmental alliance between the Sociedad Patriótica and the Movimiento Pachakutik (linked with the indigenous movement) following disagreement about the increasingly neoliberal bias of the economic policies of President Lucio Gutiérrez.

The most acute ideological and political polarization in the whole region, however, was in Venezuela. The confrontation created by the national civic strike led by the Coordinadora Democrática (CD) did not bridge the gap opened up when the same sectors planned a coup d'état to topple the elected president, Hugo Chávez. This time the opposition sectors on strike raised the stakes, inciting the population to stop paying taxes. In January 2003 there were demonstrations in favour and against the government, which left three dead and many wounded. The cycle was closed on 1 February, when the CD, the CTV and FEDECAMARAS decided to lift the strike.

To end this whole series of protests, convergences and political crises, there was the gigantic popular mobilization in Bolivia, which intensified until mid-September to mid-October 2003, against the policy of exporting gas and the general neoliberal course taken by the government. It culminated in the stepping down of President Sánchez de Lozada on 17 October. These mobilizations and protests involving the indigenous movements, peasants and main urban populations

– reaching levels unseen in Bolivia for the last fifty years – ended with massive reprisals that took the lives of 70 people. They have had a great impact on the rest of Latin America, particularly in the Andean region.

There were also general and/or sectorial stoppages and strikes at the national level in nine countries of the region during the second quarter of 2003. In Colombia, the Comando Nacional Unitario, set up by the main union confederations, called for general strikes during June and August against the economic policy and privatizing initiatives of Uribe's government, while similar action was taken by public sector employees in Brazil, Ecuador, El Salvador, Panama, Peru and Uruguay. A general strike was called in mid-August by the Central Unitaria de Trabajadores Chilena (CUT) rejecting a project for labour reform. This did not prevent the law from going through but it had important symbolic value as the first general strike in this Andean country for 13 years, since the military dictatorship ended, and it received support from some fifty unions in both the public and private sectors.

In Brazil a project for a provisional reform by President Lula's government in its early months of office triggered the first national-level labour conflict with which the new government team had to deal. On 8 July some 400,000 state employees participated in an indefinite strike convened by the CUT. In early August, a demonstration rejecting the project attracted 70,000 people in Brasilia, but at the end of the month both chambers of parliament voted to approve the project. While the CUT-led strike did not receive massive support, it triggered a debate inside the Workers Party and various social movements about the economic direction of a government elected to redistribute wealth and benefit the most oppressed social sectors in Brazil.

The protracted teachers' strike in Peru from May claimed an increase in salaries and more funding for the education budget. It culminated in a broad process of social protest, which, like the demonstration against privatization in southern Peru of mid-2002, dealt yet a further blow to the legitimacy of Toledo's weakened government.

As for Colombia, in the context of the brutal privatizing offensive of Uribe's government, combined with an increased militarization of the country, there were two general strikes. They were convened in June and August by the worker confederations CGTC, CTC and CUT against the sale and privatization of public enterprises and services (Telecom, ECOPETROL, Caja Nacional de Previsión, Instituto del Seguro Social, Cajanal). These strikes were part of an intense process of social resistance led by workers from the sectors affected, who were confronted with the militarization of the enterprises, ordered by the government on the pretext of avoiding terrorist attacks.

In various countries of Central America and the Caribbean there were many, significant conflicts in the public sector and broad social convergences in which city-dwellers were the main protagonists. In Panama, the strikes of the officials of the Caja del Seguro Social (CSS) for an increase in the budget and in their salaries, with the education community demanding extra teaching staff, were two high points in a sectorial convergence that also involved workers and students in demonstrations supporting the struggle. In mid-May there was a march against the government's economic policies, with workers, teachers, students, peasants, livestock producers and distributors demonstrating against rate rises and government tax reforms.

In the Dominican Republic a series of multi-sectoral protests was called by the Coordinadora de Organizaciones Populares, Sindicales y de Transportistas, the Frente Amplio de Lucha Popular (FALPO) and the Colectivo de Organizaciones Populares to condemn an agreement with the IMF, power cuts and a rise in fuel prices.

In Honduras the Great Dignity March at the end of August filled the streets of Tegucigalpa, protesting against approval of a law on drinking water that would privatize the service, and against the civil service law and regulations for land ownership. This march brought together some 15,000 people from union confederations, the Bloque Popular, indigenous organizations, doctors, nurses and primary and secondary school teachers.

In Uruguay a protest was led by health workers who, in mid-July, demanded a wage increase and medical supplies. The action was supported by the Sindicato Medico del Uruguay, which also decided on a work stoppage. Both sectors declared a general strike and the conflict extended across the country, with hospitals occupied on the decision of assemblies of workers. While this was happening the PIT-CNT called for the sixth general strike against the Battle government.

In Brazil the MST was active in occupying land and establishing peasant settlements, mostly in the central region (São Pãolo), the centre-west (Mato Grosso) and the northeast. Through these actions the movement was trying to step up pressure on the new government to accelerate implementation of comprehensive agrarian reform, one of the electoral promises of President Lula. Likewise the MST occupied the warehouses of the National Supply Company to denounce the lack of food in the settlements and delays in expropriating land.

There were 110 occupations between January and June 2003, often accompanied by roadblocks on the federal highways. In response to the occupations a group of large rural landowners launched the 'zero invasion' campaign, putting pressure on Lula's government to meet with a delegation of the MST. For their part, the MST denounced the creation of rural militias by landowners.

Lastly, after a period of prolonged silence and the refusal of the Mexican government and parliament to recognize the rights of the country's indigenous peoples, the Zapatista movement announced, in July, the winding up of the '*Aguascalientes*' (places of assembly) and their replacement by the '*Caracoles*' (snails), as well as the setting up of the Juntas de Buen Gobierno. The aim was to consolidate the autonomous rebel municipalities and give new impetus to the solidarity ties forged by the Zapatista indigenous peoples in the EZLN with other social movements and international solidarity networks. Also in July, in successive communications, sub-comandante Marcos ratified the opposition of the EZLN to the Plan Puebla Panamá and invited national and international civil society to participate in celebrations for the 'Caracoles'. On 8 August, in Oventik, thousands of Zapatista indigenous people and members of Mexican civil society joined social movements and militants from other continents in a ceremonial act to mark this new experience in building peoples' power through networks of autonomous peoples.

'ARMED NEOLIBERALISM' AND LATIN AMERICAN CONVERGENCES AGAINST REGIONAL TRADE AGREEMENTS

Faced with the twofold crisis in economic policy and political legitimacy that increasingly challenged the neoliberal regime, the period 2002–03 was marked by a new phase of 'armed neoliberalism'. This phrase not only refers to the policy of war and military intervention claimed as an international prerogative by President Bush. It also includes the deepening of a policy of social repression that tends to militarize social relationships within a country and covers legal reforms that encroach on democratic rights and freedoms, the criminalization of protest, the consolidation of increasingly authoritarian governments and growth of state and parastatal repression. Justified in the name of the fight against drugs, terrorism and delinquency, the 'security' ideology is attempting to reconstruct so-called neoliberal governability.

The heavy hand of the US over the region, much more evident since 11 September 2001, is trying to establish terrorism and security as a central part of the agenda in governmental meetings. The case of Colombia is symptomatic. The victory of Alvaro Uribe in the presidential elections opened up a process that not only accentuated military confrontation with the guerrillas – after the breakdown of the peace agreements of the previous period – but also applied a 'social militarization' policy in an attempt to affirm authoritarian legitimacy, particularly among the urban middle class. This was linked with US strategy, which takes the armed conflict in this country as a reflection of all social conflict in the Andean region and as requiring the 'fight against terrorism'.

Militarization in Latin America does not try to legitimize itself by proclaiming the secret existence of 'chemical or biological arms', as happened before the American invasion of Iraq. Instead the talk is of 'narco-terrorist networks' and 'narco-trade unionists', linked with the indigenous and peasant movements that for years have been contesting the hegemonic political model in the region and are particularly opposed to the implementation of the Free Trade Area of the Americas (FTAA). At the same time the US is pushing for the FTAA to become completely operative by 2005, promoting different kinds of negotiations, regional and bilateral and through other pressures and conditions.

An agenda to accentuate the neoliberal course as it confronts the crisis can be seen in the progress of negotiations on the so-called trade liberalization agreements. This process became clear with the conclusion of negotiations on the Free Trade Treaty between Chile and the US, due to become operative at the end of 2003, the coming into effect of a Free Trade Treaty between Chile and the European Union as from February of the same year, and the announcement of the start of negotiations between Central American countries and the US.

There has also been a growing protest against trade liberalization agreements as social movements and organizations become more aware of their importance and effects. This explains the consolidation of regional linkages of the different social movements as networks, campaigns and sectorial coordination. The campaign against the FTAA and the World Economic Forum, during 2002, began to expand in Latin America through the Mesoamerican Forum, the Panamazónica Forum, the Thematic Social Forum in Argentina and national forums in Uruguay, Venezuela and Colombia. The continuing preparation of the regional campaign against the FTAA, and the strengthening of the local coordinations around this initiative culminated, in October

2002, in the first national consultation organized by Brazilian social movements, who could count on over 10 million votes.

This mounting opposition to the FTAA was also to be seen in the streets of Quito during the Summit of the Economic Ministers of the Americas in November 2002, where a large demonstration, promoted by Ecuadorian indigenous movements and accompanied by delegations from social movements and organizations from the whole continent, held the Continental Encounter on 'Another America is Possible', against the FTAA. In Cuba, at the end of the same month, the Second Hemispheric Encounter to Fight the FTAA concluded by approving a document and action plan entitled 'To all the peoples of America: a call from Havana'.

During this period struggles against commercial liberalization were mainly led by the agricultural and peasant sectors. As the agricultural chapter of NAFTA came into effect at the beginning of 2003, the numerous protests by small farmers and peasants, already under way in 2002, became more widespread. Also in Peru, agricultural producers mobilized, demanding subsidies for the sector and that imports be stopped.

Accompanying this process of subordinating the region to North American capital has been a growing US military presence in the region, with the arrival of troops in Panama and Bolivia at the beginning of 2003, on the pretext of humanitarian missions, and an increase in military assistance to Colombia. Linked to this militarization and social repression, a new chapter seemed to be opening up in this country, with prolongation of the state of emergency, an increase in the number of social and political leaders assassinated or kidnapped, and the suppression of protests and emerging movements, for example in the repressive measures used in the Cauca and the police raids at the Universidad Nacional in Bogota.

This face of 'armed neoliberalism' was also visible in the harassment of the Zapatista communities in Chiapas and the removal of settlements in the Montes Azules region, carried out by the Mexican army at the end of 2002. At the same time, the repression suffered by the peasants of Chapare in Bolivia, and the detention and trial of Mapuche leaders of the Arauco Malleco Coordination in Chile showed that the policy of criminalizing the social movements was continuing.

This was given new impetus by the approval of laws increasing sentences for demonstrators and prohibiting certain forms of protest, along with a growing number of legal trials and imprisonment of social and political militants and leaders and increasing use, by some governments, of declaration of states of emergency during social conflict, the militarization of public enterprises and buildings, police hounding of workers on strike and raids on the homes of leaders. The President of El Salvador announced in July 2003 the launching of the 'heavy hand' plan, which authorized his armed forces to detain and imprison anyone suspected of 'hooliganism'. This initiative also involved the governments of Honduras and Guatemala. As part of his counter-insurgency offensive and the militarization promoted by the Colombian government, President Uribe increased his squads of peasant soldiers.

Despite the tragic balance of this social militarization and its impact on popular movements and democratic liberties, there has been great difficulty in generalizing and consolidating it. Nor has it convincingly shown its capacity, under the threat of terror, to demobilize and discipline the struggles. The best example followed the Bolivian crisis in October 2003. Militarization and savage repression had left dozens dead and hundreds wounded but it only increased the general condemnation and national and international mobilization against the government's tactics. Ultimately, the different sectors expressed in one, single voice their main demands: a popular referendum concerning the export of Bolivian gas and then the removal, voted in the national parliament, of President Gonzalo Sánchez de Lozada, who was responsible for unleashing the massacre.

It is also important to emphasize how the demonstrations in the region are directly linked to the international situation, strongly promoted by the organizations that form part of the 'movement of movements' for global resistance. While such demonstrations are not new to Latin America, they have greatly increased through the World Social Forum experience of Porto Alegre and the coordination of regional activities against the FTAA.

In the first quarter of 2003 and following increasing participation of different social sectors in demonstrating against the war in Iraq, this kind of protest grew significantly in the region: from 0.7 per cent of the total records in the last-quarter of 2002 it rose to 7.8 per cent in the first-quarter of 2003.

The protagonists of these struggles are indigenous social organizations, trade unions, human rights activists, peasants, women, ecologists, left-wing parties, etc. Also significant in producing broad coalitions are mobilizations promoted by various churches and ecumenical groups in organizing vigils and prayers for peace.

They have brought about significant levels of participation of broad collectives ranging from pacifism to anti-imperialism, and in many national cases they contest the politics of the governments or succeed in conditioning their positions.

Finally, mention should be made of the failure of the WTO meeting for trade ministers in Cancún, Mexico, in September 2003. The strength of the peasant mobilizations, the global resistance movement, the 'Summit of the Peoples', and the work of NGOs inside and outside the official summit contributed to the forming of a bloc of countries of the South, led by Brazil, which denounced the unilateral requirements of the industrial countries, weakening the chances for the negotiations to adopt the US time frame for the FTAA to be launched in 2005.

The meeting for trade ministers of the Americas in November 2003 in Miami attempted to overcome the setbacks experienced at Cancún and reschedule the timing of the agreement. This will be a new challenge for the convergences and networks organized in the north of the continent and will influence the prospects for sustaining the resistance movement against neoliberal globalization through the whole American region.

In this context, the political changes analyzed here, as well as the experiences of struggle and regional coordination forged by the movements in recent times, open up the possibility of a new Latin American resistance that could halt the policies of militarization and subordination to North American interests. However, the possibilities of starting transformations for defeating neoliberalism are not only linked to making effective changes but also, and especially, to the strengthening of popular movements and expanding their capacity for autonomy and self-management, as well as their ability to promote the broadest democratic participation by the majority in constructing the collective future.

BIBLIOGRAPHY

Algranati, Clara (2003) 'Luchas sociales y "neoliberalismo de guerra" en América Latina', in OSAL (Buenos Aires: CLACSO), no. 10, January/April

Boron, Atilio (2003) 'El ALCA y la culminación de un proyecto imperial', in OSAL (Buenos Aires: CLACSO), no. 11, May/August

Coronado Del Valle, Jaime (2002) 'Democracia, ciudadanía y protesta social: la experiencia de Arequipa y la colonialidad del poder', in OSAL (Buenos Aires: CLACSO), no. 8, September

OSAL [Observatorio Social de América Latina] (2000) (Buenos Aires: CLACSO), no. 2, September

OSAL [Observatorio Social de América Latina] (2001) (Buenos Aires: CLACSO), no. 4, June

Palau, Marielle (2002) 'Luchas sociales obligan a retroceder al gobierno y detienen el proceso de privatización', in OSAL (Buenos Aires: CLACSO), no. 8, September

Seoane, José (2001) 'La protesta social en América Latina', in OSAL (Buenos Aires: CLACSO), no. 3, January

Seoane, José (2003) 'Rebelión, dignidad, autonomía y democracia. Voces compartidas desde el Sur' (Buenos Aires), mimeo

Seoane, José and Clara Algranati (2002) 'Los movimientos sociales en América Latina. Entre las convergencias sociales y el neoliberalismo armado', in OSAL (Buenos Aires: CLACSO), no. 8, September

Seoane, José and Emilio Taddei (2003) 'Movimientos sociales, conflicto y cambios políticos en América Latina', in OSAL (Buenos Aires: CLACSO), no. 9, January

Solón, Pablo (2003) 'Radiografía de un febrero', in OSAL (Buenos Aires: CLACSO), no. 10, January/April

Taddei, Emilio (2003) 'Las protestas sociales en el espacio urbano: trabajadores asalariados y convergencias sociales', in OSAL (Buenos Aires: CLACSO), no. 11, May/August

11
Proletarian Resistance and Capitalist Restructuring in the United States

Pierre Beaudet

THE PERENNIAL AMERICAN ENIGMA

The American proletariat is, and always has been an enigma for the left and the social movement, above all in Europe. It was militant and innovative in its struggles and demands, and this used to be the trademark of a movement that was finally recognized as the Industrial Workers of the World. The IWW invoked the name of Lenin and organized an incredible series of strikes almost everywhere in the United States from the beginning of the twentieth century. Later on, during the Depression, there was a gigantic social movement, with factories being occupied and workers unionized on a massive scale, which led to a transformation of the legal structure of the State, enabling a broad participation and the expression of plurality of social forces.

In the cauldron of the 1960s, a strong grassroots union movement sowed panic among the large industrial enterprises. In Detroit the Revolutionary Black Workers proliferated, ending up with a network that was widespread in the large automobile factories. In the manufacturing sector, but also in the services and the public sector, the mass mobilizations of both working people and the young challenged the growth of militarism and imperialism, especially during the Vietnam war.

This proletarian radicalism still exists, but it has, of course, to deal with a powerful, established machine. With the emergence of the neoliberal project in the 1980s, the dominant economic and political interests took up the offensive. Trade unions, especially, were harassed and suppressed. But new forms of struggle developed, creating new protagonists and demands that infiltrated into the heart of the ruling system.

IN THE HEART OF THE MONSTER:
CAPITALIST RESTRUCTURING AND CLASS TRANSFORMATION

Once Ronald Reagan came to power in 1980, the restructuring orchestrated by neoliberalism created new power relationships, putting the social movement on the defensive. This started with the crushing of the air controllers' union (over 10,000 members), followed by an unprecedented assault against unionism in the public sector through privatization, deregulation and severe cuts in the budgets for health, education, public transport and social assistance. At the same time, the restructuring of the manufacturing sector increased, through the delocalization of certain industrial sectors (particularly automobiles) towards the southern states, which has little union tradition, and even towards Mexico, in a process spurred on by NAFTA (the North American Free Trade Area), an accord signed by President Bush senior in 1994.

The corporations also carried out a full-scale reorganization of work ('lean production', subcontracting, job flexibility, etc.), which wreaked havoc among the unions. Managements forced the unions to accept serious cutbacks in salary and working conditions. Strikes launched against this trend (e.g. at Greyhound, Dodge, Eastern Airlines) were unsuccessful.

One of the main reasons for these failures was the incapacity of the leadership of the national confederation AFL-CIO (at that time headed by Lane Kirkland) to resist the neoliberal onslaught. To a large extent official trade unionism decided to accept these reductions and concessions, hoping to recuperate and counting on the return of the Democrats. When the latter, under the leadership of Bill Clinton, took back the presidency in 1994, not only was the damage already done, but the 'modernized' Democrats actually abandoned their traditional alliance with the AFL-CIO and continued the restructuring process. The impact has been devastating on the conditions of work and wages of American workers, as well as hitting the trade union movement hard. For example, in 2002:

- The average income of waged workers after thirty years was at the same level as in 1973 (in constant US dollars). During the same period, the annual income of the richest 5 per cent (over $150.000) of the population increased by 36 per cent. The income of the 10 per cent poorest diminished by 9.3 per cent.

- Over 11 per cent of the population was below the official poverty line.Twenty-six per cent of the labour force was composed of the 'working poor': wages for full time work paid at basic minimum rates ($7 or $8 an hour, according to the state). Forty million Americans had no medical coverage.
- Unemployment affected 8 million workers officially, which does not take into account 2 million people in prison. Nearly 2 million jobs had been eliminated since September 2001. Only 48 per cent of the unemployed were eligible for unemployment insurance and they received $250 a week for 14 weeks.
- The number of unionized workers fell dramatically, from 27 per cent (1978) to 13.9 per cent (1996) of the labour force: union membership was at its lowest level since 1936.
- In 1995 the number of work days lost through strikes was 12 per cent of what it had been in 1980: the lowest in the history of industrial relations in the United States.

These developments have profoundly changed the composition of the American proletariat. The traditional industrial working class has lost in numbers and strategic importance, partly through the loss of jobs, partly through the reorganization of production to the detriment of skilled labour. The service sector, which includes many companies paying low wages (e.g. the catering sector, domestic labour), has grown enormously – hence the increase of women, young people and immigrants entering the labour market. In 1996, women constituted 39 per cent of the membership of AFL-CIO, as against 22 per cent in 1979.

A MOVEMENT UNDER WAY

At the beginning of the 1990s, the American trade union movement had reached an impasse. Concessions and compromises, far from slowing down neoliberal restructuring, had only accelerated it. As has been said, the traditional alliance between the AFL-CIO and the Democratic Party was unable to reverse the trend, even after the election of President Clinton in 1994. Meanwhile, however, things began to stir at the grassroots of the unions. Large unions, like the Teamsters, were taken over by militants at the beginning of the 1990s. In other sectors, a new generation of trade unionists began to surface.

In 1995, this led to the election of a new reforming president of the AFL-CIO, John Sweeny. Not only was there a change in tone but the confederation introduced new ideas and new tactics. The general feeling was that the union movement should rediscover its previous image, as a rallying point for social movements. New alliances were forged with community movements of Afro-American and Latino organizations and other networks involved in the struggle for civil rights and social justice.

At the end of 1995 the US government convened its 'partners' in Seattle to elaborate the foundations of world neoliberalism through the World Trade Organization. What looked set to be an international conference, like many others, proved to be more of a battlefield. The local AFL-CIO committee in Seattle, representing many teamsters and dockers (whose union had maintained a progressive tradition), decided to mobilize, with the support of Sweeny. Challenged by the events being organized by young people and the alternative world movements, the unions – who were initially suspicious – decided to immobilize the downtown area for several hours. Teamsters and 'tortoises' (ecologists, young people), side by side, stood up to the police offensive and gained a degree of public sympathy. This *rapprochement* between the unions and social movements had considerable repercussions, although the trade union movement was not yet prepared to go all the way against neoliberal policies.

In the meantime, however, the more favourable economic situation of the later 1990s enabled some union organizations to be more demanding. In 1997 the Teamsters union at multinational UPS launched a national strike, which was carried out by women, with the support of numerous communities, and won its case.

But despite the new union militancy and the economic boom, employers proved resistant. The destruction of unionism, which began in the 1980s, has had long-term effects: managements knew that they could deal with the unions and even do without them. There has been a strong reinforcement of the legal mechanisms for 'decertifying' existing unions (i.e. withdrawing their legal credentials) and preventing new unions from establishing themselves. This has complicated the task of union organizers. Large companies and even very large ones openly boast that they do not tolerate unions. This is the case, for example, with Wal-Mart, the retail shops chain, whose turnover in 2002 was greater than that of General Motors.

This has created problems for the union movement. Membership of AFL-CIO, which, at its height was 21 million, levelled out at

13 million in 2002. For the last ten years, union campaigns have succeeded in recruiting some 90,000 workers a year, a relatively small number compared with the 250,000 to 300,000 new union members joining the AFL-CIO each year in the 1960s.

The situation has worsened following the election of George W. Bush in 2000, ushering in a new era dominated by the most conservative elements in the American ruling class. The ties between Bush and the corporate sector could not be more intimate, and serious conflicts of interest have arisen through the connivance, if not complicity, between the new administration and numerous large corporations involved in shady dealings, such as Enron. The aims of the administration are evident: to dismantle the semblance of social protection that still exists in favour of privatization, to abolish protective measures and other 'irritants' that 'harm' the private sector (e.g. legislation concerning the rights of workers and the environment) and to break up the union movement, in spite of its very moderate leadership.

Since the events of September 2001 President Bush has had the opportunity to accelerate his reforms. A huge offensive has been initiated in the name of national security. The dismissals, already envisaged at the end of the boom, multiplied and particularly affected air transport and tourism. More than 170,000 workers have lost their right to collective bargaining. A witch-hunt has begun against immigrants and refugees, who make up a major part of the proletariat in industry, agriculture and services. When war was launched on Iraq, patriotic hysteria knew no bounds. 'Who is not with us is against us,' cried Bush. The Ministry of Justice, run by an ultra-conservative fundamentalist, John Ashcroft, created 'Operation Tips', which obliges businesses to 'mobilize' their employees (in distribution companies, the public sector and transport) in spying and surveillance activities. AFL-CIO's opposition to the war, even in a muted form, confirmed the conservatives in their desire to pick a fight. The federal government intervened directly to break a dockers' strike on the west coast, organized under the leadership of a militant union, the International Longshore and Warehouse Union (ILWU).

NEW FORMS OF RESISTANCE

Faced with the prolonged decline of traditional trade unionism and the current assault of the Bush administration, new forms of struggle have developed. Some are inspired by past resistance (from the IWW to the freedom marches of the civil rights movement), others are more contemporary and influenced by the new proletarian sectors, which are usually mobile, relatively unskilled and organized in networks.

New organizations have been set up that might be called para-unions, functioning outside formal union structures, often with the support of the more militant trade unions, who see this as a way of making the union movement itself more dynamic and of forging links with other communities. This is a crucial issue, especially for immigrant workers, whose demographic and 'strategic' weight in the economy has increased but who still remain on the margins of union organization and especially of its leadership. Some associations, like the Chinese Staff and Worker Association (New York), the Asian Immigrant Women Advocates (San Francisco) and the Latin Workers Center (Chicago), have helped develop solidarity and tools for struggle. This usually leads to unionization campaigns, mass resistance against discrimination and action to force the unions to listen more attentively to immigrant workers. Huge coalitions have been set up, with the help of the Hotel and Restaurant Employees Union (HERE), in various cities to organize freedom rides and ended up with a large national demonstration in New York on 10 October 2003.

Another important development has been the emergence of student–labour alliances in a number of schools and universities. These alliances are formed around issues like the unionization of unskilled workers (mostly immigrants) on campus. One example was the action at Yale, in which a coalition of unions, students and communities brought about improvements in working conditions, investment in social housing and the adoption of a code of ethics to govern the university's corporate investments. At the same time militant students set up the United Students against Sweatshops (USAS), which runs a campaign condemning the marketing of products manufactured by non-union factories in the USA and the rest of the world. This campaign was fully supported by the main union in the garment sector, UNITE.

These coalitions or networks take on specific forms, according to regions and sectors. In Connecticut, the Naugatuck Valley Project organizes over 60 union, community and Christian organizations in a permanent campaign against the closure of factories, an increasing trend as companies in the garments sector and light industries relocate towards Mexico. This coalition has also taken steps to encourage people to register as voters. In Minnesota, the

---

The National Day of Student Action

In recent years, American students have built up a strong movement against corporate greed. On 4 April 2001, the anniversary of the assassination of Martin Luther King, Jobs with Justice, the Student Labor Action Project (SLAP) and the United Students against Sweatshops (USAS) organized their third national day of action for economic and social justice. Such actions took place in 30 American states, 70 towns and 80 campuses, of which the following are some examples:

- The State University of Phoenix (Arizona): sit-in in the administrative buildings, demanding cancellation of the university's contract with the company Sodexho-Marriott, for its investments in private prisons and its anti-union stance.
- The State University of San José (California): the symbolic construction of an 'open-air factory', the size of a henhouse, with barbed wire fencing, tables and sewing machines. While the workers sewed, students collected almost a thousand signatures for a petition organized by the Consortium for the Rights of Workers to prevent university clothing from being made under low-wage factory conditions.
- Yale University (Connecticut): visits to pro-NAFTA companies by 125 student and union groups.
- Lexington University (Kentucky): students demonstrate to support workers in a company involved with the university, Solid Waste, which forces them to agree to conditions that are dangerous for their health. According to prevailing state law in Kentucky, wage earners are not entitled to federal employment rights.

Alliance for Progressive Action coalition is fighting for the conversion of military industries.

Jobs with Justice

Created in 1987 under AFL-CIO auspices, Jobs with Justice (JwJ), an independent movement, describes itself as a 'national and permanent campaign for the rights of workers'. It is a coalition of coalitions that brings together over 1,500 organizations in 25 states and 40 towns, and it can count on participation of over 50,000 militants. Over the last few years JwJ has been spectacularly successful. Its campaigns are supported by mass community mobilizations that have resulted in the unionization of over 15,000 workers, often in sectors and regions where levels of unionization are very low.

A recent example was the struggle of the janitors of Boston, organized by a relatively militant union, the SEIU. For several weeks in October 2002, over 10,000 members of the union and community groups massed in the centre of town and upset the operations of several large office buildings, with the support of students organized by the Student Labor Action Project. This struggle finally ended in victory (an increased average wage of $10 an hour and improvements in working conditions) and spread to other American towns. In Chicago a similar mobilization led 9,500 janitors to confront powerful property entrepreneurs, who have strong links with the Bush administration and the Republican Party.

Jobs with Justice is also a political rallying point, apart from its direct action and community mobilizations. In Cleveland the coalition succeeded in getting the municipality to adopt a new law enforcing the minimum wage. A candidate supported by the unions was subsequently elected to the municipal council. The campaign continues to defend community clinics (the Affordable Health Care Coalition), which serves over 30,000 residents but is threatened by privatization and budget cuts.

Encouraged by its local successes, JwJ has looked to coordinating national campaigns, which is a real challenge in an environment that is socially, racially and politically so segmented. One important campaign focuses on the right to create unions – a right that is being lost in many states. Some corporations, like the Azteca food chain and Wal-Mart are the targets of the coalitions led by JwJ. Their activities include sit-ins inside and in front of their stores, demonstrations at the homes of management personnel and seeking media coverage. The employers stand accused of violating the rights of workers, who are almost all women and immigrants.

Together with a number of unions and community coalitions, JwJ has also taken up the challenge to impede the Free Trade Agreement of the Americas (FTAA), which aims at integrating the whole hemisphere under the hegemony of the US. The previous NAFTA process has reinforced the multinational strategy of playing the lowest salaries (Mexican) against the highest ones (American and Canadian), while delocalizing or threatening to delocalize factories. According to union research, over a million jobs (mainly in the manufacturing sector) have been lost in the US through NAFTA. To oppose the FTAA process, JwJ has organized coalitions, and with the support of AFL-CIO, a petition 'No to the FTAA!' has been launched. The campaign also calls on ecological organizations to participate, because both NAFTA and the FTAA undermine environmental legislation.

JwJ has not played a prominent role in the anti-war movement, but it participated in the anti-war coalitions. Many large demonstrations have taken place, particularly in Washington and New York, as well as Chicago, where union traditions are still strong: over 30,000 people, mostly workers and immigrants, said 'No!' to Bush in March, just before the Iraq war.

Russ Davies, JwJ coordinator for Massachusetts, has explained the challenge facing the American social movement in the context of mounting militarism:

> We must maintain the principle of international solidarity at a time when military rhetoric and protectionism is feeding on massive losses of jobs. Under the present regime of the global organization of capitalism, the labor world must organize itself internationally. We should support the workers and unions in Colombia and elsewhere when they are assassinated and repressed by American corporations. We must continue to situate local struggle in the global context, with a global strategy. We must see what unites us and continue to support the struggle for the rights of immigrants against the FTAA. There will be increasingly tough battles for the right to health, jobs, decent pensions and these can become very large-scale for the social movements, mobilizing millions, rather than thousands, of people. We must create links between all these questions, like the theft perpetrated on American workers by Enron and the terrible impact of Enron practices in countries like India.
>
> At a time when union militants are trying to maintain their mobilizations and actions, our allies in the alternative world movement, locally and internationally, must understand the political realities facing the workers' movement in the United States. The demands of the movement against the war are supported by a minority of Americans at present. On the other side, there is a huge majority. Workers and their allies feel that they are part of the movement for global justice. So there is a problem. We must be patient and understand that time is needed to construct a strong social movement. We have no choice. Our password 'another world is possible' also means that 'another movement' is possible and necessary: a movement of workers, students, ecologists and all those who came to Seattle and who demonstrate in day-to-day struggles.

12
Europe:
The Challenge for Social Movements

Bernard Dreano

As the European Union expands to the east, it launches a new phase in its history. The way in which this is done will have enormous consequences, not only for the Europeans themselves but for the rest of the world too. Neoliberal policy, the alpha and omega of the Eurocrats, remains in place in spite of strong social opposition in a number of countries. The Iraq crisis has shown up the divergences between different European governments on transatlantic relationships and also rifts between certain governments and their own people. The French philosopher Paul Thibaud wonders how serious is this 'fissuring': 'its cracks can be discerned – but how far can it go?' The constitutional treaty drawn up by the 'Convention' and its president Valéry Giscard d'Estaing plans to recast European integration to give a solid base to this new phase. As the European deputy Philippe Herzog has remarked, it seems to be 'more of a crisis of the community dynamic, from which it cannot extricate itself'.

Europe is at a crossroads and governments seem to be indicating only selected paths to their population. But people have protested in all the great cities of Western Europe (and also some cities in Eastern Europe) to defend peace as well as the past gains in social protection, and are hoping for the opening up of new paths. But the social movements find it difficult to take on board the full scope of 'Europe', and hence to propose alternatives appropriate for the issues at stake. Here we shall consider a few problems on which some of these movements are now working.

NEOLIBERALISM AND SOCIAL DUMPING

A few years ago the social democratic left dominated most of the governments of the European Union. Since then, they have given way to the liberal right almost everywhere. This change has not in itself brought about a great change in policies, which continue to be markedly neoliberal. But it does indicate the tendency of public opinion to accept privatization and deregulation. The policy of going with the current, adopted by the left when dominated by social democrats, has contributed to this trend and hampered the growth of resistance. But now, another sector of public opinion, at least as important, has been refusing to accept the challenge to the Welfare State by taking refuge in abstention in elections and in different forms of populist voting – usually the extreme right – while a new (?) critical left has begun to emerge.

Blatant right-wingers, including, given its track record Tony Blair's New Labour and some other 'socialists', have thus accelerated the dismantling of the social compacts of post-war years on pensions, health insurance, public services, the right to work, training, etc. The offensive has been met in several countries (Italy, Austria, Spain, France, Germany, etc.) by strong social resistance. But trade unions have not been able to constitute a European front, mainly because social protection is perceived by many as part of national policy (much more than it actually is). Divisions in the unions (e.g. within IG-Metall in Germany, between CFDT and CGT in France, CGIL and CISL-UIL in Italy) have weakened the movement, while forms of organization peripheral to the traditional unions have strengthened: radical minority unions like the 'Groupe des 10-Sud' in France or the Cobas in Italy, small anarchist trade unionist groups in Spain and France, the coordination of teachers and performing arts professionals (musicians, actors and backstage workers), the 'without' movements – without work, without shelter, without documents (No-Vox), etc.

Some governments, starting with those of France and Germany, have intimated, somewhat ambiguously, that the 'stability pact', which is dragging the continent into sustainable stagnation and imposing financial limits, should not be respected. However, no social safety net, nor even agreed plans for one, has been announced. All-encompassing neoliberalism requires the weakening of each country, which it promotes through social dumping and reducing standards to the 'lowest social levels', as a prelude to challenging the very notion of collective rights on social issues. An alternative European and social logic would prioritise social matters to the highest level and consolidate rights, for example by setting up mechanisms for minimum salaries and social benefits. There is nothing unrealistic about this: despite a generally negative trend in recent years, certain gains have been won or consolidated at the national or European levels, e.g. in union rights, transnational 'joint production committees', training, legislation against discrimination and harassment, and so on.

The alternative to neoliberalism involves giving a new value to public action. The Common Agricultural Policy, the main European public policy, maintained in its present form by a Chirac–Schröder compromise, is clearly threatened and will sooner or later be dismantled. What will finish the CAP off is not only British (neoliberal) hostility towards it: it is just as much the French determination to maintain a production-based and export-oriented agricultural policy on behalf of the French agricultural lobby (FNSEA) as against the sustainable agriculture advocated, for example, by the Confédération Paysanne in France and Via Campesina at the international level. French arrogance in defending 'Daddy's CAP' risks ending up with a CAP that is quite meaningless. Further, the EU's enlargement brings a tragic dimension to this debate: no CAP at all, or maintaining a CAP in decline, will ensure yet more unbridled competition and devastating neoliberalism.

At least there is a debate on the CAP. The future of non-agricultural structural funds is barely discussed unless it is to criticize its management, if not its existence: the neoliberals find in it a pretext to attack the Brussels bureaucracy. These funds mainly contribute to agriculture (FEOGA) but also to regional and social development (FEDER and FSE, respectively), while other budget items enable the financing of development aid to non-EU states or assistance to particularly underprivileged and vulnerable peoples. They are thus instruments for carrying out essential policies. The general line adopted by governments is not to increase these funds, for various reasons: neoliberal budgetary austerity, the desire of leading countries not to transfer more funds to the EU, and the egoism of the richest towards the poorest. The disposition of these funds and even their management are effected mainly, although not totally, with a neoliberal vision. The working of these measures is hindered by horrific bureaucratization, which – it should be said – is more the fault of the member states than of European bureaucracy.

The enlargement of the EU should impose an increase in structural funding, but the line is to reduce it, while co-operation with the South (for example the Euromed partnership with the Mediterranean countries or with the ACP, the African and Caribbean countries) has been given short shrift as at least some money has to be found for Eastern Europe. The left is strangely silent on this subject, for it neither criticizes European budget decisions and methods of managing these funds nor does it defend the projects made possible in Europe through these funds, and demand their extension. Such funds support national development proposals, policy on inequality and discrimination, and green papers on research, energy, transport, etc. All this is flagrantly insufficient and badly oriented, but the left could be more pro-active in proposing European public policies.

ADAPTING TO EUROPEAN UNITY

The European Union is by far the largest economic unit in the world. This enables it to make itself felt especially vis-à-vis American might, if not to resist it. But if this power is used to build a new European imperialism, our planet will not survive. The imperial past of the large European powers is still a bitter memory across the world and for Europeans themselves who do not really desire a European empire on the pretext of confronting US hegemony. There are indeed many who want a different role for Europe, one that contributes to balance in international relationships and to the global future. Such a contribution will not develop solely through the political posturing of certain states (positive as this can be) and still less through diplomatic games and old-fashioned intergovernmental alliances, opposing one 'European' triple entente (Paris/Berlin/Moscow) to an 'Atlantic' triple alliance (London/Madrid/Rome).

It is true that the rulers of the large, old European powers, especially the UK and France, cannot conceive of abandoning their past prestige without giving the impression of becoming second-class powers. Tony Blair, continuing British post-war policy, aligns the country with the US in the impertinent belief that he can play the role of enlightened mentor to those 'Texan louts' in power in Washington. As we have seen, he acted in this way in the Afghan war and then tried to be the leading defender of the Anglo-American attack on Iraq. This stance gives him an apparent equality with the Americans. Jacques Chirac meanwhile stood up to Bush on Iraq. Globally speaking, from the viewpoint of the anti-war movements, he played a positive role, even though he failed to change the fatal outcome. But it was more a question of oratory than a genuinely strategic autonomy, for which France hardly possesses the means. Before 1989 France thought it could maintain its power through the Franco-German axis. Based on the historic phase of 'Franco-German reconciliation', this was a guarantee of peace and one of the key elements in the construction of post-war Europe: the 'political and military pre-eminence' of France balancing the economic and demographic strength of Germany. The Chirac–Schröder alliance against the Iraq war is no longer based on such obsolete geopolitics, although it falls short of being a coherent political policy that with the admission of other players could become a European-wide platform.

Any such development should in no way convey the idea of a dominating arrogance towards the small countries of Europe. But the 'big' Europeans, starting with Chirac at the European summit of Nice in 2000, showed contempt for the so-called 'small ones', and Chirac repeated his criticism of former Communist countries for taking the Atlantic side over Iraq. Maintaining such attitudes contributes to European paralysis. Besides, there is no need to scorn the 'small' states if the aim is to define a European policy. On the one hand, it is obvious that the 'European fracture' concerning Bush's war is above all between the 'big' governments (at the time Blair–Aznar–Berlusconi versus Schröder–Chirac). On the other hand, Belgium, composed of both Walloons and Flemings (and at that time liberal/eco/socialist) and Greece, in spite of the prudence incumbent on the EU presidency during the Iraq crisis, showed more courage and a greater sense of Europeanism than did the politicians of the 'big nations' on the most important issues.

This is particularly important in the case of the new EU members who, released from the Soviet Empire, imagine that they will rediscover, if not real sovereignty, at least some 'national patriotism' (as it was called by the Polish journalist Konstantin Gebert), and they expect to receive some consideration (from both the governments and their people). The change of direction of the small countries (and not only those of Central Europe) towards NATO is based on a deep unconscious preference for the far-off American master to the obnoxious bigwigs of London, Paris and again Berlin perhaps in the future. It is imperative to withdraw from this game if an autonomous European policy is to be defined: one that meets the aspirations of the peoples of Central Europe and extricates their rulers from their servile attitude towards Washington.

Everyone deplores the lack of European unity and audacity, but many adapt themselves to it. This attitude was perceptible even among the movements that protested against the American war in Iraq. There was both a will committing Europe to greater responsibility as well as a will to become disengaged and adopt a cool neutrality. The latter attitude can perhaps favour American hegemony objectively even more than a declared pro-Atlantic stance.

THE EU AND REGIONAL INTEGRATION

Enlargement has always been less a matter of the reunification of Europe than an instrumental model: a model that happens to be neoliberal and has not been endorsed by the people. The 'community gains' to which the candidate countries have to adhere are not presented as a political and cultural process, but as a 'structural adjustment' to the dominant economic model, a 'capacity to be competitive', with a minimum of solidarity mechanisms. This solidarity is now far more meagre than that enjoyed by the Greeks, Spaniards, Portuguese and Irish when they joined the EU. But the growing heterogeneity of the EU requires more, rather than fewer structural measures allocated to common objectives. It should leave candidate countries with their nationality enhanced, not diminished. There need to be democratic procedures for prioritizing national policies as well as adequate means for carrying out general Union aims – and not the supreme right of competition and the universal regulation of general privatization.

As for democracy, the Copenhagen criteria for political conditionality were used by the EU governments with Turkey basically in mind. But they have turned out to constitute an ambiguous barrier, a step back from the conditionality for membership of the Council of Europe (it is notable that this institution does not respect its own conditionality, for example vis-à-vis Russia and Chechnya). This ambiguity can partly be explained by the democratic limits of members of the Union themselves in certain fields (e.g. women's rights, cultural and linguistic rights, press freedom, democratic electoral systems). Also the conditionality demanded of the candidate states is not applied to present members, as can be seen in the evident abuses of the Berlusconi government in Italy. Clearly this can also be explained by the reluctance of the more ardent neoliberals to include social rights as part of the democracy issue. An additional difficulty is acceptance of candidate nations on a fully equal basis, respecting their values and history, and the persistence of paternalistic attitudes. But today this is also true within the very heart of the EU itself.

The question of the 'Union's frontiers' is a source of confusion, which is often deliberate. The current European enlargement (plus Greece and minus Croatia) seems to consist of an ethnic culture that is Catholic, Protestant, Ashkenazic, setting aside (provisionally?) its Orthodox-Sephardic elements and (less provisionally?) the Muslims. This would seem to validate Huntington's thesis on the 'clash of civilizations'. The question of Turkey is indeed symptomatic of the problem of European identity. Turkey has been associated with the EU since 1963 and has older ties than other candidates. A 'No' to Turkish membership, in these conditions, sends a message of alarm not only to the Turks but also to millions of European Muslims in the Balkans, as well as descendants of immigrants in France, the UK, Germany, etc. If Europe persists in this vein, the Muslim communities, unable to become basically European, will remain alien. Immigrant Portuguese in France or Poles in Germany could have ties as strong with their region of origin as Bretons in Paris or Sicilians in Turin, for they are (or will be) members of the Community. As for the 'extra-communitarians', they must be prepared to break with their country of origin if the European states so demand.

The membership of Cyprus is a particularly sensitive issue for the Turks and Greeks. It is also a test of the capacity of the EU to regulate the 'ethnic' conflicts at its heart, these having been frozen for thirty years. The current attitude of the Greek government and the Islamic democrats in the Turkish government, and as the mobilization of the people in the two parts of the island testifies especially, would make it possible to solve the problem on the basis of a federation. However, the Turkish military and their man in the field, Rauf Denkstash are doing all they can to derail this solution. And the nationalist propaganda on the Greek side provoked a setback in spring 2004, which is, on such an important issue, a real European failure.

The question of relationships with the EU is also posed for those European countries that are in 'purgatory'. Ion Iliescu, the old Communist *apparatchik*, now President of Romania, and Simeon Koburgovski, the old king, now Prime Minister of Bulgaria, have proved themselves the most faithful allies of Washington in the Iraq crisis. Is this really surprising for two countries the EU seems to keep at a distance rather than embrace? The welcome conveyed by the governments of the EU to the 'non-communitarians' of the Balkans is far from generous. Slovenia, lauded as the best candidate, is somehow recompensed for its flight out of the old Yugoslav federation: a flight that was one of the origins of the Yugoslav drama. The other peoples of ex-Yugoslavia and Albania will keep their status as a secondary zone, i.e. pariahs subject to visas and controls. The hoped-for integration into Europe continues to be seen in practice (by the Croats, for example) as contradictory to Balkan integration. Thus the promise of integration contributes to continuing regional disintegration.

The Europeans did however adopt a different approach in 1999 when they signed, together with all the states of the region, the stability pact of Southeast Europe, an indispensable precondition for a harmonious future for the Balkans in Europe. Unfortunately, the EU does not seem very concerned to put into practice the proposals it proclaimed, of regional integration, which would be part of continental integration. This 'insouciance' should also be seen in drawing up an EU balance sheet as the principal structure in administering the protectorates of Bosnia-Herzegovina, Kosovo and Macedonia. It is a balance-sheet that seems to interest no-one.

Nor can the countries of the former USSR (apart from the Baltic states) be ignored in any vision of Europe. There are problems of frontiers: circulation of people to and from the Russian enclave of Kaliningrad, the 'crossed minorities' of Russians and Poles in the Baltic states and in Belarus, relationships of Moldavia with Romania, etc. But the problem is more global: what relationships will an integrated Europe have with these European neighbours? What kind of association? At the present time, apart from the highly developed integration of the mafia, the European TACIS projects have not been at all conclusive. The (temporary?) entente of Paris/Berlin/Moscow against Bush is unconvincing. Finally, alas, the strongest East–West relationship is the 'peace partnership' of NATO.

But how can there be a serious association with our neighbours to the East, when one sees how the EU subordinates its association with its southern neighbours to its own strategic project? The text of the Euro-Mediterranean co-operation agreement (Euromed), finalized in 1995 at Barcelona, was presented as a 'southern Helsinki', a promising dynamic of mutual co-operation and security between the two banks of the Mediterranean, involving economic co-operation, mutual peace, respect for human rights, cultural exchanges, and so forth. In practice, this agreement has been sabotaged, deprived of financial means (the MEDA programme) and emptied of all that was not concerned with free trade (a one-way process, for the freedom of businessmen from the North to circulate has not been compensated by the freedom of workers from the South to do the same). This sabotage, carried out by the Arab governments of the southern bank just as much as the European governments on the northern bank, reaches its apogee in the case of Israel (not only because the Israelis, like the others, flout Article 2 concerning human rights in the association agreement, but also through their systematic destruction of all the civilian infrastructures financed by the Union in Palestine).

European integration does, however, raise hopes well beyond those of the neighbours of Western Europe. Rightly or wrongly, many see it as a possible counterweight to the political and military domination of the US and to the hegemony of neoliberalism. For the poorest countries, the Lomé agreements that link the European Union to the ACP (African/Caribbean/ Pacific) countries seem to offer some hope in this direction, in spite of their manifestly neocolonial aspects, dictated largely by France. However, the evolution of the Lomé negotiations, then the Cotonou agreements that followed them, have unfortunately only confirmed the tendency to align with the world dictates of liberalism. Europe as the motor of fair development assistance, the helper of the poor, remains a dream.

Sometimes there are glimpses of a timid desire for what could be a real European world policy, like the one advocated by Samir Amin when he calls on 'the Europeans (or some of them)' to redefine 'a project for an anti-hegemonic front'. On key issues, like the environment (Kyoto), international law (the International Criminal Court), public health (AIDS), alliances sometimes develop with continents or larger states (Brazil, South Africa). India and China could also constitute strategic partners in a future thrust to restore balance to the world. Then it will be necessary to go further and provide concrete solutions to questions of collective security, the construction of an international public order defined in political terms, a genuine disarmament process, advocating negotiations and mediation rather than power relationships, the advent of a sustainable development model expressed in qualitative terms. We are still far from all this as far as the governments of Europe are concerned. But perhaps citizens are not so far away from it, judging by the rapid progress of the alternative world movement.

AN 'EMANCIPATORY EUROPE'?

The European Constitution, presented by Valéry d'Estaing, president of the Convention, was hailed as a way of 'bringing the Union closer to its citizens'. But the Convention, which met in Brussels from February to July 2003, was not the real 'constitutional process' the EU needed on the eve of its enlargement, nor the democratic forum in which the peoples of Europe could have put questions to their governments about the Iraq crisis or propose alternatives. The neoliberal orientation is as constant as the stance towards the US is inconstant. Unfortunately, these power relations are retained in the constitutional treaty ratifying the European Constitution, passed at the EU summit in June 2004.

It is a socially 'dangerous' constitution, stressed the Belgian trade unionist George Debunne, former president of the European Trade Union Confederation (CES), adding: 'Everything should be done to stop this constitutional text being adopted as long as there is a unanimous vote with the right of veto in social and fiscal fields.' It is politically unacceptable, said the French journalist Bernard Cassen, in that the questions that European citizens 'are really concerned about – content of community policies and, after the Iraq war, the independence of Europe – have been relegated to second place during the convention's 16 months of work'. It is a case of putting the cart before the horse, the deciding of 'how' and 'by whom', before having faced the problem of 'what', added the founder of the ATTAC movement. 'This is not by chance. It implicitly assumes that all this is basically settled and that the profoundly liberal logic of the former treaties [the Single Act, Maastricht, Amsterdam and Nice] cannot be modified at all, except in marginal matters.'

The debate on the Convention and its result is nevertheless significant. The European social movements are not, unfortunately, sufficiently mobilized on its deadlines.

The identity of the European Union is defined partly in Title One, through its statement of values and objectives, and partly through the Charter of Fundamental Rights, which is included in the Constitution. It does in fact offer some progress. Whatever its faults, the very fact that the Charter forms the basis of a policy promoting rights can help to extend them and to prevent any lowering of targets already attained. This progress can nevertheless be criticized. It institutionalizes competition as the essential means of allocating resources. It also recommends a 'social market economy that is highly competitive, aiming at full employment and social progress, a high level of protection and an improvement of the quality of the environment', which is, to say the least, a contradiction in terms! Public services appear neither in the values nor in the objectives of the Union. Finally, certain fundamental values, for example, peace, have been 'forgotten', although they figure in national constitutions or are the objective of international charters (including those of the Council of Europe and the United Nations). The constitutional project thus represents a step back from the basic laws of several of its members, and there is no explicit clause encouraging the broadening and deepening of fundamental rights.

The project stabilizes and clarifies the various competences of the EU and member states. A qualified majority is defined as a majority of the states representing at least 60 per cent of the population of the Union. It covers a dozen fields that still require unanimity. Culture is the object of a compromise text between unanimity and qualified majority. This is not a bad thing: unanimity in an enlarged Europe is a guarantee of blockages.

Very significantly, however, fiscal and social policies are not subject to a qualified majority, thus fiscal and social dumping will continue. The six-month revolving presidency of the EU would be replaced by a president of the European Council elected for two and a half years, with a mandate that can be renewed only once. The number of Commission members would be reduced to fifteen in 2009: a president elected by the European Parliament on the proposal of the Council, a foreign affairs minister (vice-president of the Council) nominated by the European Council, and thirteen commissioners chosen by strict rotation of the member states. The president of the European Council (with limited powers), together with the president of the Commission and the minister for foreign affairs, constitute a triumvirate that will be subject to rivalry and confusion. The rotation of the thirteen commissioners will mean, for example, that Malta will have the same 'representation' as Germany and that the latter will not have a commissioner with the right to vote for five years out of ten.

The Constitution, which was finally passed in June 2004, invites national parliaments to exercise control over their own governments, in other words the work of the Council of Ministers and of the European Council. The adoption of the constitutional treaty must thus be accompanied by new arrangements to ensure that the Parliament is not just a chamber for recording votes. But the proposed democratization is not enough. An accumulation of legislative and executive power still remains in the hands of the Council of Ministers. The Commission will retain the exclusive right to propose legislation. As for decisions on matters that are the exclusive competence of the EU (monetary, commercial and competition, etc.), this is not sufficiently safeguarded for the European Parliament (and the national parliaments). Greater co-operation between states can readily be hindered by member states that do not want to take part.

The project is also less than satisfactory on the powers of trade unions and other associations in the EU. Given the disproportionate means available to trade unions and associations on the one hand

and employers on the other, the supremacy of employer lobbying is maintained. And yet this is a fundamental issue in 'getting the Union closer to citizens', in terms of the general interests of Europe. Conversely, the churches figure prominently in the constitution. Lastly, there is no opening up of resident citizenship, relevant to at least twelve million 'extra-communitarian' immigrants in Europe: 'all those having the nationality of a member state possess citizenship of the Union'.

The 'coordination of economic and employment policies' maintains the present instruments of the euro zone: the European Central Bank (ECB), the general economic policy, the stability pact and growth. The operational methods (particularly independence) and the unique objective of the ECB (stability of prices) have been made constitutional. No authority can prohibit it; no majority can control it. Nothing is said about budgetary harmonization and coordination. Decisions on fiscal matters require the unanimity of the Council of Ministers. The EU budget ceiling, introduced by the Maastricht treaty, is maintained, depriving the Union of its main political dimension. The project in no way furthers 'social Europe', the poor relation of the European Union. The proposals that the European Trade Union Confederation made to the Convention for building a social Europe have yet to be followed up. Public services remain, as they are today, essentially 'subject to the laws of competition'.

This major institutional imbalance perpetuates harmful mechanisms – macro-economic coordination is limited and the competition between states is 'constitutionalized' – all of which reinforces social, fiscal and budgetary dumping and accentuates the impoverishment and dismantling of public services.

As far as foreign policy is concerned (following Maastricht), the constitutional project stipulates that 'The Union is a juridical person'; the European Council elects, in agreement with the president of the Commission, the foreign affairs minister of the Union; and the 'necessary European decisions' are made unanimously by the European Council and the Council of Ministers. As for the European Parliament, it is consulted and informed 'regularly'. Common security and defence comes into operation whenever the European Council 'so decides' (unanimously), respecting 'the obligations that result from the North Atlantic Treaty for some state members that consider their common defence is to be carried out in the framework of NATO'. The constitutional document cobbles together the wide divide between the French position according to which the security of the world must not rely only on the will of American power, and the British position, which is exactly the opposite.

The constitutional draft superimposes two concepts of Europe and, as Alain Lecourieux has emphasized, overlooks a third one. We can see in it 'the European space', which is the British idea, with the EU reduced to a free trade zone, associated with the USA. NATO is its only political dimension. We can also see the germs of 'powerful Europe', corresponding to the dominant discourse in France, or to the 'European model' of the German government (which is wary of the powerful Europe concept). The French/German couple align themselves on this ambiguous, twofold concept and they oscillate between the intergovernmental and community pressures that come respectively from France and Germany. It is difficult to see in the document any sign of plans for an 'emancipatory Europe', as it projects a Union identity characterized by the market and competitiveness. It does not promise any democratic recasting of the EU, nor does it sketch out Europe as a political entity.

THE MOBILIZATION OF SOCIAL MOVEMENTS IN EUROPE

As stated, we stand at a crossroads for the future of Europe, and one of the most important characteristics of the present time is the return, in a number of countries, of a high level of political and social mobilization. It has taken the form of social movements resisting neoliberal policies, with large strikes and demonstrations in France, Italy, Spain, Austria, Belgium, Germany, Greece, etc., and political struggle, with the powerful anti-war movement, particularly in the UK, Spain and Italy, whose governments supported American policy, and to a lesser extent in Denmark, Hungary and the Netherlands. The movement has also been strong in countries that have not aligned with Bush: France, Belgium, Greece, Turkey, etc., while in Germany the Red/Green coalition owed its electoral revival to its critical stance towards Washington. Finally, the global resistance movement expanded with the success of the anti-war demonstrations, anti-G8 mobilizations in Genoa (2001) and Annemasse-Geneva (2003), the European Social Forum in Florence (2002), the counter-European summits in Nice (2000), Gothenburg (2001) and Thessalonica (2003), the great gathering in Larzac, France, before the Cancún meeting (August 2003), the Social Forum of Paris/St Denis (November 2003) and many local forums, from Budapest to London.

The mobilization of social movements in Europe is not yet a really European mobilization but it can become one in future. It relates to cultural and historical differences between the movements in each country, but is also a question of perception of the European political framework itself. For many of the young demonstrators, attacking the European summits of Nice and Gothenburg is the same thing as attacking the assembly of the IMF in Prague or the G8 at Genoa or Evian. However, while the EU is an imperfect construction, it is based on an essentially democratic political process: it is an instrument to be taken over, not a fortress to be destroyed. The IMF and the WTO are international institutions with questionable mechanisms (for example, IMF's qualified suffrage), with doubtful positions (e.g. the neoliberal dogma of the WTO), and should be suppressed or reformed in the framework of a global system of world regulation (an effective United Nations). The G8 is an illegitimate institution that has no justification for existing. The experience of the movements against the former institutions of more than a decade has been one of increasing demands, and mobilization against such structures is one that fundamentally contests the way they work. The G8 should be dissolved. It is disconcerting that people mix up the three levels, as this works against a definition of all progressive policy for Europe, for the relevant level for applying such a policy is continental, even if it is not the only one.

If there is to be a specific European field that includes European institutions, primarily those of the EU, it is necessary to create an effective front at this level. Why is this so difficult to set up? The obstacles hindering the creation of such a front should be identified. In their approach to Europe the movements are heterogeneous, imbued with the peculiarities of their different political cultures and histories. For example, the various positions of neutrality of certain members of the Union – Ireland, Finland, Sweden and Austria – have different historical origins, while the uncommitted behaviour of part of the left in these countries is rooted deeply in their political culture. At the same time, such neutrality has not been relevant since the end of the Cold War and often gives the impression of powerlessness or hypocrisy (to what extent is Austria 'neutral' these days?). A dominant Europeanism, both in public opinion and in the political classes of the original six countries of the Union, conceals huge contradictions on how the future of Europe is conceived (e.g. among the Italian political parties). Historical 'Atlantism', to take one example, is natural not only for the English, but also for the

Dutch (and the Poles), who never raise fundamental questions (in spite of virulent criticisms of American imperialism), judging by the feebleness of their alternative proposals.

It is important then to analyze the current varieties of response towards the integration of the peripheral countries and the disenchantment with this integration by the countries at the centre of the Union. These dynamics are created by the above-mentioned peculiarities, but also by temporary political perceptions, or by the different forms of the European debate in each country at any given moment, for example the reservations of the French to all tendencies towards EU enlargement. With careful analysis we can more easily understand the mosaic of historical and cultural 'viewpoints' in Europe and the political divergences between movements that seem to share the same global objectives. The divergences must be made explicit, discussed and, if possible, overcome, while the historical and cultural 'viewpoints' will remain part of the picture for a long time to come. For example, the 'Globalize Resistance' position, a leading theme in the alternative world movement, is referred to by an English idiomatic expression (the UK Socialist Workers Party in the vanguard) that should be identified before debating the specifically political divergences – on the European project itself, on the nature of various alliances, on the differing forms of organization of the movements, on policy-making, and so on. To take a very different example, in the European Green Federation the systematic search for a consensus has hindered the identification of the real idiosyncrasies of each of the parties, and some of the differences that should structure the debate within the Federation.

In social and economic matters it is necessary to draw up a balance-sheet of the actions – both successes and failures – of the European Trade Union Confederation, of the 'Vilvorde' strikes or those of transport workers, taking into account the mobilization of productivist peasant unions and other lobbies (including road hauliers), and of others who could oppose them. But we should not overlook the support of the European marches against unemployment, the work of the European network to relieve extreme poverty and the occasional role of more radical campaigning organizations of the No-Vox type (such as the Right to Shelter and unemployed movements in France). The field of economic policy is increasingly being taken up by expert groups (like CELSIG on the public services, certain academics, within the European Economic and Social Council, etc.) and the development of

ATTAC groups is a sign of the growing tendency for themes pertaining to 'social Europe' to be adopted.

As for the struggles against discrimination and the resistance to xenophobic ideologies, while the official Migrant Forum of the European Union has predictably failed to meet people's aspirations, other forms of mobilization continue, including the UNITED network, for the rights of the Roma peoples, pressure for rights of citizenship through residence, 'without' campaigns, etc. In certain countries (e.g. Poland, Ireland) the support of women in the movements is crucial, although sex discrimination remains a problem all over Europe. Finally, the question of 'minorities', or more exactly the denial of certain cultural and political rights for peoples and communities in Europe, is acute in several countries (including, to some extent, France), in spite of some progress in this field in the Council of Europe and the European Parliament.

The recent anti-war mobilization, which has been impressive in most European countries, has not made great progress on questions of peace and security. If that is to happen, the European peace movements should not content themselves with criticizing the US but reflect on their own recent history, the very significant experiences, in certain countries, of mobilizations against wars of ethnic purification in ex-Yugoslavia, the struggle for a just and durable peace in the Near East and the difficulties in dealing with certain internal conflicts (Ireland, the Basque territories and, at an obviously less serious level, Corsica) or other countries (e.g. Algeria, Chechnya, West Africa).

The European dynamic on peace and security will not evolve on the basis of a recasting of NATO, even if this reassures public opinion in Central Europe. Nor will it develop from the St Malo process (i.e. the French/British agreement on European defence), particularly if the probable consequences of the Iraq crisis are taken into consideration. Will they develop on the basis of the proposals made in March 2003 by Guy Verhofstadt, the Belgian Prime Minister? These are interesting in that they propose a dynamic that does not appear to express the will of French, German or British hegemony over Europe.

Are we seeing a successive and gradual unification of forces developing in Europe, forming around themes and common actions? This is constructing Europe 'from below': carrying out resolute and creative action within European structures, but without, *a priori*, worrying about limits, while fixing clear objectives and working to bring together the separate elements of a platform for mobilization and proposals that should inspire – indeed subvert – the European processes 'from above' that are at present bogged down in paralysis and false intergovernmental pretences.

RENEWING EUROPEAN POLITICAL EXPERIENCE

How can the peoples of Europe respond to the challenge of our era, in an original political construction of their continent? By keeping the best of their democratic traditions and rejecting the worst of their imperialist heritage. Can they bring the internal social movements together in a European citizens' movement that will speak to the world? There are signs of this, as we have seen, through the alternative world movement, which is reinforcing itself at the continental level. Certain political hypotheses have been put forward: we have cited, among others Samir Amin. Etienne Balibar has suggested an original philosophical path, which seems to us relevant in this brief survey of the European situation and debate:

> Europe's experience of extermination has led the continent to see itself as the upholder of the principles of international law – which, however, it very often does not apply to itself. Its consciousness of the Other does not prevent it from systematically practising exclusion, combining the criteria of culture (not to say race) and economic discrimination. ... The invention of secularism in a context of a dominating Christianity ... has reinforced rejection of the great conflicting religious universalisms (above all, Islam), while protecting 'domestic' cults (the attitude towards Judaism is highly ambiguous, haunted as it is by the bad conscience of genocide, which has not eliminated all traces of antisemitism). It also acts (or enables interpretation) as a system of resistance to multiculturalism itself, that is, it paradoxically becomes the means of an identity discourse, if indeed it is not a quasi-religion of 'Western culture'. Finally, the 'European concept' of democracy as a system for the political expression of social conflicts becomes (once again?) pure and simple corporatism at the very moment when deregulation and the globalization of the economy deprives itself of the means for 'protecting' its nationals against the vagaries of the market in collective assets and the workforce.
>
> Nevertheless the European experience can be useful to the world as its obvious contradictions are part of the attempt to prolong and renew the European political experience as from now by situating it in a project of transforming international relationships which, while depending on its forces (economic, cultural and intellectual, social and institutional), some 'inside' and others 'outside' the European space, do not stem from power

politics. Such a project consists not so much in giving birth to a new power (or even a new 'superpower'), as in launching a new power regime over which no-one, even those that history has enabled to work the most effectively for their development, can be considered to have exclusive proprietary rights. Such power is essentially relational, manifesting itself through the evolution of structures and power relationships, or through the growing weight of resistance and alternatives to the dominant discourse.

Is it possible? Or does the current crisis sound the death knell of a certain conception of European political integration, leaving behind it only dispersed and weakened national policies? Such a regression, far from making it possible to establish new foundations for a counter-offensive, will only reinforce the hegemony of the US in the world and neoliberalism's anti-social course in Europe. This is not inevitable, all the more so as a consciousness of European responsibilities is strengthening in face of the headlong rampage of the American hawks into other countries after Iraq, which they openly threaten to carry out.

Part Two

The Dynamic of Convergence
for Another World

13

The World Social Forum: Towards a Counter-Hegemonic Globalization

Boaventura de Sousa Santos

The World Social Forum (WSF) is a new social and political phenomenon. The fact that it does have antecedents does not diminish its newness: quite the opposite. The WSF is not an event. Nor is it a mere succession of events, although it does try to dramatize the formal meetings it promotes. It is not a scholarly conference, although the contributions of many scholars converge in it. It is not a party or an international of parties, although militants and activists of many parties all over the world take part in it. It is not a non-governmental organization or a confederation of NGOs, even though its conception and organization owes a great deal to NGOs. It is not a social movement, even though it often designates itself as the movement of movements. Although it presents itself as an agent of social change, the WSF rejects the concept of an historical subject and confers no priority on any specific social actor in this process of social change. It holds no clearly defined ideology, either in defining what it rejects or what it asserts.

Given that the WSF conceives of itself as a struggle against neoliberal globalization, is it a struggle against a form of capitalism or against capitalism in general? Given that it sees itself as a struggle against discrimination, exclusion and oppression, does the success of its struggle presuppose a postcapitalist, socialist, anarchist horizon, or, on the contrary, does it presuppose that no context be clearly defined at all? Given that the vast majority of people taking part in the WSF identify themselves as favouring politics of the left, how many definitions of 'the left' fit the WSF? And what about those who refuse to be defined because they believe that the left–right dichotomy is a Northcentric or Westcentric particularism, and look for alternative political definitions?

The social struggles that find expression in the WSF do not adequately fit either of the ways of social change sanctioned by Western modernity: reform and revolution. Aside from the consensus on non-violence, its modes of struggle are extremely diverse and appear spread out in a continuum between the poles of institutionality and insurgency. Even the concept of non-violence is open to widely disparate interpretations. Finally, the WSF is not structured according to any of the models of modern political organization, be they democratic centralism, representative democracy or participatory democracy. Nobody represents it or is allowed to speak in its name, let alone make decisions, even though it sees itself as a forum that facilitates the decisions of the movements and organizations that take part in it.

These features are arguably not new, as they are associated with what are conventionally called 'new social movements'. The truth is, however, that these movements, be they local, national or global, are thematic. Themes, while fields of concrete political confrontation, compel definition – hence polarization – whether regarding strategies or tactics, whether regarding organizational forms or forms of struggle. Themes work, therefore, both as attraction and repulsion. Now, what is new about the WSF is the fact that it is inclusive, both as concerns its scale and its thematics. What is new is the whole it constitutes, not its constitutive parts. The WSF is global in its harbouring of local, national and global movements, and in being inter-thematic and even trans-thematic. That is to say, since the conventional factors of attraction and repulsion do not work as far as the WSF is concerned, either it develops other strong factors of attraction and repulsion or does without them, and may even derive its strength from their non-existence. In other words, the 'movement of movements' is not one more movement. It is a different movement.

The problem with new social movements is that in order to do them justice a new social theory and new analytical concepts are called for. Since neither a theory nor analytical concepts emerge easily from the inertia of the disciplines, the risk that they may be under-theorized and undervalued is considerable. This risk is all the more serious as the WSF, given its scope and internal diversity, not only challenges the various disciplines of the conventional social sciences, but also scientific knowledge as sole producer of social and political rationality. To put it another way, the WSF raises not only analytical and theoretical questions, but also epistemological questions. This much is expressed in the idea, widely shared by WSF participants, that there will be no global social justice without acceptance of global justice as a concept. But the challenge posed by the WSF has one more dimension still. Beyond the theoretical, analytical and epistemological questions, it raises a new political issue: it aims to fulfil utopia in a world devoid of utopias. This utopian will is expressed in the following way: 'another world is possible'. At stake is less a utopian world than a world that allows for utopia. In this chapter, I deal with the WSF as critical utopia, epistemology of the South and cosmopolitan politics.

THE WORLD SOCIAL FORUM AS CRITICAL UTOPIA

Ernst Bloch says that 'utopias have their timetable'. The conceptions of and aspirations to a better life and society, ever present in human history, vary in form and content according to time and space. They express the tendencies and latencies of a given time and a given society. They constitute an anticipatory consciousness. It is therefore appropriate to ask: does the WSF have a utopian dimension? And, if so, what is its timetable?

The WSF is the set of initiatives of transnational exchange among social movements, NGOs and their practices and knowledge of local, national or global social struggles against the forms of exclusion and inclusion, discrimination and equality, universalism and particularism, cultural imposition and relativism, brought about or made possible by the current phase of capitalism known as neoliberal globalization.

The utopian dimension of the WSF consists in claiming the existence of alternatives to neoliberal globalization. As Franz Hinkelammert says, we live in a time of conservative utopias whose utopian character resides in its radical denial of alternatives to present-day reality. The possibility of alternatives is discredited precisely for being utopian, idealistic, unrealistic. Looking at the last one hundred years, Hinkelammert distinguishes three conservative utopias: Stalinism, Nazism and neoliberalism (combined with neoconservatism and Christian fundamentalism). All of them are sustained by a political logic based on one sole efficiency criterion that rapidly becomes a supreme ethical criterion. According to this criterion, only what is efficient has value. Any other ethical criterion is devalued as inefficient.

Under Stalinism, the one efficiency criterion was the plan, or planned economy. Under Nazism, the criterion was racial superiority. Under neoliberalism, the criterion is the market, or the laws of the market. In the last case, the total market becomes a perfect institution. Its utopian character resides in the promise that its total fulfilment or application cancels out all utopias. As Hinkelammert says, 'this ideology derives from its frantic anti-utopianism, the utopian promise of a new world. The basic thesis is: whoever destroys utopia, fulfils it.' What characterizes conservative utopias and distinguishes them from critical utopias is that they identify themselves with the present-day reality and discover their utopian dimension in the radicalization or complete fulfilment of the present. The problems or difficulties of present-day reality are not the consequence of the deficiencies or limits of the efficiency criteria, but result rather from the fact that the application of the efficiency criteria has not been thorough enough. If there is unemployment and social exclusion, if there is starvation and death in the periphery of the world system, that is not the consequence of the deficiencies or limits of the laws of the market; it results rather from the fact that such laws have not yet been fully applied. The horizon of conservative utopias is thus a closed horizon, an end to history.

This is the context in which the utopian dimension of the WSF must be understood. The WSF signifies the re-emergence of a critical utopia, that is, the radical critique of present-day reality and the aspiration to a better society. This occurs, however, when the anti-utopian utopia of neoliberalism is dominant. The specificity of the utopian content of this new critical utopia, when compared with that of the critical utopias prevailing at the end of the nineteenth and beginning of the twentieth century, thus becomes clear. The anti-utopian utopia of neoliberalism is grounded on two presuppositions: the illusion of total control over present-day reality by means of extremely efficient powers and knowledge; and the radical rejection of alternatives to the status quo. The WSF calls into question the totality of control (whether as knowledge or power) only to affirm credibly the possibility of alternatives. Hence the open nature (vague if you will) of alternatives. In a context in which the conservative utopia prevails absolutely, it is better to affirm the possibility of alternatives than to define them. The utopian dimension of the WSF consists in affirming the possibility of a counter-hegemonic globalization.

In other words, the utopia of the WSF asserts itself more as negativity (the definition of what it critiques) than as positivity (the definition of that to which it aspires). The specificity of the WSF as critical utopia has one more explanation. The WSF is the first critical utopia of the twenty-first century and aims to break with the tradition of the critical utopias of Western modernity, many of which turned into conservative utopias: from claiming utopian alternatives to denying alternatives under the excuse that the fulfilment of utopia was under way. The openness of the utopian dimension of the WSF is its attempt to escape this perversion. For the WSF, the claim of alternatives is plural, both as to the form of the claim and the content of the alternatives. The affirmation of alternatives goes hand in hand with the affirmation that there are alternatives to the alternatives. The other possible world is a utopian aspiration that comprises several possible worlds. The other possible world may be many things, but never a world with no alternative.

The utopia of the WSF is a radically democratic utopia. It is the only realistic utopia after a century of conservative utopias, some of them the result of perverted critical utopias. This utopian design, grounded on the denial of the present rather than the definition of the future, focused on the processes of intercourse among the movements rather than an assessment of the movements' political content, is the major factor of cohesion of the WSF. It helps to maximize what unites and minimize what divides, to celebrate interaction rather than dispute power, to be a strong presence rather than an agenda. This utopian design, which is also an ethical design, privileges the ethical discourse, quite clear in the WSF's Charter of Principles, aimed at gathering consensus beyond the ideological and political cleavages between the movements and organizations that compose it. The movements and organizations put between brackets the cleavages that divide them, as much as is necessary to affirm the possibility of a counter-hegemonic globalization.

The nature of this utopia has been the most appropriate for the initial objective of the WSF: to affirm the existence of a counter-hegemonic globalization. This is no vague utopia. It is rather a utopia that contains in itself the concretization appropriate for this phase of the construction of counter-hegemonic globalization. It remains to be seen if the nature of this utopia is the most appropriate one to guide the next steps, should there be any next steps. Once the counter-hegemonic globalization is consolidated, and hence the idea that another world is possible is made credible, will it be possible to fulfil this idea with the same level of radical democracy that helped formulate it? I shall come back to this.

THE ISSUE OF STRATEGY AND POLITICAL ACTION

The WSF is characterized, as already said, by its claim to the existence of an alternative to the anti-utopian, one-and-only-way of thinking of neoliberalism's conservative utopia. It is a radically democratic utopia that celebrates diversity, plurality, and horizontality. It celebrates another possible world, itself plural in its possibilities. The newness of this utopia in left thinking – which is eloquently formulated by the Zapatistas – cannot but be problematical as it translates itself into strategic planning and political action. These are marked by the historical trajectory of the political left throughout the twentieth century. The translation of utopia into politics is not, in this case, merely the translation of long range into medium and short range. It is also the translation of the new into the old. The tensions and divisions thus brought about are no less real for that reason. What happens is that the reality of the divergences about concrete political options gets mixed up with divergences about codes and languages of political option. Moreover, it is not always possible to determine if the reality of the divergences lies in real divergences.

It should be stressed, however, that the novelty of the utopia managed to overcome the political divergences. Contrary to what happened in the thinking and practice of the left in Western capitalist modernity, the WSF managed to create a style and an atmosphere of inclusion of and respect for divergences that made it very difficult for the different political factions to exclude themselves at the start under the excuse that they were being excluded. For this contributed decisively to the WSF's 'minimalist' programme in its Charter of Principles: emphatic assertion of respect for diversity; access with few conditions (movements or groups that advocate political violence are excluded); no voting or deliberations at the Forum as such; no representative entity to speak for the Forum. It is almost like a *tabula rasa* where all forms of struggle against neoliberalism and for a juster society may have their place. Facing such openness, those who choose to exclude themselves find it difficult to define what exactly they are excluding themselves from.

All this has contributed to making the WSF's power of attraction greater than its capacity to repel. Even the movements that are most severely critical of the WSF, such as the anarchists, have not been absent. There is definitely something new in the air, something that is chaotic, messy, ambiguous, and indefinite enough to deserve the benefit of the doubt or be susceptible to manipulation. Few would want to miss this train, particularly at a time in history when trains had ceased to travel. For all these reasons, the desire to highlight what the movements and organizations have in common has prevailed over the desire to underscore what separates them. The manifestation of tensions or cleavages has been relatively tenuous and, above all, has not resulted in mutual exclusions. It remains to be seen for how long this will to convergence and this chaotic sharing of differences will last.

Neither the kinds of cleavages nor the way the movements relate to them are randomly distributed inside the WSF. On the contrary, they reflect a meta-cleavage between Western and non-Western political cultures. Up to a point, this meta-cleavage also exists between the North and the South. Thus, given the strong presence of movements and organizations of the North Atlantic and white Latin America, it is no wonder that the most salient cleavages reflect the political culture and historical trajectory of the left in this part of the world. This means, on the one hand, that many movements and organizations from Africa, Asia, the indigenous and black Americas, and the Europe of immigrants do not recognize themselves in these cleavages; on the other, that alternative cleavages that these movements and organizations might want to make explicit are perhaps being concealed or minimized by the prevailing ones. After this caveat, let us identify the main manifest cleavages.

Reform or revolution

This cleavage carries the weight of the tradition of the Western left. It is the cleavage between those who think that another world is possible by the gradual transformation of the unjust world in which we live, through legal reform and mechanisms of representative democracy; and those who think that the world we live in is basically a capitalist world, that this world will never tolerate reforms that will put it in question, and that it must therefore be overthrown and replaced by a socialist world. This is also regarded as a cleavage between moderates and radicals. Either field comprises a wide variety of positions. For instance, among revolutionaries, there is a clear cleavage between the old left, which aspires to a kind of State socialism, the anarchists, who are radically anti-statist, and some newer left, rather ambivalent about the role of the State in a socialist society. Although they amount to a very minor proportion of the WSF, the anarchists are among the fiercest critics of reformism, which they claim controls the WSF's leadership.

The cleavage reverberates, albeit not linearly, in strategic options and options for political action. Among the most salient ones should be counted the strategic option between reforming the institutions of neoliberal globalization (WTO and the international financial institutions) or fighting to eliminate and replace them; and the option for political action between, on the one hand, constructive dialogue and engagement with those institutions, and, on the other, confrontation with them. It translates itself into opposite positions, either as regards the diagnosis of contemporary societies, or the evaluation of the WSF itself. As to the diagnosis, contemporary societies are at times viewed as societies where there are multiple discriminations and injustices, not all of them attributable to capitalism. Capitalism, in turn, is not homogeneous, and the struggle must focus on its most exclusionary form – neoliberalism. Contemporary societies are viewed as intrinsically unjust and discriminatory because they are capitalist. Capitalism is an enveloping system in which class discrimination feeds on sexual, racial and other kinds of discrimination. Hence, the struggle must focus on capitalism as a whole rather than against one or more of its manifestations.

As to the evaluation of the WSF, it is sometimes viewed as the embryo of an effective movement against neoliberal globalization, for confronting it at the global scale of maximum social injustice, although it is sometimes seen as a movement which, because it is not grounded on the principle of the class struggle, will accomplish little beyond a few rhetorical changes in dominant capitalist discourse.

What is new about the WSF as a political entity is that the majority of the movements and organizations that participate in it do not recognize themselves in these cleavages and refuse to take part in them. There is great resistance to assuming a given position rigidly and even greater resistance to labelling it. The majority of movements and organizations have political experiences in which moments of confrontation alternate or combine with moments of dialogue and engagement, in which long-range visions of social change cohabit with the tactical possibilities of the political and social moment in which the struggles take place, in which radical denunciations of capitalism do not paralyze the energy for small changes when big changes are not possible. Above all, for many movements and organizations, this cleavage is Westcentric or Northcentric, and is more useful in understanding the past of the left than its future. Indeed, many movements and organizations do not recognize themselves, for the same reasons, in the dichotomy left and right.

Precisely because, for many movements and organizations, the priority is not to seize power but rather change power relations in the many faces of oppression, the political tasks, however radical, must be carried out here and now, in the society in which we live. It makes no sense, therefore, to ask *a priori* if their success is incompatible with capitalism. Gramsci's concept of hegemony is useful to understand the movements' political actions. What is necessary is to create alternative, counter-hegemonic visions, capable of sustaining the daily practices and sociabilities of citizens and social groups. The work of the movements' leaderships is of course important, but in no way is it conceived of as the work of an enlightened avant-garde that paves the way for the masses, always the victims of mystification and false consciousness. On the contrary, as subcomandante Marcos recommends, it is incumbent on the leadership to 'walk with those who go more slowly'. It is not a question of either revolution or reform. It is, for some, a question of rebellion and construction, for others, a question of revolution in a non-Leninist sense, of civilizational change occurring over a long period of time.

Socialism or social emancipation

This cleavage is related to the previous one but there is no perfect overlap between the two. Regardless of the position taken vis-à-vis the previous cleavage, or the refusal to take a position, the movements and organizations diverge as to the political definition of the other possible world. For some, socialism is still an adequate designation, however abundant and disparate the conceptions of socialism may be. For the majority, however, socialism carries in itself the idea of a closed model of a future society, and must, therefore, be rejected. They prefer other, less politically charged designations, suggesting openness and constant search for alternatives. For example, social emancipation as the aspiration to a society in which different power relations are replaced by relations of shared authority. This is an inclusive designation focusing more on processes than on final stages of social change.

But many movements of the South think that no general labels need be attached to the goals of the struggles. Labels run the risk of acquiring a life of their own, and giving rise to perverse results. As a matter of fact, according to some, the concept of socialism is Westcentric and Northcentric, while the concept of emancipation is equally prey of the Western bias to create false universalisms. Hence many do not recognize themselves in either term of this dichotomy, and do not even bother to propose any alternative.

The State as enemy or potential ally

This is also a cleavage in which movements of the North recognize themselves more easily than movements of the South. On the one hand, there are those who think that the State, although in the past it may well have been an important arena of struggle, for the past twenty-five years has been transnationalized and turned into an agent of neoliberal globalization. Either the State has become irrelevant or is today what it has always been – the expression of capitalism's general interests. The privileged target of counter-hegemonic struggles must, therefore, be the State, or at least they must be fought with total autonomy vis-à-vis the State. On the other hand, there are those who think that the State is a social relation and, as such, is contradictory and continues to be an important arena of struggle. Neoliberal globalization did not rob the State of its centrality, it rather reoriented it better to serve the interests of global capital. Deregulation is a social regulation like any other, hence a political field where one must act if there are conditions for acting.

The majority of the movements, even those that acknowledge the existence of a cleavage in this regard, refuse to take a rigid and principled position. Their experiences of struggle show that the State, while sometimes the enemy, can often be a precious ally in the struggle against transnational impositions. In these circumstances, the best attitude, again, is pragmatism. If in some situations confrontation is in order, in others collaboration is rather advised. In others still a combination of both is appropriate. The important thing is that, at every moment or in every struggle, the movement or organization in question must be clear and transparent regarding the reasons for the adopted option, so as to safeguard the autonomy of the action. Autonomy, in such cases, is always problematical, and so it must be watched carefully. According to the radical autonomists, collaboration with the State will always end up compromising the organizations' autonomy. They fear that collaborationists, whether the State or the institutions of neoliberal globalization are involved, end up being co-opted. An alliance between the reformist wing of counter-hegemonic globalization and the reformist wing of hegemonic globalization will thereby ensue, ending up by compromising the goals of the WSF.

National or global struggles

This is the most evenly distributed cleavage among all the movements and organizations that comprise the WSF. On one side, there are the movements that, while participating in the WSF, believe that the latter is no more than a meeting place and a cultural event, since the real struggles that are truly important for the welfare of the populations are fought at the national level against the State or the dominant national civil society. For instance, in a report on the WSF prepared by the Movement for National Democracy in the Philippines, one can read:

> The World Social Forum still floats somewhere above, seeing and trying yet really unable to address actual conditions of poverty and powerlessness brought about by Imperialist globalization in many countries. Unless it finds definite ways of translating or even transcending its 'globalness' into more practical interventions that address these conditions, it just might remain a huge but empty forum that is more a cultural affair than anything else ... national struggles against globalization are and should provide the anchor to any anti-globalization initiative at the international level.

In other words, globalization is most effectively fought against at the national level. On the other side, there are the movements according to whom the State is now transnationalized and thus is no longer the privileged centre of political decision. This decentring of the State has also brought about the decentring of civil society, which is subjected today to many processes of cultural and social globalization. Furthermore, in some situations, the object of the struggle (whether a decision of the WTO or the World Bank, or oil drilling by an multinational corporation) is outside the national space and includes a plurality of countries simultaneously. This is why the scale of the struggle must be increasingly global, a fact from which the WSF draws its relevance.

According to most of the movements, this is again a cleavage that does not do justice to the specific needs of specific struggles. What is new about contemporary societies is that the levels of sociability are increasingly interconnected at local, national and global scales. In the most remote village of the Amazon or India the effects of hegemonic globalization and the ways in which the national state engages with it are clearly felt. If this is the case with levels of sociability, it is the same with the levels of counter-hegemonic struggles. It is obvious that each political practice or social struggle is organized in accordance with a privileged scale, be it local, national or global, but whatever the scale, all the others must be involved as a condition of success. The decision on which scale to privilege is a political decision that must be taken in accordance with specific political conditions. It is therefore not possible to opt in the abstract for any one hierarchy among levels of counter-hegemonic practice or struggle.

Direct or institutional action

This cleavage is clearly linked to the first and third cleavages. It specifically concerns the modes of struggle that should be adopted, preferably or even exclusively. It is a cleavage with a long tradition in the Western left. Those for whom this cleavage continues to have a great deal of importance are the same who slight the newness of neoliberal globalization in the historical process of capitalist domination.

On the one side, there are the movements that believe that legal struggles, based on dialogue and engagement with State institutions or international agencies, are ineffectual because the political and legal system of the State and the institutions of capitalism are impervious to any legal or institutional measures capable of really improving the living conditions of the popular classes. Institutional struggles call for the intermediation of parties, and parties tend to put these struggles at the service of their party interests and constituencies. The success of an institutional struggle, therefore, has a very high price, the price of co-optation, de-characterization and banalization. But even in the rare cases in which an institutional struggle leads to legal and institutional measures that correspond to the movements' objectives, it is almost certain that the concrete application of such measures will end up being subjected to the legal–bureaucratic logic of the State, thereby frustrating the movements' expectations. In the end there will be only a hollow hope. This is why only direct action, mass protest and strikes will yield success in the struggles. The popular classes have no weapon but external pressure on the system. If they venture into it, they are defeated from the start.

On the contrary, the supporters of institutional struggles assume that the 'system' is contradictory, a political and social relation where it is possible to fight and where failure is not the only possible outcome. In modernity the State was the centre of this system. In the course of the twentieth century the popular classes conquered important institutional spaces, of which the welfare system is a good example. The fact that the welfare system is now in crisis and the 'opening' that it offered the popular classes is now being closed up, does not mean that the process is irreversible. Indeed, it will not happen if the movements and organizations continue to struggle inside the institutions and the legal system.

This cleavage is not spread out at random among the movements that comprise the WSF. In general the stronger movements and organizations are those that more frequently privilege institutional struggles, whereas the less strong are those that more frequently privilege direct action. This cleavage is much more lively among movements and organizations of the North than of the South. The large majority of the movements, however, refuse to take sides in this cleavage. According to them, the specific legal and political conditions must dictate the kind of struggle to be chosen. Conditions may actually recommend the sequential or simultaneous use of the two kinds of struggle. Historically, direct action was at the genesis of progressive legal–institutional changes, and it was always necessary to combat the co-optation or even subversion of such changes through direct action.

The principle of equality or the principle of respect for difference

As already said, one of the novelties of the WSF is the fact that the large majority of its movements and organizations believe that, although we live in grossly unequal societies, equality is not enough as a guiding principle of social emancipation. Social emancipation must be grounded on two principles – the principle of equality and the principle of respect for difference. The struggle for either of them must be articulated with the other, for the fulfilment of either is a condition of the fulfilment of the other. Nonetheless, there is a cleavage among the movements and even, sometimes, inside the same movement on whether priority should be given to one of these principles, and in that case to which one. Among those who say yes to the first question, the cleavage is between those who give priority to the principle of equality – for equality alone may create real opportunities for the recognition of difference – and those who give priority to the principle of the recognition of difference, for without such recognition equality conceals the exclusions and marginalizations on which it is based, thus becoming doubly oppressive, both for what it conceals and for what it reveals.

This cleavage occurs among movements and within movements. It traverses, among others, workers', feminist, indigenous and black movements. For instance, whereas the workers' movement has privileged the principle of equality to the detriment of that of the recognition of difference, the feminist movement has privileged the latter to the detriment of the former. But the most widely shared position is indeed that both principles have joint priority, and that it is not correct to prioritize either one in the abstract. Specific political conditions will dictate which of the principles is to be privileged in a given struggle. Any struggle conceived under the aegis of one of these two principles must be organized so as to open space for the other.

In the feminist movement of the WSF, this position is now dominant. Virgínia Vargas expresses it well when she says:

> At the World Social Forum, feminists have begun ... nourishing processes that integrate gender justice with economic justice, while recovering cultural subversion and subjectivity as a longer-term strategy for transformation. This confronts two broad expressions of injustice: socio-economic injustice, rooted in societal political and economic structures, and cultural and symbolic injustice, rooted in societal patterns of representation, interpretation and communication. Both injustices affect women, along with many other racial, ethnic, sexual and geographical dimensions.

Agreeing with Sonia Alvarez, she asks for new feminisms – feminisms of these times – as a discursive, expansive, heterogeneous panorama, generating polycentric fields of action that spread over a range of civil society organizations and are not confined to women's affairs, although women undoubtedly maintain them in many ways. And she concludes: 'Our presence in the WSF, asking these very questions, is also an expression of this change.'

Many of the tensions and cleavages mentioned above are not specific to the WSF. They in fact belong to the historical legacy of the social forces that for the past century and a half have struggled for a better society against the status quo. The specificity of the WSF resides in the fact that all these cleavages coexist within it without upsetting its aggregating power.

To my mind, several factors contribute to this. First, the different cleavages are important in different ways for the different movements and organizations, and none is present in the practices or discourses of all the movements and organizations. Thus, all of them, while they tend towards factionalism, create potential for consensus. That is, all the movements and organizations have room for action and discourse in which to agree with all the other movements or organizations, whatever the cleavages among them. Second, there has so far been no tactical or strategic demand that would intensify the cleavages by radicalizing positions. On the contrary, cleavages have been of fairly low intensity. For the movements and organizations in general, what unites has been more important than what divides. In any reckoning of union versus separation, the advantages of union have overcome the advantages of separation. Third, even when cleavages are acknowledged, the different movements and organizations distribute themselves among them in a non-linear way. If a given movement opposes another in one cleavage, it may well be on the same side in another cleavage. Thus, the different strategic alliances or common actions featured by each movement tend to have different partners. In this way are precluded the accumulation and strengthening of divergences that could result from the alignment of the movements in multiple cleavages. On the contrary, the cleavages end up neutralizing or disempowering one another. Herein lies the WSF's aggregating power.

THE FUTURE OF THE WORLD SOCIAL FORUM: SELF-DEMOCRACY AND THE THEORY OF TRANSLATION

In the WSF the new and the old face each other. As utopia and epistemology, the WSF is something new. As a political phenomenon, its novelty coexists with the traditions of thought on the left or, more generally, counter-hegemonic thought, in its Western, Southern and Eastern versions. The newness of the WSF is attributed to its absence of leaders and hierarchical organization, its emphasis on cyberspace networks, its ideal of participatory democracy, and its flexibility and readiness to engage in experimentation.

The WSF is unquestionably the first large international progressive movement after the neoliberal backlash at the beginning of the 1980s. Its future is the future of hope in an alternative to *la pensée unique* (one-and-only-way-of-thinking). This future is completely unknown, and can only be speculated about. It depends both on the movements and organizations that comprise the WSF and the metamorphoses of neoliberal globalization. For instance, the fact that the latter has been acquiring a bellicose fixation on security will no doubt affect the evolution of the WSF. In light of this, the future of the WSF depends in part on the evaluation of its trajectory up till now and the conclusions drawn from it, with a view to enlarging and deepening its counter-hegemonic effectiveness.

The evaluation of the WSF is one of the exercises that best reveals the confrontation between the new and the old. From the point of view of the old, the WSF cannot but be assessed negatively. It appears as a vast 'talk-show' that hovers over the concrete problems of exclusion and discrimination without tackling them; a cultural movement without deep social roots, therefore tolerated and easily co-opted by the dominant classes; it has no definite agents or agency, because, after all, it has no definite enemies either; its inclusiveness is the other side of its ineffectiveness, which, besides having an effect on the rhetoric of hegemonic discourse, has been minimal, since it has achieved no changes as far as concrete policies go, or contributed to ameliorating the ills of exclusion and discrimination.

In this evaluation, the WSF is assessed according to criteria that prevailed in progressive struggles up until the 1980s. Such criteria do not concern strategies and tactics alone; they also concern the time frames and geopolitical units that are the reference of their applicability. The time frame is linear time, a time that gives meaning and direction to history; the temporality or duration is that of the State's action, even if the action aims to reform or revolutionize the State. The geopolitical unit is the national society, the boundary within which the most decisive progressive struggles of the last century and a half have occurred. Let's speak in this case of positivist epistemology.

It seems obvious that the positivist epistemology underlying this evaluation is completely different from the one I have ascribed to the WSF. In order to be minimally adequate, the evaluation of the WSF must be carried out according to the epistemology of the WSF itself. Otherwise, the assessment will always be negative. In other words, the evaluation must be carried out on the basis of the sociology of absences and sociology of emergences. In this case, the geopolitical unit is trans-scale: it combines the local, the national and the global. Its time is not linear. From the standpoint of linear time, many of the counter-hegemonic experiences will always be absent or impossible. The temporalities of these experiences are indeed multiple, from the instant time of mass protests to the glacial time of utopia.

In this light, the evaluation of the WSF cannot but be positive. By affirming and rendering credible the existence of a counter-hegemonic globalization, the WSF has contributed significantly towards enlarging social experience. It has turned absent struggles and practices into present struggles and practices, and shown which alternative futures, declared impossible by hegemonic globalization, were after all giving signs of their emergence. By enlarging the available and possible social experience, the WSF created a global consciousness for the different movements and NGOs, regardless of the scope of their action. Such a global consciousness was crucial to create a certain symmetry of scale between hegemonic globalization and the movements and NGOs that fought against it. Before the WSF, the movements and NGOs fought against hegemonic globalization without being aware of their own globality.

The decisive importance of this consciousness explains why the WSF, once aware of it, does everything to preserve it. It explains, ultimately, why the factors of attraction and aggregation prevail over those of repulsion and disaggregation. This consciousness of globality was decisive to make credible, among the movements and the NGOs themselves, the trans-scale nature of the geopolitical unit wherein they acted. By encompassing all those movements and NGOs, however, the WSF incorporated that same trans-scale nature, and that is why its efficacy cannot be assessed exclusively in terms of global changes. It has to be assessed as well in terms of local and national changes. Given the levels involved, the evaluation of the WSF's efficacy is undoubtedly more complex, but for that same reason it does not allow for rash assessments derived from positivist epistemology.

The WSF is today a more realistic utopia than when it first appeared. Increased realism, however, poses considerable challenges to utopia itself. The challenges consist in deepening its political existence without losing its utopian and epistemological integrity. I identify two main challenges, one short range, the other long range.

Self-democracy

The first, short-range challenge I designate as self-democracy. The WSF's utopia concerns emancipatory democracy, which in its broadest sense is the whole process of changing power relations into relations of shared authority. Since the power relations against which the WSF resists are multiple, the processes of radical democratization in which the WSF is involved are likewise multiple. In brief, the WSF is a large collective process for deepening democracy. Since this is the WSF's utopian distinction, it is no wonder that the issue of internal democracy has become more and more pressing. In fact, the WSF's credibility in its struggle for democracy in society depends on the credibility of its internal democracy.

The WSF's initial phase corresponds, as I said, to the three main forums held in Porto Alegre, together with all the others – local, national, regional and thematic – also held under the aegis of the WSF. It was a phase of beginnings and consolidation. The organizing structure, in the case of the WSF, was based on the IC (International Council) and the OC (Organizing Committee). In the case of the others, it depended on ad hoc committees constituted through 'contact groups' connected with movements and NGOs that in general had taken part in one of the editions of the WSF. For this phase, the organizing structures were, to my mind, the most appropriate. Admittedly, the criteria of representation and participation could have been better tuned to the diversity of the movements and NGOs. But it should be stressed that the successive forums of the WSF tried to respond to the criticisms advanced. If the response was not always satisfactory, I believe the reason has more to do with administrative incapacity than politically motivated design.

The challenge consists in changing the organizing structure according to the demands of the new phase, with a view to deepening its internal democracy. Two paths to reach this goal may be identified. One consists in transferring the WSF's core from the global event to the national, regional and thematic forums. The point here is that at these more circumscribed levels the issues of representation and participatory democracy are easier to solve. The WSF, as a global event, will continue to affirm the globality of counter-hegemonic globalization, but it will lose some of its centrality. The OC will continue to have a decisive role, but a role that will tend to be increasingly more executive, while the IC will continue to be charged with defining the broad thematic options and the organizing structure. The democratizing effort must therefore focus on the IC, urging it to go on reflecting the multiple diversities that congregate in the WSF. This path, which seems to be close to what some members of the IC have been proposing, assumes its continuity with the previous phase. The aim is not to take decisions that might put at risk the extraordinary successes achieved so far.

This path does not claim to solve the issue of participatory democracy. However representative and democratic the leading and organizing structures of the forums may be, the issue of the participation of the rank and file will be always there, whether participation concerns the debates or decisions taken in a given forum about future forums. Communication technologies offer today new possibilities for voting and carrying out referendums during the forums. If it is true in general that cyberdemocracy has an individualistic bias in reducing the citizen's political capacity to handling the terminal, it is no less true that such a bias is neutralized by the meetings of the forum, where intercommunication – the exchange of experiences and points of view – is so intense, precisely among the rank and file.

The second, far more structured path aims to increase the WSF's internal democracy from the bottom up. On the basis of the smaller forums, such as local or city forums, representative structures are created at the different levels in such a way that the structures at the higher levels are elected by the immediately lower levels. The result envisaged is a pyramidal organization having at the apex the WSF turned into a forum of delegates. A recent and full version of this path has been proposed by Michael Albert, of Znet. According to the proposal's author himself, it has some thoughts that 'may have some merit', 'but whether they do or not', he adds, 'certainly changes must be made'. Here are the main points of Albert's proposal:

1. Emphasize local forums as the foundation of the worldwide forum process.
2. Build each new level of forum, from towns, to cities, to countries, to continents, to the world, on those below.
3. Determine locally the decision-making leadership of the most local events.
4. Select the decision-making leadership at each higher level, as far as possible, through the local forums that are within the higher entity. Italy's national forum leadership, for example, is chosen by the smaller local forums in Italy. The European forums' leadership is chosen by the national forums within Europe, and similarly elsewhere.
5. Mandate that the decision-making leadership at every level should consist of at least 50 per cent women.
6. Charge delegates and organizations and attendees from wealthier parts of the world a tax on their fees to help finance the forums in poorer parts and subsidize delegate attendance at the world forum from poorer locales.
7. Delegate 5,000 to 10,000 people to the WSF from the major regional forums around the world. Select the WSF leadership through regional forums. Mandate the WSF to discuss proposals from around the world – not to listen again to the same famous speakers whom everyone hears worldwide all the time anyhow – and openly publish WSF discussions, as well as having delegates report back to their regions.
8. Ensure that the WSF as a whole and the forums worldwide avoid the mistake of trying to become an international, a movement of movements, or even just a voice of the world's movements. To be a forum, the WSF and the smaller component forums need to be as broad and diverse as possible. But being too broad and too diverse means the WSF simply cannot function.

9. Mandate that the forums at every level, including the WSF,
   welcome people from diverse constituencies using the forums
   and their processes to make contacts and develop ties that can
   in turn yield national, regional or even international networks or
   movements of movements that share their political aspirations
   sufficiently to work closely together, but which exist alongside
   rather than instead of the forum phenomenon.

The above proposal, besides recommending the pyramidal
construction of the WSF's democracy, includes measures that aim
to correct structural deficiencies of representation, derived for
example, from gender and North/South inequality and difference.
This proposal poses a radical break with the organizational model
adopted until now. Although there is a widespread feeling that the
present model is exhausted, one suspects that such a radical break
may stir up the fear that one might be throwing the baby out with
the bath water. It is, however, as Michael Albert himself asserts, a
proposal to be discussed.

Needless to say, any proposal, especially one so radical, must be
debated and ultimately voted. But by whom? By the current IC,
certainly not representative of the whole WSF, let alone democratically
elected by its members? By the participants of the forums? Which
forums? These questions show that there is no machinery of democratic
engineering capable of solving the problem of internal democracy at
a single blow. To my mind, such a problem will end up being taken
care of through successive partial solutions. Its cumulative effect will
be the result of a learning process that, at each level, consolidates its
force and gathers energy to venture to a higher level.

The theory of translation

The second challenge is long range. The challenge of internal
democracy concerns the processes of decision-making, rather than
the content of the decisions, let alone the practices of struggle that
may evolve. In the long run, the evaluation of the WSF will depend
on its capacity to transform the immense energy of its constitu-
ents into new forms of counter-hegemonic agency – more effective
forms because combining the strength of different social movements
and NGOs.

The political theory of modernity, whether in its liberal or Marxist
version, constructed the unity of action from the agent's unity. The
coherence and meaning of social change was always based on the

capacity of the privileged agent of change, whether the bourgeoisie or the working classes, to represent the totality from which the coherence and meaning derived. From such capacity of representation derived both the need and operationality of a general theory of social change.

The utopia and epistemology underlying the WSF place it at the antipodes of such a theory. The extraordinary energy of attraction and aggregation revealed by the WSF resides precisely in refusing the idea of a general theory. The diversity that finds a haven in it is free from the fear of being cannibalized by false universalisms or false single strategies propounded by any general theory. The WSF underwrites Ernst Bloch's idea that the world is an inexhaustible totality, as it holds many totalities, all of them partial. According to this conception of the world, there is no sense in attempting to grasp the world by any single grand theory, because any such general theory always presupposes the monoculture of a given totality and the homogeneity of its parts. The time we live in, whose recent past was dominated by the idea of a general theory, is perhaps a time of transition that may be defined in the following way: we have no need of a general theory, but still need a general theory on the impossibility of a general theory.

I cannot pursue this point here, but rather concentrate on what derives from it: what is the alternative to the general theory? To my mind, the alternative to a general theory is the work of translation. Translation is the procedure that allows for mutual intelligibility between the experiences of the world, both available and possible, as revealed by the sociology of absences and the sociology of emergences.

The WSF is witness to the wide multiplicity and variety of social practices of counter-hegemony that occur all over the world. Its strength derives from having corresponded or given expression to the aspiration of aggregation and articulation of the different social movements and NGOs, an aspiration that had been only latent up until its emergence. The movements and the NGOs constitute themselves around a number of more or less confined goals, create their own forms and styles of resistance, and specialize in certain kinds of practice and discourse that distinguish them from others. Thus is constituted the identity that separates each movement from all the others. The feminist movement distinguishes itself from the labour movement, both distinguish themselves from the indigenous movement or the ecological movement. All these distinctions have actually translated themselves into very practical differences, if not even into contradictions that contribute to separating the movements and creating rivalries and factionalisms. Here arise the fragmentation and atomization that are the dark side of diversity and multiplicity.

This dark side has lately been acknowledged by the movements and NGOs. The truth is, however, that none of them individually has had the capacity or credibility to confront it, for, in attempting to do so, they run the risk of falling prey to the situation they wish to remedy. Hence the extraordinary step taken by the WSF. It must be admitted, however, that the aggregation and articulation made possible by the WSF is low intensity. The goals are limited to recognizing differences and wishing for exchange in order to make the differences more explicit and better known. In these circumstances, joint action cannot but be limited. A good example was the European Social Forum in Florence in 2002. The differences, rivalries and factionalisms that divide the various movements and NGOs that organized it are well known and have a history that is impossible to erase. This is why, in their positive response to the WSF's request to organize the ESF, the movements and NGOs that took up the task felt the need to assert that the differences between them were as sharp as ever and that they were coming together only with a very limited objective in mind: to organize the Forum and a Peace March. The Forum was indeed organized in such a way that the differences could be made very explicit.

The challenge that counter-hegemonic globalization faces now may be formulated in the following way. The aggregation and articulation made possible by the WSF were enough to achieve the goals of the phase that has now reached its end. However, deepening the WSF's goals requires forms of aggregation and articulation of higher intensity. Such a process includes articulating struggles and resistances, as well as promoting ever more comprehensive and consistent alternatives. Such articulations presuppose combinations among the different social movements and NGOs that are bound to question their very identity and autonomy as conceived so far. If the idea is to promote counter-hegemonic practices through the collaboration of ecological, pacifist, indigenous, feminist, workers' and other movements, and if the idea is to go about this horizontally and with respect for the identity of every movement, an enormous effort of mutual recognition, dialogue and debate will be required.

This is the only way to identify more rigorously what divides and unites the movements, so as to base the articulations of practice and knowledge on what unites them, rather than on what divides them. Such a task entails a wide-ranging exercise in translation to enlarge reciprocal intelligibility without destroying the identity of what is translated. The point is to create, in every movement or NGO, in every practice or strategy, in every discourse or knowledge, a contact zone that renders it porous and hence permeable to other NGOs, practices, strategies, discourses, and knowledge. The exercise of translation aims to identify and give potential to what is common in the diversity of counter-hegemonic drive. Cancelling out what separates is out of the question. The goal is to have host-difference replace fortress-difference. Through translation work, diversity is celebrated, not as a factor of fragmentation and isolationism, but rather as a factor of sharing and solidarity.

To describe fully the procedures of the translation work is beyond the limits of this chapter. Elsewhere I have proposed translations between the concept of human rights and the Hindu and Islamic concepts of human dignity; between Western strategies of development and Gandhi's *swadeshi*; between Western philosophy and African oral *sagesse*; between 'modern' democracy and traditional authorities; between the indigenous movement and the ecological movement; between the workers' movement and the feminist movement. To be successful, the work of translation depends on demanding conditions. Nonetheless, the effort must be made. On it depends the future of counter-hegemonic globalization.

14

The World Social Forum:
A Democratic Alternative

Francine Mestrum

Is the alternative world movement an alternative to capitalism? Is it radically opposed to neoliberalism or does it limit itself to denouncing it, without envisaging a change of system? Is it, unconsciously, a believer in liberalism and only seeking to 'regulate' governance and world trade more effectively? Is it content, in a postmodern ideological context, with alternative practices without requiring theories or models? Is Thomas Friedman right when he accuses the alternative world supporters of being ' ignorant protectionists'[1] who obstruct the war against poverty? These are some of the questions that have given rise to a considerable amount of commentary, analysis and responses, often unfounded.

Here I would like to focus on this *problematique* in order to study the alternatives that have been debated within the World Social Forum at Porto Alegre, the great annual gathering of the alternative world movement since 2001. More specifically, using documents published there, I shall try to analyze the convergences and divergences that have arisen in the debates and identify some of the main divisions that explain the heterogeneity of the movement. These conclusions are provisional in that they should be seen in light of the different proposals emanating from the various schools of thought. Such proposals are often formulated too concisely and only partially portray the reality that they analyze and highlight.

CONVERGENCES: AGAINST NEOLIBERALISM AND FOR DEMOCRACY

Convergences in the alternative world movement take place at two levels: denunciations of the present situation, and demands for a democratic future. As this democracy is far from being achieved, it would be wrong to talk about performative statements that create the situation they describe.

All documents issued by organizations at Porto Alegre are unanimous in denouncing neoliberalism. It is held responsible for all the evils suffered by the planet and the peoples who inhabit it, whether through globalization as such, the debt, poverty and inequality, privatization, fiscal havens, the power of the transnationals, the lack of democracy or warfare. Apart from these general condemnations, other phenomena such as racism and discrimination are also denounced. For some, especially after 11 September 2001, neoliberalism has progressively changed into neo-imperialism and it is the United States and/or the European Union that are blamed.[2]

There is a striking unanimity when looking at the future: claims for democracy, for participation and for control by citizens. The belief in the potential of people to manage their own lives is paramount. This is repeated in many of the documents, both as an objective and as a way of dismantling the present system and constructing a new world. While this demand for democracy is a direct opening up of the path for making desired changes in the future, it is also accompanied by a certain looking back, in other words a demand to abide by existing regulations. There are many who call for a scrupulous respect for human rights and a revival of the United Nations. These demands are far from being new, but they underline the importance given both to governance and the rule of law. In actual fact, this only reiterates the demand that elites respect regulations they themselves have devised.

Apart from these two great convergences, there is almost a total absence of radical demands for a change in the system. Documents pleading explicitly for socialism or an alternative to capitalism are extremely rare. Furthermore, social rights and the fight against poverty are mentioned by only a few organizations. Development as such is not specifically analyzed.

All this could indicate that in spite of the strength and unanimity of condemnations of neoliberalism, the alternative world movement is reformist and does not declare that it is against capitalism. After all, democracy, human rights and the United Nations constitute part of the gains from liberalism. Has the latter also perverted its opponents? This is far from being the case. It is true that certain organizations demand a 'correct', 'equitable' globalization, respect for institutional regulations and the rehabilitation of State sovereignty. They seem to share the objectives of the advocates of globalization, while denouncing their failures. They only propose more effective instruments.

Nevertheless, probing deeper reveals that there are other claims less compatible with liberalism. This is particularly true for the demands that the external debt of impoverished states be cancelled, the creation of a Tobin tax, protectionism for poor countries vis-à-vis world trade as well as respect for cultural diversity, the rights of indigenous peoples and gender rights. The demand for democracy also shows a lack of confidence in political parties and representative democracy: generally speaking, there are few references to the political institutions of national states. Politics is to be found at the world level, in references to international organizations and civil society, and at the local level, through calls on peoples and citizens.

The first part of this analysis would seem to confirm that:

1. James Scott's theories[3] claiming that the rules of the game – the social contract – are constantly being violated by the elites themselves, as they impose new production relationships. The denunciations and references to rights and regulations that exist but are not applied show people's distrust, indeed rancour, over the betrayal of their elites.
2. If the above is true, the alternative world movement is reformist by only demanding the restoration of pledges made fifty years ago as concerns human rights, reduction of inequalities, peace and development.
3. Other claims, strongly oriented towards the future, indicate there are other cleavages, however. Not only is there an opposition between reformism and neo-Keynesianism and anti- or post-capitalism: there are other divisions that highlight the difficulties in arriving at more homogeneous demands. Quite apart from the question of whether this homogeneity is desirable or not, the divisions should be analyzed more carefully for a better understanding of the challenges faced by the movement. It is true that the WSF is above all a process and that the diversity of its views proves its vitality. Nevertheless, can one really speak of a 'movement' if these views are incompatible? Where does diversity end and fragmentation begin?

In the following sections, three issues are studied in greater detail:

- international trade, which directly affects globalization and, indirectly, democracy;

- solidarity economics, which opposes modernists to anti- and post-modernists;
- world governance, which opposes the economy to politics and the State to civil society.

WORLD TRADE: FOR OR AGAINST GLOBALIZATION?

World trade is one of the most important subjects for the alternative world movement. There is much criticism of globalization, particularly of the World Trade Organization and its powers which are considered excessive. There was thus considerable surprise when, in the spring of 2002, Oxfam International published the report *Rigged Rules and Double Standards*,[4] announcing a campaign on behalf of world trade. There were many reactions to this report, which I shall use to try to show the issues in the debate.

In his preface, Amartya Sen explains how economic progress has come about through interdependence. He believes that trade, along with migration and communication, 'has helped to break the dominance of rampant poverty and the pervasiveness of "nasty, brutish and short" lives'. But, he observes, the benefits from world trade have not affected everyone. 'There is a paradox at the heart of international trade. ... It is ... a source of unprecedented wealth. Yet millions of the world's poorest people are being left behind. Increased prosperity has gone hand in hand with mass poverty and the widening of already obscene inequalities between rich and poor.' Oxfam considers the human cost of unfair commercial practices to be enormous. For example, customs barriers are four times higher for the poor countries than for the rich ones. This costs them $100 billion a year: twice the amount of the aid they receive.

As a result, the campaign organized by Oxfam seeks to make the most of the potential of international trade to reduce poverty. It believes in:

- 'improving market access for poor countries and ending the cycle of subsidized agricultural overproduction and export dumping by rich countries;
- ending the use of conditions attached to IMF/World Bank programmes which force poor countries to open their markets ... ;

- creating a new international commodities institution to promote diversification and end oversupply, in order to raise prices ... ;
- establishing new intellectual property rules ... ;
- prohibiting rules that force governments to liberalise or privatise basic services that are vital for poverty reduction;
- enhancing the quality of private sector investment and employment standards;
- democratising the WTO to give poor countries a stronger voice;
- changing national policies on health, education and governance.'

Critics were swift to react. Oxfam was accused of having accepted the free trade paradigm adopted by the WTO. Emphasizing access to markets, it was said, is to overlook the fact that the beneficiaries of free trade are not the poor, but the rich.[5] A more fundamental criticism came from Vandana Shiva, who explained that the export of agricultural products from the South to the North only serves to support non-sustainable consumerism in the North, while preventing the countries of the South from meeting their own needs. Citing statistics, she shows how production for export has reduced local production and hence food sovereignty. Moreover, she pointed out, from the $100 billion profits mentioned by Oxfam, the ecological costs have to be subtracted, as they have not been taken into account.[6]

Oxfam has indeed remained faithful to its slogans and policies of the 1970s: 'Trade, not Aid'. Far from adopting the WTO regulations, it advocates changing them, as it considers the international trade system as 'indefensible'. The regulations governing trade are distorted in favour of the rich countries. Oxfam demands another system for intellectual property, price stabilization and the dismantling of protectionism in the North. It recognizes the right of poor countries to protect their agriculture and their need for specific national policies. The only question that is lacking compared with the demands of the 1970s is control over transnational corporations.

Those opposing Oxfam's stance denounce world trade while recognizing that it exists and is necessary. But what they are essentially advocating is food sovereignty and a draconian change in WTO rules, with the accent on local production and consumption, while respecting the environment. Above all, according to Vandana Shiva, farmers must remain the masters of the (mainly local) markets.

While these two approaches are in opposition as regards trade, they resemble each other in their realism and in what they do not say. In fact, the system recommended by Oxfam is rooted in the past. It is for regulated trade at stabilized prices, respecting ecological and social regulations. In theory, such a system is perfectly feasible, as indeed was the development discourse at the UN during the 1970s: almost all its demands appear in the Oxfam report. However, the WTO and the current regulations exist because the rich countries decided that they should do so. There is no sign of a change of attitude. Amartya Sen is right to say that a market economy is quite compatible with different forms of distribution of resources, regulation and development policies. But there are reasons to believe that transnational corporations will not easily abandon their privileges. They will be less interested in investing in African countries as soon as their social and ecological regimes start resembling those of the North. Oxfam preaches fair trade in a world in which the trading protagonists do not want it. It uses the globalization discourse (world trade and war on poverty) to defend a system that opposes it. Its arguments are strong and its claims pragmatic, but the chances of their being achieved seem minimal, given present power relationships.

As for the supporters of local markets, their system is radically different from that of Oxfam, but it is nevertheless not against the market, nor international trade. In fact a system of local production and consumption can coexist happily with a system of production for the world market. But while the former advocates standards that go against globalization, it does not prevent globalization from existing. The main difference is the priority given to endogenous development, respect for ecological and social standards as well as direct control by producers. While world trade is not excluded *a priori,* it involves completely different modes of protection that can threaten the existence of an alternative system.

Oxfam accepts 'equitable' globalization. Its opponents give priority to local, democratic development. To the extent that globalization implies a transfer of power to transnational actors, it works against the democracy claimed by those who oppose it.

SOLIDARITY ECONOMICS AND SUSTAINABLE DEVELOPMENT

Solidarity economics and sustainable development have three sources of inspiration. First are the reactions to the modernization and developmentalism of the 1970s.These critiques of development, often religiously inspired, were felt to be basically Eurocentric and an effort to repeat Western experiences. Authors like François Partant and Ivan Illich (in the 1970s) and Serge Latouche and Wolfgang Sachs (at present) attack the mirage of 'progress' and preach an anti- or post-development. They denounce economicism and westernization and defend the return to traditions and cultural values that are indigenous and non-material. A second source comes from political ecology in general and, in particular, the great UN conferences on the environment in 1972 and 1992. Partisans are conscious of the ecological limits of development and they denounce the non-sustainable models of production and consumption in the countries of the North. They plead for a fundamental change of attitudes vis-à-vis natural resources and commercial exchanges. Thirdly, advocates of solidarity economics and sustainable development have read, or reread the outstanding work of Karl Polanyi, *The Great Transformation,*[7] in which the anthropologist explains the need for the economy to be embedded in social relationships. This is thus the essential characteristic of solidarity economics: it is not based exclusively on the search for profits, but on the production and reproduction of social relationships.

The heterogeneity of these sources gives rise to various approaches to social change. However, they do have several characteristics in common, such as people's economics, based on local exchanges, participatory democracy, emphasizing the role of women and indigenous peoples, and a belief that respect for the natural environment imposes limits to development and the exploitation of resources.

While solidarity economics would seem to oppose neoliberal capitalism, it should be pointed out that, in fact, the two are perfectly compatible and can co-exist.[8] This has been a real godsend to international organizations: they can defend the informal sector, micro-credit and the empowerment of women. The World Bank and the UNDP have discovered 'social capital', which is their view of social security for the poor and/or shared values and they promote a 'local' economy, disembedded from the world economy. In fact, the rich no longer need most of the poor, so what better than keeping them 'at the margins' of the capitalist system by preaching a local development in which material values are delegitimized and women do the work that public authorities have abandoned? Furthermore, the informal sector, which is independent or at the service of the formal capitalist sector, enables workers to be exploited, unaffected by 'bureaucracy', taxes and/or social norms. What international organizations and certain NGOs and social movements have in common is their aversion to the State. Both of them, for different reasons, want to limit the State to a strict minimum: the former to avoid national regulations that contradict globalization and the latter to give greater autonomy to local communities.

To the extent that sustainable development sees beyond the local and is concerned with the economic system as a whole, it avoids the trap of capitalism. However, it comes up against the difficulty of putting it into operation, particularly in the countries of the North. There has been no WSF document on this *problematique*.

The coexistence of solidarity economics and neoliberal capitalism is possible. But there are also various cleavages within the 'solidarity' paradigm itself.

To the degree that anti- or post-development is based on religious values and attacks progress, it can become clearly antimodernist. The defence of community values, localism, the rejection of individualism and belief in a 'natural' social order are all evidence of an antimodernism that can be found in Gandhi as well as Khomeini. This opposition was also clear in the Catholic Church when the *Populorum Progressio* Encyclical of 1967 adopted the demands for social justice of the liberation theologists, while at the same time asserting that only God was able to change the social order. Martin Khor of the Third World Network distinguishes two paradigms: globalization and family/community self-management. Condemning industrialization, he declares for the second paradigm but, given present realities, he proposes working on both at the same time and trying to instil some of the latter into the former.[9]

There is always a risk of antimodernism in projects targeted only at the 'excluded'. Desirable as they may seem, these projects are limited to organizing 'those without' (papers, shelter, etc.), counting on community, intra-class solidarity – which is always liable to end up in an antimodernist impasse. Islands of inclusion/exclusion are quite compatible with the management of capitalist crisis, and they differ from social endeavours that 'start with the excluded' and try to involve the upper classes in social change, or at least in inter-class solidarity.

A second division concerns capitalism more directly. While solidarity economics and sustainable development can be directly incorporated into a capitalist system, most projects are launched in opposition to it. Nevertheless there are those who explicitly declare in favour of an alternative system. At Porto Alegre, three initiatives could be classed under this heading: the ecosocialist manifesto of Covel and Löwy,[10] a project of Argentinian socialist economists,[11] and a libertarian proposal of Hahnel and Albert.[12]

- The ecosocialist project rejects reformist aims and clings to the liberating objectives of socialism. It redefines its aims within an ecological framework, subjecting the limits of essential growth to the sustainability of society. It advocates a fundamental transformation of needs, giving priority to use value rather than exchange value.
- The Katz project is basically concerned with social policy measures for ending the 'social genocide' of the Argentinian crisis. It also proposes to tax the upper classes, terminate payment of the external debt and nationalize the banks, as well as preaching reindustrialization and agrarian reform. These proposals are formulated within a strategically socialist project.
- The project for participatory economics puts forward an economic model 'in which both the market and central planning have been banished ... as well as the hierarchy of work and of profits. In such an economy, consumer and producer councils coordinate their activities. ECOPAR is based on the public ownership of the means of production and planning measures that are decentralized, democratic and participatory.'

While these three initiatives are very different from one another, they distinguish themselves markedly from capitalism. They facilitate a gradual transformation and encourage co-operation at a global level.

The third division emerges when projects for solidarity economics and sustainable development are analyzed from an anthropological viewpoint. This is to be found among the French thinkers who write in the *Transversales* review: 'Human beings ... are creatures who not only have needs but also desires. All projects that are based on purely instrumental rationality are doomed to failure.'[13] Projects are then elaborated on the basis of a plural economy and 'chosen time,[14] as well as a redefinition of wealth.[15] This involves a deconstruction of economic theory, going beyond the microsocial level and differing from 'crisis management' in that they reconsider the meaning of wealth and trading systems. When they assert that 'relationships are more important than goods', they are trying to reinsert human beings into the heart of trade so that it ends up by losing its purely economic function of production and consumption.

In this all too brief consideration of projects for solidarity economics and sustainable development it is nevertheless possible to identify cleavages and contradictions at the very heart of alternative thinking. However the WSF did not originate these ideas (which are much richer than appears from this summary). Political ecology and UN conferences gave rise, during the 1980s and 1990s, to projects that have been somewhat overlooked by the alternative world movement.[16] In this field, even more than in others, the WSF is a meeting place where projects are presented and ideas and opinions exchanged.

Finally, it should be said that the partisans of solidarity economics and sustainable development are well aware of prevailing power relationships. They point to the need for transformation, but do not propose any strategy.

WORLD GOVERNANCE

Most of the alternative world projects meet and cross one another in the discourse on world governance. Indeed, it is in the way that power and decision-making are conceived that the feasibility and reality of the alternative become visible. At the same time, this discourse shows up the very real difficulties encountered by the new world social movement.

Progressive movements have always been universalist and internationalist. Hence, their opposition to globalization is curious as it could provide the material basis for an idea that has remained abstract for too long. The idea of globalization first was a moral intuition, then, later, it became concrete: it stops being a slogan and becomes the objective basis for the rights and obligations that we all have towards each other.[17] Nevertheless, globalization is rejected because the market has become the dominant and unifying element of humanity. This is why the social movement calls itself the alternative world movement, for it advocates a philosophical, not a market-oriented universalism. It is for this reason that it cherishes the watchwords of the French Revolution: liberty, equality, fraternity. The principle of liberty is extended to include the social and economic; by equality is meant the equality of rights for human beings whose diversity is recognized and protected; while fraternity is embraced by calling for world solidarity and defence of the commons. These values are to be found, in one way or another, in all the great civilizations. The history of the Universal Declaration of Human Rights bears witness to their universality.[18]

Nevertheless, what has to be done to put it into operation? Should interventions, perhaps even military ones, be used to impose it? On this question the alternative world movement is not unanimous. Even if the State does not figure much in the alternative discourse, it is evident that a large part of the movement counts on it for organizing democracy or for protecting world trade. It is also striking to see the repeated appeals to the international organizations in all the fields neglected by the nation states. This is particularly the case for women, indigenous peoples and environmental issues, and would indicate the maturity of demands for emancipation. Far from rejecting globalization *in toto*, the new social actors choose their points of reference because they are able to respect multiple identities and allegiances.

This also explains why, in spite of rejecting neoliberal globalization, the demand for democracy from a number of participants takes concrete form in the demand for world citizenship: recognizing human rights, including economic, social and cultural rights, and the juridical instruments for making them respected. At the same time, these world citizens claim recognition of their cultural diversity. Vandana Shiva defends the principle of a 'living democracy'[19] that combines freedom for all life on earth and the indivisibility of justice, peace and sustainability. The alternative world movement is for a globalization that is human and ecological, and not market-oriented. It comes out strongly against the WTO and the Bretton Woods institutions, as well as the power of transnationals. Some have no hesitation in calling for the dismantling of the Bretton Woods institutions,[20] while others demand that their powers be considerably reduced, for example those of the WTO, or perhaps put under the direct control of the UN.[21] Still others demand democratization and a greater participation of the Third World countries. No-one calls for the abolition of the United Nations. According to Samir Amin, it is the only legitimate institution for discussing globalization.[22] However, there are demands for a reform of the Security Council, the General Assembly and the Economic and Social Council. In spite of the deficiencies of these bodies, references to them are frequent, with calls for the need to reinforce them and give them greater power. As an extension of this reasoning, new world institutions are demanded, such as tax and environmental organizations.[23] Walden Bello, who calls for deglobalization, emphasizes the need for a deconcentration and a decentralization of institutional powers. However, he argues that the powers of UNCTAD, the ILO and the regional economic organizations should be strengthened.[24]

As for the power of the TNCs, few practical proposals have been put forward. They range from pronouncing their death sentence to promoting the social responsibility of business through citizen action.[25] It is pointed out that corporate responsibility – promoted by the UN – has been used by many TNCs to improve their brand image and to avoid accountability measures, i.e. mechanisms that would oblige them to abide by the regulations and criteria that have been adopted.[26]

Two things are very clear in this discourse on world governance. First, the alternative world movement is not against globalization as such, but against neoliberal capitalism. There is a belief in the UN as a supreme body, if not as world arbiter, and a number of organizations want its powers reinforced. In this field, the only cleavage seems to be the one between the opponents of capitalism and the opponents of its neoliberal version, but this is inferred rather than openly stated. A second cleavage concerns the role of the nation states. Greater sovereignty is demanded for them and also that they be put at the service of their peoples. As has already been said, the role of nation states is not one of the most popular topics among the alternative world movement. While the demand for democracy and the State's role in civil society seem to predominate in the discourse, the rejection of economic globalization and the demand for local and regional production and consumption automatically attribute more power to the State. There is some opposition to this, although it is more implicit than explicit. Many of the movements are still very sceptical about public authorities, only trusting civil society, while others call for the State to regulate economic life.

As far as world governance is concerned, the alternative world movement can be placed in the camp of the international organizations that are considered 'progressive', such as the UN, UNDP, UNCTAD and ILO. These are the ones that support a more or less radical reform. It was the UN that commissioned the independent Carlsson report[27] on world governance, which envisaged a 'people's assembly'. Since the beginning of the 1990s,[28] UNDP has formulated some very concrete measures for a 'new world order'. However, as their power declined, these organizations adapted their future projects. In his report to the Millennium Summit[29] Kofi Annan talks only about 'loose and temporary global policy networks', the idea of central world government having become an 'anachronism'. Today the UN presents itself as the mouthpiece of the peoples, but it has abandoned its projects to regulate the behaviour of all the nation states. Nowadays power is in the hands of the WTO and the Bretton Woods institutions, which are more under the control of the G8 (the rich countries) than that of the UN.

What is interesting in the world governance debate is to see the attachment of the alternative world movement to a certain idea of world order that is close to the ideals of the UN fifty years ago. At the same time it sheds a cruel light on real power relationships. The opportunities to carry out projects, reformist or radical, are extremely limited.[30] Rich countries do not dream of giving more power to poor countries. Within the G8, they try, on the one hand, to adapt to the hegemony of the USA, on the other, to rid themselves of the burden of the poor. This informal encounter, which originally was meant to coordinate the macro-economic policies of the rich countries, has become an organization that brings together ministers for social affairs, justice and the interior, even development. It is in the process of developing as an alternative to the UN, in close co-operation with the Bretton Woods institutions and the WTO. Faced with this reality, the powerlessness of the alternative worlders is striking. While alternative practices in the field of trade and sustainable development can be put into operation, in this field the movement can do little.

CONCLUSIONS

The World Social Forums of Porto Alegre have resulted in a considerable number of partial alternative proposals, which have often come from single-issue groups. This explains why the projects that are debated are extremely heterogeneous. What unites the different movements is their denunciation of neoliberal capitalism and their demand for democratic participation, which makes it possible to refer to the movement as denouncing neoliberal globalization. However, as the alternative worlders are far from sharing the same political, economic, social and cultural objectives, the Social Forum must be seen essentially as an 'open space for meetings',[31] a place for reflection, debate and mobilization.

The main cleavage dividing the different movements is not reformism versus post-capitalism. This difference does indeed exist, but most proposals avoid making declarations on this point and advocate measures that can evolve in either direction. Reformism continues to be what it has always been, but it is difficult to imagine post-capitalism without reformism.[32] The basic philosophy of the former is different but the paths leading to the two projects will part ways only in the longer term.

A second cleavage at least as important concerns progress and modernity. A return to the local community and so-called traditional values can move in an antimodern direction. This would constitute a rupture with political liberalism.

Finally, a third cleavage concerns the State, civil society and world governance. Few proposals are clear about the role that should be attributed to the nation states. They are fundamentally Keynesian, but they come up against both globalization on one hand and, on the other, their traditional adversaries who preach a return to the local. This cleavage is intimately linked to the crisis of political representation and demands for a more active participation of civil society. While it is true that politics have to be reinvented, it would seem necessary to do more thinking about the role of the State. As the social movement is for an alternative world, it is for a political globalization in which the different levels – from the local to the global – must find their place. It is by making intelligent linkages between these levels that civil society can play an important role. As neoliberalism also advocates a reform of the State, the movement should be clarifying its ideas on this.

On various other questions the WSF does not give clear answers. This is particularly true concerning redistribution, development and sustainable development, poverty and global inequalities. While social justice and solidarity are on the political agenda of the movement, indeed could be called its *Leitmotiv*, very few concrete proposals have been made in this sense. The theme of social rights is more commonly brought up in the rich countries than in the Third World. As for sustainable development, some valuable principles have been formulated, but there have been no proposals on how to put them into operation in the rich countries – particularly in terms of economic growth.

One question that deserves a more in-depth analysis is surely the one that constitutes the novelty of the alternative world movement: its opposition to neoliberalism – a variant of capitalism – and its great enthusiasm for democracy. True, this can be defined in various ways. However, development and democracy have not always got on well.

Today the movement for the Third World aspires to a democracy that contributes to development, that is self-reliant, more human, inclusive and participatory. There has to be serious work on redefining democracy and development, giving them new meaning. Likewise, politics needs to be reinvented as well as political, economic and social reorganization. As neoliberalism is also in the process of redefining – and restricting – democracy, more in-depth thinking on this becomes urgent.

Finally, this analysis has thrown up a crucial question, which is the lack of serious thinking about power relationships. Only projects for solidarity economics give some importance to this, without however answering the question about the transformations that have to be made. This is of course intimately linked to the movement's strategy. Here, it seems, serious thinking has only just started. It requires a far greater effort than formulating alternative projects but, in the short term, it could turn out to be much more useful.

The different WSF documents are silent on the issues defended by the traditional left: anti-capitalism, socialism and revolutionary strategies. Clearly the lessons of the past – the failure of historical socialism – have been learnt. The movement aims at different relationships with power, rather than changing the system. It wants a redressing of the balance and appears to have renounced taking over power. It seems as if it has taken a postmodernist turn. It boasts, quite rightly, of its diversity and that its lack of unity is a strength rather than a weakness. But there is a real risk of atomization. It is true that the new realism is more concerned with practice than with theory and that it is in practice that new values are created. However, theory is still necessary and it has to be built up patiently and at the same time as the development of practice. This is why encounters like Porto Alegre are extremely important. They facilitate exchanges and the search for convergences. There is much work still to do, but the collective development of awareness can actively help to promote the maturing process of the different alternatives.

As for the three conditions formulated by François Houtart for a genuine alternative,[33] only the first one seems to be met, as far as I can see. The 'delegitimization' of the existing situation has been achieved by the movement. As for the 'convergence of resistance and struggles at the same level', this is far from being accomplished. The movement is still a 'simple sum of alternatives'. It does not need an alternative one-and-only-way of thinking, but a mobilizing project on to which different variants can be grafted. There has to be a sustained effort to seek convergences to reduce the risk of fragmentation. At the time of writing, the WSF is only three years old. It represents an important step in creating a political actor that can take on the challenge of neoliberalism. This would be a liberating movement that will finally give a voice to the 'third worlds' of the North and of the South. Through the organization and democratic functioning of the movement itself these alternatives will become concrete.

This analysis confirms what is undoubtedly the most important element of the alternative world movement: the failure of the dominant discourse. Neoliberalism has not succeeded in making it accepted. In fact, once again, it has become evident that a dominant ideology is not impenetrable. Capitalism, which has betrayed the values with which it has been able to impose itself, is now being combated by the arguments that it has used to promote its own interests. The demands of the alternative world movement are based on the promise of emancipation made by capitalism. Once again, hegemonic ideology has supplied the arms that make it possible to fight it.[34] This is the main sense of the demand for democracy: freedom to receive as opposed to freedom to express, using the spaces of resistance that are included in every dominant discourse. As Eric Hobsbawm has already observed, the revolution does not need revolutionary ambitions.[35]

NOTES

1. The International Forum on Globalization (2002) *Alternatives to Economic Globalization* (San Francisco: Berret-Koehler Publishers), p. 2.
2. Ken Coates (2003) *WSF: An alternative to war, domination and exploitation,* or *An appeal to social movements,* January (www.attac.info/poa2003).
3. J.C. Scott (1985) *Weapons of the Weak. Everyday forms of peasant resistance* (New Haven and London: Yale University Press), p. 345.
4. Oxfam (2002) *Rigged Rules and Double Standards: Trade,globalisation and the fight against poverty* (London: Oxfam).
5. Walden Bello, 'What's wrong with the Oxfam trade campaign', *ATTAC Newsletter,* no. 126.
6. Vandana Shiva, 'Export at any cost: Oxfam's free trade recipe for the Third World', *ATTAC Newsletter,* no. 129.
7. Karl Polanyi (1957) *The Great Transformation. The political and economic origins of our time* (Boston: Beacon Press).
8. See, for example, OECD (1996) *Reconciling Economy and Society.Towards a plural economy* (Paris: OECD), and G. Aznar *et al.* (1997) *Vers une économie*

plurielle. Un travail, une activité, un revenue pour tous (Paris: La Découverte et Syros).

9. Martin Khor, 'Conflicting Paradigms', in International Forum on Globalization (2002), p.13.

10. J. Covel and M. Löwy (2003) *Manifiesto ecosocialista* (www.portoalegre2003. org/publique).

11. C. Katz *et al.* (2003) *Siempre existen otros caminos*(www.portoalegre2003. org/publique).

12. R. Hahnel and M. Albert, *Une proposition libertaire: l'Economie Participative*; M. Albert (2003) *What are we for?* (www.portoalegre2003.org/ publique).

13. P. Viveret (1997) 'Repères', *Transversales Science/Culture*, no. 43, January/ February. Jacques Robin, Roger Sue, René Passet and André Gorz can also be cited.

14. For example, F. Plassard (ATTAC, France) (2003) *Le développement durable et le temps choisi* (www.portoalegre2003.org/publique).

15. P. Viveret (2001) 'Reconsidérer la richesse', *Transversales Science/Culture*, no. 70, August. Viveret's documents were not published at Porto Alegre although he gave several seminars.

16. See, in particular, the work of Alain Lipietz and Ignacy Sachs.

17. C.S. Kessler (2000) 'Globalization: Another false universalism?', *Third World Quarterly*, vol 21, no. 6, pp. 931–42.

18. S. Waltz (2002) 'Reclaiming and rebuilding the history of the Universal Declaration of Human Rights', *Third World Quarterly*, vol 23, no. 3, pp. 437–48.

19. Vandana Shiva (2003) 'The living democracy movement: Alternatives to the bankruptcy of globalization', in W.F. Fisher and T. Ponniah, *Another World is Possible. Popular alternatives to globalization at the World Social Forum* (London and New York: Zed Books).

20. International Forum on Globalization (2002), p. 221; M. Albert (2003).

21. ATTAC, France (2003) 'Financial capital', and Walden Bello (2003) 'International Organizations and the Architecture of World Power' in Fisher and Ponniah, pp. 41, 285.

22. Samir Amin (2003), in Rikkilä and Sehm Patomäki (eds), *From a Global Market Place to Political Spaces* (Helsinki: NIGD), p. 34.

23. Patomäki *et al.* (2002) *Global Democracy Initiatives: The art of the possible* (Helsinki: NIGD).

24. Walden Bello (2002) 'Future of global economic governance', in H. Ginkel *et al., Human Development and the Environment. Challenges for the United Nations in the new millennium* (Tokyo: United Nations University Press).

25. International Forum on Globalization (2002), p. 131.

26. Fisher and Ponniah (2003), p. 55.

27. Carlsson Commission (1995) *The Report of the Commission on Global Governance. Our Global Neighbourhood* (New York: Oxford University Press).

28. See UNDP (1992, 1994) *World Human Development Report*.

29. Kofi Annan (2000) *We the Peoples. The rôle of the United Nations in the 21st Century* (New York: United Nations).

30. See Patomäki *et al.* (2002), Table 11.
31. *Carta de principios do Forum Social Mundial,* 8/6/2002 (www.portoalegre2003. org).
32. M. Husson (2001) *Le grand BLUFF capitaliste* (Paris: La Dispute).
33. F. Houtart, *Des alternative crédibles au capitalisme mondialisé* (www. forumsocialmundial.org.br/bib/houtartfra.asp).
34 . Scott (1985).
35. Hobsbawm in Scott (1985).

15

The African Social Forum: Between Radicals and Reformers

Mondli Hlatshwayo[1]

There were over 300 participants at the Second African Social Forum (ASF), held in Addis Ababa (Ethiopia) on 5–9 January 2003.[2] Delegates ranged from members of NGOs and academics to (a very few) people from social movements and trade unions. This second forum was intended to make progress on the issues raised in the First African Social Forum, held in Bamako (Mali) in 2002. It was also seen as a preparation for the World Social Forum (WSF) that took place a few weeks later in Porto Alegre.

The choice of venue, an upmarket United Nations building, should have warned us from the start about the whole orientation of this ASF. Outside, only a few metres away, poor people greeted us, begging for money and food. Desperation was written on the faces of these children, youths, men and women, condemned to poverty and disease by a system that benefits only the few. They are the ones who have been betrayed by the African middle classes who have chosen to collaborate with the imperialist forces rather than work with their own people. I could not help recalling Frantz Fanon's prediction: 'If it so happens that the unpreparedness of the educated classes, the lack of practical links between them and the masses, their laziness, let it be said, their cowardice at the decisive moment of the struggle will give rise to tragic mishaps.'[3]

Then there was the opening address given by Ammara Essy, the interim chairperson of the African Union Commission. This had not been announced in the programme circulated in advance to the participants. As Essy extended an invitation to the forum to participate in the AU civil society structures, the clear intention was to orient the whole proceedings towards subordinating the social movements and other organizations to government structures.

Our South African delegation felt that this was most inappropriate before the forum had had the chance to define its objectives and strategies and identify its friends and enemies. The AU, for example had endorsed the NEPAD (New Partnership for Africa's Development), whereas, according to us, the ASF should be part of an anti-globalization movement that is independent and has a grassroots orientation.

PRE-FORUM PREPARATIONS BY SOUTH AFRICAN GRASSROOTS MOVEMENTS

Our delegation was representing the Social Movement Indaba (SMI) of South Africa, a network of grassroots organizations opposed to the neoliberal policies of our country, and it is perhaps appropriate here to mention the preparations it had made prior to the forum. Several meetings were held, and the delegates to the ASF agreed on the following:

- There had to be an orientation towards the popular classes because these are the forces capable of struggling for an egalitarian society in Africa and the rest of the world.
- NEPAD should be rejected. We also wanted the ASF to reject the AU because it is a structure imposed over the heads of the African people.
- But we needed to move beyond rejecting NEPAD and the AU. The forum should be used to build solidarity, struggles and campaigns against these programmes and institutions.
- Clearly, not all African forces and organizations are at the same level of political and organizational development: there will always be countries lagging behind in terms of struggles and we should listen attentively to their concerns and issues. At the same time we must develop certain principles such as non-collaboration and democracy that cannot be compromised.
- We need to show that the reason why we are opposed to NEPAD is because we believe it is a programme for the recolonization of Africa by the South African State and big capital. For us, coming from South Africa, this must be a primary concern.
- As the ASF was to precede the anti-AGOA (African Growth and Opportunity Act) civil society meeting, due to take place in Mauritius later on in the month, we thought there should be links between the Second Forum and the anti-AGOA meeting.
- The war against the Iraqi people was looming. We wanted the ASF to discuss this and support the Iraqi people, as well as pledging solidarity with the Palestinian people who continue to be killed by *apartheid* Israel, supported by the US.[4]

COLLABORATION WITH THE AFRICAN UNION AND THE UNDP?

It was clear, however, that we were going to have difficulties in pursuing these issues in the Addis Ababa Forum, given that the reformers formed the majority of the participants – most of them representing NGOs. They held that the AU was an important body as it gave Africans a chance to unite at the continental level. Therefore, they argued, the forum should participate in the civil society structures of the AU – indeed, some of the delegates already formed part of them. They were aggrieved when the more radical delegates pointed out that the AU had adopted NEPAD, which had already been rejected by the First Social Forum, and therefore there was no basis for co-operation with that body. The reformers, for their part, contested that the AU had not adopted NEPAD – although there was written evidence of such adoption in Durban 2002.

The forum organizers, again without a mandate, had invited the AU ambassadors to attend the meeting. However, given the opposition to the involvement of the AU, the invitation was cancelled. The whole thorny question of relationships with the AU was assigned to a working group on the second day, but the differences of opinion were too strong not to re-emerge. Supporters of the AU resorted to dubious tactics to impose their views: for example, the working group report to the plenary did not mention that there had been differences of opinion and even stated that there had been consensus on participation in the AU structures. This led to the question being brought back to the plenary again, but as both sides stuck to their positions the matter was not resolved.

Paradoxically, the rejection of NEPAD as a neoliberal project, which had been passed at Bamako, was reaffirmed by the Addis Ababa Forum, which also committed itself to developing alternatives. But the problem lay in how to translate this rejection into political strategy and practice. This issue bedevilled the entire forum. There were those who saw participation in the power structures as a way of influencing government policy: this was the view, it should be said, of NGOs that claimed to be speaking on behalf of the African masses. On the other hand, there were the others who saw mass mobilization and the building of structures of resistance as important.

Another bone of contention was that the organizers had also invited the United Nations Development Programme (UNDP) to present its 'Millennium Development Goals'. These were criticized as being all too similar to the objectives of NEPAD and the Structural

Adjustment Programmes (SAPs), and also because the emphasis was not on debt cancellation, but rather debt relief, and they did not call for poverty eradication, but poverty reduction. UNDP requests NGOs and civil society to monitor their implementation but, while some felt the need to engage with the UNDP's Millennium Objectives, others believed that the main aim was to incorporate the ASF into the power structures. Instead of dealing with the real issues confronting the masses, the forum seemed to be mainly preoccupied with the opinions of the power structure.

Towards the end of the meeting a document entitled 'Addis Ababa Consensus' was presented. Although it met with majority support, some still found it too radical. However, the thematic groups did manage to reach agreement on some issues. They called for:

- rejection of all forms of privatization of social services in Africa. It was further argued that social services are part of human rights to life and dignity;
- cancellation of debt and reparations. Debt was seen as the instrument of control and domination imposed by the imperialist forces and their institutions. If creditors do not cancel debt, the meeting agreed that there should be mass mobilization for debt repudiation;
- opposition to the trade liberalization imposed on Africa by the World Trade Organization (WTO). This trade liberalization has destroyed the continent's agriculture and emerging industries;
- opposition to AGOA/Cotonou type of trade agreements, which do not benefit the majority of the people;
- collaboration to be established with other social movements in Europe, Asia, North America and Latin America for the building of another world. If led by peasants, workers, women, young people and all other oppressed classes, this is possible.[5]

IS THERE DEMOCRACY IN THE ASF?

The structure of the African Social Forum was another issue left unresolved. African regions had come with proposals on the principles and structure of the ASF, but the chairperson of the plenary session, who is also a member of the secretariat, was not in agreement with this democratic process proposed by the regions. He ruled that the status quo would remain, which means that a less democratic steering committee, representing thematic groups and regions, will continue to run the show. The proposal from South Africa, for instance, was that the new council be elected and that representatives from anti-neoliberal mass movements should dominate it. Grassroots movements that have not been part of the forum should be incorporated later, according to this proposal. Not only was that not accepted, but some of the people belonging to the radical bloc were subsequently arbitrarily removed from the steering committee.

Consistently the delegates from the SMI attacked both the undemocratic nature of the African Social Forum as well as collaboration with the African Union. Some of the key issues, such as the struggles of the peoples of Africa, the AGOA, the war on Iraq and the Palestinian question, were not discussed. Instead, the forum was obsessed with the AU. For sure, many NGOs present see it as a funder for their projects and do not want the ASF to adopt a radical position that would upset their bosses and hence jeopardize future financial aid. These NGOs do not represent the interests of the masses. But they formed a majority in the forum and attempted to influence its political direction through often fraudulent manoeuvres. Their main objective seems to be to orient the ASF towards the AU and other government-type structures. They are the ones who control the ASF's resources, who decide who is to be invited to meetings and who set the agenda.

A RADICAL PLATFORM FOR AFRICA?

Clearly, the radical and reformist forces have different starting points and approaches on the future of Africa. The reformists base their activities on lobbying and appeasing power structures. But how can the others build up a radical platform in Africa?

It will require patience and confidence in the ordinary people to build such a platform. For it is workers, peasants, women and all other oppressed peoples who can bring about radical change in the region. This is the principle that should guide a radical platform for Africa and NGOs, students and academics who want to be part of it have to accept such a principle.

We need to define the kind of society for which we are struggling. In general we can say that we are struggling for an Africa and for a world that is free from hunger, diseases such as HIV/AIDS, wars, oppression of women, environmental degradation, debt and capitalist exploitation and subjugation. We are struggling for an Africa and for a world that is based on true democracy and the rule of ordinary people.

This perspective requires the participation of organizations and people who are opposed to collaborating with the existing power structures, capitalists and their multinational companies. The implications for ASF and its structures are obvious. The forum should be completely restructured, with the secretariats having various regional and thematic representations, while preference be given to representatives of organizations of ordinary people.

The ASF should also be a forum where like-minded organizations and individuals can meet and discuss social and environmental issues: debating with reformers is a waste of time. Those who are struggling against landlessness, privatization, the oppression of women, etc., should be able to meet separately in the ASF. This will help them to discuss people-to-people solidarity, develop an alternative vision to neoliberalism and build grassroots campaigns and struggles.

In South Africa we have been trying to build links with radical organizations in Mauritius, and these are being consolidated. There are comrades, too, in countries like Swaziland who have come closer to radical politics. We have also invited a comrade from Kenya to come and discuss issues of concern to radical politics in Africa.

There is a crying need to link up with radical forces in other parts of Africa, particularly in the francophone countries. There should be a continental-wide audit of such forces, and those organizations and individuals with some resources ought to start making such an audit as soon as possible. This should help in bridging the language and regional divides, an issue raised by the radical bloc in its caucus during the second ASF. It is also necessary to build strong links with radical movements in other regions of the world, particularly with the Landless Workers Movement in Brazil, as well as other organizations in Asia, North America and Europe.

NOTES

1. M. Hlatshwayo (2003) 'Report of the African Social Forum', *Khanya Journal*, no. 3, March.
2. African Social Forum (2003a) 'Another Africa is Possible', Draft General Report, Addis Ababa.
3. F. Fanon (1967) *The Wretched of the Earth* (Harmondsworth: Penguin).
4. Social Movement Indaba (SMI) (2002) Minutes on Preparations for International Events.
5. African Social Forum (2003b) 'Addis Ababa Consensus'.

16

Convergences and the Anti-war Movement: Experiences and Lessons

Paola Manduca

The reason for writing these notes is not to recall the events created by the opposition to the war in Iraq waged by the USA and its allies. Nor is it to summarize the escalation of new laws, declarations and political decisions by the US government: the lies and the restrictions on civil liberties since 11 September 2001. Others have done this. I can only note that these negative developments have helped the growth of self-respect, consciousness and determination against this war among an unprecedented number of people all over the world. In fact, the breaches of international and national laws have only emphasized the legitimacy of laws of reason and humanity.

What I want to do here is to try to describe the experience of the past two and more years of participating in organizing the anti-war movement, as well as draw some lessons from this experience.

Many of the European social movements, NGOs, associations and some trade unions were trying to digest the significance of the protests against the G8 meeting in Genoa after 21 July 2001 and recover from the physical wounds resulting from this event, in what could have been the largest peaceful demonstration against the world powers. Then, on 11 September, the Twin Towers of the World Trade Center in New York were attacked and destroyed.

Since the protests in Seattle in November 1999, more and more people have been protesting against US domination of the planet through the World Trade Organization (WTO) and the International Monetary Fund (IMF). And they realized that the immediate response of the US government to the attack meant the world was rapidly going to change. It was very soon evident that the collapse of the Twin Towers gave the US administration the chance it had been seeking to escalate its attempts at absolute domination of the world, a trend that had already been set in motion with the fall of the Berlin Wall in 1989. Now it saw the opportunity of enforcing plans that had already been put forward in non-official documents like the Project for the New American Century (PNAC), which had been produced by cronies of the Bush regime. Throughout the last decade the US had been pursuing the reorganization of the world through a hierarchy of powers, with itself at the peak. Successive US governments had been seizing more and more control over essential global resources and using increasingly violent means to do so.

Many people in the anti-globalization movements had opposed the US and NATO military interventions during the 1990s. We were well aware that the military expenditure of the US and leading countries in the European Union had been growing. We had witnessed, in the mid-1990s, the establishment of the WTO to govern and enforce a global economy, and we had protested their imposition of development plans that were having such devastating effects on the inhabitants of countries producing primary commodities and/or with natural reserves of oil, gas, minerals and water. We had got to know the most affected social groups of those countries and developed ties of solidarity with them.

As a consequence of American policies over the last few years, the will to resist the changes being forced on their lives and aspirations had been growing in the hearts and minds of many people throughout the world. The 'earthquakes' that had overtaken them made it difficult for them to take action to protect themselves, either through hard work or through traditional social relationships. Their experience of enforced changes, poverty and subordination have alerted people to expect the worst. Many of them, not only activists and the politically informed, now understand that the US recourse to armed warfare threatens, not only the lives of the people in the country under attack, but the lives of everyone on Earth.

In many parts of the world there were demonstrations against the war in Afghanistan, which was the US response to the attack on the Towers. In the US, Europe and in some Arab states, national coalitions against war came together from the convergence of pacifist groups, anti-globalization organizations and social movements. The war on Afghanistan then produced convincing evidence of the strategy of the US, and it was clear to all. It was soon confirmed that this was only the beginning of an 'unending war', undertaken against most of the world's peoples. The military actions were accompanied by the introduction of anti-terrorist legislation, like the Patriot Act in the US, but also laws along similar lines in most of the other Western countries. These were supported by increases in government spending to meet military and security costs and decreases in social expenditure, as well as new directives for the role of State and international police through the world.

During the war there was a black-out on independent information, while the international conventions on prisoners of war were ignored: for example the Guantánamo camp for detainees still remains outside the reach of international and US law. There were also changes in national laws that enabled Arab nationals in the US to be imprisoned without any charge or accusation. All this was combined with the use of non-conventional operations and weapons (like the use of depleted uranium) that deliberately targeted the civilian population.

Meanwhile the rest of the world was deafened by loud assertions of the power and supremacy of the US (and Western) democracy and declarations of 'pre-emptive, extensive' aggression and repression. None of these actions came under the control of the United Nations, which was unable to intervene. During this period, which lasted almost a year, people's vision sharpened. What was waged as a campaign of hypnosis and persuasion by the US government turned into a campaign that alerted people and roused their concern about the possible outcome of the proclaimed new order. This concern took on different forms in different contexts and with different emphases, but people were united by being equally opposed to, or suffering from, the implementation of American imperial aims, even if they often had diverse perspectives on possible alternatives and strategies for resistance. The period of protesting against the war on Afghanistan was the first stage of our collective movement against war, and it involved organization at the national level.

It soon became obvious to everyone that a new war was on the horizon. The US and its British partner focused their aggression on Iraq unilaterally and on grossly false 'evidence' of weapons of mass destruction – contrary to the views of the UN inspectors on the ground. As some Western states did not agree, the USA, Britain and Spain withdrew the resolution to involve the UN. The structural incapacity and political unwillingness of the UN to prevent the conflict was evident. Those against the war continued to organize, this time opposing the attack on Iraq, by holding campaigns of protest and information in many countries. It was clear that there existed a widespread, if extremely diffuse opposition to the war among the population of all Western countries, the Middle East and the Arab countries. From spring until autumn 2002, new anti-war organizations were formed, while existing ones attracted new participants and attention from that part of the press concerned with public opinion.

Resistance to globalization and participation in the World Social Forum in Porto Alegre had already created a network of relationships and reciprocal solidarity between social movements and anti-globalization organizations. This network was the channel for exchanging the awareness that many of us had reached, that opposition to war expressed the feelings of the majority and that the 'endless, pre-emptive war for worldwide, US-brand democracy' was worrying many people. This network shaped a common determination that preparation for another war should be opposed by a call for mass resistance.

The first action was taken at the end of the European Social Forum in Florence, on 9 November 2002, when one million people marched against the war in Iraq, calling on the social movements to organize a European day of action. Anti-war representatives from some ten European nations held a first, informal meeting, which proved to be the beginning of the European anti-war coalition. The groups present decided to broaden the movement and called for an organizational meeting of all anti-war groups and social movements in Europe. At that time, the anti-war groups differed from country to country in their strength and level of organization, varying from national coalitions to small groups of activists. But all agreed on the urgency of organizing to oppose the war before it started. Many of us felt we had a responsibility to express the general feeling that we had witnessed among people over previous months and show that a majority of Europeans were against the war. The discussions in Florence focused on calculating how much time was needed to organize internationally and within each country, and how long we could risk waiting before holding a coordinated mass demonstration before the war started, in order to give weight to public opinion on the issue.

The anti-war demonstration in Florence started the second and really new phase of European action against war. New, because of the number and kinds of theme involved; because of the methods and languages we had to work out in order for us all to act together; because this brought about changes in the methods of working by the groups and organizations concerned, which resulted in many people and groups joining in; and, finally, new because it produced the first act of worldwide resistance in history.

The first meeting of the coalition took place in Copenhagen on 15–16 December 2002, hosted by the local anti-war groups.

Participating were representatives of 11 countries: Belgium, Denmark, France, Germany, Great Britain, Greece, Italy, Macedonia, Norway, Sweden, Turkey and an anti-war activist from the US. Those present were members of national coalitions or, in some cases, of the most active anti-war group in their country. The coalitions included social movements, political organizations, peace associations and anti-globalization organizations.

This was the founding meeting for the coalition. Our discussions lasted two days, winding up with an agreement on a few simple points essential for our future work. We confirmed 15 February 2003 as the day of mass action in the capitals of Europe against the war in Iraq. We agreed that this would take place whether or not the UN gave its consent to the war. And we were to coordinate and collaborate with all the groups, movements, NGOs, trade unions, churches, associations and Arab migrant groups in our own countries, on the basis of being 'against the war on Iraq, with or without the UN'. We would all bear a common banner, 'No to the war on Iraq' in the demonstrations. In each country, we would concentrate our efforts on getting the maximum number of people to show their dissent by participating with their physical presence at the demonstration. Each country would finance its own organization, as far as possible. We would have a mailing list as a working tool to link up among ourselves and share information and news. A website would be created for the event.

A few days after our meeting in Copenhagen there came a call against the war on Iraq from a meeting, held in Cairo, of anti-war coalitions in the Arab world. And we soon established contacts with US anti-war coalitions, which, as in Europe, had started campaigning against the possible war in Iraq, as well as against the anti-Islam policies of their government. Activists in the US had the impression that there was growing opposition in their country to this second unilateral war.

The hopes and energies of the European movements were triggered by the 15 February date. As from December, activists were working full time, and all over Europe movements and groups were organizing to show their opposition to the war before it started. With this support, the most active members in the European coalition asked whether they could present, at the World Social Forum in Porto Alegre, the European coalition and its appointment for 15 February. In fact, the anti-war assembly in Porto Alegre lasted a whole day and was structured to give the maximum time for interventions from the floor. It was attended by a great number of people from all round the world and was useful for the following reasons:

- First, it was where the European coalition acknowledged, for the first time, the connection with the Arab world and with the Asian and US anti-war coalitions.
- Second, it was when the Latin American anti-war groups decided to participate in the 15 February demonstrations, and when Brazilian trade unions and peasant movements took up and supported the anti-war movement.
- Third, it gave us all the energy, solidarity and legitimacy to continue our work.

One of my comrades, with whom I shared some responsibility for organizing the Porto Alegre meeting, jokingly said that 'we were very lucky'. Yes, we were, because the intention to oppose the war was widespread and everyone present supported the European decision, made in Florence, for a coordinated action on 15 February. And it helped to create the best conditions for the demonstrations in each country.

Meanwhile, the aggressive positions adopted by the US and UK governments, all their unproven accusations against Iraq, the attempts to dismiss the UN, and the US declarations against the Islamic people: all this stimulated debate, including within the churches of the world. The Pope and other Christian leaders declared their opposition to any aggression against Iraq, criticized the invention of a 'clash of civilizations' with Islam and encouraged Christian believers to stand against the war. This helped to increase participation in the national anti-war coalitions during the preparations for 15 February.

Trade unions in many European countries became part of the national anti-war coalitions, and some sectors of civil society were encouraged to join by the anti-war stance taken by France and Germany. In Britain there was even conflict within the government caused by the absurd justifications given by Prime Minister Blair for entering into war. The last days before the demonstration saw support growing rapidly, in terms of mobilization in each country, as well as the number of nations that were mobilizing. At one point it became difficult to keep track of all the support that was being received. In the end, mass demonstrations, with numbers varying from 500 people to three million, were held in 74 countries. Altogether many millions of people in all five continents and hundreds of cities and towns joined in solidarity and opposition to the war.

We, the organizers, were to draw several lessons from our experience. We learnt that we live at a time in history in which there is a broad convergence of concern, individually and collectively, for maintaining peace through dialogue and for opposing war to resolve conflict. It became evident to us that this concern can bring together millions of individuals and hundreds of organizations around the world to organize and act in coordination. They include organizations against neoliberalism, peasant movements, environmental associations, women's and artists' groups, churches and social movements. We also saw that, by choosing a broad, but radical position on the misdeeds of power, we can attract this large convergence and thus generate widespread awareness of the issue. (Similarly, in September, the opposition to the WTO meeting in Cancún produced worldwide consciousness of the stakes involved in WTO governance of the world economy, as well as the intentions to include agriculture and services in the agreements. There was considerable satisfaction all round that the meeting failed in most of its objectives.)

Another important lesson was that networking is a method of developing political analysis and involving relationships that differs from those of elective democracy and representation. (This was not news for some sectors of the movements, including those with feminist experiences and peasant groups, but what is new is how this idea has been extended and the understanding of its potential in sustaining peoples' efforts, like the 15 February global march.) We discovered that it is possible and necessary to articulate local initiatives with national and global events (the local anti-war networking and demonstrations held throughout 2002 made possible the national, coordinated action on 15 February). And we came to realize that people have the autonomy and capacity to organize around the issues that they choose as relevant for them, even without any central committees. Finally, we proved that the debate facilitated by repeated national and international encounters like the social forums and meetings linked to anti-globalization demonstrations enables agreement to be reached on analysis that is commonly shared and that this can determine significant political events around the whole world.

However, although what we helped to happen does indicate that a new world is possible, both in terms of structural choices and social and political relationships, this world is still only in embryo. And, in spite of all our efforts, we did not succeed in preventing the war. The US and Britain are still in Afghanistan and occupy Iraq (receiving aid from a few more well-disposed states, and with the ambiguous support of UN Resolution 1511). Did all the people who came on to the streets really believe they were going to stop the war? Has it been a defeat for us that we did not prevent it? We all knew that US plans would not easily be arrested by one large demonstration, even a global one. What motivated most of those people was one or two concerns (and usually both): one, that it was ethically, intellectually and politically necessary to oppose this war; and two, this war was one more step in a strategy to take control of the planet's resources and one more aspect of the economic and social pursuance of global governance led by the US.

When, at the end of our meeting in Porto Alegre 2002 we proposed marching against 'war and the FTAA' (Free Trade Area of the Americas), this was not only in solidarity with the Brazilian population and their organizations: it expressed this understanding of the situation, an understanding that was the basis of the widespread participation in the 15 February demonstration.

Judged in terms of the above, we did what was necessary and, indeed, with considerable fanfare. We won the battle we had staged, even beyond our hopes: many people all round the globe saw it was possible to resist, understood our reasons for resisting and got an idea of how to organize resistance. And the powers of the world came to know that there are limits to their abuses. This was a 'victory', not only because it challenged the global empire. It also inspired the movement. Those who had come together in the common task to oppose war joined a coalition having their own history and their own local and national perspectives of political and social action. All of them came out of this experience having seen new possibilities for global action. Their self-perception was changed and they acquired new horizons, to which they are having to adjust in their local or national strategies. This has been happening ever since, as can be seen from the events that followed the huge demonstration.

In various places in Europe there was civil disobedience, and the transportation of weaponry being moved towards Iraq was delayed. When war actually broke out there were more demonstrations in many countries during the week 20–27 March, and again on 12 April 2003. There were fewer people than before, but the events were nevertheless very well attended. Those struggling against the war had not given up. Maybe we lost the idealists and the opportunists, the discouraged ones, but still there were many of us. Of course, this time we had less media coverage, and this started a trend of disinformation among the conventional media, which sometimes completely omitted to cover the protests.

From spring to autumn 2003 the global coalition against war has made a few significant steps forward, not only through mass meetings, although these have been taking place in many countries, including the demonstrations against the occupation of Iraq in Washington and San Francisco on 25 October.

One of the aims we had agreed on in Porto Alegre in 2002 was to identify common perspectives and link action with the Latin American and North American movements and trade unions. However, we had not managed to have continuing ties with the people and movements of Asia, Africa and, most relevant at this moment, with those of the Arab world, the Islamic countries of the Middle East and Africa.

In June 2003 there was a meeting to analyze and debate the situation, convened in Jakarta by the Asian networks. This succeeded in organizing the networking of the European coalition with the people and movements of South Asia. It produced a general agreement on the aims of the global anti-war coalition and adopted a methodology of working through global events and campaigns. The events that have since taken place, in Evian in June and around the WTO meeting in Cancún in August/September, were organized against social, economic and military warfare. An international peoples' tribunal to pass judgment on the perpetrators of the war, investigate war crimes and establish compensation for the victims has been set up. It involves sessions in countries all over the world, and it will close with a final session in Turkey. As well as the task of global disarmament, there are campaigns against military expenditure and the production of nuclear weapons in favour of European disarmament being spelt out in the European Constitution, which is still under negotiation. Campaigns against the creation of a European army, for the dismantling of NATO and for freeing the world from US and NATO military installations, are also taking off at the global level.

A campaign has been started in the US and other war-supporting countries to end the occupation of Iraq, demanding the withdrawal of military contingents. An 'Occupation Watch Committee' is active in Baghdad, observing and reporting on war crimes and occupation. Missions of solidarity are being discussed for Palestine, Iran, Iraq and Kurdistan, and there are campaigns for the end of the colonial occupation of Palestine, the dismantling of the Israeli wall and all their settlements, and for the right of return for all Palestinian refugees.

These are the ways we are trying to fulfil the trust and efforts that so many people put into opposing this war and the US attempt to take over all the resources of the planet. It is a task that sees us aligned with all those occupied in contesting globalization in other, and no less relevant aspects. This connection gives us support, tools for analysis and understanding, and the possibility of reaching more and more people in more and more countries in debate and action.

In conclusion, the following is an attempt to summarize what we have done and how we have been transformed by doing it:

- we have acquired new tools for horizontal decision-making and sharing priorities;
- we have learnt languages that can reach outside our own local and national horizons;
- we have connected opposition against armed aggression to economic and social issues;
- we have been enriched through the experience of acting and putting our efforts to the test of the world's peoples;
- we are articulating the global lessons to the local and national situations and continuing work through campaigns.

In terms of emotions, which have been shared with many people in the European and then the global coalition, as well as in terms of ethical and intellectual experiences, we went from determination to fear (at the start of the coalition), to surprise and elation (when we saw that people all over the world were supporting the opposition to war), to dismay (when war was finally launched), to the feeling of challenge (when we had to rationalize and understand the changes we had gone through), and now we are slowly developing a stubborn determination and accepting the ethical and intellectual challenge to continue bringing about transformation.

We learnt a lot from each other and from many other people. We learnt through the network, we learnt how to organize at the right time and in a productive way, and we learnt about the world around us and far away from us. They are lessons of facts and analysis, of humanity, of strengths and of fragility. Among the organizers of the coalition, we are still very grateful to each other for our work and reciprocal support.

17
The Trade Union Movement and the Social Movement: Towards A New Dialogue?

Pierre Beaudet

The first European Social Forum (ESF) took place in Florence in November 2002. More than 60,000 participants from some fifteen countries met and exchanged ideas and information in over 400 workshops and seminars. The question of alternatives to neoliberal globalization was discussed at length, as well as the need to put a stop to militarization and imperialism. It was from these discussions that the idea arose of getting movements to converge against the war in Iraq, and on 15 February 2003, more than 15 million people (of which 5 million were in Europe) responded to the call. But the impact of the ESF was probably even more important in creating a new dialogue between the union movement and the social movements. This development should be seen in the context of the unions almost everywhere having been driven on the defensive.

THE EUROPEAN SOCIAL FORUM

In the past, participation by the unions in the World Social Forums (at Porto Alegre) had been relatively modest. But in Florence, strong contingents came from the countries of Southern Europe, particularly the Confédération Générale du Travail (France), the Confederazione Generale Italiana del Lavoro (Italy), the Confederación Sindical de Comisiones Obreras (Spain), the Confederação Geral dos Trabalhadores Portugueses (Portugal) and the Geniki Synomospondia Ergaton Ellados (Greece). The professional federations were also very much present, including the European federations for transport, metallurgy and public services, as well as the European Confederation of Trade Unions. Besides these large trade union organizations there were smaller, but very militant ones, like the Cobas (Italy), SUD-G10 Solidaires (France) and others. However certain absences were noticeable, particularly IG Metall (the largest German trade union) and the British and Scandinavian trade unions.

CONSULTATION OR CONFRONTATION?

Over the last few years the European trade union movement has taken on a new urgency, particularly because of the rise of the right almost everywhere on the continent. During the 1980s, a number of European trade unions had developed close relationships with the governments in power. For the French CGT and the Italian CGIL, the pluralist left-wing governments were more partners than adversaries, even when these governments adopted neoliberal policies (privatization, deregulation, the imposition of so-called 'flexible' work, etc.).

More radical union initiatives like the Cobas in Italy or the SUD in France then emerged because parts of the union movement were uncomfortable with this accord between the social democrats in power and the trade union movement. Thus the SUD unions managed to build a base in the railways, health, education and telecommunication sectors, which then created an alliance with other dissident unions (the alliance known as the G10). This brings together over thirty independent unions, former members of the Confédération française du travail (CFDT). These small unions also broke off at the structural level, acting in a very decentralized way, without a rigid hierarchy and with a strong emphasis on direct action, rather than negotiation. For most unions, however, union action should remain within the structures that had been established fifty years ago, essentially through the network of the tripartite institutions that governed the working world. The priority was to protect this tripartite arrangement and the system of collective bargaining that stemmed from it. The viewpoint of the German unions (like IG-Metall) was the point of reference: a framework of negotiation including the economic sectors, moderation on wages and an acceptance by the employers and the State of the need to work with the unions – a strategy that in general avoided confrontation (including strikes).

These two approaches, consultation and tripartite arrangements on the one hand and direct action and struggle on the other, confronted each other within the ESF framework. The large unions (e.g. CGT, CCOO, CGIL) insisted on the need to organize a European-level strategy. The idea was to force the hand of the European Union and thus of the member states, within the framework of the 'social market' that the unions hope to impose as a response to unrestricted neoliberalism. For the CGT, for example, the rights of workers must be guaranteed by pan-European negotiations.

However, for the more militant unions, this strategy does not work. They give, as an example, the difficulties of the German unions, who have been forced, as has the social-democratic government of Schröder, to accept important concessions, even if, in Germany, the 'social partnership' still prevails. At the beginning of 2003, a five-week strike orchestrated by IG-Metall to defend the 35-hour week was unsuccessful.

Strikes in France against the reforms being imposed by Raffarin's right-wing government to increase the qualifying time for salaried earners to secure a pension also failed to block the process, even though the main trade union organizations (CGT, CFDT, SUD, FSU, etc.) all mobilized and called out two million workers on 13 May. At the critical point, the main unions, including the CGT, refused to call for a general strike.

DIFFICULT DIALOGUE WITH THE SOCIAL MOVEMENTS

As the strike strategy does not function any better than consultation, the European unions face a challenge. How, then, can they then resist neoliberalism?

In Florence this question was discussed at length. For the more militant, the path to follow was to make alliances between unions and the social movements. The simple defence of waged workers, even carried out in a militant way, was no longer sufficient because the strategy of neoliberalism is to accentuate the division between the world of work and the world of insecurity. Demands to defend wages, stable employment and social benefits are easily got round by employers who confront the 'privileged' sectors (who are unionized) with the reality of insecurity, exclusion and poverty. For the SUD militants, the struggle of those 'without papers', for the legalization of so-called illegal immigrants, thus becomes as important for the union movement as the preserving of teachers' pensions because without convergence between these 'two worlds' it is not possible to offer resistance. In the same way, the struggles to preserve social security, health and public education are also priority issues because they involve everyone, not only the unionized workers. In February 2003, Belgian trade unions and associations like ATTAC came together to demand that the EU impose a moratorium on the privatization of public utilities, particularly water.

This viewpoint is gradually penetrating the more traditional unions – through necessity, if for no other reason. There are visible signs of linkages between unions and social movements throughout Europe, particularly in the anti-war movement. Trade unions are increasingly aware that, on the broader front, resistance to neoliberal policies requires huge social coalitions. But they are not ready to make a real and direct investment in the process of mobilizing against neoliberalism. At the end of the day they want the social movements to accept more limited demands, to 'civilize' neoliberalism and reconstruct alliances with the social democrats at the political level. They hope, finally, to lead a battle to reform the EU, which, in their eyes, constitutes the best chance of imposing a 'social' Europe, functioning within and through a market economy, but regulated to avoid its excesses and pauperization. The social movements, like the militant unions, are far more sceptical about the project for the construction of Europe, which they feel is locked into the neoliberal process, and contributes, not to expanding but to restricting social rights, as in the Maastricht Treaty and the so-called Stability Pact.

TOUGH CHALLENGES LIE AHEAD

Neoliberal policies have been imposed in Europe and elsewhere in the world since the 1980s. For some years now, however, the project has been strongly opposed – even though it remains hegemonic, including among broad sectors of the social democrats. A new social coalition, involving the unions, is emerging, but it is still essentially an obstructive rather than a constructive force. The absence of political 'interlocutors' is certainly a major factor, but there are others. The alternative world movement, as one might call it, has initiated a field of action that is still very much open. A tough 'war for position' lies before us.

18
The New Agrarian Issue:
Three Billion Peasants Under Threat

Samir Amin

Capitalist agriculture, governed by the principle of profitability, is to be found almost exclusively in North America, Europe, the southern cone of Latin America and Australia. It employs only a few dozen million farmers, who are not really peasants. But their productivity, as a result of mechanization (to which they have almost exclusive access at the global level) and the amount of land at their disposal, yields about 10,000 to 20,000 quintals of the cereal equivalent per worker per year.

In contrast, peasant farmers represent almost half of humanity – three billion human beings. Their agriculture is in turn divided between those who have benefited from the Green Revolution (fertilizers, pesticides and selected seeds, although not often mechanized), whose annual production varies from 100 to 500 quintals per worker, and those who have not experienced this revolution, whose production is around 10 quintals per person.

The gap between the productivity of agriculture that is better equipped and that of the poor peasantry has increased enormously over the last half-century. In other words, the rhythm of progress in the productivity of agriculture has greatly surpassed that of other activities, bringing about a reduction of relative prices from 5 to 1.

In such conditions, if agriculture is integrated into all the general regulations governing 'competition', reducing agricultural and food products to 'goods like all the others', as the World Trade Organization has been insisting since the Doha conference in November 2001, what will be the certain consequences, given the gigantic inequality between agro-business on the one hand and peasant production on the other?

Some twenty million additional modern farms, if given access to the land they would need and if they had the access to capital markets enabling them to obtain the necessary equipment, could produce most of what urban consumers (those with 'effective demand') still purchase from peasant production. But what will happen to those billions of peasant producers who are not competitive? They will be inexorably eliminated in a brief period of a few dozen years. What will happen to those billions of human beings, most of whom are already the poorest of the poor, but who feed themselves as best they can – and for a third of them, not very well (three-quarters of the undernourished in the world come from the rural areas)? In fifty years, no industrial development, which was more or less competitive – even given the far-fetched hypothesis of a continual annual growth of 7 per cent for three-quarters of humanity – could absorb even a third of this labour reserve.

What should be done, then? Peasant agriculture has to be maintained for the foreseeable future of the twenty-first century. Not because of romantic nostalgic reasons for the past, but quite simply because the solution to the problem means moving beyond the logic of liberalism. There must be policies for regulating the relationships between the 'market' and peasant agriculture. At the national and regional levels, such regulations, especially adapted to local conditions, must protect national production, thus ensuring the indispensable food security of nations and preventing food from being used as a weapon. In other words, internal prices must be disconnected from the so-called world prices. Through continuing productivity in peasant agriculture, which will be slow but continuous, this would make it possible to control the transfer of the rural population towards the towns. At the level of what is called the world market, the regulation would probably occur through interregional agreements, for example between Europe on the one hand and Africa, the Arab world, China and India on the other, thus meeting the needs of a development that integrates instead of excludes.

SUPPORT TO AGRICULTURE IN THE REAL CONTEMPORARY WORLD AND THE 'FAILURE' OF CANCÚN (SEPTEMBER 2003)

The World Trade Organization ignores this gigantic challenge confronting the societies in the South. Indeed, the items on its agenda (the question of 'subsidies' to agriculture) have been chosen for the exclusive purpose of opening the markets of the South to the exports of agricultural surpluses from the North.

• *In 1995 the global volume of public expenditure on agriculture, according to WTO, was US$286 billion. At least 90 per cent of this was* *spent in the countries of the Triad (United States and Canada, the European Union and Japan).*

WTO classifies this agricultural public expenditure into four categories of 'boxes': red, orange, blue and green. The criterion is the degree of influence of this expenditure on production and above all on the 'prices' of agricultural products (price of production, price of sale by the farmers, price to the consumers). WTO puts into the red and orange categories the expenditure that it considers to have an impact on the prices in question, while it allocates to the blue and green categories those that do not, according to its own judgment.

For the red and orange categories, its estimate is $124 billion, while for the blue and green, it is $162 billion.

This classification is important for WTO, as the so-called 'liberalization' measures for agriculture, aiming at treating agricultural products as ordinary commercial goods, only concern expenditure in the first two categories, which are supposed to be gradually reduced, according to a timetable fixed through negotiations at WTO. Countries are therefore free to maintain expenditures classified as blue and green, or even to increase them. This has in fact become a *fait accompli* over the last ten years.

The criterion used by WTO for its classification system does not hold water. In actual fact, the four categories are only one, which is rightly called the 'black box'. All expenditure has an obvious impact on both the volume and effectiveness of production and hence prices. Its very objective is indeed to have such an impact – and it does. Thus the concept of 'linking' or 'de-linking' that defines the different forms of public expenditure in this field on the one hand, and production and price on the other, has no solid foundation. It belongs to the realm of 'pure economics' alchemy and just serves as an argument to enable manipulation in one way or the other, according to whether the requirement is to legitimize or delegitimize an economic policy objective.

• *The nature and the impact of agricultural policies in the countries of the North must be replaced, in view of the challenge outlined at the beginning of this chapter and must not be based solely on terms set by the WTO agenda (under the title 'subsidies').*

The advantages to the North in this area (as in others) are structural. Furthermore, the very success of the agricultural policies implemented in Europe (particularly the CAP) and in the US sustain these countries' productive capacities, which greatly exceed what their internal markets can absorb. The EU and the US have thus now become aggressive exporters of their overproduction. Their desire to 'open' the markets of the South to their agricultural and food exports, for which the WTO serves as the instrument, follows on from this.

But looking beyond these questions on the agenda (particularly that of WTO and the Cancún conference) and the way they are each given special treatment, it is essential that there be an overall alternative to agricultural policies – in the North and the South – starting with those concerning world trade.

The countries of the South do not have the means to imitate the agricultural policies implemented in the North, even if this made sense under their own conditions (which is doubtful). Although they do not have the means, that certainly does not mean that they have no need for their own policies for development and agriculture, bearing in mind their desire both to accelerate productivity and to control social change (avoiding the disintegration of the rural areas and the building up of slums in the cities). These policies must also integrate national objectives, first of all food autonomy (at the level of the nation states and in appropriately defined regions).

If they do this, the countries of the South not only have the right but the duty to protect these policies by a series of appropriate measures, not only through choosing the customs duty demanded, but also perhaps by adopting quantitative measures, such as quota systems. Apart from these direct measures, the protection of the development of the national economy certainly involves coherent national policies in a variety of fields, and first of all in managing their national currency and exchange rates.

Besides their subsidies to agriculture, there are other fields in which the aggressive policies of the North should be taken into consideration. The super-monopoly that agro-business uses to protect its own profit, under the pretext of 'protecting intellectual and industrial property', by imposing manufactured selected seeds by corporations in this sector, should be opposed outright by the countries of the South, among others. This question is also one of the aspects of the huge problem of the ecology and the environment. The practices that are defended by liberal thinking in this field range from pure and simple pillage of knowledge accumulated by the peasants in the South over the centuries to the destruction of biodiversity and support for options the long-term dangers of which could be tremendous (GM crops, for example).

These ideas and the construction of an alternative project (alternative world solutions) have made headway in people's opinions and are reflected in the exchange of views that took place at Kuala Lumpur in the conference of the Non-Aligned States in February 2003.

• *The 'failure' of the Cancún conference (September 2003) should be welcomed as a victory of the peoples. The fact that the countries of the South rejected the diktat of the WTO was itself a victory. But there were ambiguities. Because what the countries of the South rejected was not the 'principle of liberalism' (the free and reciprocal opening, proposed by WTO, of all markets to everyone) but only the ways proposed by WTO to implement it: ways that treat countries, whether of North or South, in a scandalously unequal manner. It is necessary to move well beyond this position, because the implementation of 'authentic liberalism' would be catastrophic for the peasants in the South in any circumstances (that is, with or without subsidies to the agricultural exports in the North).*

Do the demands and the struggles of the peasant movements make it possible to trace the outline of an alternative? Let us take the examples of the Chinese and the Egyptians in trying to respond to this question.

THE FORMING OF A PEASANT COUNTER-POWER IN CHINA

In 2000 China had a population of 1,200 million, of whom two-thirds (800 million) came from rural areas. A simple 20-year projection to 2020 shows that it would be illusory, indeed dangerous, to believe that urbanization can greatly reduce the number of rural people, even if it could help to reduce their two-thirds ratio.

By 2020, a demographic growth of 1.2 per cent a year will increase the Chinese population to 1,520 million. Let us suppose that China manages to sustain a reasonable growth of its modern industries and services in the urban areas, at an annual rate of 5 per cent. In order to attain this, modernization and the requirements of competitiveness will certainly oblige this growth not to be produced exclusively through extensive accumulation (the 'same industries and services' as at present, but more numerous), but by a partially intensive mode of production, associated with a great improvement in work productivity (at an annual rate of 2 per cent). The growth of urban jobs would then be 3 per cent a year, bringing the total number of the population that can be absorbed into the urban areas to 720 million. This last figure would include the same amount of the urban population that are currently unemployed, in insecure jobs or in the informal economy – and that is not a negligible figure.

Nevertheless their proportion will be notably reduced (which would be a positive result).

A simple arithmetical sum shows that 800 million Chinese will have to remain rural – the same number as today, but a smaller proportion of the total population, from 67 to 53 per cent. If they are forced to emigrate to the towns because they have no access to land, they can only increase the marginalized population of the slums, as has been the case for a long time in the capitalist Third World. A longer-term projection, say 40 years, would only confirm this conclusion.

• *Since the middle of the nineteenth century, the ruling classes of modern China have been acutely aware of this challenge. It is in fact a double challenge: to increase subsistence crops, not only to feed all the peasants (without constant famines) but also to support necessary urbanization/industrialization/modernization. The objective would be to promote agricultural growth itself and to ensure the political and military independence of China.*

The peasant movements are evidently determined to take as their starting point the impacts that successive 'models' laid down by the authorities have had on the peasantry as a whole and for each of the different classes that constitute it. The struggles they have waged have crystallized around objectives that are essentially defensive ('to adjust cleverly', 'to resist without proclaiming it'), and they have sometimes managed to get the governing classes to backtrack from imposing their projects. But the peasants have also, apart from their defence strategies, begun to express their own alternative objectives, even if only partial ones. It is true that the political and social forces in power have sometimes succeeded in channelling these movements of 'response' by the peasant classes, but they have often failed to do so. In fact, the authorities have used all the measures at their disposal to prevent the unification of the peasant movement at the national level. So it remains fragmented and is unable to present itself as a spokesperson/actor/participant on equal footing with other sectors of society (the bourgeoisie, the urban popular classes, the authorities) in drawing up global strategies for the development of the country. By forcing them to 'look after their own affairs' only, the governing classes have prevented the peasant movements from understanding the exact degree of interdependence between their aspirations and the requirements of urbanization/industrialization/modernization, of which they know nothing.

• *The Maoist model was inspired by the Soviet model of collectivization, which was in turn modelled on the thinking of Mao Tse-Tung.*

Kautsky started it off: modernization must be accelerated, freeing up surplus workers so that they join the rural exodus to urbanize as much as is needed and transfer part of the agricultural surplus produced by this modernization to the benefit of industrial accumulation. Socialism, seen as substituting the State for private landowners, ought to make it easier to do this than capitalism. The large agricultural holding (perhaps in the juridical form of a co-operative), which is equipped and mechanized, is from the start considered more efficient (in terms of productivity per hectare and work productivity) than the small peasant holding, as is the case in industry. Besides, agricultural and industrial exchanges, now 'planned', can also escape the laws of value, such as they are expressed in the 'free' market.

The application of this model has certainly given positive results, in terms of agricultural and global growth, which are better in China than anywhere else in the Third World and, above all, infinitely less unequal: 6.2 per cent annual growth in GNP; 3.4 per cent growth in agriculture (one and a half times more than all the rest of the Third World). It creates a Lorenz curve that is incomparably better than in other parts of Asia.

However, the limits of the model were apparent after two successful decades. Intensification of labour reached its limits (200 to 270 days of work per worker annually, as compared with 160 days before collectivization); inequalities increased between villages and provinces (because the same radical reform was applied in situations that were very unequal in terms of collective potential); while inequalities between town and country fluctuated and were poorly managed by non-commercial planning.

• *At the present time the Chinese peasantry are organizing, mainly to resist the liberal offensive. There is an acquired right that the peasants insist on defending, and it is known that they would defend it still more forcefully if the authorities were to challenge it brutally. This is the equal right for everyone to have access to the use of land, which was obtained by a radical agrarian reform that the Chinese peasants actively supported.*

The decollectivization undertaken by Deng Xiao Ping did not question this right : on the contrary it fully reaffirmed it and, for this reason, it was well received. In addition, the forms of collective management, which were authoritarian and rigid, had ended in 'fatigue' and they lost legitimacy, blocking the path towards improving living standards.

A new chapter was opened for the Chinese peasant economy by this decollectivization. Within a few years, the great majority of the peasants (as has been observed) became aware that the small family unit was not equipped to meet their aspiration to live better (and to do that, to produce more). On their own initiative they then moved towards the reconstruction of co-operative forms of production. But, in contrast with the preceding collectivization movement, this came from below: the initiative did not arise with the party or the State, but from the peasant themselves. The forms of these new co-operatives should thus be examined more closely.

What is clear is that the peasant movements strongly supported the expansion of the new co-operative forms, particularly from 1992 to 1995, although it was apparently carried out in a very disorganized way. At least this is what the authorities said, who declared their aim was to 'dissolve' these co-operatives as from 1999, so that they would give way to 'classic capitalist' forms of agricultural credit. But, according to observers in the field, the co-operatives are resisting, cleverly adapting to the succession of directives that try to regulate their activities. The battle has been joined …

However, the question of the new co-operatives cannot be analyzed in isolation from the other dimension of the challenge facing the Chinese: the financing of urban modernization and industrialization.

The authorities, through their new formulas, thought that they could leave the market mechanism and public financial policies (taxation and subsidies) to resolve the problem, as happened in classic capitalism. In overall terms the results have been considerable: in 1950, 400 million peasants fed 50 million urban dwellers; in 1980, 800 million fed 200 million; and now 800 million peasants feed 400 million urban dwellers. But the town/country relationship is far from being definitively resolved: taxation and subsidy systems are disorganized and are subject to successive revision, without achieving effective stabilization, as the markets for food crops fluctuate wildly.

  • *The ideological debate on the prospects of reforming the system ('market socialism') is no less important than the lessons to be learnt from the movements that express the aspirations of the peasants.*

This debate is highly polarized. On the one hand there are the 'liberals', infected, as everywhere in the world, by the 'liberal virus'. Their agenda is well known: the question of access to land is reduced to the principle of creating stable and definitive forms of private property in its broadest sense ('commercialized land'). The Chinese partisans of this approach deliberately turn their backs on the lessons of their own history even though these lessons belie the conclusions of the shallow rhetoric of American institutionalism and its discourse.

Conversely, there are the 'radicals'. It is easy for them to show that the liberal way leads to what they rightly called the 'Latin American impasse'. What they mean by that is, while China is a poor country where one does not see many (very) poor people, in rich Latin America (with the enormous potential of its arable land), one only sees the poor. This is 'actually existing capitalism': the only possible one.

It is indeed hard to renovate the doctrine of the 'new democracy' and reinforce its ability to support progress that is both economic and social. However, China does have one major advantage – the inheritance of its revolution – which enables it to produce one of the possible 'models' for what must be done. Equal access of all to land is in fact a fundamental right, still recognized in China (and Vietnam). The supreme irony would be that if this right is renounced, in other words if land is given the status of merchandise, as proposed by all the propagandists for capitalism in China and elsewhere, one could 'accelerate modernization'.

Hence the creation of alternatives is the decisive function of the movements that have sprung up at the grassroots (the peasants in this instance): movements that are managed by themselves and autonomous vis-à-vis the authorities. The radical Chinese that are closely following these movements are perfectly aware of this.

Here we come back to the fundamental question of democracy, conceived not as a formula that has been worked out once and for all, that only has to be 'applied', but as a process that is never achieved, which is why the term 'democratization' is more appropriate. It has to find a way of combining, in formulations that are increasingly complex, the essential needs of defining them in terms of precise 'procedures' (the rule of law in simplified language) as well as in 'substantial' terms, meaning the capacity of the democratization exercise to reinforce the impact of socialist values on the decision-making process at all levels and in all fields.

It is a question of genuine social movements and their convergence serving as a point of departure for identifying objectives, stage by stage, and the progress that is possible as an alternative to actually existing capitalism. This formula is no less valid for China than it is for all other countries in the world. We shall not move far in this direction so long as the initiative for change remains the monopoly of the governing classes and while the social movements (the peasants in this instance) limit themselves to 'resisting' those initiatives that come into conflict with their own aspirations (or supporting others). The renewal of democracy can only be genuinely democratic.

In spite of its difficulties, the movement of Chinese peasants is sufficiently powerful (apparently there are 300 million rural people who are more or less 'organized' in this movement) for the authorities to consider them already as a 'counter-power' with which they have to come to terms.

REBIRTH AND LIMITS OF THE PEASANT MOVEMENT IN EGYPT

• *The economic system of Egypt from 1880 to 1950 was built around the monoculture of cotton, upon which were grafted financial and commercial activities as well as some light industry that developed with the expansion of cotton exports.*

The system, which was managed by the hegemonic social alliance associating large capitalist landholdings with foreign capital, based its growth on that of the consumption of the minority. In this system, agriculture both supplied the main exports and covered essential food needs at prices that made it possible to maintain wage labour at very low levels. The State performed no functions at all beyond that of maintaining public order. It was indeed a form of peripheral, dependent capitalism, but it was a fully coherent system.

The national populism of the Nasser period proposed changing this system to one based on industrialization. The role of agriculture was then seen as having to help finance this industrialization, while the relative stagnation in the living conditions of the peasants that this involved would be compensated by a reduction in the inequalities within the rural world (the objective of agrarian reform). Maintaining agriculture's capacity to cover the country's food needs, even to the detriment of the former policy of growth in the exports of cotton – which were to be substituted by exports of manufactured products – was consistent with the overall logic of the project. The State became the active agent for change, through its social expenditure (the education and health needed for modernization and industrialization), its interventions in redistributing income (control of prices and subsidies) and its role in planning the economy (facilitated by the preponderance of public property).

This model was sucessful for only a short period, about a decade, from the Suez war in 1956 to the 1967 war. It was rapidly eroded by a combination of its own deficiencies and the aggressive strategies conducted by imperialism and its regional agent (Israel). Then followed, with the 'liberalism' of the following three decades (1970s, 1980s, 1990s), the dismantling of the 1960 model. It was not, however, replaced by any really coherent alternative project.

• *Egyptian agriculture provides less than 50 per cent of the country's wheat consumption. There is no doubt that it has been in decline for the last three decades of the twentieth century.*

The import of food products, which compensates for the growing food deficit, has terminated agriculture's former role, that of being the main supplier of the means to pay for the imports required by industrial development. The deficit in the agricultural balance of trade is now a third of the deficit in Egypt's overall commercial balance of trade.

Reducing the food deficit is not only a political requirement, that of limiting the vulnerability of the country to the political manoeuvres and logic of imperialism's economic strategies. It has become, for Egypt, an essential condition for pursuing any industrial development, as the capacity for covering the imports it needs is reduced insofar as the agricultural balance of trade is in deficit because of the growing dependence on imported food.

• *The agrarian reforms of the Nasser period certainly had some effect, but it was limited, however. They enabled the transfer of land from the large landowners to the middle peasants, but they excluded those without land and the overwhelming majority of smallholders, with less than one feddan of land (half a hectare).*

As the agrarian reform was gradually challenged over the last three decades of the twentieth century, so social polarization set in increasingly rapidly. The rich peasants and agrarian capitalists (including companies managed by agro-business) – those whose land exceeded ten feddans – now controlled over a third of agricultural land. The middle peasants were thus caught between the ambitions of the rich peasants and capitalists, anxious to take over more land, and the poor peasants whose dramatic situation they became more and more likely to share. The middle peasants were thus the backbone of the re-emergent peasant movement that has been visible since the 1990s.

There was an important peasant movement in Egypt in the 1940s and 1950s, at a time when the old King Cotton system had exhausted its capacities to pull along the whole economic system with it. Influenced by the communists, the watchword 'land to those who work it' was then heard throughout the countryside and it brought about, for the first time, a movement combining peasants without land, poor peasants and middle peasants, which led to a series of bloody encounters (Behietam, Koufour Negm).

The 1952 reform thus came just in time to avert the danger of civil war. But the reform, while it satisfied the middle peasants, abandoned the poor ones to their fate. However, they reacted and demanded the radicalization of the reform, as could be seen in the violence that took place in the village of Kamsheesh. The severe repression unleashed by the authorities – and the withdrawal of the communists to positions of support for the regime as from 1955–56 – put a stop to all pretences of radicalization.

• *The movement that has been reborn is so far that of the middle peasants. The rural proletariat and the poor peasantry do not participate.*

Moreover, the movement seems to have been very slow in reacting to liberalization measures. In its latest demands – based on the law of 1992 which, in principle and for the first time, treats agricultural production and the land as 'ordinary merchandise' – it even adopts the discourse of the 'American experts' on mission to Cairo and the WTO. Its demands are very moderate, only asking the Government to 'amend' the law – nothing more.

There are two basic causes for this. Firstly, the cleverness of the State apparatus (including the law courts) in implementing these laws only gradually in order to avoid conflict. Secondly, the effects of the massive Egyptian emigration towards the oil-producing countries, as from 1973. Millions of people have migrated and, as there has been a certain rotation, it has benefited almost all families, particularly the rural ones, as two-thirds of the emigrants are from medium-sized villages or poor ones. The middle peasants have thus been able to finance the modernization, not only of their living conditions such as housing, but also of their farms.

The poor peasants and the rural proletariat have also profited as best they could from migration, going in for modest sideline activities (purchase of a taxi or a small van) and able to meet their consumption needs for survival through the economies they have made abroad. Their mass emigration has also had a beneficial effect in that the labour necessary at certain times in the production cycle having become scarce, the wages of the seasonal workers have considerably increased.

There is no doubt, however, that the massive migration has helped to delay collective struggle, both in the country and in the towns, where it is responsible for the weakening of trade union militancy. But this migration seems to be coming to an end. The organized political parties have of course reacted, each responding in its own way to the rebirth of the peasant movement. The two left-wing parties, the Tagammu and the Nasser Party, have openly and formally supported the assemblies of many thousands of peasants throughout the country, in all the prefectures and sub-prefectures in the north and the south. These have been particularly numerous in the second half of the 1990s. But they have not 'organized' them and they do not dare to offer them a framework for unified national representation. They are fearful; they preach restraint and cool the ardour of the demonstrators. Strangely enough, the Islamic parties have remained on the sidelines.

The peasant movement itself thus continues to be fragmented, which enables the left-wing parties to speak in its name through small coordination committees that they have set up for this purpose. The proposals of these committees are moderate and concentrate on three main issues.

One is the amendment of the law on tenant farming and a return to the ceiling on rents imposed by law. Another is support for the reconstruction of co-operatives that are independent from the authorities and administered democratically and freely by their members. The aim is to correct the imbalances of the market (in inputs, sale of products and credit) in favour of the peasants. The third demand is that the State takes back its responsibilities, particularly in its duty (which has been traditional in Egypt) to decide the choice of crops on farms, the aim being to protect the food autonomy of the country.

This programme is perhaps acceptable and credible in the short term and can thus become more effective, enabling greater unification of the middle peasants and attracting the sympathy of the whole nation towards its demands. Nevertheless, the programme overlooks the principle of the right of equal access to land by all peasants, including the poor ones and those without land, which had been the basis of the Egyptian communist programmes up until the 1950s. Thus the above programme, put forward in the name of the peasant movement, continues to exclude the poor peasants, who form two-thirds of the total peasant population. There can be no solution to the fundamental problems of the country and no effective long-term strategy as long as the demands – legitimate as they are – are limited to those of the middle classes threatened by the unbridled forces of liberalism.

SIMILAR NATURAL CONDITIONS, DIFFERENT SOCIAL RESPONSES: THE NEED FOR A WORLD CAMPAIGN FOR THE RIGHT TO LAND

China, Vietnam, Egypt and Bangladesh all suffer from an extreme scarcity of arable land in relation to their peasant populations.

China and Vietnam have undergone radical revolutions, based on the principle of the equal right of all peasants to land – first of all, those without land and the poor peasants. It has been by putting this principle into practice (however bureaucratic the framework has been) that these two countries have managed to maintain their food autonomy (China decently feeds 22 per cent of the world's population using 6 per cent of its cultivated land). They have succeeded in achieving a minimum of inequality that is second to none in the world. It is true that the very principle of equality in access to land, and even more so, the methods of making it effective, are threatened by what has been happening over the last twenty years. But that is another problem.

The authorities in Bangladesh and Egypt have never adopted the principle of equal access to land – not even, in Egypt, when radicalization was at its height during the Nasser period. Aside from the flagrant social inequalities that result from this refusal, it also renders the society, the nation and its economy extremely vulnerable. Hence, in both countries, the adoption of the principles of globalized liberalism has produced a devastation that is ravaging the social and national fabric in record time. As far as Egypt is concerned, this alignment with liberalism has already resulted in dramatic food dependency, increasingly rapid social inequality and the dislocation of the economic system.

This comparison renders meaningless the dominant conventional discourse that attributes the reason for the failure of Bangladeshi and Egyptian rural development and overall development to the poverty of their 'natural' conditions and to their demography.

• *The two examples of China and Egypt – and there are others – bear witness to the rise in peasant resistance throughout Asia and Africa, from India to South Africa, from the Philippines to Ethiopia and West Africa.*

If there were to be a global-level campaign for the recognition of the right to land of all the peasants in the world, it would be a means of creating solidarity between this vast peasant front (which is beginning to be anti-liberal) and its potential natural allies, the worker and urban worlds. It is indeed an essential right for the survival of half of humanity. And yet this right has not yet found its place in the different 'charters of rights' adopted by the international community.

Part Three

The Strategic Challenge

19
The Alternative Movement and its Media Strategies

Victor Sampedro

'Communication, culture and counter-hegemony' was one of the five major fields for the meetings of the Second World Social Forum of Porto Alegre. The choice of this theme showed the central importance of social communication for the movement, at least as far as media visibility and institutional impact are concerned.[1] The present review of the initiatives now being undertaken may help to give a picture of the strategic challenges that face the movement. In assessing its communication arrangements, their potential and limitations, a fundamental issue is raised about the redistribution of symbolic power and communication in the era of globalization. How should we construct a pluralistic and trans-scale communication network that reflects and strengthens our struggles and resistance?

The thousands of proposals put forward on communication at Porto Alegre can be divided into five main categories: (1) the First World Audiovisual Forum, the principal aim of which is to put a halt to the capitalist globalization of the information and cultural industry; (2) the CRIS campaign in preparation for the December 2003 World Summit on the Information Society, convened by the United Nations; (3) the setting up of Media Watch Global to analyze and denounce corporate communication media; (4) the strengthening of the networks of alternative media; and (5) the new technologies (computers and Internet), which reinforce information and coordination networks, both about the movement and originating from it, with both a global and horizontal reach. The movement has shown that it is aware of all these challenges and that it has the energy to tackle them. As we examine them, we also note some risks.

THE FIRST WORLD AUDIOVISUAL FORUM

This forum brought together all professional bodies and industrial sectors in the audiovisual field along with the educators and artists present in Porto Alegre. They advocated coordinated international action so that civil society and governments can progress towards a 'genuine world audiovisual democracy'. Looking beyond principles and the somewhat abstract overall objectives, in practical terms the main aims can be summed up as follows:

- encouraging a 'high-intensity' democracy that provides for participation and deliberation;
- creating alternative systems of production and distribution;
- fostering multi-culturalism and making equality compatible with diversity;
- promoting collective knowledge and counter-hegemony, and consequently
- helping to build the concept of the global citizen, understood as an active actor both in international institutions and at lower levels.

In the forum the stale rhetoric of 'cultural imperialism' was revived. But the above-mentioned objectives address new problems. Some reflect the crisis of representative democracy and conventional journalism, now muzzled in the 'developed' world because of restrictive laws on the right to information (for example, the Patriot Act in the US). Then there is the oligopolistic domination of corporate communication, which is not only limited to US-based production. Paradoxically, the extension of a global and homogeneous mass culture coincides with the emergence of an infinite number of alternative communication initiatives. A 'global public opinion' is dawning, but it can count on very little institutional support in giving it an effective voice.

The extraordinary campaign of disinformation used in the permanent global war unleashed since 11 September is a good example of all this. The international governmental institutions were disarmed and the credibility of the corporate media was damaged as it transformed into an impressive war propaganda machine. In spite of this, millions of people all over the world came out against the war. But they were unable to stop it. They were unable even to penalize electorally the national leaders that had conducted it. The warlike and xenophobic hegemony (against the Arabs) has perhaps never reached such levels in the conventional media. But their weaknesses were perhaps never so evident either, thanks to the emergence of an alternative public sphere, facilitated by the Internet.

Even the 'free market' promoted the 'glocalization' of new media hostile to US hegemony. This would have been unthinkable in the past, but the satellite television chains Al Jazeera and Abu Dhabi are good examples. Nevertheless, the global war went ahead. It seems that the communication aims of the movement need more backing from institutions that are impervious to corporate pressures and the governmental manipulation of public radio stations. The CRIS initiative, described below, is a step in this direction.

THE CRIS (COMMUNICATION RIGHTS FOR THE INFORMATION SOCIETY) CAMPAIGN

This was also present at Porto Alegre. It assembled the various initiatives in the communication development policies of the world social movement, in preparation for the World Summit on the Information Society (WSIS), held in Geneva, 10–12 December 2003, and in Tunis in 2005. The WSIS aims at producing two basic documents: a declaration of the ethical principles and rules of conduct, and an action plan, with operative priorities and specific measures to ensure equitable access to the opportunities provided by the information society.

The United Nations has invited member states, private enterprise and civil society to take part in this intersectorial dialogue. The invitation includes the academic and education world; the scientific and technological community; business and cultural creators and promoters; municipal and local authorities; unions and parliamentary bodies. Priority is given to NGOs and social groups that are traditionally marginalized by the media and/or with little access to technology (young people, women, indigenous peoples, the handicapped).

This will be an excellent opportunity (as has happened in other world summits) to participate in the official meeting and, at the same time, to hold a counter-summit like the 'Tidal Wave Cancún', coinciding with the WTO meeting in September 2003. Taking part in the official meeting and organizing parallel summits or its own forums is essential for the movement, in spite of the tremendous efforts that this requires.[2] Communication is seen by the movement of movements as a global public good, a right to collective possession and enjoyment, on equal terms. In contrast, the information and voter market (private communication enterprises and state radio/ television systems) promotes privatization, commercialization and homogeneity of the public space. The difference in these viewpoints makes it necessary to create alternative forums to the institutional summits. Is it, in fact, worthwhile participating in the summits at all?

The pessimists maintain that a charter of the rights of peoples to communication cannot be forced through legally and that it will therefore not affect the structures and inequalities of the information society. In any case, they add, it will be used as rhetoric to cover up the practices that we know all too well. In fact, the corporate media sell commercialized information as a public service and 'interaction' of the media as 'teledemocracy', even if the audience has no other role than as consumers and spectators. The instrumentalizing rationality of communication as simply business is all too often used by governments when they utilize public radio/television systems for electoral purposes. When these systems are privatized, they fall into the hands of media corporations that are close to governments (as happens with almost all neoliberal privatization).

The recent veto of the UN preventing Reporters without Borders from attending the WSIS, on the instigation of certain governments in the South (Cuba and Libya), is certainly bad news. The dangers do not always come from the North, as can also be seen in the votes of the 'liberticide' governments of Algeria, China, Morocco, Pakistan, Russia, Sudan, Syria, Vietnam and Zimbabwe, all of which impose restrictions on the freedom of the press and access to the Internet. There is a certain irony in the summit being held in Tunisia, a country with a number of journalists in prison. Its organization is to be the responsibility of Abib Ammar, a general accused of being a torturer by the UN itself.[3]

More optimistic spirits, although aware of these contradictions, have joined in the CRIS campaign in the belief that it provides an opportunity to present formal arguments to those who want to democratize the information society. For human development must come before technology or, better still, the latter should be seen as a function of the former. The lack of the 'social' in the summit means it will be an open field for those who are pushing corporate interests and privatizing development of the Internet, while imposing censure and suppression of its socio-political usage. The (counter) World Summit on the Information Society therefore once again takes up the twofold strategy that has become essential to the movement: interacting with the more open international institutions and utilizing them as legitimizing platforms without, however, being co-opted by them.

The charter of rights for the information society will be important if it is the result of a real communication process. In other words, if it questions the institutions that are examining it. This could start with the UN (bypassed, but finally strengthened by the failed occupation of Afghanistan and Iraq) taking the role that Unesco once played in commissioning the MacBride report, which was the reference document on anti-cultural imperialism in the third quarter of the twentieth century. Member states would be called upon to recompose their national public spheres, which have fallen into decline, and make them more plural and open to civil society, which now has its own communication resources. Private communication corporations would come up against new anti-monopoly legislation to preserve communication spaces that are linked, not only to the nation state, but to regions, municipalities and communities.

The movement's communication strategies will continue to give weight to national and local interests (as in other fields). Nations without states and communities without rights will continue to be the concern of the peoples who are demanding emancipation. They are also the priority issues in the international struggles in which the social organizations, parties and unions that meet within the movement have their own roles and can make their voices heard. The (counter) WSIS must give greater strength to these actors, eager as they are to bring about change, benefiting from the coordination of efforts at the global level. This is the sense in which independent observers of the media and the new networks will be working, bringing together the communication experiences of the movement.

MEDIA WATCH GLOBAL

This was presented in Porto Alegre by *Le Monde Diplomatique* and publicized by that journal in its October 2003 issue.[4] The idea of a media watch originated in the US, resurrecting the figure of the Ombudsman, as defender of the readers, and academic criticism. Two organizations have been important pioneers in this respect. One is FAIR (Fairness and Accuracy in Reporting), which was created in 1986 during the Reagan era and publishes a bi-monthly journal called *Extra!* Its conservative counterpart is *Accuracy in the Media* (which is more inclined to call attention to 'liberal' deviations and criticism). In France, the *Observatoire de la Presse* was set up in 1995, but it focuses more on the training of professionals. The *Observatórios da Imprensa* of Portugal and Brazil combine professional criticism with a civic dimension. In almost every case these are linked to university centres that train journalists.

Media Watch Global aims to cover the three classic fields of mass communication: information (the press), mass culture and publicity. It believes that private commercialization and the expansion of multimedia oligopolies have broken down the frontiers that previously existed between these different fields. It intends to restore power to the weaker parties: to give a voice to citizens rather than consumers and to independent journalists rather than to staff journalists who are employed on an insecure basis. It intends to provide a critical platform of the 'superpower of the corporate media', which is a 'power without counter-power'. It plans to bring together media professionals and specialists in media studies, as well as active members of the public. In sum, it wants to establish criteria for an 'information ecology', which can be used to establish an 'organic information' label, based on accuracy and social responsibility.

This initiative describes its strength as being 'above all, moral: denouncing, in terms of ethics, and spotlighting dishonesty in the media through reports and studies that it will prepare, publish and disseminate'. Its immediate objective is to make itself heard at the World Summit of the Information Society. Those objecting to this praiseworthy initiative feel that it runs a twofold risk of intellectualism: firstly, because importance is given to professionals and researchers rather than to associations using the media (they are always mentioned last of all, as 'persons recognized for their moral stature'); and, secondly, because it is doubtful whether 'moral' criticism is in itself enough to bring about change.

In other words, there is a danger that Media Watch Global will become an elite circle with a 'self-referential' critical discourse, concentrating on the 'prestigious' communication media and contents and thus emphasizing the voices in the global movement that already have media visibility. But 'consumers', thanks to the new technologies, are now able to move beyond the limits of their traditional means of expression. As well as criticizing and denouncing the media and its contents, they can start (in fact they have started) to produce materials themselves. Media Watch Global could also confuse – as happened with critical intellectuals in the 1960s – 'moral criticism' with political practice. Criticism is essential, especially as a permanent and open task that is also oriented towards the media of the movement, which (naturally!) also shows elitist tendencies. What the movements really need are platforms to make themselves heard and seen among themselves. Only in this way will they acquire the active public status that is appropriate for global citizenship. To attain this there are the two methods of media intervention, described below.

NETWORKS OF ALTERNATIVE MEDIA

The global resistance movement has begun to create networks that use the classic technologies of print and audio-visual, now reinforced by the personal computer and digitalization. An interesting project is that of ALAI (Agencia Latinoamericana de Información), which wants to democratize communication from below. It is a web-based community of social movements that strives to be a forceful and strategic presence for these movements on the Internet. Among its publications is *América latina en movimiento* (Latin America on the move) in digital and printed versions. Another important network, which collects together local, popular and community radio, is ALER. It is closely related to the thought of Paulo Freire and contributes to 'constructing democratic and participatory societies in which the poor are the protagonists in their own development'. These initiatives have arisen from development communications programmes (also seen in Africa and Asia) and have been the driving force in setting up social movements in the South. Without them, the growth of the indigenous organizations, the MST and Vía Campesina would have been impossible.

These networks have managed to gain admittance into international institutions. For example, Unesco is developing a programme of multimedia community centres, which brings together the local media (particularly radio broadcasts in indigenous languages). The new technologies increase the interaction and participation of communities at different levels. Community telecentres have been devised to promote communication and exchange of information at both the local and global level. Some are linked to community radios, which are low-cost, with a strong local base, so that it is possible to create data banks and audio-visual archives with libraries and documentation centres. The example of the Ejercito Zapatista de Liberación Nacional (EZLN) has been important in helping to protect these developments against ethnic risks (the folkloric or the anthropological) and linking the indigenous communities to global solidarity networks, to transnational campaigns and to their growing political activities at state level.

In the North, paradoxical as it may seem, the classic alternative media of the movement against capitalist globalization, have been less effective. There are various factors at work here. The commodification of public space by the corporate media leaves little room for social initiatives. The fragmentation and individualization of the technologies (just as with lifestyles) have destroyed many of the social networks that used to feed the cultural industry and alternative media: for example, worker culture and counter-culture. The press belonging to parties and trade unions has practically disappeared and the underground media has become commercial. At the end of the twentieth century there still remained some media from the extra-parliamentary left, but they cannot compete with the main conventional media or compare with the media networks of the South in terms of social outreach.

Where civil society is more vigorous the traditional left-wing media have managed to launch combined operations. Worth noting is the co-operation established by the newspapers *L'Unitá*, *Il Manifesto* and *Liberazione* in Italy. They succeeded, after the G8 Counter-Summit in Genoa (in June 2001), in distributing a video, a white paper and a CD-ROM through the news-stands. They doubled the distribution of the weekly magazine *L'Espresso*. Also in Italy, the *Global Magazine*, a review linked to the experience of the self-managed social centres, headed by Toni Negri, was started in spring 2003. These represent the 'new generation' of intellectuals of the movement (who have been theorizing for decades), as compared with the more traditional model of *Le Monde Diplomatique*.

Nevertheless, one may well wonder to what extent the above media are representative, beyond the critical vanguard. Are they open to the plurality of the new movements? The more critically inclined maintain that they are, first of all, vehicles for the globalized elite, somewhat similar to the *Financial Times* (although diametrically opposite ideologically). They project the thinking and initiatives elaborated by a small group of intellectual activists who benefit more from the opportunities of globalization than they suffer from its costs. The risks of intellectualism, already mentioned in connection with Media Watch Global, could be repeated here. All these developments have audio-visual or radio ramifications, although the colonization of the frequency waves by the corporate media does not give them high visibility and they therefore cannot reach a very large public. Here should be mentioned, though, the potential of some free radio networks, which, in certain countries in the North, have been playing the same mobilizing role as the community networks of the South.

TELEMATIC INITIATIVES

Such initiatives are based on the new technologies of PCs connected to the Internet and have become the hallmark of the movement's communication identity, which, like the technology itself, largely transcends spatial-temporal barriers. They are used in several ways:

- websites set up specifically for the counter-summits and transnational campaigns;
- websites of classic counter-information;
- cyber activism;
- weblogs, in which the user is at one and the same time the source, the journalist and the commentator, e.g. the Indymedia network.

Let us look at each of these to assess their strengths and weaknesses in communication strategy.

Counter-summit websites

These sites serve as tools for convening meetings and conveying information. They are basically of three different kinds: theme-oriented, logistical and organizational, and legal assistance. Since the first counter-summits, a certain model has developed in the social forums that aims at transmitting information to traditional media (print and audio-visual), both alternative and corporate. This is reflected in *A Ciranda Internacional da Informação Independente,* on the Porto Alegre website in 2003, which brings together about a hundred journalists and dozens of media that share information between themselves. With its six languages it has given quality coverage of the World Social Forum, attracting more than 60,000 daily visits during the event.

Copy-left principles are applied: each publication has the right to reproduce the articles of the others without payment.[5] To belong participants only need accreditation to cover the forum. Participants of the Ciranda can combine the roles of reader, journalist and distributor. At the same time they have access to the free software necessary for publishing messages, participating in chatrooms, etc. All this puts into practice the idea of communication as a common good, reinforcing it against commercial and technological privatization plans. Its advantages are obvious: a lowering of costs, a great range of distribution, lack of editorial controls, horizontal and two-way communications.

There are, however, limitations. Access to the new technologies is an insurmountable barrier for large numbers of people who have been marginalized by social class, educational level, gender, political regime, the technological development of the country or community of origin. This could be rectified by social policies to spread the new technologies and promote 'technological literacy'. Copy-left and free software aim at this, but they only make significant breakthroughs when supported by the local administration. Also, the websites of the Social Forums and campaigns seem to have a very short life. They concentrate on the event and mainly serve as tools for coordination. This is not so much a limitation of this media in itself: it raises the question of the existence of a real movement, which in fact functions around campaigns and counter-summits. It could reflect the real limitations of the 'anti-globalization forces', in their present state of development and the diversity of their natures: time alone will tell. Lastly, the websites could be criticized for all the publicity and promotional material they contain. Sometimes they give too much importance (as in the e-economy) to the actors and organizations who use their space. But the realm of the virtual is not the realm of the real. And this is an objection that can be applied to the applications of telematics described below.

Counter-information websites

Such sites are the way in which the vast majority of organizations in the movement make themselves known. Economic benefits and technical simplification have helped in their wide dissemination. Setting up a website is one of the first resources adopted by a group and sometimes becomes its 'foundational act' (and, unfortunately, its only one). Links with other sites weave the movement's networks together, but there is a certain risk of compartmentalization because the coordination through mailing and distribution lists is sectorial. This, one supposes, could give rise to common agendas and identities that are in fact antagonistic. For this reason there are websites with 'glocalized' portals, which act as information agencies and promote interrelationships between organizations of the movement classified by territory, field of activity, affiliation, etc.

Cyber activism

The Internet is not only a shop window: it is also a field of activism. Hacker culture is composed of a network of experts that promote access to the new technologies and their free and collective development. There are many cyber actions, ranging from 'softer' to 'harder'.[6] Through many of the sites it is possible to receive gifts and solicit subscriptions from new members. Massive mailings of requests or petitions through the transmission of a form are relatively easy. Cyber demonstrations are virtual representations of a collective action or demonstration. Mailbombing consists of sending so many messages that they saturate a server or cause it to break down altogether if it can host only a certain number of pages. Cracking enables people to access the information or reserved spaces of a server in order to disable or sabotage it. The list of possibilities continues, given the infinite variety of these initiatives. There is no doubt that some manage to convene more participants than direct actions, which require a physical presence. However, this advantage is offset by the fact that the level of involvement decreases exponentially.

Cyber activism is a symptom of technological reappropriation by the grassroots, of a communication media that owes its widespread popularity to its virtual communities. However there are some reservations. It can turn into mere, self-referential virtuality, without any real effects beyond the Internet. It could also be argued that its effects are trivial, compared with the use made of this media by the State and the market. The keywords linked with the global movement represent a very small percentage in the searches using the main research engines, where the principal use is instrumental and individual. The flows of alternative communication are insignificant, compared with those related to financial capital and commercial transactions. Nevertheless, this should not prevent recognition of the enormous tactical potential of the new technologies. They do not guarantee media and institutional visibility but they do provide the necessary coordination to achieve it.

Weblogs

Weblogs consist of pages to which we have already referred (e.g. *A Ciranda* in Porto Alegre). However, Indymedia merits special mention. It was born during the heat of the Seattle events of 1999 (at that time it received 1.5 million hits), reaching its high point at the counter-summit of Genoa (5 million hits). It calls itself 'a collective of independent communication media organizations and hundreds of journalists covering the grassroots and who are not commercial'. Its objective is 'the radical creation of real and impassioned narratives'.[7] The network includes over 500 local centres of independent communication (mostly in Europe and America), and it carries out indispensable internal and external functions for the movement. It has become the key information provider for the counter-summits and campaigns, both for sympathizers and for the conventional media.

The principle of 'open publication', which is both instantaneous and uncensored, is the definition of Indymedia, whose watchword is 'Don't hate the media, be part of it!' They maintain that there is no editorial committee *sensu stricto*, although there are collectives that have this function and are completely open, or else closed, with an editorial line. News is ranked according to the ratings given by users. Reports that are suppressed are withdrawn because they duplicate other reports, have commercial aims or 'do not meet the editorial line'. However they do remain accessible as 'hidden articles'. In other words, while the mediation is not absolute, there is transparency in the criteria of selection and its effects. The key to the filter is that the previous discussions in the forums, chatrooms and mailing lists neutralize possible noise or dissonant or contradictory messages. Thus there is no monolithic model of Indymedia.

The very growth of Indymedia has forced them to move beyond the mere functions of the coordination and dissemination of events. The crisis of the counter-summits as a basic strategy has forced Indymedia to define their objectives more clearly. There is a certain falling back on local content except when the cycles of mobilization at this level and at state level coincide with global campaigns. The desire for continuity and permanence has led them into trying to establish themselves as a 'world council of spokespersons'. But this would involve moving away from direct deliberation to delegation. The plans to set an editorial line, which is necessary to maintain coherence and eliminate noise, also present problems.[8] Basically it is a question of the networks of the global movement, which defines itself more by what it opposes than by what it defends. It is mobilized more through opposition to common enemies than by common solidarities and interests. The need to move beyond this stage is a question to be discussed. But the objective of communication that is trans-scale, diverse and unifying is the same, in terms of strategy and content, as the one facing the movement as a whole.

BY WAY OF CONCLUSION

The Internet has been presented, far too frivolously, as the public sphere of the movement. Such a description does not however fulfil the requirements of responsibility and obligations (personal and collective) demanded by communication aiming at social transformation. The movement occupies a public space at the margin of the hegemonic public space. It will have an effect on the latter when the movement reaches the power institutions and the market. Then alternative messages will be introduced into the corporate media, parliaments and international organizations. That is, alternative communication has the transforming value of the social fabric that supports it, and when it succeeds in upsetting the imbalances of existing power. And this happens outside (far further than) the discourse that we present in the movement's media: in the interactions and struggles that are closest to us, in the daily challenging of the practices of dominion and oppression.

The Internet articulates the collective action and cycles of protest that have succeeded in making the movement visible to the institutions and the media. And this is the image and the public agenda of the movement, as opposed to those that are woven on the Net. If the symbolic production of the movement has gained such strength and visibility, it is as a response to the parallel process of 'mediatization' of the economic and political centres that it opposes. The mediatic and cybernetic paraphernalia of 'popular capitalism' and the Love Parades happen at the same time as cyber activism and the counter-summits. At both levels there are problems of banalization, representativity and manipulation. To present them in the hegemonic public sphere and ignore them in 'our own' is, to say the least, a sign of complacency. Almost all the studies made on the subject indicate that the new technologies tend to reflect and not to overcome inequalities. Another generalized conclusion is that the alternative communities and identities need more personal relationships than technological extensions.[9]

Radical democracy is based on democratic communication, which is a necessary but not sufficient condition. A media victory (access to and favourable coverage in the conventional media) is not a guarantee of political success. Rapid saturation, because of the trivial commodification of the movement and the routine coverage of official sources, creates indifference and silence in the short term. Our windows on to media opportunity are very small.[10] The power centres adopt political and repressive measures to guarantee an information flow that is favourable to the hegemonic public sphere. A good example was the entry of the Zapatista March into the Zócala Square of Mexico City. This extraordinary symbolic spectacle did not guarantee the political and juridical recognition of indigenous rights. And the EZLN returned to the communities to devise a new, socially based strategy.

Both on the practical and symbolic level, all actors and actions that we have considered are necessary. Everyone takes action on different levels and in tasks that are complementary. Forums and watch committees, conventional media and telematics must all become intertwined, drawing strength from each other, in order to build platforms together eventually. The movement must accept that strategies to infiltrate the corporate media are complementary with the strengthening of the alternative media. It is a question of embarking on a massive communication effort to get visibility and the capacity to interact with the public and the institutions. This is not in order to become one more media product. We have to generate counter-information, maintain transversal discussions and make progress in coordination, not to impose identities or brands in watertight compartments. The real network goes in and out of both conventional and alternative communication, without getting bogged down in the process. The 'target areas' that have to surround it remain outside.

NOTES

1. The demand is for reform and incremental changes: approaches and proposals that are 'feasible', as opposed to the Acción Global de los Pueblos, which demands 'anti-capitalistic' structural change, so that protest is also proposal. In fact, the antagonistic action of the latter has pushed the former into the corporate media and institutions. I am limiting myself to the more 'consensual' part of the movement and communication practice in Europe and America.
2. This has developed into the strategy of the movement since it first started and it still continues.
3. *El Pais*, 9 October 2003.
4. Ignacio Ramonet, 'Le cinquième pouvoir', *Le Monde Diplomatique*, no. 96. The quotations are taken from this article.
5. This is an appropriate way of covering a forum in which over 1,500 conferences, panels, seminars, workshops and political and cultural demonstrations take place. The list of participating organizations includes: *Le Monde, Le Monde Diplomatique* and *Media Solidaire* (France), *The Nation* and *Zmag* (USA), *Il Manifesto, Liberazione* and *Carta* (Italy), *TaZ* (Germany),

One World (UK), *Rebelión* (Spain), *Focus on the Global South* (Australia/ Thailand), *Caros Amigos, Correio da Cidadanía, Reportagem, Carta Maior, Agência Adital* and dozens of publications from the Brazilian and Latin American trade unions and social movements. The proposed Ciranda Brasil, as a permanent news agency, had not yet come into being at the time of writing.

6. Taken from Sara López, Gustavo Roig and Igor Sádaba (2003) *Nuevas tecnologías y participación politica en un mundo globalizado* (Bilbao: Hegoa). Also, Igor Sádaba (2002) 'Solidaridad y nuevas tecnologías. Transformaciones, obstaculos y realidades', in *Jornada CommunicAcción para la solidaridad y la accíon colectiva* (Bilbao: Hegoa). Bilbao.

7. 'Qué es Indymedia', FAQ www.indymedia.org

8. For example, Indymedia Madrid represents the extreme of this process, demanding a 'declaration of intent' and a description of the user, which includes 'some questions about yourself', before they evaluate the information. See 'The editorial process'.

9. See the bibliographical review of Mario Diani (2001) 'Social Movements' Networks: Virtual and Real', in Frank Webster (ed.), *Culture and Politics in the Information Age* (London: Routledge).

10. Victor Sampredo (2000) 'Media, Social Movements and History: An Agenda-building Case Study', in D. Fleming (ed.), *Formations: 21st Century Media Studies Textbook* (Manchester and New York: Manchester University Press).

20

The European Union and the 'Internal Threat' of the Alternative World Movement

Ben Hayes and Tony Bunyan

It has been argued that States have three options when faced with large public demonstrations (Brewer *et al.*, 1988). The first is to accommodate the demands of the protesting group – or at least recognition of these through dialogue and debate. A second option is to criminalize the protesters' motives and actions. Third, there is the suppression of the actual demonstrations, political activities, and ultimately of the right to protest. We would add to this a fourth option, containment, which characterized the more benign approach of governments to the massive anti-war demonstrations across the world in early 2003. Where States have faced sustained political protests, we have seen precious little of the first and much of the second and third reactions. And so it has been with the more recent development of the European Union and its response to the growth of the anti-globalization movement, where containment is increasingly replaced by suppression and criminalization.

THE SCHENGEN INFORMATION SYSTEM (SIS)

Well before the high-profile demonstrations in Gothenburg and Genoa in 2001, the Schengen and EU member states had agreed a number of police co-operation measures on public order and security.[1] Perhaps the most significant was the creation of the Schengen Information System, an extensive database that went online in 1995 and presently covers 15 countries.[2] Participating states contribute data to the SIS on people wanted for arrest; people to be placed into custody, under surveillance or subject to specific checks; people to be refused entry at external borders (on either national security or immigration grounds); and lost or stolen items.[3] Protesters and political activists have been entered into the SIS under the 'national security' provisions

258

(Article 96).[4] Inclusion carries a legal sanction – the prevention of entry to the specific countries (or the entire Schengen area for non-EU nationals) – and amounts to a *quasi*-criminal record, even though those entered may not actually have been convicted of any criminal offence. An example of this 'political policing at its most obvious' (Peers, 2000, 224) is the case of Stephanie Mills, a Greenpeace activist who was denied access to the entire Schengen area on 25 June 1998 because the French government had entered the names of a number of Greenpeace staff into the SIS.[5]

It is not known how many protesters are held on the SIS because statistics breaking down the different categories have never been produced. Basic figures were issued every year until 1998, but these disappeared under an 'informal' decision following the incorporation of Schengen into the EU structure.[6] Unreleased documents obtained by *Statewatch*, show that on 5 March 2003 the SIS included a total of 877,655 persons.[7] Eighty-nine per cent are registered under Article 96: most of them will be rejected asylum-seekers. A report on the legality of entering protesters into the SIS, being compiled by the Schengen Joint Supervisory Authority on data protection, is awaited with interest.

THE 1997 EU JOINT ACTION AND AMSTERDAM DEMONSTRATIONS

The first substantive EU measure on public order was the 1997 Joint Action on 'law and order and security'.[8] This measure was a Dutch initiative and it is notable that it was agreed just before the 50,000-strong 'Eurotop' demonstrations at the EU summit in Amsterdam in June 1997, where 317 people were arrested. All were entirely peaceful (albeit noisy in trying to disrupt the sleep of the heads of state), but all were charged under legislation criminalizing 'membership of an organization that aims to commit crimes' – apparently the model for the EU Joint Action on 'membership of a criminal organization' agreed the following year.[9] The policing of the Amsterdam summit set the tone for future policies and operational conduct.[10]

The EU Joint Action on law and order extended existing provisions in a 1996 EU Council Recommendation on co-operation against football hooliganism (often a testing ground for policies later applied to public order in general). This placed an obligation on member states to provide each other with information, 'upon request or unsolicited, via central bodies, if sizeable groups which pose a threat to law and order and security are travelling to another Member State in order to participate in events'.

ARTICLE 2(2): BORDER CONTROLS TO COUNTER PROTESTS

Another little-noted provision in the 1990 Schengen Convention would also come into play as governments concerned themselves with the suppression of the protests. Article 2 of the Schengen Convention implemented the underlying commitment to abolish internal borders (though this is far from the reality[11]). Article 2, paragraph 2 allows Schengen states to reintroduce border checks 'Where public policy or national security so require... for a limited period'. The Belgian government was the first to invoke this 'exception', during an immigrant regularization programme early in 2000; it was first used to prevent protesters from attending a demonstration during the French presidency of the EU, where both France and Spain reintroduced border controls for the Biarritz summit in December 2000. Since then, by early 2003, Article 2(2) had been used at least 14 times to counter demonstrations taking place at international summits.[12] The policy does not just mean that identity checks take place during the limited periods, but that hundreds (and in some cases thousands) of people are refused entry to the member states to which they are travelling – a spectacular curb of the supposedly fundamental freedom of movement. By way of an example, some 2,093 people were turned away at the Italian border in the run-up to the Genoa G8 summit.[13] At the G8 summit in Evian, France (1–3 June 2003) border controls were reintroduced among six countries, for a two-week period starting ten days before the meeting![14]

GOTHENBURG, GENOA AND 11 SEPTEMBER: CRIMINALIZING THE LEFT

The EU summit in Gothenburg (Sweden) on 14–16 June 2001 brought protests into the media spotlight when two demonstrators were shot by the police. Some 50 people were detained in custody for a lengthy period, and around 400 names are said to have been added to the SIS. By the time of the protests in Genoa a month later, EU justice and home affairs ministers had agreed on a broad strategy for 'security at meetings of the European Council and other comparable events'.[15] It aimed to increase police co-operation, intelligence gathering and exchange, internal border checks, judicial co-operation and joint organizational measures. 'Operational control' at the EU level was delegated to the EU Police Chiefs' Task Force, which had been created at the Tampere summit (Finland) in October 1999. It still has no legal basis for its activities and is subject to no meaningful democratic control or public accountability whatsoever (see below).

The horrific scenes in Genoa, where Carlo Giuliani was shot in the head at close range by a *carabiniere* conscript, were overshadowed less than two months later by the terrorist attacks in America. Eleven September had immediate and lasting implications for national and EU policy agendas and would feed directly into the framework for countering protests. Within a week, the European Commission had presented a draft proposal for a Framework Decision on combating terrorism.[16] This was 'politically agreed' just six weeks later, an unprecedented time frame for EU decision-making (and all the more astonishing given the EU's record on harmonizing criminal law).

Protests were immediately implicated in the proposed definition of terrorism, which listed a number of less serious offences including theft, robbery and the 'unlawful seizure' of 'places of public use' or 'state or government facilities'. 'Damage' to these places was also covered. However, these offences could only be considered acts of terrorism if the *purpose* was terroristic. Here the definition in the Commission proposal beggared belief, covering offences:

> intentionally committed by an individual or a group against one or more countries, their institutions or people with the aim of intimidating them and seriously altering or destroying the political, economic, or social structures of those countries, [they] will be punishable as terrorist offences.

Like almost any political, industrial or environmental protest, it was clear that the Gothenburg and Genoa demonstrations could easily be construed as having the clear aim of 'seriously altering or destroying the political, economic, or social structures'. The Council of the European Union (representatives of the 15 governments) responded by *widening* the definition, changing 'altering' to 'affecting', which could have covered almost anything.[17] It also added 'international organisations' to the 'political, economic, or social structures'. The adopted definition (politically agreed on 6 December 2001 and formally adopted six months later) is:

> – seriously intimidating a population, or
> – unduly compelling a Government or international organisation to perform or abstain from performing any act, or

– seriously destabilising or destroying the fundamental political, constitutional, economic or social structures of a country or an international organisation (Article 1(1)).[18]

During the negotiations, the European and some national parliaments expressed concerns about the breadth of this definition. However, with no power to 'codecide', amend or reject policies, their concerns were all but ignored. In fact, the texts had been politically agreed by the governments *prior* to formal consultation and, in the political climate engendered by 11 September, dissent was mute. There were, however, three apparent concessions to the civil society groups, lawyers and parliamentarians who had campaigned against such a broad definition.[19] The offence of 'seizure ... of a public place' was replaced by 'causing extensive destruction to ... a public place'. Secondly, a recital was added to the preamble:

Nothing in this Framework Decision may be interpreted as being intended to reduce or restrict fundamental rights or freedoms such as the right to strike, freedom of assembly, of association or of expression, including the right of everyone to form and to join trade unions with others for the protection of his or her interests and the related right to demonstrate (Recital 10).

A minority of EU governments had wanted to refer explicitly to the anti-globalization movement but, significantly, this was not included. Instead, respect for fundamental freedoms should only be guaranteed in relation to trade union work and not, apparently, for wider political protest. Finally, a statement of the EU justice and home affairs ministers was added to the Framework Decision:

Nor can the [definition of terrorism] be construed so as to incriminate on terrorist grounds persons exercising their legitimate right to manifest their opinions, even if in the course of the exercise of such rights they commit offences.

Again, this apparent concession does not amount to any kind of concrete guarantee. Political statements have no legal force, they are *only* statements. Thus, despite public assurances to the contrary, the member states have left open the possibility of applying terrorist legislation to protests. The acid test will be in how member states use the definition in practice.

A somewhat clearer statement of intent from the Spanish government would follow in February 2002, with their presidency proposal for an EU Council Decision on 'exchanging information on terrorist incidents'. This innocuous sounding measure started out by asserting that:

> The [EU Terrorism] working party has noticed a gradual increase, at various EU summits and other events, in violence and criminal damage orchestrated by radical extremist groups, clearly terrorising society... These acts are the work of a loose network, hiding behind various social fronts, by which we mean organisations taking advantage of their lawful status to aid and abet the achievement of terrorist groups' aims.[20]

Moreover, the Spanish argued that:

> The Union has reacted by including such acts in Article 1 of the Framework Decision on combating terrorism.

Information was to be exchanged on 'individuals with a police record in connection with terrorism', apparently referring to a record of a criminal conviction (even if only minor public order offences). But it then went on to say this requirement is not necessary where domestic law allows the exchange of 'intelligence' (suspicions and suppositions).[21] A number of governments publicly distanced themselves from the Spanish proposal, and the fifth draft – by now a non-binding EU Council Recommendation – stated that 'the Netherlands delegation backed by some other delegations considered the description of individuals concerned by the decision is too vague'.[22]

The measure was finally adopted in November 2002, still referring to the 'risk that terrorist organisations will use larger international events for carrying out terrorist offences as defined in Article 1 of the Framework Decision on combating terrorism'; acts carried out by 'various loose networks of terrorists' and the 'need for analysis and proactive monitoring'.[23] As a non-binding Council Recommendation, those member states that wish to exchange information on protesters in the name of combating terrorism are effectively free to do so.[24] Adopting the provisions in the form of a Recommendation also meant that national and European parliaments did not have to be consulted.

The spurious link between protest groups and terrorists was also promoted by Europol's annual situation report on terrorism in the

EU. Two new categories were included in the report of February 2002 for the first time: 'anarchist-terrorism' and 'eco-terrorism'.[25] Although no definition or examples of the latter were given, the report claimed that 'Radical environmentalists and animal rights movements have maintained a limited campaign. Nevertheless, the material damage they caused was extensive.' In respect to 'anarchist-terrorism', the report cited the possibility of the 'resurrection of left wing terrorism' and referred to a series of terrorist attacks 'in the southern part of the Union'. In fact, all the examples provided came from Italy and at least one of them, an explosion outside the Palazzo di Giustizia in Venice after the G8 summit (in July 2001), has been attributed to right-wing extremists (the far right is not mentioned at all in Europol's report). The efforts of the Spanish government to criminalize more and more Basque activists (for example youth and prisoner support groups) by linking them to ETA were also reflected in Europol's 'threat assessment'.

TROUBLEMAKERS' DATABASE, TRAVEL BANS, AND PARAMILITARY POLICING: SUPPRESSING THE PROTESTS

After the Gothenburg and Genoa demonstrations, EU justice and home affairs ministers called for the creation of national databases of 'troublemakers', again based not on the criminal process, but on suspicion and supposition and with no reference to legal standards or data protection rules governing the exchange of this data.[26] They also wanted domestic legislation to allow EU member states to pass laws to prevent people from going to protests in other countries if their names have been recorded or if they have been convicted of minor public order offences. Echoing Tony Blair's depiction of the protesters as an 'anarchists' travelling circus',[27] seven EU governments – Germany, Sweden, Portugal, Italy, Belgium, Luxembourg and the UK – wanted to go even further and create an EU-wide database and to introduce travel bans for suspected 'troublemakers' across the EU.[28]

A month after the 11 September attacks, the wishes of the seven were reflected in a Belgian presidency proposal to extend the SIS to cover 'potentially dangerous persons' to be prevented from entering countries for 'sports, cultural, political or social events'. Under the plan the scope of the SIS would be widened to allow for 'alerts' to be placed on people 'known by the police forces for having committed recognised acts of public order disturbance' under Article 99 of the

Schengen Implementing Convention.[29] This currently allows police forces to enter the names of people to be placed under:

> discreet surveillance or specific checks... where there are real indications to suggest that the person concerned intends to commit or is committing numerous and *extremely serious offences* ... (emphasis added).

The proposed extension of Article 99 would allow the inclusion on the SIS of those:

> with the intention of organising, causing, participating or fomenting troubles with the aim of threatening public order or security.

An 'alert' on these 'troublemakers' 'would cause the person to be barred from entering the country during a limited period before and after the event takes place'.

In April 2001, these proposals were included in the plans for SIS II, a 'second generation' system with extended scope and function that would incorporate the EU accession countries.[30] Though discussions are now apparently on hold,[31] the scenario remains one of targeting 'known individuals' based on information gathered at national level (by police and internal security agencies). A database of suspected 'troublemakers' held on the SIS will then be accessed by police and internal security agencies when there is an assumed 'threat' for a particular event in that country. This would deny people their right of free movement in the EU and the right to protest. As suggested earlier, it would also constitute a quasi-criminal record. Moreover, the construction at national level of a register of 'known individuals' means that quite ordinary and everyday political activity of groups and organisations will be placed under regular surveillance.

EU RIOT POLICE

Soon after Genoa, the German interior minister, Otto Schily, backed by his Italian counterpart, Claudio Scajola, called for the creation of an EU anti-riot police. While this was seen as unworkable in the short term, the prospect of the EU's future Rapid Reaction Force being used *inside* the EU was raised.[32] The Schily–Scajola calls were followed by a formal German proposal for the creation of 'Special Units' to implement 'joint and harmonised measures against travelling offenders committing violent acts'; a 'common tactical framework';

training for 'large-scale (emergency) situations' [thus linking protests and 'emergencies']; 'standard common equipment with command, control and operational means (e.g. radios, weapons, special devices)'; and 'the preconditions… to enable one Member State to request the support of special units from other Member States'.[33]

Bilateral and multilateral arrangements are equally important, and member states have increasingly requested the presence and assistance of police officers from neighbouring states during protests. These practices may in time lead to a formal system for the movement and deployment of specially trained national units to police public order situations in the host country. Observing the 'increasingly militarised approach to demonstrations', Jude McCulloch suggests (2002, 56) that

> Protestors are not seen as citizens who may be breaking the law and subject to arrest and charge, but instead as 'the enemy within', to be defeated by use of overwhelming force.

OPERATIONAL MATTERS

In December 2002, the EU Justice and Home Affairs Council noted the production of a 'security handbook' for international summits.[34] This manual formalizes intelligence exchange, and 'personal data' on 'potential demonstrators and other groupings expected to travel' should now be supplied to the hosting state on a monthly, weekly and finally daily basis in the run-up to the protest. 'Preventative patrols and controls at land borders' and 'necessary arrangements for a quick and efficient' expulsion should be in place. Again, the legal basis for this 'co-operation' is quite unclear.[35] The power to revise the security handbook is reserved to the EU Police Chiefs Operational Task Force (PCTF), assisted by the Security Office of the general Secretariat of the EU Council. The PCTF has no formal legal basis and is subject to no formal democratic control. Nonetheless, the deliberations over the EU constitution suggest it will be given a central role assisting a committee of permanent officials from the member states in 'coordination and oversight of the entire spectrum of operational activity in police and security matters' – including public order.[36] A questionable distinction between 'legislative' and 'operational' matters means that national and European parliaments will continue to be excluded. There is also a distinct possibility that protesters will be denied their fundamental rights as a result of EU policies or practices (implemented by national agencies). In the event, there may be few clear lines of democratic or judicial accountability.

Neither are there any safeguards in the EU Council Recommendation of April 2002 'establishing multinational *ad hoc* teams for gathering and exchanging information on terrorists'.[37] Discussions made clear that the object of these *ad hoc* teams is not to arrest and bring suspects to court. Rather, small groupings of EU states – led by Spain and Italy – will set up unaccountable, undercover teams of police and internal security officers and agents to target and place under surveillance suspected groups and individuals.[38] There is also a question mark over the role of Europol, the European Police Office. Despite having no mandate to address public order matters, there was much to suggest that prior to 11 September the agency was taking an interest in protesters under the banner of terrorism.[39] While there can be little objection to the creation of teams to combat *genuine* terrorists, this comes with a strict proviso that they act under the rule of law, according to rules of procedure and are accountable legally and democratically for their actions.

This ideal brings us on to *unspoken* policy options open to governments facing political protests. Political spin against demonstrators, negative portrayal in the mass media, surveillance, information collecting, infiltration, informers, *agents-provocateurs*, harassment, intimidation and the destabilization of activist groups: State subterfuge is alive and well across the world, including in Western democracies. Ideologically, and often strategically, countering protests and counter-subversion are two sides of the same coin: 'operating on behalf of a government against people who want to upset its authority' (Kitson, 1969[40]). In this way the legislation and policy of the EU complements the efforts of the more zealous authorities among the EU member states.

CONCLUSION

At the time of writing, the Italian presidency is commencing and the Berlusconi government has long made clear its attitude toward the demonstrations. The exchange of information on protesters, banned lists and the denial of entry for football fans, joint investigation teams and a terrorist suspects' database are all on the agenda[41]; work on the proposals discussed above will continue behind the scenes. While a number of member states and elements in the Commission and Parliament are clearly uncomfortable, they are in a minority. The dominant approach is also incompatible with fundamental rights to freedom of association, to demonstrate and to privacy.[42] Regardless of public order policy, unless EU governments spend time and resources resolving the underlying issues that are bringing people on to the streets, the protests are unlikely to subside. The question that remains is the extent to which the EU's McCarthy-style approach to an enemy within will further radicalize civil society.

NOTES

1. The Schengen Agreement was signed in 1985 and the Schengen Implementing Convention in 1990. The Amsterdam Treaty, which entered into force in 1999, incorporated the Schengen arrangements into the EU structure. All Schengen articles referred to in this chapter are in the 1990 Convention.
2. The UK and Ireland are the only EU member states not yet participating in the SIS, though plans to incorporate them into the police co-operation aspects are well under way. Norway and Iceland participate under a Protocol to the Amsterdam Treaty. Countries acceding to the EU will also participate, in 'SIS II'.
3. For a detailed analysis of the SIS and other EU databases, see Mathiesen (1999).
4. Protesters may also have been 'flagged' for surveillance or specific checks such as searches under Article 99.
5. French hostility towards Greenpeace dates back to its protest against French nuclear testing in the South Pacific and the subsequent French torpedo attack that sank the Greenpeace flagship *Rainbow Warrior* (see also *Statewatch Bulletin*, vol. 8, no. 5, September–October 1998). Another infamous case is that of the Boore brothers, two Welsh football fans who were deported from Belgium after their names had been passed by the UK NCIS, who had in turn been passed the names by the Luxembourg authorities, who had wrongly claimed they had 'caused disorder' during a security check. They were detained for 16 hours and then deported in handcuffs. It took the brothers six years to get their names removed from national and Schengen records (Peers, 2000, 188; *Statewatch Bulletin*, vol. 6, no. 4, July–August 1996).
6. *Statewatch News Online*, April 2001, http://www.statewatch.org/news/2001/mar/07accountab.htm.
7. Officials *estimate* that there are 'approximately 125,000' terminals with access to the SIS in the 15 countries.
8. Joint Action 97/339/JHA, OJ 1997 L 147/1, http://www.statewatch.org/news/2001/aug/japubord.htm.
9. Joint Action 98/733/JHA, OJ 1998 L 351/1.
10. 'The protesters paid a high price for disturbing the sleep of Jacques Chirac and Tony Blair ... Over a hundred [protesters] were immediately deported before they could challenge their detention in court (a spectacular breach of EC free movement law); some were deported without their belongings;

the Danish consul was barred from visiting the detained Danes; some were sent back to Denmark in a military aircraft with a Dutch fighter-bomber escort; and information on those charged was handed over to at least some of police intelligence agencies – despite the gross abuse of prosecutorial discretion in laying charges. It is not known how many were entered onto the EU's various databases or circulated within the *ad hoc* meetings of EU public order specialists. Those not expelled were held for three days and then released, some alleging mistreatment by the police and denial of their right to make a phone call; none was ever convicted' (Peers, 2000, 225).

11. *Statewatch Bulletin*, vol. 3, no. 1, January–February 2003.
12. *Statewatch European Monitor*, vol. 3, no. 4, February 2003.
13. *Statewatch Bulletin*, vol. 11, no. 3/4, May–July 2001.
14. EU Council document 9537/03, 23 May 2003.
15. EU Council document 10916/01, 16 July 2001, http://www.statewatch. org/news/2001/jul/10916en1.pdf.
16. *Statewatch News Online*, September 2001, http://www.statewatch.org/ news/2001/sep/14eulaws.htm; see also Mathiesen (2002).
17. *Statewatch News Online*, October 2001, http://www.statewatch.org/ news/2001/oct/08counterr.htm.
18. *Statewatch News Online*, December 2001, http://www.statewatch.org/ news/2001/dec/07terrdef.htm. Framework Decision published in OJ 2002 L 164/3.
19. *Statewatch News Online*, November 2001, http://www.statewatch.org/ news/2001/nov/26appeal2.htm.
20. EU Council document 5712/02, 29 January 2001, http://www.statewatch. org/news/2002/feb/05712.pdf.
21. *Statewatch News Online*, February 2002, http://www.statewatch.org/ news/2002/feb/07protest2.htm.
22. EU Council document 5712/5/02 rev 5, 9 April 2002.
23. For adopted Recommendation, see http://www.statewatch.org/news/2003/ apr/spainterr.pdf.
24. *Statewatch Bulletin*, vol. 12, no. 2, March–April 2002; *Statewatch News Online*, April 2003, http://www.statewatch.org/news/2003/apr/16spainterr. htm.
25. EU Council documents 5759/02, 31 January 2002 and 5759/1/02 rev 1, 20 February 2002, for full text, see report on *Statewatch News Online*, February 2002, http://www.statewatch.org/news/2002/feb/10anarch.htm.
26. EU Council document 10916/01, 16 July 2001, http://www.statewatch. org/news/2001/jul/10916en1.pdf.
27. *The Guardian*, 21 July 2001.
28. *Statewatch News Online*, August 2001, http://www.statewatch.org/ news/2001/aug/12poreport.htm.
29. *Statewatch News Online*, November 2001, http://www.statewatch.org/ news/2001/nov/19sis.htm.
30. *Statewatch News Online*, April 2001, http://www.statewatch.org/ news/2002/apr/01sis.htm.
31. The less contentious proposals are scheduled for adoption in legislation to extend the capabilities of the current SIS (EU Council documents 10054/03

and 10055/03, 24 June 2003). There has been no recent discussion on the scope and function of SIS II, including the 'troublemakers' database'. These seem to have been frozen while the technical capabilities and call for tenders are being discussed (8989/03, 5 May 2003).

32. The EU's Rapid Reaction Force is to be used *externally* against 'growing violence destabilising law and order, breaches of the peace'.
33. *Statewatch News Online*, October 2001, http://www.statewatch.org/news/2001/oct/01paramilitary.htm.
34. *Statewatch Bulletin*, vol. 13, no. 1, January–February 2003.
35. The earlier German proposal alluded to the 1997 Joint Action on law and order and security (see above), but this only provides a legal basis for the exchange of information, not operational matters.
36. *Statewatch News Online*, April 2003, http://www.statewatch.org/news/2003/apr/TBART.pdf.
37. EU Council document 5715/6/02, 22 April 2002.
38. *Statewatch Bulletin*, vol. 12, no. 3, May–July 2002.
39. Hayes (2000), 10. After 11 September, most of Europol's resources were diverted into combating 'extremist Islamic terrorism'.
40. Inspired by the mass demonstrations against the Vietnam war, Kitson saw not only a new role for the army but also for the use of military tactics in the preservation of internal order. He did not base his arguments on the Vietnam demonstrations, but rather the need to reconsider the role of the armed forces in the face of the likely détente brought about by nuclear proliferation, independence from colonialism and a decline in the likelihood of 'conventional' warfare. His underlying concern, however, was clear enough: 'If a genuine and serious grievance arose, such as might result from a significant drop in the standard of living, all those who now dissipate their protest over a wide variety of causes might concentrate their efforts and produce a situation which was beyond the power of the police to handle' (1969, 25).
41. EU Council document 10874/03, 25 June 2003.
42. These rights are laid down in the EU Charter of Fundamental Rights, the European Convention on Human Rights (ECHR) and the UN Universal Declaration on Human Rights (UNDHR). The Charter guarantees everyone 'the right to freedom of peaceful assembly and to freedom of association at all levels, in particular in political, trade union and civic matters' (art. 12 (see also art. 11, ECHR and art. 20, UNDHR)), 'the right to freedom of expression... [including] freedom to hold opinions and to receive and impart information and ideas without interference by public authority' (art. 11 (see also art. 10, ECHR and art. 19 UNDHR)), 'the right to respect for his or her private and family life' (art. 7 (see also art. 8, ECHR)) and 'the right to the protection of personal data concerning him or her' (art. 8).

BIBLIOGRAPHY

Brewer, J.D., A. Guelke, E. Moxon-Browne and R. Wilford (1988) *The Police, Public Order and the State* (London: Macmillan)

Hayes, B. (2000) *The Activities and Development of Europol: Towards an unaccountable FBI in Europe* (London: Statewatch)

Kitson, F. (1969) *Low Intensity Operations: Subversion, insurgency and peacekeeping* (London: Faber)

Mathiesen, T. (1999) *On Globalisation of Control: Towards an integrated surveillance system in Europe* (London: Statewatch)

Mathiesen, T. (2002) 'Expanding the concept of terrorism', in P. Scraton (ed.) *Beyond September 11: An anthology of dissent* (London: Pluto)

McCulloch, J. (2002) 'Either you are with us, or you are with the terrorists': The war's home front', in P. Scraton (ed.) *Beyond September 11: An anthology of dissent* (London: Pluto)

Peers, S. (2000) *EU Justice and Home Affairs Law* (London: Longman)

21

Police Measures Against the New Global Protest

Donatella della Porta and Herbert Reiter

In its interactions with social movements, the State is often the target of various demands concerning more or less general measures. However, as soon as the social movements, which can be considered as 'powerless' actors with few or no institutional resources (Lipsky, 1965), use non-conventional forms of action, the State enters into relationships with them as the partner with the monopoly of legitimate physical force. In fact, social movements have been defined as challengers, addressing their demands to the institutions (Tilly, 1978), mainly through different forms of protest. Some of these, although legal, interrupt the daily routine (e.g. processions and demonstrations), others are illegal, whether or not they are non-violent (e.g. civil disobedience), while still others use various degrees of violence. By their very use of protest, the social movements engage the State, not only a counterpart in eventual negotiations about the objectives of the movement, but also as a guarantor of public order.

A key aspect of the institutional reponse to protest is its strategy for maintaining public order (protest policing). This is important in relationships between the police and the movements, particularly the tension between the State's duty to maintain public order and its role as the main guarantor of citizens' liberties and rights of participation. In fact, the control of protest is one of the most delicate tasks facing the police in modern democratic countries, for what is at stake is not 'only' respect for personal liberty, but also the rights of citizens to political participation – and hence the very essence of the democratic system. The concept of public order, on which the police base their action and the strategies they use to maintain it thus have a considerable impact on the perception of citizens for the respect shown by the State for their rights and liberties. The policeman who intervenes in order to control demonstration is seen not only as the representative of political power, but also as an indicator of the quality of democracy in a political system – all the more so in that such interventions attract the attention of the mass media, which increases their impact and therefore potential criticism.

In the eyes of the demonstrators, police forces represent the most tangible face of the State, and this has important repercussions on the choice of strategies. Traditionally, the more repressive the strategies, the greater the radicalization of the forms of protest. At the same time, protest policing is a key element for the development and self-definition of the police as an institution and profession.[1] The gradual affirmation of the police as the main specialized agency in this task was of fundamental importance in the process of the modernization and professionalism of European police forces during the nineteenth century. Also, the waves of protest have had considerable impact, both on the strategies and organization of the police, as Jane Morgan has observed in her research on the British police (1987). In contemporary democratic societies the way in which the police handle protest seems to be a significant, if not dominant aspect of its self-image (Winter, 1998a).

Numerous research findings hold that, as from the 1970s, the style of controlling protest became more tolerant in Western democracies, with less recourse to force and more importance given to the development of negotiation strategies (della Porta and Reiter, 1998a). Recently, however, this trend seems to have been interrupted. For decades, studies on the social movements in Europe focused on the process of their institutionalization, if not their 'entry into the mainstream', while studies on the police were mainly concerned with the changes in strategies in reaction to the waves of protest of the 1960s and 1970s. But, today, once again questions are posed about the dangers of the radicalization of political and social conflicts.

In the history of the 'globalization from below' or alternative world movement, which is still only a few years old, there have been frequent clashes between police and demonstrators. Looking back, even before Genoa in 2001 there had been violence: in Gothenburg, at the EU summit with the US, in June; in Quebec City, at the start-up meeting of the Free Trade Area of the Americas (FTAA) in April; in Naples, at the Global Forum of the OECD in March, and in Davos at the World Economic Forum in February. Earlier, in 2000, there had also been big clashes in Prague, during the meeting of the international council of the World Bank and the IMF in September; in Washington, at the summit of these two organizations, in April; in Davos, again, at the World Economic Forum in January; in the previous year in Seattle, for the WTO Summit in November and in Cologne, at the G7 Summit, in

January. While many other demonstrations had taken place peacefully – particularly those preparing the counter-summits – there has clearly been a high proportion of clashes between police and demonstrators in the more visible events organized by the movement.

THE PROTEST POLICING STRATEGIES: DE-ESCALATION OR ESCALATION OF REPRESSION?

Sociological research has distinguished three main strategic approaches to the control of protest, which in different historical periods have been given preference (della Porta and Reiter, 1996). These are: *coercive* strategies, that is, the use of arms and physical force to control or disperse demonstrations; *negotiating* strategies, in which all efforts to control the protest are made through prior contacts with the activists and organizers; and *information* strategies, consisting of collecting and distributing information as a preventative measure in controlling protest and collecting information, and using modern audiovisual techniques to identify those who violate the law, without having to intervene directly. Police interventions can vary in response to the behaviour considered illegitimate (fluctuating between repression and tolerance), strategies of controlling the various actors (in general or selectively), the moment of intervention by the police (preventative or reactive), the degree of force (hard or soft), extent of formal respect for procedures (legalistic or opportunistic) and the development of mediation institutions (negotiated or authoritarian) (della Porta, 1995).

Combining all these dimensions makes it possible to define two coherent models for controlling public order (see Table 1): one, more tolerant, selective and flexible with limited use of force and frequent negotiations; the other, more repressive, diffused and rigid, with a massive use of force and methods that are also illegal (like *agents-provocateurs*) and little use of negotiations with those responsible for the demonstrations (della Porta and Fillieule, 2004). It is thus possible to differentiate a style of public order based on escalated force and a style of negotiated control. In the first case, little priority is given to the right to demonstrate, the more innovatory forms of protest are not greatly tolerated, communication between the police and the demonstrators is reduced to the essentials and there is frequent use of coercive measures. In the second case, the right to demonstrate peacefully is considered a priority, forms of protest, even disruptive, are tolerated, communication between protesters and police is considered fundamental if the demonstration is to proceed pacifically and the use of coercive measures avoided as much as possible (McPhail, Schweingruber and McCarthy, 1998, 51–4). In addition, there are the types of information strategies that the police adopt to control the protest: it is possible to distinguish between general control and a control that concentrates on those possibly responsible for criminal acts.

Table 1   Strategies for controlling protest

	Escalated force	Negotiated control	New global demonstrations
Coercive strategies	Massive use of force to repress violations, even minor ones	Tolerance of minor violations	Massive use of force, including against peaceful demonstrators
Negotiating strategies	Intimidating use of relationships with the organizers	Partnership to ensure the right to demonstrate	Little confidence in negotiations
Information strategies	General collecting of information	Concentration on collecting data on punishment of violations	General collecting of information and using it to raise alarm

Following the great waves of protest in the Western democracies that culminated at the end of the 1960s, strategies for maintaining public order, as well as their operative practices and techniques, underwent a radical change. While the diffuse concept of respect for people's right to demonstrate their disagreement tended to become more inclusive, the intervention strategies moved away from the model that had predominated until then. Through the 1970s and 1980s, although with some temporary hiccups, there was a trend towards increasing tolerance of violations of the law when considered of minor importance. Among the changes of strategy in the control of the public order there was: less use of force, greater emphasis on 'dialogue' and the investment, in terms of resources, in collecting information (della Porta and Reiter, 1998a).

These strategies, which could be called 'de-escalation' (or prevention, in the Italian case), were based on specific routes and certain assumptions. Before the demonstrations, representatives of the protesters and the police had to meet and negotiate in detail the route to be followed and the behaviour to be maintained during the demonstration (including certain symbolic violations that were more or less allowed). But there was never to be any assault on peaceful groups, and the agreements reached with those responsible for the demonstration were never to be countervened, communication between the organizers and the police forces had to be kept open for the whole demonstration; the police should above all guarantee the right to demonstrate peacefully; and violent groups had to be stopped without endangering the safety of the demonstrators (Fillieule and Jobard, 1998; McPhail *et al.*, 1998; Waddington, 1994; Winter, 1998b; della Porta, 1998).

The negotiated model has not been applied consistently in many of the demonstrations of the movement for globalization from below, particularly those against the international summits, even before Genoa. In fact, as these movements emerged on to the public scene a new, long 'escalation' got under way. Above all, the management of public order during the summits often seemed unable to defend the rights of peaceful protesters to demonstrate, with restrictions of citizens' rights of movement and non-selective coercive interventions. In fact, once again maintaining public order involved: an escalation in coercive means, also inflicting them punitively; chaotic communication between the demonstrators and the police; and diffuse intelligence activities, with restrictions on the right to demonstrate.

THE INCREASING USE OF REPRESSION

It seems that negotiation is increasingly giving way to the use of physical force, even against peaceful protesters. Already in 1999, at Seattle, the police were accused of being unprepared for maintaining public order and of making repeated charges against non-violent demonstrators. According to four commissions of enquiry,[2] on 30 November, even before the 'black bloc' had broken a few windows, the police resorted to force to disperse the non-violent sit-ins, using tear-gas and pepper-sprays (Smith, 2000, 13; Morse, 2001). After the curfew was imposed, police blockades and assaults were repeated, day and night, for three days, until the intergovernmental summit ended (without having reached agreement).

In Gothenburg, too, according to many witnesses, the action of the police in the streets was at first weak, confronted as it was by the violence of the black bloc, but then it became unusually tough: accounts by protesters and activists of the behaviour of the police during the demonstrations, publicized mainly on the Internet, are full of the confusion among the police and their unpreparedness, ending up in violent charges against peaceful demonstrators, the use of firearms (three demonstrators wounded, one of them seriously) and gratuitous brutality, both in public and towards the people who had been taken into custody. More than a hundred complaints were lodged by demonstrators against the Swedish police for wrongful treatment. The reports were particularly critical of the assault on a school that served as a dormitory for the demonstrators in the night after the most violent clashes. The special paramilitary unit justified its action by claiming to be looking for an armed German terrorist. According to the demonstrators involved, they were subjected to verbal and physical abuse during the incident. That it was an ineffective intervention was confirmed by the fact that of the many people who were taken into custody (539), only a few were charged (23), most of them foreign citizens. This also happened in Prague (859 taken into custody, 20 charged) and was repeated in Genoa. If nothing else, these figures would seem to prove the incapacity of the police to stop the violent protesters – who, according to the figures provided by the police themselves, were much more numerous – or to present sufficient proof to the magistrates to justify all those having been taken into custody.

While before Genoa there were deviations from negotiated public order, at Genoa itself the choice of means to control the protest totally abandoned this system. When the police spokesmen came before the parliamentary commission of enquiry they repeatedly emphasized that they had taken measures to ensure maximum respect for the rights of the demonstrators. However, many described the Genoa days as episodic police riots, in other words rebellions by police agents who disobeyed the orders of their superiors. As for the maintenance of public order in the streets, while the demonstration of the 19th was peaceful, the two successive days saw frequent punitive forays, also against peaceful demonstrators (see Andretta, della Porta, Mosca and Reiter (2002), Chapter IV, for a reconstruction of the events). As for the Friday, reporters' accounts agreed, repeatedly during the day, on the provocations by the black bloc, which were followed by indiscriminate arrests by the police. The main escalation took place in the afternoon when the *carabinieri* loaded up a procession of the 'disobedient' that was still moving along a route that had been authorized and, according to various witnesses, had been peaceful. While there had not been any incidents up to that point, 'the disorder' – according to Giulietto Chiesa of the newspaper *La Stampa* (2001, 44) – 'from that moment on was the direct and unequivocal consequence of the choice made by the police'. After the first charges, 'the progress of the *carabinieri* met with resistance that soon became inevitable: "accept to be beaten or defend yourself!" Thus, before my eyes, those two or three thousand young people who headed the procession were transformed into active and furious combatants' (*ibid*, 45).

It was precisely during these clashes, three hours after the first arrests, that, between Via Tolemaide and Corso Gastaldi where various parts of the procession had been blocked, the young Genovese Carlo Giuliani lost his life. According to the report of the parliamentary enquiry commission (composed mostly of right-wing members) the episode had to be seen 'in the context of furious clashes between groups of violent demonstrators and the forces of order' (*Relazione I*, 223). The minority report contested this scenario by pointing out 'the dramatic scenes that were filmed, in which so many youths were being loaded up or chased by agents' (*Relazione II*, 148), and drew up a 'dramatic' balance-sheet at the end of the day: 'thousands of tear-gas canisters were thrown by the police and Digos agents, hundreds of people were wounded, dozens taken into custody. And in 24 years there had not been a death [in Italy]' (*ibid*, 145).

During Saturday's procession, the black blocs, which the protesters had tried to drive back, were carried away by the charges of the state police who that day were in the frontline, as opposed to the *carabinieri* who were more scattered, following the clashes of the previous day. This time the police used tear-gas (launched also from helicopters and the tops of buildings) rather than armoured vehicles, keeping at a greater distance from the demonstrators. Once again the police reacted to the violent actions of the black bloc, charging at the procession, blocking all ways of escape and involving peaceful and non-dangerous demonstrators, who were often holding up their hands. It was at this moment that armed vehicles drove at high speed into the crowd (*Relazione II*). That same evening, the police broke into the Pertini-Diaz school. And 62 out of the 93 demonstrators who were sleeping there were taken to hospital afterwards, where they stayed from one to five days, some in a critical condition. These police brutalities were denounced by hundreds of women and men arrested by the police and kept in the Bolzaneto barracks. Some stated that they had been beaten several times, forced to sing anti-communist, anti-semitic and anti-homosexual songs and threatened with sexual violence. In most cases meetings with lawyers were delayed and often the foreigners who had been taken into custody were expelled from the country without even having seen a magistrate.

REFUSING NEGOTIATION

In spite of affirmations of principle, the negotiating strategy was not followed in a convincing or coherent way. Before the Gothenburg summit, the social-democrat government of Sweden – a country with a very long history of left-wing governments but with hardly any experience in violent political demonstrations – had however declared that it wanted the police to engage with the movement.[3] For the first time in its history, the Swedish police had thus set up, in the preparatory phase of the summit, a group responsible for contacts with the organizers of the protest. But this group was not consulted or involved when the police decided to clear the large school complex that had been given to the demonstrators for holding their counter-summit seminars. The police saw this as a preventative measure before the summit started, in spite of there having been no violent incidents up until then. This eruption, justified by the search for illegal arms and violent activists, bore little fruit. Worse still, it seemed to have robbed the contact group of all credibility and to have exacerbated the anger of most of the peaceful demonstrators against the police, especially those involved, in spite of themselves, in the clashes that took place in the clearing of the school.

As for the G8 Summit at Genoa, while the police chiefs repeatedly said that they had tried to establish relations and open communication lines with the protest movement, it was the commissioner himself, the highest official responsible for maintaining public order, who declared that he did not have any real contact with the spokesperson of the Genoa Social Forum (GSF) until the second or third round, given that the previous contact had been with the *prefetto* (hearings of 28 August 2001, 38). He also said that he had only once seen the architect Paolini, who had been charged by the government to engage with the GSF, and that he had not considered him a serious interlocutor (*ibid*, 43). The meetings between the GSF spokesperson and the authorities about the organization of the demonstration, which had been requested several times by the movement, got under way very late – a few weeks before the G8 Summit.

In spite of all this, at the commision of enquiry, all representatives of the central and local authorities emphasized their efforts to establish dialogue and collaboration with the movement. The relationships between the authorities and the GSF had however followed a tortuous 'stop-go' course, marked by repeated misunderstandings and constant distrust. The hope of the movement to be able to organize a large counter-summit, encouraged in the first contacts with the centre-left Italian government at that time, were disappointed and even the more specific negotiations on the organization of the street protest were interrupted several times.

The amorphousness of the processions and the incapacity of the organizers to maintain order is traditionally seen by those responsible for public order as risky, potentially multiplying the number of groups with whom to negotiate and reducing their ability to control their followers.[4] The very heterogeneity of the movement is, according to the police, a forewarning of disorder. Also, the 'remoteness' or, at least, the abstraction, of the problem being raised in the demonstrations does not help the agents to understand the motivations of the protesters (della Porta and Reiter, 2002). These tendencies seem to have been particularly accentuated in Genoa: in the eyes of the police force, the GSF protesters were essentially dangerous and violent, and this image was partly created by the analyses made of the different components of the pre-summit protest: the 'red bloc' of the pacifists, who seek visibility through actions to prevent, boycott and delay the work of the summit; the 'yellow bloc' of the 'white overalls' (who then became the 'disobedient'), ready for civil disobedience and direct action, not excluding a resort to violence; the 'blue bloc' of the more radical social centres, ready to take direct, violent and provocative action against the police; and lastly the 'black bloc', the group considered the greatest risk to public order (La Barbera, hearing of 28 August 2001, 60).[5] This judgment of the yellow and blue blocs does not seem to have taken into account the evolution of many of the social centres, which, during the 1990s, had abandoned more violent forms of action in favour of 'protected civil disobedience'. Thus constructive dialogue, which requires reciprocal respect and trust, was undermined from the start.

This impression was reinforced by the judgments of the movement that were expressed after Genoa. In retrospect, the whole GSF was portrayed as being untrustworthy and a large number of the protesters as co-responsible for the violence. The ex-commissioner of Genoa, Colucci, who was dismissed from his post after a ministerial inspection (together with the assistant head of the police, Andreassi; the head of Ucigos, La Barbera; and the assistant head of the Genoese Digos, Perugini, who was photographed kicking a youth lying on the ground), declared to the parliamentary commission of enquiry: 'the people with whom we entered into contact were completely unreliable and did nothing to contribute to proper management of the street protest'. And again: 'We knew that within the GSF there were associations that were quite untrustworthy, but every time we tried to establish the right contact, the encounter was always very, very evasive' (hearing of 28 August 2001, 34, 52). Those responsible for the violence and damage were, according to them, not only the 2,500 protesters supposed to belong to the black blocs, but at least 7,000 to 8,000 protesters from the blue and yellow blocs (including the 'white overalls'), creating veritable hotbeds of revolt (La Barbera, *ibid*, 64). A still greater number, according to them, had not tried to stop the violent ones or denounce them to the police.

The representatives of the forces of order also affirmed that they had not given the militants the formal – yet essential – permission to demonstrate. For a long time it was affirmed that the demonstrations of 20 July had not been authorized, whereas, as it emerged during the parliamentary enquiry, the normal notice had been presented and accepted by the *questura,* who had however forbidden access to certain squares and banned the procession of the 'disobedient' from going beyond Piazza Verdi.[6] The accusation of illegality, however, goes beyond this formal act. During his hearing, the ex-commissioner of Genoa, Colucci, repeatedly declared that there had been no processions in Genoa, but occupation of territory by tens of thousands of people and that the police found themselves confronted, not by a situation of public order, but by urban guerrilla warfare.

Lists of the actions considered illegitimate included not only those of the 'disobedient' but also those of the 'pacifists'. As for the statement of the 'disobedient', that they wanted to prevent the summit peacefully, blocking the entrances, ex-commissioner Colucci said to the parliamentary commission of enquiry: 'Do you think such an intention can be described as peaceful? At that point it was already quite clearly being announced that the confrontation would not just be verbal, but also physical' (hearing of 28 August 2001, 52). Citing the effort of the pacifists to create a human cushion between the violent and the police, Colucci declared: 'I ask myself: "to create a human cushion between the black bloc and the police": does that not mean to try and stop the police from intervening?' (*ibid*, 15).

INFORMATION STRATEGIES AND RESTRICTING
THE RIGHT TO DEMONSTRATE

As for information strategy and the restriction on the right to demonstrate, at the summit meetings at Davos, Prague and Nice, the freedom of demonstration had already been subordinated to the security of the heads of state and government, with massive intelligence operations and hundreds of protesters blocked at the frontiers. There were also limitations on the freedom of movement in large areas around the venues of the meetings. At Gothenburg, the 'preventative' strategy adopted by Sweden – particularly refusal of people at the border, based on suspicions, even general ones, of demonstrators coming from other countries in the European Union – were already being seen as provocative and also problematic for a modern democracy, which must guarantee participation. This created doubts about the effective respect for individual rights in the new European institutions.[7] In Germany – most of the violent demonstrators at Gothenburg were German citizens – the efforts to prevent the violence of the 'summit hooligans' before Genoa concentrated on the use of *Ausreiseverbot*, banning people from leaving the country during international meetings. The juridical basis for the preventative action of the German police was the measures developed to stop the ultras (after the clashes during the football World Cup in 1998, the law on passports was changed to make it possible to prohibit hooligans from leaving the country) and certain measures formerly applied against neo-nazi activists.

After Genoa, these practices and the criteria adopted for identifying and keeping records on activists who were or were suspected of being violent came under increasing criticism (see *Der Spiegel*, 31/2001; *Die Zeit*, 37/2001, 4ss.; Griebenow and Busch, 2001). However, at the conference of the EU interior ministers of 13 July 2001, which had been called to agree on greater collaboration between the various police forces to ensure that summits could take place peacefully, Minister Schily proposed to 'Europeanize' German practices, creating a European data bank of the 'violent' and introducing the use of *Ausreiseverbot* into all the other countries. In the end, the result of this conference was to assign prevention responsibility to individual member states, while giving them directives to improve their collaboration according to the model developed to deal with stadium hooliganism (Griebenow and Busch, 2001, 64ff). As has been documented by a Belgian report on the intervention of European police forces at the EU Summit at Laecken, co-operation seems to be difficult because of the varying quality of the information coming from the different countries as well as the limited competences of the international liaison bureaux (Busch, 2002, 54f).

At Genoa the strategy of physically isolating the venues of the summits was confirmed through massive border controls, partial closing of access roads to the city, a buffer zone (the yellow zone) in which the freedom to demonstrate was restricted and a red zone, which was fortified and prohibited to protesters. In the preparations for the G8, the attention of governments was in fact concentrated on holding the demonstrators far away from the venue of the summit and keeping potentially violent individuals outside the city. On 11 July the Schengen convention on the free circulation of people was suspended until midnight on 21 July. Militant activists and those suspected as such were turned back at the frontiers: in his report to the parliamentary enquiry, the head of the police, De Gennaro, mentioned 140,000 controls and over 2,000 people turned back, among them 147 Greek activists, including some of the leaders of the Greek coordination against the G8, who arrived by ship at Ancona and were forcibly expelled. The red zone, with 13 openings and a perimeter of 8 km (at Prague it had been barely 2 km and at Quebec City less than 6 km), not only closed the areas being used by the summit, but also some streets of the city, such as Via XX Settembre.

The proposal of Minister Schily – which met with the resistance of France, Austria, Denmark, Sweden, the Netherlands, Finland, Ireland and Greece – could be cited as an almost exemplary case of the kind of arrangements decided at international summits and criticized by the movement. In fact, an effort was made to introduce, at supranational level, repressive measures that existed only in a rudimentary form (if indeed they existed at all) in those laws and institutions of control that were democratically legitimate, for which liberal, democratic and socialist movements have had to battle for so long within the framework of their nation states.

Instead, the displacement of decision-making power to the supranational level led to the gradual recognition of the need to expand democratic rights, including the right to protest, rather than to restrict them. In fact, at the EU level, the Watson report on the liberties and rights of citizens, justice and internal affairs of the European Parliament (European Parliament A5-396/2001), which was the basis for a recommendation to the plenary of the European Council of 12 December 2001, requested, *inter alia*, that internal frontiers not be blocked so as to stop people from participating in demonstrations that had been properly announced, that the police desist from excessive use of force, that interventions should be based on the principles of de-escalation and that the rights of individuals be protected, even in confused scenes of mass mobilizations in which violent activists participate, alongside peaceful citizens. Above all certain recommendations – such as the elaboration of a common European definition of 'public order' or of a European manual for police forces involved in public demonstrations – show that the existence of internal standards that are substantially comparable among the member states is not enough to guarantee, at a supranational European level, the exercise of the rights of citizens to demonstrate and protest.

CONCLUSION

In the 1990s the maintenance of public order appeared to be 'civilized' – with some exceptions – as de-escalation strategies were preferred. However, in managing protest against neoliberal globalization strategies of escalating force have re-emerged. This return to the past cannot be attributed to the particular propensity for violence of a movement, which, in fact, in an overwhelming majority, seems basically more oriented towards non-violence (for conviction, or for opportunistic reasons) than other movements in the past. While the management of international summits, in particular, certainly creates delicate situations for public order, the characteristics of the movement should make it possible to implement negotiated strategies. In the case of Genoa, it seems as if this strategy was discouraged by the prejudices that the police had of the demonstrators – prejudices that were mainly created by unreliable reports from the secret services.

This shows up the limits of a partial reform of the police, which has maintained certain, not very democratic characteristics in its organizational structures. These included, especially: its militarization, lack of democratic accountability, partial separation of some forces from civil authorities, insufficient professionalism in handling public order and a culture of public order that does not give priority to the right to demonstrate (della Porta and Reiter, 2003; Andretta, della Porta, Mosca, Reiter, 2002). The organizational structures and the know-how of the police are in fact important elements in building a police force capable of acting to protect the democratic rights of citizens, apart from the orders given by the political powers. The hypothesis that the brutality of the police intervention at Genoa derived from a political order from above does however require, as a corollary, a police force that has an organizational structure and a culture that predisposes it to carry out interventions that are not only 'tough', but go beyond the legal limits.

All this indicates, though, that one of the main explanations for the hardening of police response to the movement for globalization from below is the (lack of) political response to the protest. One of the evident effects of globalization in its neoliberal version has been the illusion – proclaimed by the right and often believed by the left – that there are no more politics. According to this view, which had acquired a certain currency during the 1990s, technological changes, accelerating capital movements across borders, would undermine the capacities for political intervention over markets until they disappeared altogether. Even though an understanding of the need for political control over the economy has now reappeared, neoliberal globalization seems to have had an enduring effect on the political sphere. There appears to be a sharper separation between a representative conception of politics and a participatory conception, which is symbolically expressed in the opening slogan of the Saturday procession at Genoa: 'You are the G8, we are six billion!'

While the conceptions of representative and participatory democracy have always been in a state of mutual tension, they nevertheless came together at times – for example, in mass political parties, especially left-wing ones, which for a long time combined the function of selecting the governing class with that of forming collective identities and values, but also in the social movements of the past, which had found militants in left-wing parties who were ready to listen to and pass on their demands. But the lack of social 'embeddedness' of political parties – which has been precipitated by globalization – has polarized the two conceptions. A reciprocal distrust has been growing between the political and institutional class and the activists of the movement. The parties that no longer have militants concentrate their attention on the electorate, considering voters as isolated individuals whose pulse can be taken through opinion polls, rather than trying to convince them of other values. If, therefore, they are convinced that the electorate is mainly at the centre, there is increasing hesitation vis-à-vis the movements who are demanding typically left-wing interventions – such as greater social justice. The hunt, at all costs, for the 'average' elector thus distances the parties of the institutional left from a large portion of 'the people of the left'.

NOTES

1. For a definition of protest policing, see della Porta (1995), chapter 3. For a discussion on the various styles of protesting policing in Europe and the United States, see della Porta and Reiter (1998a).
2. Conducted by the American Civil Liberties Union, the Seattle National Lawyers Guild, WTO Legal Group, the Committee for Local Government Accountability and the WTO Accountability Review Committee.
3. This reconstruction of the events at Gothenburg is based on Peterson and Oskarsson (2002); *Frankfurter Rundschau*, 16 June 2001; *Tageszeitung*, 16 and 18 June 2001.
4. See, for example, Waddington (1994), on the maintenance of public order in London.
5. The extreme fringes of the movement are then connected with the recent re-emergence of terrorist actions (see La Barbera, hearing of 28 August 2001, 66; Andreassi, hearing of 28 August 2001, 101).
6. It is useful to recall that Article 17 of the Italian Constitution stipulates, for meetings held in public places, that notice should be given to the authorities, thus cancelling the authorization stipulated in the Single Text of the laws on public security, issued under Fascism. The authorities can prohibit demonstrations 'for proven motives of security or public order' or impose certain conditions concerning, for example the route of the demonstration. Minister Scajola stated before the parliamentary commission of enquiry: 'Non-authorized demonstrations do in fact self-authorize themselves. The duty of the State is to intervene to protect citizens from possible acts of violence. If today we ask Italian citizens whether demonstrations should be authorized or if they are legitimate in themselves, they would reply that all of them should be authorized. This is a fact' (hearing of 7 September 2001, 86).
7. According to the *Tageszeitung* (18 June 2001), during the days of the summit meetings, 130 Germans were denied entry at the frontier, including two completely full coaches, while after the clashes ' hundreds' of protesters were expelled.

BIBLIOGRAPHY

Andretta, M., D. della Porta, L. Mosca and H. Reiter (2002) *Global, noglobal, new global: La protesta contro il G8 a Genova* (Bari-Roma: Laterza)

Busch, H. (2002) 'Vor neuen Gipfeln. Ueber die Schwierigkeiten internationaler Demonstrationen', in *Bürgerrechte & Polizei/Cilip*, no. 72, pp. 53–7

Chiesa, G. (2001) *G8/Genova* (Turin: Einaudi)

Della Porta, D. (1995) *Social Movements, Political Violence, and the State: A comparative analysis of Italy and Germany* (Cambridge: Cambridge University Press)

Della Porta, D. (1998) 'Police Knowledge and Protest Policing: Some reflections on the Italian case', in D. Della Porta and H. Reiter (eds), *Policing Protest: The control of mass demonstrations in Western democracies* (Minneapolis: University of Minnesota Press), pp. 228–51

Della Porta, D. and O. Fillieule (2004) 'Policing Social Movements', in H.P. Kriesi and D. Snow (eds), *The Blackwell Companion on Social Movements* (Oxford: Blackwell)

Della Porta, D. and H. Reiter (2003) *Polizia e protesta. L'ordine pubblico dalla Liberazione ai 'noglobal'* (Bologna: Il Mulino)

Fillieule, O. and F. Jobard (1998) 'The Policing of Protest in France. Towards a model of protest policing', in D. della Porta and H. Reiter (eds), *Policing Protest: The control of mass demonstrations in Western democracies* (Minneapolis: University of Minnesota Press), pp. 70–90

Griebenow, O. and H. Busch (2001) 'Weder Reisefreiheit noch Demonstartionsrecht in der EU?', in *Bürgerrechte & Polizei/Cilip*, no. 69, pp. 63–9

Lipsky, M. (1965) *Protest and City Politics* (Chicago: Rand McNally)

McAdam, D. (1983) 'Tactical Innovation and the Pace of Insurgency', *American Sociological Review*, vol. 8, pp. 735–54

McPhail, C., D. Schweingruber and J. McCarthy (1998) 'Policing Protest in the United States', in D. della Porta and H. Reiter (eds), *Policing Protest: The control of mass demonstrations in Western democracies* (Minnesota: University of Minnesota Press), pp. 49–69

Morgan, J. (1987) *Conflict and Order. The police and labour disputes in England and Wales, 1900–1939* (Oxford: Clarendon Press)

Morse, D. (2001) 'Beyond the Myths of Seattle', *Dissent*, Summer, pp. 39–43

Peterson, A. and M. Oskarsson (2001) 'Policing Political Protest. A Study of the Police Handling of Protest Events in Conjunction with the EU Summit meeting in Göteburg' (unpublished manuscript)

Smith, J. (2000) 'Globalizing Resistance: The Battle of Seattle and the future of social movements', *Mobilization*, vol. 6. no. 1, pp. 1–19

Tilly, C. (1978) *From Mobilization to Revolution* (Reading, MA: Addison-Wesley)

Waddington, P.A.J. (1994) *Liberty and Order. Public Order Policing in a Capital City* (London: UCL Press)

Winter, M. (1998a) *Politikum Polizei. Macht und Funktion der Polizei in der Bundesrepublik Deutschland* (Münster: LIT)

Winter, M. (1998b) 'Police Philosophy and Protest Policing in the Federal Republic of Germany, 1960–1990', in D. della Porta and H. Reiter (eds), *Policing Protest: The control of mass demonstrations in Western democracies* (Minneapolis: University of Minnesota Press), pp. 188–212

SOURCES

Hearings: Italian Parliament, Hearings before the Commission of Enquiry on the 'events that occurred at Genoa on 19, 20, 21 and 22 July 2001 on the occasion of the G8 Summit', verbatim record of the sessions of 8, 9, 28, 29, 30 August and 4, 5, 7 September 2001. Accessible on website www.camera.it

Report I: Italian Parliament, Final Document approved by the Commission of Enquiry on the 'events that occurred at Genoa on 19, 20, 21 and 22 July

2001 on the occasion of the G8 Summit', attached to the Session of 20 September 2001

Report II: Italian Parliament, Alternative Proposal of the Final Document of the Commission of Enquiry on the 'events that occurred at Genoa on 19, 20, 21 and 22 July 2001 on the occasion of the G8 Summit' presented by deputies Luciano Violante *et al.*, attached to the Session of 20 September 2001

22
New Powers, New Counter-Powers

Raoul-Marc Jennar

The neoliberal tidal wave that has been inundating the planet over the last twenty years or so has brought about a continual weakening of the State to the benefit of both private interests and supranational institutions. Considerable powers have been transferred to them without, however, ensuring the democratic control and accountability that exist at the national level. New centres of regional power (e.g. the European Union) and international power (e.g. the World Trade Organization) have emerged, imposing on member states legislation and regulations that have no democratic approval, apart from an almost automatic procedure of ratification. Nor are they submitted to any counter-power, an indispensable guarantee against arbitrary measures.

The governmental political parties, both right and left, have participated in this process. Sometimes they have encouraged it: they have never halted it. And a huge chasm has been created between citizens and these new centres of power. The political parties operate without external communication, cut off from those they are meant to represent, like the blind and deaf bureaucracies that they are. Citizens do not feel that their representatives do in fact represent them. The traditional political class has fallen into considerable disrepute. And this is responsible for the protest vote, populist politics of all kinds and the emergence of manufactured personalities like Bernard Tapie and Arnold Schwarzenegger.

The fact that the political parties are becoming increasingly weak and unable to counteract the trends that are dispossessing citizenship has driven people into reappropriating that part of the political field they had entrusted to representative democracy. A new kind of citizenship is developing that is merging into what is now called civil society.

THE BASTIONS THAT MUST BE STORMED BY CIVIL SOCIETY

'Civil society' is in fact a highly ambiguous term. It represents an effort to rehabilitate a concept that Gramsci and then Bourdieu have analyzed particularly well. Civil society is a complex collection of associations, non-governmental organizations, producers of ideology such as the media, universities, churches, scientific, cultural and artistic milieux, political parties and, lastly, business circles.

The concept of civil society refers to a reality that is extremely heterogeneous, and those involved are likely to have quite contradictory projects for society. It is thus a challenge for those who want to maintain and reinforce the established order through their domination and exploitation relationships and for those who, wanting to change these relationships, call this order into question. Both do their best to create consensus for their project. In the long run, as they do not have the same weapons at their disposal, the former succeed better than the latter. And as the press has moved from its role of the 'fourth power' or 'fourth estate' – i.e. counter-power – to that of watchdog for the dominant way of thinking, this has accentuated the relative importance of the politically correct.

But nothing is for ever, and the search for consensus creates a permanent tension that transforms society into a turmoil of unstable forces. What Gramsci called 'the solid bastions of civil society' do not necessarily uphold unchanging relationships indefinitely. The circulation of ideas shakes these bastions: nothing is predestined. The confrontation between voluntary work enriched by knowledge and the economic and bureaucratic apparatus can bring about change. That is the hope.

The emergence of a new citizenship means winning back the knowledge that leads to the recovery of power. There are now new forms of resistance, after years of resignation. The withdrawal of the Multilateral Agreement on Investment, Seattle and Cancún, Porto Alegre and all the gatherings that come together at the G7 meetings, the general assemblies of the World Bank and the IMF, and the European summits constitute the various stages in this reconquest. An international citizenship was born between 1998 and 2000, and it is increasingly asserting itself. It intends to act on civil society in order to act on the new regional and international powers. At the global level, it is renewing the remarkable work of popular education carried out at the end of the nineteenth century and the beginning of the twentieth, which led to democratic progress (e.g. universal suffrage), as well as social progress (e.g. social security, trade union rights). Neoliberalism is doing its best to dismantle all this or to render it ineffective. Confronted by what Bourdieu called a 'conservative restoration', this international citizenship, which is also called the alternative world, has undertaken the formidable task of decoding the abstruse texts that regulate globalization, in order to make people aware of the tremendous issues at stake and to mobilize them.

The new regional and international powers (European Commission, the World Trade Organization) have lost no time in reacting and, with the huge means at their disposal, are carrying out a systematic operation of mental intoxication and manipulation.

THESE NEW POWERS AND CIVIL SOCIETY

The European Commission has an ambiguous relationship with civil society. It uses the NGOs involved in emergency or development activities, making them serve its own orientations. The considerable sums that it gives to co-finance projects presented by these NGOs creates a power relationship that some cannot resist, especially those proclaiming, as their creed, that they are neutral and apolitical. As if the very notion of development and its practical details are not in themselves a major political problem! So it is no surprise to see NGOs whose mission is to fight world hunger rejoicing in the tons of rice, maize and powdered milk dumped upon such and such a country each year, without ever questioning the causes of famine and thinking about what would be necessary to end it. These NGOs have become the docile executors and therefore appreciated partners of the Commission.

As for the other NGOs and associations that are directly questioning the Commission's decisions, the latter goes to great lengths to create confusion among them by organizing what it calls a 'dialogue with civil society'. Thus in these meetings, which actually have no influence on the Commission's orientations, the representatives of the agro-business, biotechnology and pharmaceutical companies and of the financial, manufacturing and textile sectors are seated beside the delegates of Oxfam, Médecins Sans Frontières, Friends of the Earth, etc. The Commission makes a big fanfare about this so-called dialogue. It wants to give the impression that it is prepared to listen equally to both the business world and the non-profit organizations, whereas before taking any initiative it has already been in close touch with these very same business circles. But this action gives an illusion of being open and transparent as far as governments and European parliamentarians are concerned. It enables the Commission to make the rest of the world believe that it really practises the values that it claims to promote.

By manipulating civil society in this way, the Commission pushes for a consensus that benefits itself. Simulating a dialogue that appears to be participatory strengthens the invisible hegemony that it exercises over Europe.

Of course the employers' pressure groups play the game too. But there are also, in the NGO galaxy, some who refuse to analyze their own function in a global context, proclaiming their 'apolitical' stance. They help to reinforce the consensus.

As for the WTO it also tries to do likewise, but with far less success. Each year it organizes a symposium to which businessmen, NGOs, diplomats and parliamentarians are invited. All kinds of viewpoints are put forward. But this kind of exercise has no impact whatsoever on the dominant orientations imposed on the WTO by the US–EU–Japan–Canada quartet. However, it does enable the WTO to claim that it wants to listen to civil society. During the ministerial conferences, a kind of observer status is conferred on the main protagonists of this civil society whose numbers, however, are half those accorded to the employers' groups.

NEW COUNTER-POWERS

As we have seen, NGOs are refusing the commodification of the planet and the glorification of 'everyone for himself'. The international citizenship formed by many networks of associations and NGOs (the International Forum on Globalization, the Third World Network, Focus on the Global South, Vía Campesina, the From Seattle to Brussels Network, Oxfam International, etc.) carry out intensive information and awareness raising. They also produce files on WTO issues, providing an expertise that is difficult to find in universities as they fall increasingly under the influence of private interests.

Such expertise is often lacking among many governments of the countries of the South, even if this has greatly improved recently. But what is still missing is the capacity to respond to the totally false presentations made by WTO experts sent to their countries by the World Bank and the IMF. The negotiations for Cambodia's accession to the WTO are typical of this manipulation. Recalling these negotiations, the Cambodian trade minister declared: 'It was supposed to be the way leading to paradise. In actual fact, it was only a path through the jungle, full of mines and ambushes by guerrillas, tigers and piranhas.'

One of the novelties highlighted at the WTO ministerial conference at Cancún was the expertise provided by alternative world NGOs to some governmental delegations. Certain NGOs, having adopted a less sermonizing attitude and a more discreet profile, worked closely with various delegations from the countries of the South, exchanging notes and evaluations during the whole conference.

This co-operation had in fact started after the preceding ministerial conference held in Doha in November 2001. When it became obvious that the promises made to the developing countries agreed at Doha would not be kept by the rich countries, the Geneva offices of several alternative world networks published in-depth analyses that the developing countries found to be far-sighted and relevant. A working co-operation got under way, and at Cancún its effectiveness was evident. This helped to maintain resistance to those proposals of the rich countries that favoured only themselves.

In this way the increasing influence of the planetary citizens' movement has been reinforced and expanded. With the total failure of the political parties confronted by the neoliberal catastrophe and with the determination of the government parties of both right and left to subordinate politics to economics, the citizens' response develops, consolidates and affirms itself, far from all forms of populist reaction.

23

International Law, a Decisive Issue for the Alternative World Movement

Monique Chemillier-Gendreau

In recent years the rapid and threatening advances of liberalism have had the salutory effect of triggering resistance at the most appropriate level, the global. But the Berlin Wall had to fall for this movement to get under way. Until then, the forces opposing the dangers created by the evolution of industrial, then finance capital were concentrated in the communist regimes, or communist parties elsewhere. These regimes and parties, although claiming to be inspired by international proletarianism, had all been bent – to different degrees – on their national interests, and thus they no longer defended general issues that were of universal concern. And the communist doctrine was particularly weak on the question of international law,[1] which, in its view, consisted of summary norms. The institutions created to enact international law (e.g. the International Court of Justice) were also felt to be instruments of the bourgeoisie.

It is true that the participation of the Soviet Union in the creation of the United Nations (following its alliance with the West against Nazism during the Second World War), followed by the entry into the UN of other communist states, led these countries during the 1960 and 1970s into contributing, together with Third World states, to a different discourse on international law. However, the movement faded out during the 1980s without having had any practical effects. It became increasingly clear that these two groups of countries were unable to give a dynamic content to the idea of a new world order (either the new economic order or the new juridical one). The end of communism then caused some to believe that, with its demise, the end of history had come and liberalism would now follow its course without let or hindrance.[2]

This illusion was restricted to a relatively small circle and it did not last long. Never has humanity been so mistreated and so dangerously menaced as at the present moment. Never has it been so evident that resistance at the national level cannot produce satisfactory and sustainable results. Hence, gradually resistance has built up at the global level and is trying to organize itself as a coherent collective. But it is unable to set itself general and far-reaching objectives. It concentrates on very heterogeneous struggles, like the fight for access by the poor countries to generic medicines, rejection of GM crops and opposition to the war against Iraq.

Thus the struggles are about situations that people wish to change. In the list of their demands there is no explicit reference to the norms of international law that would bring about respect for the desired objectives, nor of the general principles underpinning these norms, nor the relevant juridical categories whereby the defined norms would be guaranteed. It seems that, in conformity with the secret wish of many jurists, law continues to be an unintelligible technique, the understanding and manipulation of which eludes most citizens. And, while this is true of national law, it is still more so of international law. Not only does opinion not influence the way regulation works (How to put it into practice? What has a legal basis and what does not? What procedures are accessible?), it cannot grasp legal issues clearly in terms of values.

The teaching of international law is responsible for this state of affairs. First of all, law is generally not taught, or only very partially, at the pre-university stage, which means that many citizens are not at ease with juridical reasoning. Moreover, in most countries, the teaching of international law has evolved in volume and content in a way that reflects the power relationships between peoples and financial actors, because it is often only an optional subject that jurists are not obliged to study to get their degrees. This is the case in most American universities. In France, the proportion of international law courses that are obligatory was greater thirty years ago than it is today. This subject was then obligatory for teaching public law, and it constituted one of the four examinations in the competition for recruiting university teachers. But it has now been reduced to the level of an option, which means that one can become a professor of public law without having studied international law.

An analysis of the structure of legal studies is also instructive, for it shows the importance given by the global community to the different aspects of the norms that should govern it. The doctorate that leads to teaching and research in the discipline is mostly oriented towards laws covering international business, world trade and, perhaps, diplomacy, as well as the law of the sea. A certain number of universities offer degrees on human rights. The setting up of an international penal judiciary has recently created interest and led to many conferences and more teaching on this sensitive subject. But the weak point is the general teaching, which should clarify the theoretical, and even philosophical, framework that serves as a basis for contemporary international law, and the teaching concerning the norms of the rights of peoples, the right to peace, treaty law and law concerning international institutions.

However, it is the general basis of international society that is undergoing a violent crisis, as can be seen by the critical phase the UN is going through, as well as the wars, the terrorist and assassination attacks, the consignment of whole populations to the rubbish heap, the chaotic uncertainty about the definition of a people, the rise in international criminality, the resurgence of piracy, the insufficient lack of authority of the International Court of Justice, which a major power like the US can flout by not carrying out its decisions. Examples have been the Lagrand affair, whereby the Court demanded unsuccessfully that the US suspend the execution of a German citizen. The same fate befell its decision of 5 February 2003 on the comparable case of Avena and other Mexican nationals.

International law is indeed more concerned with the rights of business than the rights of peoples or the relationships between states, and this is a dangerous drift. International law has been incapable of providing a framework for a world that has become extremely complex and whose characteristics stem from being made up of two different layers. This is because of the co-existence of, on the one hand, an inter-state society, which believed it had set up an adequate institutional system with the Charter of the United Nations (but the inequalities between states and the widespread recourse to military and violent solutions to their conflicts have caused the system to fail); and, on the other hand, a genuinely globalized society, in which relations between individuals and groups are established direct, without passing through the inter-state system. The juridical framework is thus discreet and very flexible because it consists of international contracts that leave all parties completely free.

The peoples of the world are doubly victims of this situation because the weakness of the UN prevents it from protecting them, while the flexibility of international contracts makes it possible to pillage them. This imbalance between the rights of business and a general international law at the service of peoples should be examined from the viewpoint of the juridical forms being used and their impact on the values that lie at the basis of law, the two being closely interlinked.

As complex societies became organized in the West, the great juridical systems that later influenced the whole world tended to make a *summa* distinction between law and other sources of law, particularly the contract. The law was linked to sovereignty and its roots go back to the late medieval times. It expressed the will of the sovereign: a monarch to begin with and later the people's representatives. It thus had a unique level of authority and generality. Because of this the values upon which a society decided to build became obligatory. All other sources of law (except the Constitution) were subordinate to it.

In most legal systems, contracts entered into between individuals or collective bodies express the free will of those concerned – on the condition, however, that they are framed within the law. In this way the coherence of the juridical order was ensured. The juridical system, which was itself based on constitutional principles and organized by legislation, is a guarantee of this coherence and may annul a contract that contravenes laws governing the public order. There is no doubt that the contract, which freely expresses the will of the contracting parties, is a precious instrument for freedom and creativity. It enables parties to fix the limits of their actions in relationship to those of others. But it cannot be denied that the concepts so dear to the civilizing theory of autonomy and the juridical equality of the partners in the contract are but myths. If the inequality (financial, access to information, military power, etc.) between the contracting parties is too great, the weaker ones cannot claim equality before the law to defend their interests, and the content of the contract will reveal the power relationships (e.g. work contracts during a period of underemployment, 'glass bead treaties' during the colonial era, international contracts between powerful companies and small, dependent states) and will perpetuate or deepen inequality.

Thus it is that a society that is only contractual is inevitably an unjust society because human beings do not renounce advantage unless they are forced to do so by the political power in the name of the collective interest. This is the role of law within a society. Exercised in the name of the sovereign (and after a public debate, if the sovereign is the people represented in democratic institutions), it gives authority to the prevailing values at any given moment. Of course, it also expresses power relationships – and the social drift experienced by the Western democracies testifies to this – but although it does not consolidate justice, it does at least produce order. And while there can be many injustices in a system of order, there are still more of them in chaos.

In the decolonization era, the liberated populations were promised that they would accede to their sovereignty with an order that they themselves would define at the national level. The UN framework was an effort to organize international society on an inter-state model, crowned by a range of supranational institutions to guarantee the peace and independence of all states. But there was a lot of bad faith in proclaiming the principle of equality between all peoples and states, and indeed this principle was immediately denied when the regime of permanent members was set up, placing them above all others. Above all, the system remained essentially contractual. The Charter itself is a treaty, and the promotion of international law, declared as an objective of the UN, did not go as far as posing questions about the juridical and procedural means enabling the general and obligatory rules to be imposed on everyone and which would organize international society around common values. The treaty, that is, the contract between states in which the power relationships were likely to be reflected, remained almost the only source of international law.

At the same time, directly globalized society, which consists of economic exchanges, mobility of persons, capital, goods, particularly non-material ones (knowledge, information, etc.) has developed on the basis of international contracts. The more complex these exchanges are, the more the juridical set-up lacks transparency. These contracts are not subject to national jurisdiction (because the different partners do not belong to the same nationality and reside in different countries) and they therefore do not come under the authority of any juridical order.

Since the Second World War, globalization has accelerated and contracts that accommodate the dynamic of these exchanges have multiplied. As they are free from any principles, they have allowed the organized exploitation of people's resources (e.g. the huge oil contracts in Africa, the tourist development of the Maghreb and Latin America by foreign companies) and they have greatly contributed to the weakening of countries' sovereignty. Also, judging by all the litigations, the questions of competent tribunals and applicable laws have clearly not been settled, so their solutions are based on power relationships. Negotiations on the Multilateral Agreement on Investment, which for the time being are uncompleted, show the desire of private actors and the governments that support them to weaken still further the internal law system of countries so that international investors do not encounter any obstacle in their search for huge and rapid financial gains.

In the period after independence the elites of the developing countries were quite militant. But those times are gone. They then tried to use existing juridical categories to establish protective principles, without realizing that the appropriate categories had yet to be invented. In fact, classic legal systems as constructed by the Western states had favoured the contractual form, which was adapted to the respect of sovereignty. But they were a relatively homogeneous group of states. Treaties, which are contractual law, make it possible to avoid having more general instruments that would necessarily restrict the powers of the sovereign. This was not the case for societies that had become very heterogeneous through the integration of their country, because their size made them barely viable and also because they were weakened by wars or underdevelopment. For these countries, the contract is a real danger if it is not drawn up within a framework of intangible principles that would make it possible to prevent flagrant plundering. However, the representatives of weak states, concerned about maximum respect for their sovereignty, which had sometimes been acquired through great sacrifice, were no more willing than the other states that their sovereignty should be fettered by regulations beyond their control. They were thus content with passing a few protective principles, both in the general treaties and in the resolutions of international organizations. But in the former case it is impossible to arrive at a norm of general application as the states are free not to subscribe to the texts that are submitted to them and the relative effect of treaties is a hindrance to their overall obligations.[3] As for the resolutions, the question whether they are juridically binding has been settled in the negative. They are thus considered as 'soft law' and states are not bound to respect them.

The system has been tied up to the advantage of the more powerful states in that international justice itself is voluntary. Nothing can force a state to accept the jurisdiction of the International Court at The Hague. And it is the same for the new International Criminal Court, whose statutes do not include economic or environmental crimes, which thus go unpunished.

In this way, the principles formulated in the 1970s concerning the rights of peoples in terms of the economic order, such as the requirement that a specific proportion of the budget of the developed states be earmarked for development, or those related to the control of foreign investments, remain disconnected from realities. International contracts between very unequal actors, particularly between the large international investors and weak countries, have led ineluctably to pillage without meeting any juridical obstacles. At the same time, international law manuals have continued to consign non-negligible developments to 'phantom' categories. To take an example: the general imperative law, introduced into positive law by the Vienna Convention of 27 May 1969 where it is stated that a treaty is null and void if it is contrary to a peremptory norm (*jus cogens*). These are the regulations accepted at a given moment by the community of states as a whole, but the norms are imprecise and no-one knows what procedures could put them into operation. Doubtless they refer to another category, a little less spectral: that of international custom. This is made up of all the norms that have been constituted over time by habitual behaviour that is accompanied by an explicit feeling of obligation. But if law is not written, custom has to be proved as existing on the basis of recognized practice. If there is disagreement on the existence of such a rule, a judge has to resolve the disagreement by first of all deciding on the existence of customary law.

As can be seen, we have underlined the weakness of international justice. The impasse stems first of all from the lack of a juridical instrument establishing the intangible values of the world that could protect it from extremes of injustice as well as from its own destruction. Of course, this does not encourage progress along the difficult path of defining such values. We are now at a moment of very great danger when it is urgently necessary to affirm values that can serve as a brake on the devastating effects of industrial and financial development. The planet is now in a situation that becomes daily more difficult to reverse. Apart from being destroyed by an excess of industrialization, it is also being devastated by an unbridled capitalism that demands increasingly large and immediate profits. Whole peoples are sinking into destitution or being overtaken by chaos. Rivalries between sovereignties, the obstacle that prevents the enactment of general norms that are valid for world society as a whole, as well as the uncontrolled incursions of actors determined to increase their profits, have led to situations like that of the trade in generic medicines whereby pharmaceutical companies shamelessly defend positions in the commercial negotiations of the WTO, the direct consequences of which condemn millions of human beings to death. The resistance movements, incapable of taking offensive action after the shipwreck of communism, have accepted that the free market has become a universal principle and have been driven into adopting a defensive position, only fighting for a few exceptions to be made.

Thus the very idea of the common good has been caught up in this disaster. This is a radical inversion and urgent action should be taken. The principle is the defence of the common good, in other words a solidarity society in which all human beings, simply because they share the adventure of life, have the right to live in the best possible conditions. The planet, our 'common home', must not be endangered by anyone. This principle, developed in all its applications, should be defined in texts that are inviolable and have universal impact. It means that other norms are subordinated to it, particularly the contracts that express the balance or imbalance of private interests. Thus the market and its ambitions should be considered as an exception, providing that it is subordinate to the aim of attaining the common good. This revolution is to be achieved through the due process of law.

NOTES

1. The French reference book was Grégory Tounkine (1965) *Droit international public* (Paris: Pedone).
2. Francis Fukuyama (1992) *The End of History and the Last Man* (New York: The Free Press).
3. As we can see, the major powers evade international commitments that protect indispensable common interests (e.g. France refusing to subscribe to the Convention on the Non-Applicability of Statutory Limitations to War Crimes of 1968 or the US remaining outside the Kyoto Protocol on Climate Change in 1997, as well as the Rome agreement on the International Criminal Court of 1998).

Contributors

Clara Algranati, **José Seoane** and **Emilio Taddei** (Argentina) are researchers at the Latin American Social Sciences Council (CLACSO), Buenos Aires

Samir Amin, Egyptian economist, is the director of the Third World Forum and President of the World Forum for Alternatives

Pierre Beaudet (Canada) is the director of the Alternatives network, based at Montreal, Quebec

Verity Burgmann is professor of political science at Melbourne University

Monique Chemillier-Gendreau (France) is professor of public law and political science at the University of Paris VII – Denis Diderot

David Coetzee is a South African journalist and political scientist based in London and Washington. He runs the SouthScan News Service, covering South Africa, southern and central Africa

Boaventura de Sousa Santos is a Portuguese sociologist, professor at the University of Coimbra and director of its Centre for Social Studies at the Economics Faculty. He is also director of the *Revista critica de Ciencia Socia* and is visiting professor at the University of Wisconsin-Madison, the London School of Economics, the Universidade de São Paulo and the Universidad de Los Andes

Donatella della Porta (Italy) is professor of sociology at the European University Institute at Florence

Bernard Dreano (France) is facilitator at the Centre d'Etudes et d'initiatives de solidarité internationale (CEDETIM) in Paris

Ben Hayes and **Tony Bunyan** are British researchers, responsible for *Statewatch*, an independent body monitoring respect for public liberties in Europe (http://www.statewatch.org/). The Internet site includes an observatory on the mobilization projects of the European Union (http://www.statewatch.org/observatory3.htm)

Mondli Hlatshwayo (South Africa) is member of the social movement 'Indaba'

Raoul-Marc Jennar is a Belgian political scientist and researcher for Oxfam Solidarité (Brussels) and for the Unité de recherche, de formation et d'information sur la globalisation (URFIG – Paris; Mosset) (http://www.urfig.org)

Azza Abd al-Mohsen Khalil (Egypt) is researcher at the Arab and African Research Center, Cairo

Lau Kin Chi is professor at the Department of Cultural Studies, Lingnan University, Hong Kong and member of the network Asian Regional Exchange for New Alternatives (ARENA)

François L'Écuyer (Canada), anthropologist, is in charge of African programmes for the Canadian NGO Alternatives

Francis Loh is professor of political science at the University Sains Malaysia of Penang, head of Aliran (a Malaysian NGO) and member of the network Asian Regional Exchange for New Alternatives (ARENA)

Opiyo Makoude (Kenya) is in charge of lobbying for ACORD (Agency for Cooperation and Research in Development)

Paola Manduca, an Italian geneticist, is one of the key figures in the European Anti-War Platform and a member of the World Women's March

Francine Mestrum (Belgium) has a doctorate in social sciences and is author of the book *Mondialisation et pauvreté*

Vinod Raina, an Indian physicist, has participated in an organization of the victims of the Bhopal disaster and the Narmada Bachao Andolan. He is also one of the founders of the People's Science Movement and he currently presides in the Council of Fellows of the Asian Regional Exchange for New Alternatives (ARENA) and Jubilee South – Asia/Pacific. He is also a member of the India Organizing Committee and the International Council of the World Social Forum

Herbert Reiter is a German historian. He works with the Groupe de recherches sur l'action collective en Europe (GRACE) at the Department of Political Science and Sociology at the University of Florence

Victor Sampedro (Spain), sociologist, is professor of communication and sociology at the Rey Juan Carlos University in Madrid

Andrew Ure (Australia) is an anti-capitalist militant with a master's degree from the University of Melbourne

Index

Abkhazia, conflict in Georgia 45–6,
  49
Afghanistan
  Asian NGOs against US attack on
    38
  Blair's support for war on 148
  demonstrations against war in
    213
  failed occupation of 247
  mujahidin fighting in 43
  Russian and British 19th century
    imperialism 42
  Tajiks of Northern Alliance 45
  war on 42, 52, 53
Africa-Caribbean-Pacific countries
  (Lomé and Cotonou
  agreements) 96, 147, 153, 209
African Growth and Opportunity
  Act (AGOA) opposition to 207,
  209
Agricultural products
  Oxfam on agricultural trade
    191–3
  impact of price drop on Sudanese
    farmers 77
  WTO and agricultural subsidies
    227–30
AIDS/HIV
  alliance on 153
  Congolese population affected by
    88
  Treatment Action Campaign 105,
    106
Algeria
  internal conflicts in 160
  plurality of syndicates weakens
    labour in 75
Amin, Samir 69, 153, 161, 198,
  204n22
Annan, Kofi 200, 204n29
Anti-war coalition 212–21
  campaigns against US and NATO
    military interventions 213, 220
  civil disobedience 219

coalition meeting in Copenhagen
    215–16
  growth of military expenditure
    213
  linkages with other continental
    coalitions 216, 220
  Occupation Watch Committee
    220
  participation of European unions
    217
  Pope and other Christian leaders
    against war 217
  role of ESF and peace march 215
  solidarity missions for Palestine,
    Iran, Iraq and Kurdistan 220–1
Arab world
  anti-globalization movement
    77–9
  economic policies of
    independence states 68–9
  elite dependency on West 70–1
  elitism of social action
    frameworks 81–2
  labour movements 72–5
  peasant movements 75–7
  privatization and parasitic
    practices 70
  return to authoritarianism 71
  social movements 68–84
  State/civil society relationships
    79–80
  see also Algeria, Egypt, Palestine,
    Sudan, Syria and Tunisia
Argentina
  economic crisis and social effects
    121
  mobilization of unemployed 124
  neoliberal legitimacy challenged
    120
  popular assemblies in Buenos
    Aires 121
  protests force president's
    resignation 116
  questioning of traditional repre-
    sentative democracy 119–20

Argentina *continued*
'social territoriality' 119
solidarity production and trade
in occupied factories 119
Thematic Social Forum 131
Armenia
assassinations in parliament 48
citizen dialogue with Azerbaijan
50
historical nationalists of
Dachnaksoutioun 48
Nagorno-Karabakh question 45,
46, 47
Russian and Iranian relationships
47
'unachieved self-determination'
48
Asia Pacific Economic Cooperation
(APEC) 37
Asian Development Bank (ADB) 37
Asian Peace Alliance (APA) 37, 39,
40n12
ATTAC movement 154, 160,
204n14, n21, 224–5
Australia
Aboriginal contribution to
alternative world vision 57–8
as regional US deputy 52
Baxter and Woomera detention
camps 55, 64n18
Community Active Technology
60
culture of dissent 59–60
Fortress Australia 54–5
labour movement 56, 58–9,
65n39
neoconservative think-tanks 60
new security measures 59–60
plight of asylum seekers 53–5
political parties 56
resistance to neo-globalization
52–67
S11 52, 58, 59, 62n2, n3
Tampa incident 54
unpopular 'War on Terror' 52, 53,
55
Azerbaijan
Baku-Ceyhan and Baku-Erzerum
pipelines 47

Center of Religious Faith and
Protection of Freedom of
Conscience 49, 51n7
conflict with Armenia over
Nagorno-Karabakh 45
new leadership ability questioned
47
strategic position and
hydrocarbon wealth 45
US firmly installed 46

Balkan countries 151–2
Bangkok Declaration (1993) 36
Bangladesh 239
Belgium
government courage on Iraq war
issue 149, 157
deportation of Boone brothers
268n5
PM's proposals for EU peace and
security 160
support for Mobutu regime 85
trade unions against utility
privatization 224–5
union leader: EU constitution
'socially dangerous' 154
Bello, Walden 199, 203n5, 204n21,
n24
Berlin Wall fall of 212, 294
Bloch, Ernst 167, 185
Bolivia
anti neoliberal bloc 124
arrival of US troops 132
Aymaras of Chapare and Yungas
against crop eradication 113,
115, 125 132
Coordinadora por el Agua y la
Vida de Bolivia *ix*, 125
Coordinadora por la Defensa del
Gas en Bolivia 123
'gas war' *x*
electoral successes of Movimiento
al Socialismo and Evo Morales
125
gigantic mobilization against gas
exportation 127
militancy of peasant and
indigenous movements 115,
132

opposition to budget reform 126
removal of president 133
'water war' in Cochabamba 113,
122, 125;
Bourdieu, Pierre 289, 290
Brazil
consolidation of MST 115
CUT relations with government
viii
CUT-led strike against Lula
government 128
financial crisis 114
huge increase in social conflict
127
land occupations 119
MST denounce landowners
creating rural militia 130
Lula as president 124
see also Landless Rural Workers
Movement (MST)
Bretton Woods institutions 59,
66n42, 111, 171–2, 200
see also World Bank and IMF

Cambodia at WTO meeting 292–3
Cancellation of Third World debt
advocated by Kanagawa
Declaration 40n11
campaigns against *ix*
cancellation felt incompatible
with liberalism 190
concern of SA social movements
107
Freedom from Debt Coalition in
Philippines 29
pressure for 96, 97
Carlsson report on world
governance, 199, 204n27
Caspian Sea, hydro-carbons
transportation 46–7, 51n5
Catholic Church
antimodernist stance 195
Filipino NGOs linked to 29
International Movement of
Catholic Students 37
opposition to Iraq war 217
Populorum Progressio encyclical
195
role in the Congo 85, 86

Central Asia
collective security treaty of ex-
USSR states 43
disappointing progress of
democracy 43
Shanghai Forum 44
US rearguard base 42–45
war on terror benefits despots
43–4
see also Kazakhstan, Kyrgyzstan,
Tajikistan, Turkmenistan and
Uzbekistan
Chechnya 43, 45, 46, 150
Chile
Central Unitaria de Trabajadores
Chilena 128
free trade treaties with US and EU
131
health workers against reforms
123
Mapuche Indians and the
Coordinador Arauco-Malleco
115, 132
China
peasant counter-power 230–5,
239
Dark Dragon Pond 22–4
James Yen Institute for Rural
Reconstruction 25
land access 233–4
'market socialism' 233
Nanjie Village 21–2
new co-operative forms 233
Peoples' Communes 17, 20
Pingdu County 18–21
population growth 230–1
rural China's resistance to
globalization 15–26
Rural Cooperative Funds 18,
20–1, 26n5
Two-Land-Use Scheme 18–20
Uighur nationalists 44
Wanli-Luxia Women's Credit
Union Cooperative 24
Xiaogang Village 16
Christian fundamentalism 167
Ciranda Internacional da
Informação Independente, A
251, 253

Colombia
Comando Nacional Unitario 128
general strikes 128–9
increased military aid 132
militarization of political life 121
mobilization against labour
reform and FTAA 124
National Social Forum 131
police raids at Universidad
Nacional 132
social militarization 131
US strategy in 131
Congo, Democratic Republic of the
Alliance of Democratic Forces for
the Liberation of the Congo
86
Angolan/Rwandan/Ugandan/
Zimbabwean invasions 85, 86,
87
Congolese Union for Democracy
86, 87
foreign intervention and human
rights violations 85–90
French and US imperialism 85,
87
Laurent and Joseph Kabila
presidencies 86, 87
Mobutu dictatorship 85, 86
MONUC 89, 90
pillage and massacre 90
spheres of interest 88
'Tutsiphobia' 87
Union for Democracy and Social
Progress 85
Union of Congolese Patriots 90
unsuccessful peace agreements
87
Cuba 132
Cyprus 151

Dominican Republic
opposition to IMF from
the Coordinadora de
Organizaciones Populares,
Sindicales y de Transportistas,
Frente Amplio de Lucha
Popular (FALPO) and the
Colectivo de Organizaciones
Populares 129

East Africa
African activists in trade
negotiations 97
challenging 'legalities of
participation' 101
democratization and citizenship
93–5
demonstration effect of 'real-time
transmission' 93
economic governance 96–7
grassroots movements 97–100
international solidarity
campaigns 99
'quiet encroachment' 92, 101
social movements 91–102
Ecuador
Confederación de Nacionalidades
Indígenes del Ecuador
(CONAIE) 113, 125
Confederación de Pueblos de
la Nacionalidad Kichwa del
Ecuador (Ecuarunari) and the
government 127
great increase in social conflict
127
demonstrations in Quito 125,
132
Movimiento Pachakulik 124–5,
127
Egypt
anti-globalization movement
77–9
Arab Research Centre 78
boycott committees 78
Centre for Socialist Studies and
Research 78
Centre for Syndicate Services 78
Coalition of Egyptians 78
continued exclusion of poor
peasants 238–9
cotton monoculture 235
decline in wheat production 236
demand for agricultural reforms
238
'disreputable laws' 71
Egyptian Group for Combating
Globalization 78
emergence of peasant movement
76

emigration to Gulf countries 237
fragmentation of peasant
   movement 238
growth of food imports 236
impact of liberalization on
   agriculture 76
increase in social polarization
   236
labour movement 72–3
Land Centre 78
Nasser national populism 235–6
new industrial cities 75
Open Door Policy 76, 78
Peasants' Union 76
rebirth and limits of peasant
   movement 235–9
resistance to agricultural rental
   law 77
Tagammu and Nasser Parties 237
Union of Labour Syndicates 75
El Salvador
conflict on privatization of social
   security 123
involvement of Honduras and
   Guatemala in government's
   repression 133
launching of 'heavy hand' 133
European Union
'internal threat' 258–71
   Schengen Information System
      258–60, 264–5, 268n1, n2,
      n3, 269n31
   definition of terrorism
      broadened 261–2
   denial of protesters'
      fundamental rights 266–7,
      270n42, 281–2
   increasingly militarized
      approach to demonstrations
      266
   Joint Action on law and order
      259–60, 270n35
   McCarthy-style approach to
      dissent 268
   protest policing strategies
      274–6
   restriction of right to
      demonstrate 281–2

role of Europol 263, 267
summit protests at Amsterdam
   259, 268n10
summit protests at Genoa 258,
   260, 261, 283
summit protests at Gothenburg
   258, 260, 261
Watson report on citizen
   liberties and rights 283
treaties and other agreements
   Charter of Fundamental Rights
      154
   Constitution (Convention) ix,
      145, 153–7
   Convention on Human Rights
      270n42
   Council of Ministers retain
      accumulation of power in
      new Constitution 155
   European Central Bank 156
   former treaties 154
   Maastricht, Stability Pact and
      restriction of social rights
      225
   new Constitution
      institutionalizes
      competition to allocate
      resources 154
   peace 'forgotten' in new
      Constitution 154
   new institutional arrangements
      155–7
policies and strategies
   as instrumental model for
      neoliberalism 150
   as new international power
      centre 289, 291
   big powers as bullies to small
      countries 149
   Common Agricultural Policy
      (CAP) 147
   East European countries in
      purgatory 151
   European fracture' on Iraq 149
   frontiers and issue of Turkey
      150
   neoimperialist role 188
   political conditionality 150
   powerful Europe' concept 157

European Union *continued*
    reduction in non-agricultural
        structural funding 147–8
    regional integration 150–3
    relationships with Israel,
        Palestine 152
    relationships with South 147,
        152–3
    St. Malo process 160
    treatment of minorities 160
    Stability Pact of SE Europe 152
challenges to social movements
    145–62
    action on immigrants and
        minorities 159–60
    Commission and NGOs 291–2
    European Trade Union
        Confederation 159
    great anti-war mobilization
        160
    lack of criticism on budgetary
        decisions 147–8
    mobilization against neoliberal
        policies 157–8
    need to distinguish between
        different summits 158

Fanon, Frantz 18, 206
Feminism need for new feminisms
    178
Focus on the Global South
    international social movement
    network 40n12, 292
Food sovereignty, importance of
    192
France
    agricultural lobby (FNSEA) 147
    Chirac/Schröder alliance on Iraq
        war 149
    Chirac/Schröder compromise on
        CAP 147
    Confédération Paysanne 147
    denial of cultural/political rights
        for communities in 160
    French thinkers on solidarity
        economics 193–7
    French/German reconciliation
        148
    government ambiguity on
        Stability Pact 146

international law at universities
    295
intervention in the Congo 85, 87
No-Vox campaigns 159
oil interests in Azerbaijan 46
presence in Kyrgyzstan 42
presentation of Media
    Watch Global by *Le Monde
    Diplomatique* 247
reluctance to abandon past
    prestige 148
strikes against Raffarin
    government 224
trade unions 222–4
widespread social resistance to
    neoliberal offensive 145
Free Trade Agreement of the
    Americas (FTAA)
    campaigns against *ix*
    Continental Campaign against
        the 118
    LA coordination against 133
    march against war and the 219
    region-wide demonstration in
        Quito against 132
    Second Hemispheric Encounter
        to fight the 132
    Columbian unions, peasants and
        students mobilize against 124
    US coalitions against 143
    US time frame for 134
Freire Paulo 249
Friedman, Thomas 188
Friends of the Earth 291
From Seattle to Brussels
    international social movement
    network 292
Fukuyama, Francis 301n2

G7, G8
    as an illegitimate institution 158
    control over WB, IMF and WTO
        200
    gatherings against 158, 212,
        273–4, 290
Gandhi, Mahatma 5, 6, 7, 10, 12,
    13, 195
General Agreement on Trade and
    Services (GATS) 107

Generic medicines
campaign against pharmaceutical
companies in SA 105
fight for 295
WTO involvement in 300–1
Genetically Modified Organisms
(GMOs) dangers of 229
rejection of 295
Georgia
Abkhazia conflict 45–6
Abkhazian refugees in 49
Association of Displaced Women
51n10;
decision to leave CIS 46
development of self-management
schemes 49
disastrous economic situation 46
lack of control over Southern
Ossetia 46
Russian accusations of help to
Chechen fighters 46
Germany
government ambiguity on
Stability Pact 146
Heinrich Böll Foundation and
Fredrick Ebert Stiftung 96
IG-Metall 146, 223, 224
interior minister call for EU anti-
riot police 265
interior minister proposes to
Europeanize German police
practices 282
Lagrand affair 296
red/green coalition 157
Schröder/Chirac alliance on Iraq
war 149
Schröder/Chirac compromise on
CAP 147
'social partnership' still prevails
254
use of *Ausreiseverbot* 282
violent German demonstrators at
Gothenburg 282
widespread social resistance to
neoliberal offensive 146
Gramsci, Antonio 60, 173, 289, 290
Green Revolution, farmers
benefiting from 226

Greenpeace activist refused entry to
Schengen area 259
French government hostility to
259, 268n5
Guantánamo, illegality of camp 214

Helsinki Citizens' Forum 50, 51n9
Hobsbawm, Eric 203
Honduras, Great Dignity March 129
protests against privatization of
water 123
Houtart, François 202–3, 205n33
Huntington, Samuel 150–1

Illich, Ivan 194
India
Ambedkar, B.R. 6, 10, 11
anti-dam movement 10
Chipko Andolan (Hug the Trees)
8–10
dalits x, 4, 6, 7, 10–11
Mahatma Gandhi and his legacy
5, 6, 7, 10, 12, 13
Mumbai Resistance 2004 13
National Alliance of People's
Movements (NAPM) 10
Panchayati Raj 5, 7, 12
Pandit Nehru and industrial
modernization 6
People's Science Movement
12–13
Phule, Jyotirao 10, 11
professionally-staffed NGOs 12
social movements 3–14
Indonesia
Alliance of Independent
Journalists 34
Association of Indonesian
Muslim Intellectuals 33
Centre for Information and
Action Network 34
election of Abdurachman Wahid
and Amien Rais 34
financial crisis and reform
movement 33
Forum Demokrasi 34
Indonesian Environmental
Forum 33
Legal Aid Institute 33

Indonesia *continued*
Lembaga Studi Pembangunan 33
Muslim extremists 35
Nadhatul Ulama and
Muhammadiyya 34
People's Democratic Party 34
Seikat Buruh Sejahtera Indonesia
34
Indymedia
network of 500 local centres 253,
257n7, n8
role of Community Active
Technology 60
Inter American Development Bank
113–14
International citizenship, birth of
290–1
International Court of Justice (ICJ)
294, 296, 299
International Criminal Court (ICC)
153, 299, 301, n3
International Day of Protest against
War on Iraq 39, 216–18
International Federation of Human
Rights Leagues 48, 50, 51n6,
n9
International Forum on
Globalization 203n1, 204n25,
292
International Labour Organization
(ILO) 103, 104, 199
International Monetary Fund (IMF)
need for policy change 16
African activists lobbying of 96,
97
conditionalities 191
crisis of political legitimacy
113–14
general assemblies 158, 290
impact of decisions by 175
imposition of SAPs on SE Asian
countries 27, 35
insistence on privatizations in
Latin America 123
reform or replacing of 171–2
protests against 59
qualified suffrage, a questionable
mechanism 158
US domination through 212

Internet, role in alternative world
movement strategy 243–57
Iran
as 'Axis of Evil' 42
importance for Pentagon 45
avoidance of pipeline through 47
Iraq
international opposition to war
in 212–21, 295
Latin American demonstrations
against war in 133
African solidarity with Iraqi
people 207
UN inspectors 214
US presence in 44
US war on 42
Israel
apartheid Israel 207
as regional US agent 236
campaign against Israeli Wall 221
destruction of Palestinian
infrastructures 152
flouting of human rights 152
Italy
abuses of government 150
Berlusconi's attitude to
demonstrations 267
Blair/Aznar/Berlusconi stance on
Iraq 148, 149
ESF, Florence 222–4
Genoa Social Forum 279–81
Italian newspapers and the ESF
250
police violence at G8 Summit,
Genoa 277–84
widespread social resistance to
neoliberal offensive 146

Japan 45
John Paul II, Pope opposition to
Iraq war 217

Kanagawa Declaration (1992) 40n11
Kazakhstan
competition with Uzbekistan for
regional hegemony 44
rich oil resources 42
Russian military presence and
minorities in 43

Kenya
    Arap Moi regime 91, 93, 94, 95
    Central Organization of Trade
        Unions 97
    civil society lobbying 96
    Export Processing Zones 97–8
    Ogiek community 93, 98–100
    symbolism of *saba saba* 95
Keynes, John Maynard 103
Keynesian and neo-Keynesian
    economics 104, 111, 190, 201
Khomeini, Ayatollah 195
Khor, Martin 195, 204n9
Kyoto Protocol on Climate Change
    61, 153, 301n3
Kyrgyzstan
    corruption of rulers 43
    once 'little Switzerland' 45
    poverty of country 42
    selling of territory to China 51n2
    substantial Russian military
        presence still 43
    US troops in 42

Labour movements
    Algerian 75, Australian 56, 58–9
    Egyptian 72, 73, 74, 75
    European 222–4
    German 223, 224
    Kenyan Central Organization of
        Trade Unions 97
    new radical unions in France,
        Italy 146, 222–4
    Seikat Buruh Sejahtera Indonesia
        34
    South African 104, 105, 106, 107,
        108, 109, 110
    Sudanese 73
    Syrian 72
    Tunisian 73
    unions and social movement
        relationships 224–5
    US 136–40
Lagrand affair, 296
Landless Rural Workers Movement
    (MST), Brazil
    consolidation of 115

land occupations by 115, 119,
    129
occupation of warehouses 129
pressure for agrarian reform 129
strike against Lula government
    128
Latin America
    Agencia Latinoamericana de
        Información (ALAI) 249
    ALER (community radio) 249
    exploitation by tourist companies
        298
    growing opposition to neoliberal
        policies 112–18
    increasing repression and
        militarization 118, 130–3
    regional demonstrations against
        free trade agreements 118,
        131–4
    social protest in 112–35
    see also individual countries
Latin American presidents
    Battle, Jorge (Uruguay) 123, 129
    Chávez, Hugo (Venezuela) 125,
        127
    de la Rua, Fernando (Argentina)
        116, 121, 126
    de Lozada, Gonzalo Sánchez
        (Bolivia) 127, 133
    de Melo, Collor (Brazil) 112
    de Souza, Lula (Brazil) 124, 128,
        129
    Grau, Cubas (Paraguay) 113
    Gutiérrez, Lucio (Ecuador) 124–5,
        127
    Peréz, Carlos Andrés (Venezuela)
        112
    Toledo, Alejandro (Peru) 125,
        126, 128
    Uribe, Alvaro (Colombia) 121,
        128–9, 131, 133
Latin American Social Observatory
    (OSAL) CLACSO, studies of LA
    social protest 112, 120, 126
Latouche, Serge 194

Maghreb countries
Euromed 152
exploitation by tourist companies
298
Malaysia
Bakun Dam Hydro Electric
Project 32
Barisan Alternatif 33
coercive laws (ISA) 32, 38
Consumer Association of Penang
32
environmental groups 32
growth of multi-ethnic and
multi-religious NGOs 33
human rights groups 32
Islamic movements 33
Malaysian TUC 33
NGOs 31–3
Peneroka Bandar 32
United Malays National
Organization 31
Women's NGOs 32
Manipulation of civil society
291-292
Médecins sans Frontières 291
Mexico
army removal of Zapatista
settlements in Chiapas 132
Avena case 296
financial crisis 114
Frente Nacional contra la
Privatización de la Industria
Electrica 123
Frente Nacional por la Defensa
de la Soberania y los Derechos de
los Pueblos 124
government's abortive attempts
to privatize electricity 124
see also Zapatistas
Migration
Asian Migrant Centre 37
EU Migrant Forum 160
rights of immigrant descendants
in Europe 151, 160
Millennium Summit 200, 204n29

Ministerial summits of the Americas
Cancun 134, 157
Miami 134
Quito 132
Multilateral Agreement on
Investment (MAI) 290, 298–9
Multinational corporations see
Transnational Corporations
(TNCs)

NAFTA (North American Free Trade
Area)
encouragement of industrial
delocalization 137, 143
negative effects on environment
143
Nagorno-Karabakh
Armenian/Azerbaijan conflict
over 45, 46, 47, 48, 50
National Social Forums
Colombia: 131
Uruguay 131
Venezuela 131
Neo-Keynesian economics (see also
Keynesian economics) 190
New Partnership for Africa's
Development (NEPAD),
opposition to ix, 207, 208
New Zealand/Aotearoa
Aotearoa Educators 56
globalization seen as extension of
colonialism 56, 58
in forefront against neoliberal
globalization 56
Maori claims x
Tino Rangatiratanga movement
56, 64n24
North Atlantic Treaty Organization
(NATO)
Eastern Europe's attitude to 149
EU respect for obligations to
156–7
EU's only political dimension 157
opposition to military
intervention by 213
'Peace Partnership' 43, 152
recasting of 160

Oceania
    Australian intervention in
        Solomon islands 61
    imprisonment of asylum seekers
        on Pacific islands 55
    Papua New Guinea students
        killed protesting IMF/WB 59
    liberation struggle in West Papua
        61, 67n57, n58
    IMF structural reforms forced on
        Solomon islands 61
    struggles against rising sea levels
        61, 66n52
Organization for Economic
    Cooperation and Development
    (OECD) 273
Organization for Security and Co-
    operation in Europe (OSCE) 48
Oxfam International 191–3, 291

Palestine
    African solidarity with
        Palestinians 207
    EU aid to 152
    Palestinian refugees' right of
        return 221
    participation in pan-Arab
        conference, Cairo 78
Panama, strikes of insurance
    officials and education
    community 129
Paraguay
    Congreso Democratico del
        Pueblo 116, 122
    failure of privatization offensive
        124
    Federación Nacional Campesina
        (FNC) 122
    Mesa Coordinadora Nacional de
        Organizaciones Campesinas
        122
    peasant mobilization 113
    worker/farmer protest against
        rate rise and economic reforms
        124
Partant, François 194
Patriot Act 38, 213, 244
Peasant movements, counter-power
    in China 230–5
    in Arab world 75–7

    see also Chapter 10 for many
        Latin American references
Peru
    failure of privatization offensive
        124
    Frente Amplio Cívico against
        electricity privatization in
        Arequipa 116, 122
    Frentes Cívicos spread elsewhere
        113, 125
    massive protest forces end of
        Fujimorismo 113
    protracted teachers' strike 128
Philippines
    Caucus of Development NGO
        Networks 29
    Coalition for Peace 29
    Congress for a People's Agrarian
        Reform 29
    Freedom from Debt Coalition 29
    Movement for National
        Democracy 175
    National Confederation of
        Cooperatives 29
    National Council for Fisherfolk
        and Aquatic Reform 29
    NGOs in local government
        29–30
    People's Media Network 29
Plan Andino, opposition to 118
Plan Puebla Panamá
    movement against 115, 118, 123
    opposition of EZLN to 130
Polanyi, Karl 194, 203n7
Political parties
    Australian Greens and Labour
        Party 56
    European Green Federation 159
    Indian political parties and their
        social movements 5–8
    New Labour (UK) 146
    Seikat Buruh Sejahtera Indonesia
        34;
    Socialist Workers Party (UK) 159
    South African Communist Party
        104, 105, 107
    US Democratic Party 137, 138
Project for the New American
    Century (PNAC) 212–13

Protest policing strategies 286n1,
    272–6

Refugees
    Fortress Australia 53–5
    in Southern Caucasus 49–50
    in the Congo 88
Regional Social Forums:
    African Social Forums
        African Union 206–8
        Arab participation in 79
    ASF 206-11
        at Addis Ababa and Bamako
            206, 208, 210
        contesting of ASF organizers
            208–10
        criticism of SAPS and UNDP
            208–9
        Indaba 207, 210
        international solidarity links
            211
        opposition to NEPAD 207–8
        radical African platform
            210–11
    Asian Social Forum
        Arab participation in 79
        at Hyderabad 37, 39
    European Social Forums
        at Paris/Saint-Denis 157
        limited objectives at Florence
            186
        peace march 215
        social movement/union
            relationships 223–5
    Latin American Social Forums
        Mesoamerican Forum 131
        Panamazónica Forum 131
Reporters without Borders 246
Russia
    imperialism in19th century 42
    free hand in Chechnya 43
    pressure on Georgia 45
    salvaging of economy 114
    Shanghai Forum 44
    see also USSR
Russian Federation, Northern
    Ossetia, member of 46

Sachs, Wolfgang 194

Scott, James C. 190, 203n3, 205n34
Seattle, 1999 protests in 59, 212,
    276
Sen, Amartya 191, 193
Shiva, Vandana 192, 198, 204n19
Sivaraksa, Sulak 31
Solidarity economics 193–7
South Africa
    African National Congress 103,
        104, 105, 106, 108
    Anti Privatization Forum 106
    Black Economic Empowerment
        (BEE) programme 104, 106,
        110
    coalitions against privatizations x
    Congress of SA Trade Unions
        (COSATU) viii, 104, 105, 107,
        108, 109
    Freedom of Expression Institute
        110
    Growth, Employment and
        Redistribution (GEAR) plan
        103, 104, 109
    Indaba Social Movement 105,
        207, 210
    labour movement fragmentation
        108–10
    Landless People's Movement 106
    old and new social movements
        103–11
    Soweto Electricity Crisis
        Committee 106
    Treatment Action Campaign 105
Southeast Asia
    four main types of NGOs 28
    bail-out of national economies
        114
    imposition of SAPs on countries
        in 27, 35
    regional human rights and social
        issue coalitions 37
    social movements and NGOs in
        27–41
    see also Indonesia, Malaysia,
        Philippines and Thailand
Southern Caucasus
    'democratures' 50
    GUAAM alliance 47
    old and new conflicts 45

refugees 49–50
social self-management 49
see also Armenia, Azerbaijan and
    Georgia
Spain
    'Atlantic' triple alliance: Blair/
        Aznar/Berlusconi 148, 149
    government proposal to EU on
        'terrorists' 263
    small anarchist trade unions 146
    union participation in ESF 222
    widespread social resistance to
        neoliberalism 146
    withdrawal of UN Resolution 214
Structural Adjustment Programmes
    (SAPs), 27, 35, 208–9
Subcomandante Marcos
    ratifies EZLN opposition to Plan
        Puebla Panamá 130
    views on leadership 173
Sudan
    labour movement 73
    development of peasant unions
        77
    crop prices drop 77
Survival International 99
Sweden, police violence at
        Gothenburg Summit 276–7,
        282
Syria
    labour movement 72, 73
    Union of Labour Syndicates 73
    National Committee for
        Boycotting Imperialist Goods
        and Interests 78

Tajikistan
    ethnic-religious civil war 43, 45
    main Islamic groups officially
        reject terrorism 43
    movements defend civic rights
        49
    US troops in 42
Tanzania
    authoritarian regime 93–4
    Civic United Front 94
    Maasai pastoralists against
        mineral companies 98
    Nyerere's *ujamaa* 92, 94

political organizations develop
        94
    private sector-led growth 96
Thailand
    Assembly of the Poor *ix*
    Campaign for Popular
        Democracy 30–1
    constitutional reforms 31
    Coordinating Group on Religion
        for Society 31
    Local Development Institute 31
    NGO Coordinating Committee
        on Rural Development 30
    Thai Development Support
        Committee 30
    Thai Inter-Religious
        Commission for Development 31
Third World Network 195, 292
Tobin tax 190
Transnational Corporations (TNCs)
    16, 56, 111, 137, 139–40, 144,
    175, 189, 192, 198, 199, 291
Triad, The 228
Tunisia
    General Federation for Students
        78
    Bourguiba's individualist policies
        influence unions 74
    Tunisian Labour Union 73
    venue for next WSIS 246
Turkey
    oil and gas pipelines 47
    possible integration with EU
        150–1
    salvage of economy 114
    strategic importance for US 45
    venue for final session of peoples'
        tribunal 220
Turkmenistan
    American tolerance of
        dictatorship 44
    gas reserves 44
    Turkmenbashi personality cult
        44, 51n3
    waiting in the wings 45

Uganda
    Acholi Religious Leaders' Peace
        Initiative 100

Uganda *continued*
  Amin Dada and Obote II regimes
    94
  liberalizer, the 96
  Lord's Resistance Army 93, 100
  poverty eradication/reduction
    programmes 96
  Uganda Debt Network 96
UNCTAD (United Nations
    Conference on Trade and
    Development) 37, 199
Unesco
  MacBride report 247
  multimedia community centres
    249
Union of Soviet Socialist Republics
    (USSR)
  participation in creation of UN
    294
  release from Soviet Empire 149
  problems of states of former 152
  see also Russia
United Kingdom
  ACORD workshop, Nairobi 98
  ActionAid 96
  as aggressive exporter of
    agricultural overproduction
    228–9
  as US partner in Iraq war 214
  Blair justification for Iraq
    intervention 217
  Blair's 'anarchists' travelling
    circus' 264
  Blair's attempt to influence
    Washington 148
  Blair-Aznar-Berlusconi alliance
    on Iraq 149
  British hostility to CAP 147
  historical Atlanticism of 158–9
  idea of Europe 157
  impact of protests on British
    police strategies 273
  imperialism in 19th century
    Afghanistan 42
  New Labour dismantling public
    services 146
  reluctance to abandon past
    prestige 148
  Socialist Workers Party 159

United Nations
  contractual nature of UN system
    298
  present critical phase of 296
  MONUC 89, 90
  need to reform structures of 16,
    198
  paralysis of 214
  resolutions on Iraq 214, 219
  role in world communication
    245, 246, 247
  'soft law' of UN resolutions 299
  UN Charter 296, 298
  UN inspectors 214
United Nations Conference
    on Environment and
    Development, Rio 36, 194
United Nations Development
    Programme
  advocacy of new world order 199
  Millennium Development goals
    similar to SAPs 208–9
  'social capital' 194
United Nations World Conference
    on Human Rights, Vienna 35
United States of America
  'armed liberalism' policy in Latin
    America 13g0–133
  Accuracy in the Media 247
  Affordable Health Care Coalition
    143
  AFL-CIO 137, 138, 139, 140, 142
  Alliance for Progressive Action
    coalition, Minnesota 141–2
  anti-war coalitions in 216
  anti-war demonstrations in 143–4
  as aggressive exporter of
    agricultural overproduction
    228–9
  as counterweight to Russian
    tutelage 43
  Asian Immigrant Women
    Advocates 141
  attack on World Trade Center 62,
    212
  blame for changing neoliberalism
    to neoimperialism 189
  Bush's anti-terrorist crusade 120

capitalist penetration in LA 115, 118

capitalist restructuring and worker resistance in 136–44

Central Asia as rearguard base of 42–8

Chinese Staff and Worker Association 141

Consortium for the Rights of Workers 142

corporations (*see also* TNCs) 136–40, 144

domination of world economy and geopolitics 39

Fairness and Accuracy in Reporting (FAIR) 247

flouting of ICJ rulings 296

Free Trade Agreement with Australia 63n7

Free Trade Treaty with Chile 131

growing military presence in Panama and Bolivia 132

Hotel and Restaurant Employees Union 141

imperial aims 214

Industrial Workers of the World 136, 140

international law at universities 295

International Longshore and Warehouse Union 140

Jobs with Justice *ix,* 142–4

John Ashcroft and 'Operation Tips' 140

labour movement 136–40

Latin Workers Center, Chicago 141

Lexington University, Kentucky 142

military adventurism 39

military presence in Latin America 130–3

Naugatuck Valley Project, Connecticut 141

neoconservative think tanks 60

new forms of resistance to system 138–44

NGOs in Central Asia and Southern Caucasus 43, 49

oil and strategic interests in Southern Caucasus 45, 46, 47, 48

opposition to US military interventions in 1990s 213

Patriot Act 38, 213, 244

Project for a New American Century (PNAC) 212–13

restrictions on civil liberties in 212

Revolutionary Black Workers 136

Soros Foundation 49

State University of Phoenix, Arizona 142

State University of San Jose, California 142

Student Labor Action Project (SLAP) 142–3

support for 'social militarization' in Colombia 121, 131

support of Mobutu dictatorship 85, 87

Teamsters 138, 139

time frame for FTAA 134

tolerance of Turkmenistan dictatorship 44

troops in Kyrgyzstan, Tajikistan, Uzbekistan 42

troops sent to Philippines 38–9

Ugandan petition to Bush 100

unilateralism *vii,* 27, 39

United Students against Sweatshops 141, 142

USAID 49, 77

Wal-Mart 139, 143

Yale University 141, 142

Universal Declaration of Human Rights 198, 204n18, 270n42

Uruguay

Frente Amplio-Encuentro Progresista 122–3

health workers strike 129

National Social Forum 131

PIT-CNT calls general strike 129

PIT-CNT lead anti-privatization struggle 122

privatization of telephones rescinded 123

Sindicato Medico del 129

Uzbekistan
  ecological disaster of Aral Sea
    44–5
  Karimov uses Islamic spectre to
    crush opposition 43–4
  US troops in 42

Venezuela
  abortive *coup d'état* against
    Chavéz: 125
  aim of *coup* to privatize State oil
    company 125
  'civic' strike called off 125
  failure of further efforts to
    destabilize government 127
  National Social Forum 131
  role of business, church and army
    in *coup* 125
Vía Campesina 118, 147, 249, 292
Vienna Convention (1969) 300
Vietnam 234, 239

'War on Terrorism' *xi*, 39, 43, 52,
    53, 55
Washington Consensus
  Latin American opposition to
    113–14
  South African resistance to 111
World Bank
  conditionalities 191
  crisis of political legitimacy
    113–14
  general assemblies 290
  impact of decisions 175
  insistence on LA privatization
    123
  PNG students killed protesting
    against 59
  policies as source of problems 16
  qualified suffrage, questionable
    mechanism 158
  reform or replacing of the 171–2
  'social capital' 194
  support for Indian NGOs 12
  US domination through 212
  withdrawal of support to
    Narmada dam 10
World Economic Forum
  Asia Pacific Economic Summit,
    Melbourne 52

clashes of police and
    demonstrators at Davos 273
  'Crown Casino' 55, 64n20
  difficulties of policing meetings
    65n35
World Rainforest Movement 99
World Social Forum (WSF), Mumbai
  participation of *dalits* in 11
  preparations by Indian social
    movements for 13–14
World Social Forums, Porto Alegre
    165–87, 188–205
  a new social and political
    phenomenon 165, 179
  absence of Central Asian
    participants 50
  affirms possibility of counter-
    hegemonic globalization 168
  African preparation for WSF 206
  alternative structures proposed
    182–4
  as critical utopia 167–70
  challenge of self-democracy 181
  Charter of Principles 169, 170
  cleavages in the movement
    171–9, 199–201
  consensus on non-violence 166
  convergences in the movement
    118, 188–9
  failure of dominant discourse
    203
  'impact on Indian social
    movements 13–14
  need for new social theory and
    analytical concepts 166
  present organizational structures
    181–2
  communication strategies 243–57
    alternative media networks
      249–51
    Communication Rights
      for Information Society
      campaign (CRIS) 245–7
    First World Audiovisual Forum
      243–5
    Media Watch Global 247–9
    new technologies 251–5
World Summit on the Information
    Society (WSIS) 245–7

World Summit on Sustainable
Development (WSSD) 105
World Trade Organization (WTO)
agenda on agriculture 227–30
as new international power
centre 289, 291
campaigns against *ix*
criticisms of excessive power of
191–3
Doha conference 226, 293
expertise of alternative world
NGOs at recent meetings
293
failure of Cancún conference
230, 290
forcing privatization in LA 123
impact of decisions by 175
ministerial meetings at Quito,
Cancún and Miami 132, 134
need for more democracy 192
neoliberal dogma of 158
reform or replacing of 171–2
relations with NGOs 292
Tidal Wave Cancún 245

US domination through 212
water, electricity highlighted at
Cancún 107

Yugoslavia (former), problems of
states constituting 151–2

Zapatistas
ceremony of 'caracoles' 130
communications policy as
example 249
EZLN opposition to Plan Puebla
Panamá 130
first uprising 112
villages harassed by Mexican
army 132
Juntas de Buen Gobierno 130
March for Dignity 115, 249
national significance of the
movement 113
radically different vision of
utopia 170
role in anti-neoliberalism struggle
64n27